Urban Friendships and Community Youth Practice

Urban Friendships and Community Youth Practice

Melvin Delgado

OXFORD
UNIVERSITY PRESS

OXFORD
UNIVERSITY PRESS

Oxford University Press is a department of the University of Oxford. It furthers
the University's objective of excellence in research, scholarship, and education
by publishing worldwide. Oxford is a registered trade mark of Oxford University
Press in the UK and certain other countries.

Published in the United States of America by Oxford University Press
198 Madison Avenue, New York, NY 10016, United States of America.

© Oxford University Press 2017

Library of Congress Cataloging-in-Publication Data
Names: Delgado, Melvin, author.
Title: Urban friendships and community youth practice / Melvin Delgado.
Description: Oxford ; New York : Oxford University Press, [2017] |
Series: Social justice and youth community practice series | Includes
bibliographical references and index.
Identifiers: LCCN 2016019903 | ISBN 9780190467098 (alk. paper)
Subjects: LCSH: Youth—Services for—United States. | Urban youth—United
States—Social conditions. | Urban youth—Social networks—United
States. | Youth development—United States. | Community organization—United States.
Classification: LCC HV1431 .D445 2017 | DDC 362.7083/0973—dc23
LC record available at https://lccn.loc.gov/2016019903

9 8 7 6 5 4 3 2 1
Printed by Sheridan Books, Inc., United States of America

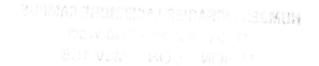

To Laura, Barbara, and Denise whose support and patience were instrumental in making this book possible.

CONTENTS

SECTION II **Case Illustrations**

ACKNOWLEDGMENTS

Dr. Tish McGhee (Barry University), Ms. Leah Krieble (Columbia University School of Social Work graduate student). Finally, I wish to acknowledge and thank the anonymous external proposal and final draft reviewers whose affirming and constructive advice was invaluable in writing the final draft of this book.

Urban Friendships and Community Youth Practice

SECTION I

Conceptual Foundation

1

Setting the Context

Introduction

I can think of very few topics that elicit as wide a range of emotional responses as "what does it mean to have a close dyadic friendship and all that goes with it, including the highs and lows, the roller coaster associated with some friendships?" Friendships come in many different shapes, sizes, and shades, and this makes them intriguing and difficult to categorize. However, there is no denying their importance regardless of how they are categorized and labeled.

Not unexpectedly, the subject of friends is so popular that this theme was responsible for one of the country's most popular television series, as evidenced by the ratings and longevity of *Friends*, a show that lasted 10 years (1994–2004), consisted of 236 episodes, and is currently in syndication as this book goes to press. Although friendships have always played a prominent role in television shows, *Friends* was the first show to focus on this form of relationship from numerous perspectives, highlighting its multifaceted manifestations. Appearing even earlier, the 1985 coming-of-age movie *The Breakfast Club* has a cult-like following, and its central theme of friendship's struggles and rewards has played a large part in its popularity over the past 30 years.

Grayling (2013, p. 1) starts off his book *Friendship* by grounding the topic and its prominence within the human constellation of relationships: "The highest and finest of all human relationships is, arguably, friendship. Consider the fact that we regard it as a success if we become friends with our parents when we grow up, our children when they grow up, our classmates or workmates even as they remain classmates or workmates, for in every such case an additional bond comes to exist, which transcends the other reasons we entered into association with those people in the first place." Grayling points out that the bond created makes friendships a special form of social relationship.

This introductory chapter provides readers with a theoretical grounding and roadmap for this book and highlights both the immense rewards and incredible challenges in understanding friendships when applied to urban youth. Social interventions, and none more so than those that are urban and targeting highly marginalized groups and communities, must be based on a sound foundation of knowledge and be social-justice driven (Mayer & Boudreau, 2012).

Community social work practice targeting urban friendships takes on added importance because it seeks to alter a cherished basic social fabric in peoples' lives. In the case of marginalized youth, these friendships can mean the difference between success and failure in life and even life or death in situations where environmental circumstances can severely compromise well-being.

Ontological Approaches

Three ontological approaches have dominated the understanding of youth, and youth peer and friendship networks can be viewed within these ontological worldviews (Hopkins, 2013): (1) life course, (2) intergenerationality, and (3) intersectionality. The life course perspective is arguably the most commonly used approach in the social sciences. The intergenerational approach can be considered the second most popular, followed by intersectionality. More recently, youth resistance research has started to gain traction, although it has garnered favor within a relatively small sector of the youth research field (Tuck & Yang, 2013).

This book will not favor any one of the three popular approaches, although intersectionality and youth resistance will be drawn on quite extensively because of the emphasis placed on power relations and marginality. A socioecological approach will be used because of the importance of environmental or contextual forces in shaping urban youth of color and the prominent role it has played in social work education (Tietjen, 2006, p. 70): "The ecological model has always been associated with the goal of understanding and promoting environmental conditions that optimize development for all children. . . . Findings generated by this model suggest that interventions at the level of the individual or the microsystem are unlikely to be effective if the structures in which they are embedded do not support the intervention."

Youth friendships are best grounded and understood within a socioecological foundation, and nowhere is this more relevant than when discussing youth who are urban and marginalized. This does not mean that many different concepts and constructs will not be introduced in this book to help increase our theoretical grounding. The reader will no doubt be familiar with many, if not all of them: strengths/assets, social identity, social/natural support, social capital, youth individuation, positive youth development/youth-led, intersectionality, praxis, and social agency will be the most salient in this book.

An ecological grounding allows the introduction of factors and considerations that are individual-based as well as taking into account social forces shaped by where youth live and evolve. A socioecological approach does not make our understanding of youth friendships easier to grasp; it does, however, provide key concepts that make it more responsive to capturing the multifaceted complexities of the subject matter.

It is well understood and widely accepted that individuals tend to operate within overlapping social networks of family, close friends, coworkers, and acquaintances (Pyrooz, Sweeten, & Piquero, 2013), and these networks are responsive to ecological forces or events. Children, however, develop within a complex system of relationships and within ecological structures and forces (Spencer & Swanson, 2013; Zaff, Donlan Jones, & Lin, 2015).

Although this network overlaps, not all segments are of equal importance, and friendships certainly wax and wane in importance depending on life stage and ecological circumstances, and the same can be said about all other groups in the network. Nevertheless, friendships do constitute an essential element in any social network, and one of the key questions is to *what extent* they influence individual outlooks and behaviors rather than *if* they influence. Thus, it becomes a question of degree (Vitaro, Boivin, & Bukowski, 2009).

Friendships and Animals

Human beings, it should be noted, are supposed to excel at making friends (Terrell, 2014). However, before focusing on friendships and humans, it is appropriate to touch on the point that friendships are not restricted to humans. Even the topic of the potential of having robots as friends has not escaped scrutiny (Emmeche, 2014). Friendships can also involve animals, which brings additional challenges to our understanding of this phenomenon (Gaita, 2009). These "special" friendships involving animals can encompass many of the key aspects associated with close friendships, and they introduce the concept of friendship between animals, too, thus further advancing the universality of friendships (Dagg, 2011; DeScioli & Kurzban, 2012).

Wood et al. (2015) discuss the multifaceted role that companion pets can play in friendship formation; although this type of relationship seems relegated to older adults, it certainly cuts across the life span:

> This research suggests companion animals can be a catalyst for several dimensions of human social relationships in neighborhood settings, ranging from incidental social interaction and getting to know people, through to formation of new friendships. For many pet owners, their pets also facilitated relationships from which they derived tangible forms of social support, both of a practical and emotionally supportive nature. Given growing evidence for social isolation as a risk factor for mental health, and, conversely, friendships and social support as protective factors for individual and community well-being, pets may be an important factor in developing healthy neighborhoods.

Being there when needed is considered a hallmark of a "true friend," be it an animal or a fellow human being (Hoagland, 2013). Accessibility, as a result, becomes a key aspect of a close and meaningful friendship, be it in person or through social media.

Maher and Pierpoint (2011) report on a unique study involving friends and the use of dogs as status symbols and weapons in youth groups and gangs, with dogs being used primarily for socializing, companionship (friendship), protection, and enhancing of status with peers. As a result, these dogs fulfilled multiple roles and needs. Friendship, in essence, is a complex social relationship, one unlike any other type of relationship. For some of us, friendship is a perpetual search, and there is no one path to achieving this goal or enriching our understanding of the subject (Bond, 2014; Greif, 2008; Mabee, 2014).

Academic Views of Friendships

Anthropologists have long struggled to determine whether friendship is universal and an integral part of human beings since the beginning of time or a modern-day phenomenon that has evolved over time to assume its present form(s) (Friese, 2013). The answer(s) goes beyond an academic interest and enters into the realm of everyday existence, becoming a subject worthy of policies, programs, and activities that can foster this form of social relationship.

Academics are certainly not at a loss for ways to view and measure friendships. Friendship is widely acknowledged to pervade the entire human social landscape (Brent, Chang, Gariépy, & Platt, 2014) and interest in understanding friendships, as a result, has transcended eras, demographics, academic disciplines, and geographical borders (Al-Shaar, 2014; Garrison, 2014; Leaman, 2014). Friendships can be conceived of as a naturally occurring social phenomenon, but not for every youth. As a result, friendships that are "normal" or "typical" rarely gain the attention of scholars and practitioners until something goes wrong.

The subject of friendship knows no national boundary; it is not unique to any historical period; ethnic or cultural values; age, racial, socioeconomic, or religious group; sexual identity; physical or intellectual abilities; or political ideology. This signifies its saliency in the lives of individuals and, indirectly, in the communities where they reside (Amichai-Hamburger, Kingsbury, & Schneider, 2013; Anagnostaki, 2006; Roach, 2012). Its transcultural relevance introduces a perspective that serves to enrich our understandings of how friendship concepts overlap and deviate based on cultural context.

Why a Focus on Friendships?

Why friendships and not peer networks? E. E. Cummings, the renowned American writer, stated it quite eloquently in the following statement: "We do not believe in ourselves until someone reveals that deep inside us something is valuable, worth listening to, worthy of our trust, sacred to our touch. Once we believe in ourselves we can risk curiosity, wonder, spontaneous delight or any experience that reveals the human spirit." That someone is called a friend, and that is why it is worth our focus.

Youth "hang out" with other youth, some of whom can be designated as friends, thus bringing a degree of overlap between those youth who are friends and those designated as peers. Obviously, peers do exert influence and their presence cannot be ignored, but they do not wield the same level of influence as relatives over a sustained period of time. Peers and friends, in turn, are part of crowds, an even larger unit of analysis that brings its share of challenges in understanding the degree and nature of influence (Bagwell & Schmidt, 2011).

Crowds, in turn, come together because of shared interests or backgrounds and represent multiple peer networks. Crowd labels such as "jocks," "nerds," and "druggies," for example, are common and can often be included as a peer network. Labels can also be attached to particular neighborhood or street residents. Growing up in neighborhoods such as the South Bronx (New York City), Prospect Avenue, 149th and Third Avenue, Fox Street, Longwood, or a particular public housing development, for example, serves to unite youth as a crowd; the neighborhood becomes part of an identity that goes beyond ethnicity or race by introducing a geographical identity and having influence on friendship development opportunities. Determination of peer networks, as a result, is not without its conceptual and empirical challenges (Donlan, Lynch, & Lerner, 2015).

The value of friendships, or lack of them in cases of concern, is often used as a key indicator of health, social status, emotional well-being, and determination of social connections or grounding within a community (Cherng, Turney, & Kao, 2014; Theobald, Danby, Thompson, & Thorpe, 2014). Furthermore, their value extends far beyond the present, and they are considered essential in assisting youth to enter intimate relationships in adulthood (Bukowski, Motzoi, & Meyer, 2009; Sakyi, Surkan, Fombonne, Chollet, & Melchior, 2014). It certainly is no wonder that the subject is worthy of social interventions specifically focused on these types of relationships.

Dale Carnegie's (2010) *How to Win Friends and Influence People* is a book that was first published in 1937 and one whose popularity can be measured by the millions of copies sold and the multiple languages it has been translated into. This book is obviously more about influencing people than making friends in the conventional sense of the word. Nevertheless, it highlights the importance of social relationship skills in all facets of life, both personally and professionally. Bryan's (2012) *Top 10 Tips for Building Friendships,* in turn, targets youth with "friendly" advice on establishing and maintaining close friendships. Friendships do not automatically emerge or disappear, and their success or failure can often be traced to relationship skills.

It would be foolhardy, as a consequence, to write a book on urban youth friendships without examining youth who have difficulties establishing friendships, close or otherwise. As noted by Erwin (1998, p. 120): "Deciding that a child has relationship problems worthy of intervention can be a considerably more complicated matter than might at first be imagined." Lack of close friendships, for example, may be the result of many different social and interpersonal factors and needs to be understood from a developmental stage perspective. These types of friendships may be arduous to initiate, or, if they can be initiated, they may be difficult to be maintained on a daily basis over an extended period of time. Terminating friendships, too, as addressed later in this book, brings its own set of rewards and challenges.

The value of friendships extends beyond social meaning and encompasses a wide range of conditions, sets of being, potentials, health states, identity formations, protective factors, and self-worth (Anthony & McCabe, 2015; Crépel, 2014; Demir & Özdemir, 2010; Fletcher & Ross, 2012; Hiatt, Laursen, Mooney, & Rubin, 2015; Shin, Daly, & Vera, 2007). Friendships seem to reach and touch almost all spheres of life. The expression "the start of a beautiful friendship" captures a relationship filled with hopes and aspirations for being transformative for both parties.

Bagwell and Schmidt (2013) argue that if we were to think of our favorite childhood books, the ones highlighting friendships will stand out in meaning and lasting memory. The role of female friendships in Jane Austen's novels, for example, is illustrative of the ideal for girls and young women (Todd, 2012). In essence, friendships are very important from an early developmental perspective and across the life span, and early stages set the context for succeeding stages, thus making early friendships particularly important (De Goede, Branje, & Meeus, 2009).

Friendship is a subject that is of tremendous importance, yet we have a propensity to take it for granted and not think of it until there is a major disruption or life event in our lives. Its importance transcends ordinary people and professionals, rich and poor, making it a concept that is ever-present in a community and society. Thus, there is good reason why friendship is considered a significant social concept (Cocking, 2013; Geddes, 2014; Lawson, 2006), and its significance seems to defy social conditions and demographics. Friendship, for example, has even been found to play an important role in the lives of older adults with dementia (de Medeiros, Saunders, & Sabat, 2012; Harris, 2012; Ward, Howorth, Wilkinson, Campbell, & Keady, 2012). Age and health status know no boundaries when it comes to friendships.

Friendship is so important that it even traverses long distances. Geographical distance is no longer a barrier in making and maintaining friendships. The advent of the Internet and Facebook, for example, has introduced a new dimension that no longer depends on physical proximity and in-person contact to enter into a definition of what constitutes a close friend (Becker et al., 2009; Merry, 2014; Vallor, 2012). A. Lambert (2013) argues that Facebook holds a premier place within social media, offering a different form of dialogue, intimacy, and friendship. Texting and mobile phones, too, have emerged as a prominent form of communication between friends, one that takes into account busy schedules, geographical distance, and other social factors (Lenhart, Ling, Campbell, & Purcell, 2010).

Online friendships, for example, can duplicate many of the qualities found in in-person contacts between friends (Henderson & Gilding, 2004). However, it should be noted that one study of the perceived difficulty in online friendship maintenance found that geographic location does have an impact on the perceived ease of friendship maintenance, and this may be the result of particularly hectic schedules and other demands, with the Northeastern United States being rated as more arduous for maintaining online friendships than other regions (Holmes, 2012).

Historical Understanding of Friendships

Why should community practitioners be interested in any historical understanding of friendships? Our current understanding of friendships is not possible without a historical appreciation of how these forms of relationships were valued, observed, recorded, and understood (Chung, 2014; Lochman, López, & Hutson, 2011). How can we appreciate where we are going when we do not know where we have been? Readers not interested in history, however, need not worry because this section is meant to provide a brief overview rather than an in-depth historical accounting.

Philosophy has played an instrumental role in shaping modern-day thoughts about the meaning of friendships, and this is no doubt due to the attention given this subject in the writings of the giants of philosophy. The significance of the subject has been the focus of philosophical debates over centuries (Amichai-Hamburger et al., 2013; Alfano, 2015; Leaman, 2014) and even drew the attention of such noted philosophers as Plato and Aristotle (Annas, 1977; Boje & Jørgensen, 2014; Price, 1989; Stern-Gillet, 1995). Confucius, too, weighed in on the value of a good friendship (Mullis, 2010).

Aristotle answered the question of what constitutes a friend: "What is a friend? A single soul, dwelling in two bodies." Aristotle's Books VIII and IX of *The Nicomachean Ethics* divides friendships into three distinctive types (those involving utility, pleasure, and good), with each type addressing a different dimension of friendships (Rohrer, 2014). Vernon (2005), in *The Philosophy of Friendship*, notes that friendship is often "heralded as the defining relationship of our age." In turning to the social sciences, German sociologist Ferdinand Tonnies (1887) is widely credited with being one of the first sociologists to address friendships in his influential book *Gemeinschaft und Gesellschaft (Community and Society)*.

One would be hard pressed to find someone who does not believe in the value and power of friendships across the life cycle. Any retrospective view of our lives will invariably touch on someone we considered to be a strong friend who played an instrumental role at a critical juncture in our lives, be it positive or negative.

This perspective applies equally to those of us who are ordinary and those of us who have accomplished great achievements and are celebrities (Hellstern, 2008; Hruschka, 2010). Adler's (2013) *Soulmates from the Pages of History: From Mythical to Contemporary, 75 Examples of the Power of Friendship* certainly attests to the extraordinary power of friendships. Friendships, in essence, have played an influential role in all spheres of life and history and, as a result, are worthy of being better understood and appreciated.

Needless to say, there has been a historical bias when it comes to recording and understanding children and youth. It can be argued that it is impossible to fully understand adolescence without paying attention to friendships and peers (Hirsh & Renders, 2014). The same conclusion can be made about adolescent low-income/low-wealth urban youth of color. History, it can be argued, is written by adults for the benefit of adults. For example, the role and importance of children and youth in this nation's civil rights movement is essentially uncovered in books about this movement (Delgado & Staples, 2008). However, youth were critical players, and they replaced adults who were jailed during demonstrations. These youth, in turn, grew up to become influential leaders in social justice campaigns, having had their start as children and youth in these events.

Historians West and Petrik (1992) argued almost 25 years ago that, in historical accounts (in this case during the 1850–1950 period), children and adolescents in America have suffered from neglect, and, when addressed, it has been to gain a better understanding of adults rather than of the children and youth themselves. An updated version of their book, unfortunately, will not produce significant new findings and added chapters to take into account the massive outgrowth in research in grounding youth within a historical period.

I believe that friendships remain an understudied topic, particularly when examining marginalized urban youth of color. This book is an attempt to redress this situation and help bridge this knowledge area with a practice field with a history of being urban-focused.

Friends as Family?

Thinking of friends as family certainly complicates our understanding of kinship and relationships. Nevertheless, when looking at friendship from an intervention viewpoint (as is the case in this book, focused on community practice and urban youth), for example, the issue of friends-as-family takes on added significance within urban settings and with highly marginalized groups, particularly those who are facing multiple jeopardies or intersectionality and are subject to oppressions' consequences (Matheson, Olsen, Weisner, & Dykens, 2009; Mayo, 2007; Singh, 2013).

For youth to think of friends as family is not a stretch of imagination, particularly in the case of street youth (Petrucka et al., 2014). Davies and Heaphy

(2011, p. 6) comment on the increasingly important role of friendships in society: "theorists . . . suggest friendships to be a model for the kind of relationships deemed to be personally important in late modernity because it embodies the principles of reciprocity, choice and autonomy. . . . In a similar vein, a number of Western European and North American studies suggest that families themselves are being reconfigured in these terms and that family relationships are nowadays so thoroughly social that friendships can be families." Grounding friendships within sociocultural and geographical (spatial) settings illustrates the interrelationships that these contacts have in shaping behavior and social networks (Morgan, 2013), a topic addressed later in this book. It is not unusual to refer to significant friends as "family" or as being "as close as family" because of the influential role close friends play in shaping lives; this is probably no more so than when youth have fractured families or are living in nonfamilial situations.

Digeser (2013, p. 34) argues that friendship can be understood through an embrace of a family resemblance concept: "How should we understand friendship given the extraordinarily diverse forms that it can take? Building on the idea that friendship is a family resemblance concept . . . friendship can be understood as a set of social practices in which certain norms and expectations govern not only the actions, but also the motivations of the friends." In essence, Digesar posits that different understandings of friendship bear no more than a family resemblance to one another, necessitating the use of a set of rule-governed social practices.

Allan (2008, p. 4), however, comments on how friendships differ from family relationships by allowing friends to respond to particularistic situations and needs, but this also makes friendship more arduous to research and understand:

> In comparison to family relationships, ties of friendship are inherently more open to individual negotiation. How friends define their relationship, what they do with each other, and what expectations they have are matters that are for them to determine. In most regards, these matters are not seen as legitimate concerns of those outside the relationship. Thus, while issues of equality and reciprocity tend to loom large in these ties, friendships nonetheless have flexibility built into their content in a way that marks them off as different from other types of relationship. As we have seen, this does not mean that friendships are unaffected by the social and economic contexts in which they are enacted, but it does mean that friendships tend to be understood as individualized and personal. Indeed where these characteristics are for some reason problematic, as for example with sociable contacts restricted to a particular setting such as a workplace, there is often a degree of uncertainty as to whether they really match the category of friendship.

There is no denying that family and friends share commonalities and are often included in any effort to discern the nature of social networks, but they also bring distinctive differences that cannot be easily ignored. When their influence is understood, these networks can be tapped to create social change (Bartos, 2013).

Grounding the Evolution of the Study of Friendships

The social science literature is replete with social constructs that can help ground friendships beyond the conventional peer network approach. The construct of *life satisfaction* (bringing together emotional, social, and behavioral constructs) provides a good backdrop to urban youth friendships even though this subject has only received attention more recently regarding youth (Huebner, Gilman, & Ma, 2012; Proctor, Linley, & Maltby, 2009). Life satisfaction is a natural extension of health, both physical and emotional. Life satisfaction, incidentally, can be closely related to neighborhood satisfaction and the presence of daily hassles for urban youth of color (Shin, Morgan, Buhin, Truitt, & Vera, 2010), thus giving a robust grounding for friendships.

The availability of social support and its various manifestations is considered an integral component for youth coping with the stresses of everyday life (McGrath, Brennan, Dolan, & Barnett, 2014). Rueda, Williams, and Nagoshi (2015, p. 219) studied help-seeking and help-offering among acculturating Mexican-American adolescents facing dating violence and determined their support network:

> Friends and supportive family members were primary sources of help, although adolescents voiced a number of barriers to help-seeking. The most prominent barrier was fear they would be told to leave the relationship, an anticipated message that aligned with their tendency to tell others to do so. Help-seeking was viewed as a weakness, and help-offering was reserved for friends that asked for it. Recommendations for programs and practice with youth include promoting culturally and gender attuned teen dating violence services that emphasize confidentiality, and working at the family, peer, and school levels to foster healthy relationships.

Social support systems involve kinship, friendship, and peer networks, and the configuration of these supports is contingent on the issue being presented and the sociodemographics of the parties involved.

Youth with higher levels of social connectedness are more likely to report higher levels of well-being as manifested through life satisfaction, confidence, positive affect, and aspirations (Jose, Ryan, & Pryor, 2012). Holder and Coleman (2015, p. 81), in a rare publication specifically focused on children's friendships and positive well-being, found a close and positive relationship between the two:

> Children's friendships are closely associated with children's positive well-being. Children who enjoy close friendships are more likely to experience higher levels of happiness, life satisfaction and self-esteem and less likely to be lonely, depressed or victimized. Friendships during childhood are predictive of greater self worth and coping skills later in life but the direction of the relationship between children's well-being and their friendships (i.e., whether well-being is a cause or consequence of friendships) is not firmly established.

Though the study of the links between children's happiness and friendships is relatively sparse, recent developments in measures of children's well-being are encouraging.

Creating activities that nurture mindfulness and the creation of supportive friendships and positive peer networks can enhance life satisfaction and well-being (Greenberg & Harris, 2012; Mendelson et al., 2010; Morgan et al., 2011; O'Donnell et al., 2014).

Our understanding of friendships can be viewed from a modern evolutionary historical perspective, in similar fashion to any other social science concept or construct, in order to more fully appreciate how our understanding has changed over time (Grayling, 2013; Lewis, Al-Shawaf, Russell, & Buss, 2015; Roberts, Arrow, Gowlett, Lehmann, & Dunbar, 2014). The systematic study of children's peer relationships, including friends, can be traced back to the 1920s, but it was not until the 1970s that theories were advanced to integrate empirical knowledge (Erwin, 1998). It seems as if no academic discipline has eschewed studying friendship because of its importance in shaping human relationships (Adams & Allan, 1998; Bagwell & Schmidt, 2013). Incidentally, friendship as an area of study is not restricted to humans, as noted earlier (Seyfarth & Cheney, 2012; Weinstein & Capitanio, 2012).

The influence of friendships can span many different social arenas, and it can be experienced in many obvious and less obvious and unusual ways. The foundation of the social work profession, for example, can be traced back to the influence of friendships. Stebner's (1997) study of the role and influence of women in the creation of Chicago's Hull House highlights the power that an inner circle of friendships, sharing a common background and embracing certain social values, had among these social work pioneers, and how they supported each other during periods of great adversity.

Blatterer (2014) argues that the history of Western thought can also be considered the history of friendship, as noted earlier in this chapter. The importance of friends can be traced back to ancient writings, and this has been well-documented in various well-known histories (Jusdanis, 2014; Konstan, 1997; Stern-Gillet & Gurtler, 2014; Trumbull, 1908). A number of outstanding history books have been written on the subject. Williams's (2012) book, *Reading Roman Friendship*, for example, highlights the role and the study of friendship in antiquity, again showing the timelessness and importance of friendship from a historical perspective.

Caine's (2014) *Friendship: A History* traces the social history of friendship in Europe from the Hellenistic period to the modern day and explores the language of friendship, including its significance in relationship to ethics, social institutions, religious organizations, and political alliances. Cicero's *Laelius de Amicitia* views friendship from a life span perspective, taking into account how friendship evolves and manifests itself differently during key developmental stages (de Luce, 2009). Finally, Good's (2014) *Founding Friendships: Friendships Between Men and*

Women in the Early American Republic illustrates the importance of friendships in the establishment of the United States of America.

Allan (1998, p. 685), almost 40 years ago, laid out a sociological perspective on studying friendship that highlights the role and influence of context that still applies today:

> This article is concerned with the contribution that sociology has made to our understanding of the ways in which friendships are socially patterned. Rather than treating these ties as individual or dyadic constructions, it examines how the social and economic contexts in which they develop influence their form. It focuses particularly on the impact that social location has on friendship, arguing that both class and status divisions are important for understanding the character of informal solidarities. However, both of these must be seen as dynamic, for neither class nor status characteristics are fixed; both alter biographically and historically, and as they alter they pattern the friendships individuals sustain.

The sociocultural forces shaping how friendship gets defined and manifested calls for a contextual grounding with an understanding that, like any other social construct, friendship is dynamic and responsive to changes in the surroundings.

There is no denying that friendship is a dynamic concept and highly responsive to life circumstances and sociocultural and socioenvironmental factors; friendships are elastic and can change in response to our life circumstances (Digesar, 2013, p. 35):

> Evidence of friendship's flexibility and breadth of character is not difficult to find. Not all of our friendships are the same and none is immune to change. The friends with whom we go to the movies, out to dinner, or celebrate the New Year may not be the friends at work or the bridge group or in the mosque. The friends that we have made simply because they lived next door may not be the friends with whom we confide our secrets and seek consolation. Our friendships at work may be extraordinarily important and, in many respects, fulfilling but those may not be friends with whom we feel most relaxed and ourselves. These differences that we experience are not hard and fast. Sometimes our closest friends fade out of our lives and other times a mere acquaintance, known for years, is transformed into a close and loyal friend. At any given time, different friends and sometimes the same friends play different roles. The diversity of the relationship is astoundingly rich and important to us.

Not all friendships are the same; friendships are dynamic, evolving over time to take into account different social and emotional needs. Helping professions understand and embrace how the lifecycle of human development brings changes in the nature of social relationships. However, this author does not believe that it has paid special attention to the role of friendships.

As this book will highlight, friendships take on even greater importance in life circumstances where youth have been marginalized and have limited access to influential resources. These youth encounter restrictions that curtail their geographical mobility or limit their access to those public spaces where they are validated and even liked or admired (Baiocco, Laghi, Di Pomponio, & Nigito, 2014; Bolzan & Gale, 2012; Kullman, 2014). Youth who are marginalized or facing particularly challenging situations can benefit from having friends help them in their struggles.

Urban friendships that transpire in what is referred to as *third spaces* (open public spaces) expose youth to increased opportunities to expand their friendship networks. Witten, Kearns, and Carroll (2015) highlight the importance of public places in assisting youth to learn about, interact with, and even befriend strangers: "The diversity of people living in a city is often most visible on inner-city streets. These streets are also the neighborhood of children who live in the central city. In the past, the wellbeing and sensibilities of children have been marginalized in planning practices in western cities but this is beginning to change." Creating public spaces that expose youth to other age groups and people from different backgrounds helps break down stereotypes for all involved.

Youth friendships are not limited to peer networks, can cross other social divides, and can even involve adults of all ages. However, there is no denying that youth social networks are very age constricted, making the options for friendships limited and thereby increasing the importance of the limited number of potential friendships that are possible. Youth often lead highly structured or scripted lives.

Social factors and considerations related to when during the day youth have an opportunity to engage with friends require further study, as in the case of friendship relationships during the nighttime, for example (van Liempt, van Aalst, & Schwanen, 2015). Urban youth living in high crime areas face challenges in undertaking outside activities with friends without risking potential physical harm. This makes public spaces that are safe and conducive to social interactions that much more meaningful in their lives (e.g., youth programs).

Urban Friendships as Community Assets

Community assets can come in many different forms. Entertaining the possibility that friendships can be thought of as community assets opens up immense possibilities for developing a more in-depth understanding of this form of relationship in the lives of youth. When friendships are included as possible assets, one international study (Spain) found that friends came in second only to family in importance (Pérez-Wilson et al., 2015). Embracing social relationship skills that help one make and retain friendships is an internal youth asset (Oman et al., 2015; Sesma Jr., Mannes, & Scales, 2013). In similar fashion to any other form of asset, internal assets can be enhanced or undermined, as evidenced by the work of the

Minneapolis Search Institute addressed later in this book; if we ignore assets or systematically seek to extinguish them, it will cause consequences that can last a lifetime.

Morgan and Ziglio (2010, p. 3) discuss how a focus on deficits provides a very distorted, narrow (and we add unethical) view of communities that does a tremendous disservice to those living there:

> Deficit models tend to define communities and individuals in negative terms, disregarding what is positive and works well in particular populations. In contrast, "asset" models tend to accentuate positive capability to identify problems and activate solutions. They focus on promoting salutogenic resources that promote the self-esteem and coping abilities of individuals and communities, eventually leading to less dependency on professional services. Much of the evidence available to policy makers to inform decisions about the most effective approaches to promoting health and to tackling health inequities is based on a deficit model. This may disproportionately lead to policies and practices which disempower the populations and communities who are supposed to benefit from them. An assets approach to health and development embraces a "salutogenic" notion of health creation and in doing so encourages the full participation of local communities in the health development process. The asset model presented here aims to revitalise how policy makers, researchers and practitioners think and act to promote a more resourceful approach to tackling health inequities.

Although Morgan and Ziglio specifically discuss community assets and health, clearly their comments are not bound by this focus and can be extended beyond these boundaries.

Privileged communities have no difficulty in listing assets and strengths, and projecting an image of self-confidence. However, marginalized communities are rarely thought of as having assets (Delgado & Humm-Delgado, 2013). Rather, deficits, needs, and problems are more closely associated with these communities and project an image of a community in disarray (Delgado, 1999; Van Willigen, 2005). A focus on assets, in similar fashion to the more conventional perspective that emphasizes problems, introduces new language that is affirming rather than damning (Benson, 2003; Green & Haines, 2011; Mathie & Cunningham, 2003). Policies that effectively disempower youth of color through emphasis on merit, deservingness, and blame emanate from a deficit paradigm (Fine & Ruglis, 2009).

According to Oliver (2001, p. x) community assets can be defined as "An 'asset' in this paradigm is a special kind of resource that an individual, organization, or an entire community can use to reduce or prevent poverty and injustice. An asset is usually a 'stock' that can be drawn upon, built upon, or developed, as a resource that can be shared or transferred across generations." Oliver's definition brings a strong social justice focus, making it particularly relevant to youth, their communities, and urban youth community practice.

Delgado and Humm-Delgado (2013) categorized seven major types of assets by taking into account how local social-cultural-economic-political factors shape how they become manifested at the local level: (1) political, (2) cultural, (3) social, (4) human, (5) economic, (6) physical, and (7) intangible ("invisible"). These seven assets can exist in various manifestations and strengths, but urban community practitioners must first be willing to envision these assets as existing before assessing, enhancing, and mobilizing them in social interventions. Friendships can easily fall into these assets categories, with the exception of physical assets.

Whiting, Kendall, and Wills (2013) discuss the need for asset-based strategies to be based on how children/youth conceptualize these internal/external resources, in this case related to public health but also applicable for community practice. Furthermore, although children's assets have been considered in the health realm, the information gathered has not been from a child's perspective, thus raising serious concerns about the value of this information.

The role and importance of urban youth friendships must be grounded within a community's assets paradigm for the purposes of developing an assessment and intervention. This type of grounding takes on even greater significance because we rarely think of friendships from a strengths or asset perspective when discussing urban youth (Elias Rodas, 2011). A paradigm shift from deficits to strengths, assets, and resiliency is occurring, but youth of color have not been significant beneficiaries of this shift (Borrero, Lee, & Padilla, 2013; Travis & Leech, 2014). Unfortunately, the general reaction is one that sees urban youth of color as deficits and, by extension, their families, peers, and friendships (Creasey & Jarvis, 2013).

Nicolas et al. (2008) argue that a deficit perspective relies on a certain vocabulary to reinforce a negative stance:

> The strengths of Black youths lie in their abilities to resist the barriers that they encounter in the various environments in which they exist. Yet the media and social science literature have defined the youths in terms of the pathology of their environments rather than focusing on the assets that Black youths use in such environments. Thus, terms such as *inner city*, *urban*, and *at-risk* are used as proxies for the youths' personality attributes and themes, such as violence, substance abuse, school underachievement, and family instability are used to define their life experiences. In doing so, the literature suggests that the negative behaviors that it ascribes to Black youths are normative in actuality.

This stance gives significant new meaning to the concept of "person-in-environment" by criminalizing youth simply because of their age, color of their skin (phenotype), and where they reside.

Gaylord-Harden et al. (Gaylord-Harden, Burrow, & Cunningham, 2012) advocate for a culturally based asset developmental approach and framework for tapping indigenous resources to aid youth of color in combating racial discrimination, but this approach has a much broader reach potential to include other assets or capital generally overlooked when discussing reaching urban youth (Neblett, Rivas-Drake, & Umaña-Taylor, 2012). Community assets, as touched on earlier in this section and which will be addressed in the following chapter in much greater depth, are multifaceted and often invisible to those outside of the community who are using a deficit paradigm to guide their interventions.

A capacity enhancement paradigm that is predicated on systematically tapping community assets holds much promise for informing youth community practice that integrates friendships into an intervention. When youth strengths/assets are integrated within community development or community capacity enhancement through youth participatory mechanisms, the potential increase in the significance of peers and friends is made even more possible (Brennan, Barnett, & Lesmeister, 2007; Serido, Borden, & Perkins, 2011).

Cox (2008, p. 20) emphasizes that any efforts to enhance youth strengths must first start with an in-depth assessment, which will then serve as the basis for a strategic intervention:

> The model for building on youth strengths suggested here begins with a thorough assessment of the child or adolescent's capacities, interests, and resources. It progresses to a formal process of strengths recognition and, finally, the development of strength-based intervention focused on 1) creating an enabling niche and 2) utilizing this niche as a vehicle for furthering the youth's progress toward improved functioning."

Such an assessment would not be complete or comprehensive without including friends and peer networks (Reynolds & Crea, 2015). However, such an assessment will be challenging and will necessitate innovative thinking and methods that go beyond the conventional; this will be addressed in Chapter 6.

Research on African-American youth has found the power and influence of family to be a protective and resilience influence (Li, Nussbaum, & Richards, 2007). The importance of family among Latino youth necessitates that we have an understanding of how family relations translate into friendship development (Delgado, 2006). However, research on the associations between parent–adolescent relationships and friendships among Latinos is very limited. Research has shown that among Mexican-American adolescents, the nation's largest Latino youth group, there is a close relationship between their parents and same-sex friends (Rodriguez, Perez-Brena, Updegraff, & Umaña-Taylor, 2014).

There is no disputing the importance of family in the lives of youth and the role that family can play in helping children develop social skills that can help them make friendships (Ferrer-Chancy, 2012). However, youth peers and particularly friends must be accounted for in this assessment of strengths and assets. Morch and Andersen (2012, p. 509) make important observations concerning the role of peers and friends and why they wield such influence in meeting youth needs:

> Although parents want to help their children, the worlds of parents and youth are so different that it can be both difficult for parents to lend support and

irrelevant for the young people to take up the offers of support. So the need for social support and advice gives the peer group its entirely new significance. The peers who are in the same situation as their friends are seen as the local and contextual experts. However, friends often have the same kind of challenges, circumstances, and future prospects as the young person himself/herself. So, when young people become dependent on a friends support, friends help reproducing typical attitudes and practices bound by gender, social class, and ethnicity.

When viewing friendships from a social-ecological perspective, influencing a youth may ultimately result in influencing the lives of their immediate social circle of close friends in the process, thus putting social interventions focused on friendships into a prominent place among interventions overall.

The increasing importance of friendships makes friendship-focused social interventions that much more relevant. Healy (2011) notes that the importance of youth friendships is such that schools must pay conscious and purposeful attention to it. Friendships are a critical concept, but schools rarely address it beyond instances where friends engage in disputes and are disruptive to the educational process. A call to educators and schools to address the subject of youth friendships is in order, and a similar call can be made to helping professions (Epstein & Karweit, 2014). The bringing together of schools and out-of-school settings can be quite powerful in reinforcing this form of relationship.

Gathering information on friendships in a purposeful manner will serve to rectify a dearth of information on the topic, which, in turn, can help guide community practice. Neighborhood- and community-level influences, including peers and friendships, must be systematically identified and considered when designing youth development interventions to reduce risk behaviors (Kegler et al., 2005). Once cast against an assets backdrop, these relationships increase in prominence to be worthy of urban community practice interventions.

Increasing the pool of youth who understand what it means to be a friend, become strong friends, or even become part of a cadre of friends in a community increases social capital (bridging and bonding), and friends helping friends increases human capital and can be an innovative use of resources in community practice. Creating programmatic opportunities for youth to engage in activities that help create, maintain, and enhance friendships that can assist them in navigating urban life's trials and tribulations can be either an explicit or implicit goal.

Critical Place Theory

The reader may initially wonder what critical place theory is doing in a book on urban youth friendships since friendships are relationship-based and, some would argue, universal and are not inherently tied to geographical place. Critical place theory provides practitioners and scholars with a frame within which to understand and appreciate how place—in this instance urban—shapes relationships of all kinds, and youth friendships are no exceptions.

Critical theory, not unexpectedly, was never intended to be a formula or cookbook recipe for how to undertake and achieve social justice and social change: it is first and only a theory, with all of its strengths and foibles, yet having great influence on how a theory comes to life based upon local circumstances (Brenner, 2012). This stance helps explain its wide appeal, reach, and variety of interpretations.

The concept of place enters into the discussion of critical place theory from a geographical perspective. Rios, Vasquez, and Miranda (2012) provide an excellent description that complements critical place theory:

> From a scholarly perspective, "place" does not represent a coherent single idea. The concept has been defined by multiple disciplinary threads ranging from philosophy, geography, and architecture to cultural anthropology and environmental psychology. Broadly defined, place refers to territorized local communities, collective memories by local actors, phenomenological associations with locales, and social relationships among people in territorial communities. . . . In other words, place is a setting for the everyday, the location of ideas and practices, and identity produced by place.

This encompassing viewpoint of space, when combined with critical theory, provides a conceptual frame through which relationships can be understood, challenged, and addressed through practice.

Mayer (2012) argues that cities are contested spaces and that residents often take a backseat to development, businesses, and profit, causing them to have to engage in protest in an effort to take back their communities. However, unlike adult counterparts, youth face severe restrictions and penalties associated with how they live their lives and socially navigate urban places and the consequences of establishing friendships across multisectors (Burke, Greene, & McKenna, 2016). This argument, however, must be cast against a background where there is considerable debate about the scope and limits of urban theory (Kratke, 2012; Scott & Storpes, 2014).

These forces shape how youth in inner cities conceptualize their environment and how to best socially navigate their surroundings, and this shapes housing options, which, in turn, shape the degree and nature of interactions (Darrah & DeLuca, 2014). The limited open space becomes a contested ground for control. Parks and playgrounds, for example, are often too small to address community needs, rarely kept up, and unsafe (Delgado, 2013).

How urban communities are conceived of and perceived profoundly influences how we go about deciding whether or how to intervene within their defined boundaries (Schmid, 2013). However, how neighborhoods define themselves can be at odds with how City Hall defines them. Neighborhood perceptions, as a result, are not inconsequential. Shared ethnic/racial backgrounds, histories, and struggles, particularly when consisting of histories of oppression, shape identity and relationships, including how friendships are defined and acted upon. At the opposite end of the continuum, it certainly is no mistake that the Occupy Movement transpired in very symbolic sections of cities because of how the identity of these spaces was associated with greed and abuse of power (Lubin, 2012).

Schmid (2013, p. 50) provides an eloquent description of how urban space comes to life, with implications for how practice unfolds and takes into account local circumstances:

> Space has, first of all, a perceptible component that can be grasped with the five senses. It relates directly to the materiality of the elements that contribute space. Spatial practice combines these elements into a special order, an order of synchronicity. Urban space is therefore a place of material interaction and of physical encounter. . . . This means that urban space can be empirically observed. What is happening in the streets? Who is present? Primarily, what is meant here is the physical presence of people in urban space.

Space without people to inhabit and interact within it is just that: space. Thus, Schmid's observations regarding urban space as context and shaper of interactions provides a backdrop for contests to transpire.

Critical theory has roots in philosophy and the history of the social sciences, and it has a long history that can be traced back more than one century to a select group of philosophers and social theorists (the Western European Marxists) and the Frankfort School. Brenner (2012) argues that the Frankfort School is "unapologetically abstract." Brenner (2012) applies critical place theory to urban settings through the use of four key critical elements or propositions: (1) critical theory is first and foremost about theory, (2) it is reflexive, (3) critique plays an instrumental role, and (4) it is centered on the disjuncture between the actual and the possible. Each of these four elements are highly interrelated and cannot be understood or appreciated in isolation from the others.

Critical place theory has found particular prominence and manifestations in a variety of scholarly and practice areas dealing with groups that are oppressed, most notably as critical race theory, critical youth theory, critical place theory, critical ethnography, critical feminist theory, critical class theory, critical colonial theory, critical queer theory, and critical disability theory. Critical theory has provided social scientists and helping professionals with a lens and language that facilitate reflectivity and praxis, essential elements in any effort to redress social ills. The various groups that critical theory examines share a fate of having experienced "dis-citizenship" and being relegated to second-class citizenship status.

Social science disciplines and the helping professions have not escaped the reach of critical theory: critical sociology, critical anthropology, critical communication, critical criminology, critical education, critical economics, critical planning theory, critical geography, critical history, critical psychology, critical participatory action research, critical social work, critical nursing, and critical youth practice are examples. It has found other manifestations, as well: critical service learning, critical civic engagement, and critical research are but three prominent examples that have found a place when focused on the nation's youth. Critical urban theory seeks to break down the social totality of cities by focusing on what is broken and/or contradictory, and this helps to explain how the theory has managed to permeate so many different professions and fields of practice (Brenner, 2013).

Urban places have historically been contested places in this society, and select communities within the urban environment have been particularly contested, as evidenced by the upsurge in police-related shootings that have resulted in the deaths of men of color, many of them young (Gualini, Allegra, & Mourato, 2015; Felluga, 2015). Unauthorized or illegal immigrants are another group that often lives in contested space. It is impossible to read a newspaper or watch a national news program without having the topic of unauthorized immigrants be fuel for a debate about the need to control our borders. The urban spaces that immigrant children and youth occupy have become even more contested in light of increasing political stances that demonize them and their families (Aitken, Swanson, & Kennedy, 2014).

These urban places are also home to high percentages of youth and low-income/low-wealth people of color, and such places are widely considered to be feeders to those schools and other systems that have been conceived of as pipelines to the nation's prisons or graveyards. The militarization of urban public schools and police departments is one of the latest manifestations of critical place theory with particular significance for youth. Critical place theory brings together groups (intersectionality) that on the surface appear to be disparate but that share marginalization and a contested geographical setting.

There are numerous other examples of contextualized urban places that can be viewed from a critical place theory perspective. Gentrification and the struggle for rights in urban communities is yet another and increasingly frequent example of how critical place theory can help practitioners and scholars (Jennings & Jordan-Zachery, 2010a). Another example relates to crime. One study of violence in Newark, New Jersey, found that almost one-third of all shootings occurred in a social network that consisted of fewer than 4% of that city's total population (Papachristos, Braga, Piza, & Grossman, 2015). Although not reported, a comparable study involving zip codes will reinforce the interaction of physical space and its residents, and, in this case, those who were victims of shootings.

The spatial aspects of conflict provide a geographical frame or lens through which we can view urban dynamics, how contested space unfolds, and oppression (Brown, 2006). The use of eminent domain as a legal tool has a long history of displacing marginalized groups in the interest of economic development (Jennings & Jordan-Zachery, 2010b). Seeing eminent domain as an apolitical contest strategy misses key elements, and critical place theory helps rectify this stance. The discussion of anti-urban sentiments in this country in Chapter 4 contextualizes the role and importance of space in shaping attitudes and corresponding policies and programs. Critical place theory provides scholars and practitioners with a language, analysis lens, and intervention goals.

The concentration of select groups within the confines of very rigid geographical boundaries helps ensure limited contact with outside groups but also makes it easier to monitor and control. As a result, urban youth of color in these communities are very restricted in developing relationships outside of their immediate neighborhoods and the institutions that serve—and some argue control—their movements. Schools are an important example (Aitken, 2001), as is the relevance of the education that is offered (Kawai, Serriere, & Mitra, 2014; Weller, 2003). These schools as contested spaces are neither comfortable nor affirming, and they do not engender feelings of belonging and inclusion (Burke et al., 2016).

High population density, as is the case of many urban schools and communities, makes it easier to interact with large numbers of individuals, which is different from rural areas. Opportunities to engage in the lawful pursuit of economic ventures are limited in communities where there has been systematic disinvestment by government and the private sector, as in the case of inner-city neighborhoods (Brown, 2006). Gangs, as a result, bring an economic enterprise to these neighborhoods and can become an integral part of the informal economy.

Research has shown that youth with multiple groups of friends experience greater constraints on behavior and are less likely to engage in antisocial acts, and population density plays an influential role here, with lower density situations lending themselves to more successful interventions (Roman, 2012). This finding makes prosocial friendships even more important in highly dense urban communities.

Those residing in the nation's inner cities, and who are excluded or marginalized have rights, and these rights must be safeguarded (Marcuse, 2012). Urban centers must not be conceptualized as "war-torn," with the language and imagery that accompanies this viewpoint. Urban youth, in turn, are not war casualities and should not be labeled as such through the use of terms such as "at-risk," "damaged," or "super predators," to note but three common labels.

How does contested urban space impact youth friendships? Youth who believe they are under siege from outside forces will gravitate toward each other to face a common force or enemy. These alliances may not form without this viewpoint. Friendships resulting from shared adversary can give these youth a sense of protection but also may result in unlawful criminal activities, as in the case of gangs, that can further target them for deleterious consequences.

Youth Community Social Work Practice

The field of youth community practice goes by many different names; this brings its share of rewards and challenges and is worthy of attention in this book. Youth development can go under many different names related to prevention without mentioning youth development, for example, making it challenging to obtain an accurate measurement of the extent of this field. Service-learning initiated through schools and community-based organizations, too, can be based on youth development principles and methods, but, to the outside world, there is nothing in the program titles that would give the impression that they are youth development influenced and directed (Bird & Markle, 2012; Delgado, 2016a; Samuelson, Smith, Stevenson, & Ryan, 2013).

Flexibility in how this field is named allows practitioners to claim a definition that best matches their preferences and allows for local circumstances to dictate how this field unfolds. "Youth work" and "community work" are probably the most popular terms used to describe this field, and these reflect a strong European influence (Banks, 2012; Chanan & Miller, 2013; Fusco, 2012; Jeffs & Smith, 2010; Spence, 2008; Twelvetrees, 2008).

It is not unusual, however, to see the subject of what constitutes practice closely tied to community work/practice (Edwin & Rosenblatt, 2015, p. xii): "some community workers describe themselves as educators. Others may view themselves, first and foremost, as organizers (of groups and activities) or as animateurs and developers. As a result, community work can take various forms. . . . Thus, community work can be approached as work that fosters peoples' commitment to their neighbors, and participation in, and development of, local democratic forms of organizations." Community-centeredness or community-centrality is clear in this form of practice regardless of the age group being addressed. Coussée's (2009, p. 1) description of youth work practice conveys both the excitement and challenge of this field of practice in Europe but also sets a wonderful context for understanding European parallels with community social work practice in the United States:

> Youth work is a polyvalent and multi-faceted practice. It takes place in a wide range of settings, it varies from unstructured activities to fairly structured programmes, it reaches a large diversity of young people, touches a lot of different themes and is on the interface with many other disciplines and practices. This versatility is one of the strengths of youth work. Young people grow up in very different situations. Youth work has the power to respond in a flexible way to this diversity. The fragmentation and methodical differentiation originates in the unremitting attempt to increase the reach of youth work, but at the same time this versatility leads to fragmentation and product vagueness.

This description illustrates why community work or practice can easily incorporate youth work or youth development as it has been conceptualized in other parts of the world, and most notably in Europe (Bradford, 2012).

Youth work, however, must endeavor not to further marginalize youth in the process of helping them if it is true to its goals and mission (Davies, 2015; Skott-Myhre, 2006). This statement may seem obvious to the reader. However, marginalization, it is important to emphasize, can transpire in both obvious and subtle ways, and the latter can be done under the best of intentions.

In the United States, there is no such field as "youth work." In general, most child- and youth-focused practice falls within the purview of child welfare, most notably foster care, and interventions focused on therapeutic services. Social work, not surprisingly, plays an instrumental role in this field, with micro-level social work practice arguably dominating the service-provision field (Holland, 2010; Webb, 2011). Youth-focused work, as a result, cuts across helping professions, including education, recreation, psychology, and social work, to note but four that stand out in my view.

The emergence of youth development as a field of practice in the late 1980s and 1990s (positive and youth-led) has opened up new arenas that are not micro-therapeutically focused. Youth development, as a result, has been conceptualized as belonging within the pantheon of community social work practice. Insertion of the prefix "youth" (youth social work practice or youth community practice for short) broadens practice that transpires within a community context, making it age-specific. For example, sport coaches in urban communities can expand their role from a narrow focus on athletics to one encompassing activities that can be defined as community practice and youth development (Richardson Jr., 2012).

The same can be said about coaches in elite sporting contexts because of their great influence in shaping character and not just athletic abilities (Strachan, Côté, & Deakin, 2011). Slam poetry, which will be addressed in Chapter 2, has strong competitive elements and has been compared to a sporting event, bringing an urban-friendly perspective to competition, social justice, and personal narratives (Waite, 2015). (Although the reader may have difficulty comprehending how poetry can be a competitive "sport," so to speak, contests are used to eliminate competitors and crown winners in a way very similar to sporting events.)

Having laid out a brief overview of youth and community work in Europe, we must ask: Is the topic of friendship integral to this form of practice there, or have our European counterparts, too, eschewed this form of social relation in their practice? A review of several major youth work books revealed no significant references to friends or friendships. When friends were mentioned, they invariably were addressed in passing reference and not considered of sufficient importance to warrant specific and in-depth attention, as evidenced through a section of a book or even a chapter devoted to the subject.

Nybell, Shook, and Finn's (2013) edited book *Childhood, Youth, and Social Work in Transformation: Implications for Policy and Practice*, for example, falls into this latter category but still manages to make important observations concerning youth friendships. In essence, youth work/youth community practice can cross conventional lines of practice through embracing innovative thinking (Batsleer, 2008; Coburn, 2010; Cooper, 2012). Engaging in friendship enhancement is an extension of this creative potential perspective on youth community practice (Lewis, 2011). Unfortunately, youth-focused work on friendships is still in its infancy, but this is not to say that peer relationships are not part of certain interventions. The specific focus on friendships is missing. For example, youth community practice can focus on helping youth cultivate positive peer and friendship networks through a variety of methods, including development of publications and social media that can be accessed by both program and nonprogram participants (Furgang & Furgang, 2012).

Community Practice and Friendships

Interestingly, the significance of friendships has generally not translated into community practice-specific intervention goals. It seems as if the topic has been relegated to therapists and addressed on a one-to-one (micro) basis. This approach, although helpful to individuals, has ignored the role of social glue that friendships play within communities and how they are essential in creating a social fabric that results in a sense of community that is essential in any well-functioning community. An individualized approach is not the focus of community social work practice, however.

Community practice expands the concept of friendships beyond individuals to the broader community or specific subgroups, as in the case of youth. For example, our understanding of the role of youth friendship networks in public places such as libraries is seriously understudied (Valdivia, 2013). The same can be said about urban youth friendships in urban museums, playgrounds, and parks, too. These social arenas and other urban public spaces are excellent venues for community practice initiatives focused on friendships.

I remember doing a case study of a midnight basketball youth development program in the Midwest that covered many different activities during high-crime hours. The program emphasized teamwork, communication and social skills, sexually transmitted disease (STD) prevention, and school academic subjects, and even had an entrepreneurial dimension with program youth selling food and t-shirts at the basketball games to raise money for program activities.

Neighborhood-based organizations are venues that can be thought of as sanctuaries where urban youth can be reached and community practitioners can tap community assets and enhance social skill development (Delgado, 2002; Quane & Rankin, 2006). These types of settings are ideal places where youth can "hang-out" with friends and potentially make new friends if there is an organizational climate that is safe, affirming, and understands the value of this form of social relationship (Strobel, Kirshner, O'Donoghue, & Wallin McLaughlin, 2008).

Outstanding Books on Friendships

This book seeks to carve out a scholarly area that has generally escaped serious attention by having the entire volume devoted to urban youth of color friendships. This is not to say, however, that outstanding books on the subject of friendships do not exist, because they do, and this book seeks to openly build on that scholarship in moving the field of urban youth community practice forward. It is appropriate to pause and credit these scholarly works.

Friendship has certainly been the focus of scholarship, as evidenced by the enormous amount of articles and chapters written on the subject, and this book draws on much of this literature, although there is a paucity of literature on youth of color from a developmental and nondeficit point of view, as the reader will see. The absence of a book on the subject that not only synthesizes this literature but also introduces community practice implications is much needed. Just because a book has not been written on a topic, however, does not mean that one should be written. That is clearly not the case in this instance.

A number of books cover some of the key elements addressed in this book, and all are excellent. Five books stand out because of their importance. Chen, French, and Scheider's (2006) edited book *Peer Relations in Cultural Context* is a well-edited work, and I cite several chapters in this book because it brings a socio-cultural multifaceted perspective to peer relationships, including friendships. However, it covers a wide variety of topics and does not focus on urban youth of color, although its emphasis on culture makes it a meaningful contribution to the literature that embraces a socioecological focus on relationships.

Greg Dimitriadis's (2003) *Friendship, Cliques, and Gangs: Young Black Men Coming of Age in Urban America* follows the lives of two African-American youth with dramatically different pathways and touches on key aspects of urban youth friendship, including a treatment of how environment shapes these relationships. However, it is dated, its review of the literature is limited, and it does not focus on intervention strategies. Bagwell and Schmidt's (2013) *Friendship in Childhood and Adolescence* provides a comprehensive review of and foundation for how friend-ships change and the potential interventions that can be used to help them during various developmental stages. Unfortunately, this book does not focus specifically on urban youth of color or on community practice.

Hruschka's (2010) *Friendship: Development, Ecology, and Evolution of a Relationship* (vol. 5) takes a broad overview of friendship across the life span and provides a very good contextualization of how friendships are influenced by a host of social forces, and it has a specific chapter devoted to the childhood-to-adulthood period. Finally, Whalon's (2014) book *Friendship 101: Helping Students Build Social Competence*, is signaled out because of its focus on youth with developmen-tal disabilities and the specific challenges they face in establishing and maintaining friends. This book integrates key concepts related to social competence and offers practical suggestions in this area, although it is not urban youth-focused.

My Interest in Urban Youth Friendships

Tracing the origins of an interest in a topic of sufficient significance to devote several years to the writing and production of a book is an arduous task, and that is certainly the case regarding this book on urban youth and friendships. My personal interest in youth friendships goes back to my own youth in the South Bronx, New York City, where I experienced the difficulty of socially navigating a challenging environment and peer groups representing the entire spectrum from positive to negative—and all in a day's work, so to speak.

It was impossible for me to focus exclusively on positive peers because both positive and negative networks overlapped within buildings, streets, and institutions such as schools, houses of worship, and neighborhoods. In other words, these peer networks were never concentrated in one setting. Negative peers were also impossible to avoid because they could be found alongside positive peers, and there were instances where they were close family members of positive peers or even members of my own family.

The trick was to maintain sufficient contact with the negative peer group without being drawn into that world and losing touch with the positive peer world. In essence, it became a balancing act. Mind you, it wasn't that the positive peer network was always all positive. They, too, had a similar navigational challenge. Carefully choosing friends, as a result, became a process that took on immense significance because, in addition to family, friends were a constant factor in my environment and it was impossible to succeed without "a little help from my friends."

Upon entering the world of practice and eventually entering academia, the interest in urban youth friendship persisted, and it is one that I have dealt with from a distance as I pursued various other scholarly community practice writing projects. This book represents my first "scholarly" entry into the urban youth friendship world with friendship as a central focus and goal. True, friends are part of a peer network, but there is no denying that friends occupy a special place within this constellation.

More specifically, this book is a continuation of my interest in urban community practice and urban youth of color, one taking a strength, resiliency, youth development/youth-led, and/or assets perspective in shaping social interventions and research. These youth face incredible challenges and many survive, and even thrive, despite harsh social conditions and the odds being stacked against them (Bird, 2011). I believe that friends have, and can continue to play, a significant life-changing role in their lives and that we, as community practitioners and academics, must strive to enhance this asset.

Book Goals

The goals a book wishes to accomplish are integrally grounded within the audience it seeks to reach. In other words, authors have a distinct audience that they want to influence. When there is clarity on this, the book becomes easier to write because an author is not tempted by distractions. The question of who best benefits from reading this book is an important one for me. This question goes far beyond what publishers think of as "target audiences" and enters the realm of who this book wishes to influence and support in their quest to use urban youth friendships as a vehicle for supporting youth who reside in socially challenging situations.

This book seeks to bridge three distinctive audiences: (1) graduate-level community social work practice students, (2) urban community practitioners, and (3) urban practice scholars interested in the subject of friendships from an assets/positive youth development intervention paradigm. Each of these groups presents unique needs and challenges, making this a tall order but one worth embracing with fervor because of the importance of the subject. It also increases the impact of this book on urban-focused community practice.

An emphasis on urban youth does not automatically equate with problems and issues (Sukarieh & Tannock, 2011, p. 675): "The field of youth development, long given over to discussions of youth as a time of storm and stress, raging hormones and problem behavior, has increasingly turned to look at the 'sunny side' of youth—at their agency, insights, capabilities and contributions. Youth, we are now regularly told, are not problems but resources and assets." It cannot be emphasized enough that negative stereotypes have predominated youth services. However, we must endeavor to avoid engaging in positive stereotypes, too.

This book is not meant to idealize or romanticize youth friendships or engage in positive urban youth stereotyping (Heaphy & Davies, 2012). Stereotypes of any kind distort reality. Instead, this book simply tries to highlight the potential of these friendships to shape behaviors, perceptions, and outcomes for urban youth while acknowledging that not all friends exert positive and affirming influence.

As a result, this book seeks to accomplish four goals: (1) provide a state of knowledge on the definition, role, and importance of friendships in general and specifically on urban youth of color (African American, Asian, and Latino); (2) draw implications for community practice scholarship and practice; (3) illustrate how friendships can be the focus of a community capacity enhancement assets paradigm through the use of case illustrations; and (4) provide a series of recommendations for how urban friendships can be addressed in graduate-level social work curriculum, but with implications for other helping professions.

Definition of Youth and Age Range Covered in this Book

Any attempt to define what is meant by "youth" is bound to get entangled in philosophical, physiological, and theoretical discourses and debates associated with a social construct that will have many variations and debates (Boocock & Scott, 2005; Jones, 2009). Delgado (2016b) advances the argument that there are no spoken and unspoken assumptions when defining youth: "The social construction of 'youth' or 'adolescence' is predicated on critical notions and assumptions that are not fixed in stone. It is subject to interpretation and debate and must be contextualized to have significant meaning. Youth, too, are not one-dimensional and can be considered as complex as adults, and maybe even more so."

Youth, for the purposes of this book, will primarily cover the period of 11–20 years of age, although youth as young as 5 years and as old as 21 years of age will also be addressed. The younger and older age groups will be covered when literature addresses them. The paucity of literature on urban youth friendships is quite striking, and I do not have the luxury of focusing on a very narrow age range. Thus, the net was purposefully cast widely, although it proves challenging when developing an in-depth understanding of youth programming because it covers such a wide expanse and introduces different developmental needs.

Book Outline

This book consists of three sections and seven chapters and a conclusion: Section I, Setting the Context (four chapters); Section II, Case Illustrations (two chapters); and Section III, Reflections (one chapter and a conclusion). The section on case illustrations, it should be noted, has four case illustrations of varying lengths. I have deliberately elected to cover multiple case studies rather than concentrate on one or two cases that could be covered in greater depth. In other words, a breadth versus depth debate has been settled on the side of breadth. Increasing the number of case illustrations broadens the practice arena but not without sacrificing theoretical depth, details, and clarity.

Conclusion

Youth friendships are very often taken for granted, and, when addressed in the professional literature, they are often part of a broader discussion on peers and peer social relationships. Children's abilities to maintain friendships in more contexts has been found to be positively associated with increased odds of the friendships being longer term, an important outcome in maintaining social stability in their lives and an indicator of potential future strengths in establishing and maintaining relationships (Troutman & Fletcher, 2010).

Some youth have no trouble in establishing and maintaining friendships, whereas others never seem to achieve this goal regardless of how hard they try. The importance of friendships is well established, and it is widely accepted that these relationships are quite complex to understand from a programmatic and scholarly point of view (Grace, 2008). Urban youth friendships as community assets and as possible targets of social interventions have not received the attention and resources they warrant.

The professional literature on the subject will only increase in importance for academics and the helping professions in the foreseeable future as we discover the power and potential of these relationships for youth and their communities and as the field of youth community practice continues to expand into new arenas. The explosion in interest in friendships will span the entire age spectrum, including baby boomers, a notable population bulge.

This introductory chapter has laid out a foundation for and parameters on urban youth friendships and why community practitioners must address these types of peer relations. Friendship has existed since the beginning of time, and these relationships have persisted for very good developmental and social reasons. Friendships in general, and no more so than when discussing marginalized urban youth, must be better understood and appreciated for social interventions to be effective. The next chapter addresses youth community practice and why this form of intervention has a major contribution to make regarding urban youth friendships.

2

Urban Community Practice/Capacity Enhancement

Introduction

As initially addressed in the introductory chapter, there is certainly no disputing that urban youth friendships are important enough to be addressed as a focus in youth community social work practice. The question, however, is how to do this in a manner that is socioculturally grounded and affirming of an urban community's social fabric and that takes into account youth voices on the subject matter (Bernat & Resnick, 2006) and social work's traditional embrace of social justice. This social justice embrace will manifest itself throughout all aspects or phases of youth community practice, including any effort to expand and enhance youth friendship networks and their social skills within an oppressive environment.

A "cookie-cutter" approach to this focus will ultimately do more harm than good because no two urban communities are identical and no two youth groups are identical either, even when sharing the same social and public space (Urban, Lewin-Bizan, & Lerner, 2009). An embrace of an explicit set of values, as addressed in this chapter, helps guide practitioners through the difficult waters of turning theory into practice in an ever-changing world—one that is highly politically charged as a result—and do so in a manner that eschews both negative and positive stereotypes.

Community practice must systematically identify and build on existing indigenous community resources, otherwise referred to as capital, assets, and strengths, and not disempower residents or youth in the process; in addition, it must conceptualize intervention as a team-centered and collaborative effort between professionals and residents to ensure that interventions have significant social, cultural, economic, and political meanings to communities (Chanan & Miller, 2013; Nelson & Adams, 2011). Community interventions that actively seek to eschew local political issues or tensions will be misguided at best and counterproductive at worst, especially when these issues or problems have social justice root causes and, in the case of youth, impinge on their social relationships.

These partnerships must actively seek to have youth as meaningful team members in all facets, including evaluation, and this may cause negative reactions from adults in the community. Because their benefits extend far beyond youth themselves and enter into the realm of community well-being, in the case of interventions targeting youth friendships, we must ask ourselves how do we create, repair, and enhance youth friendships in our role as community practitioners? It must be stressed that youth friendships do not have to conform to their adult counterpart conceptions. Furthermore, these friendships do not have to have universal qualities across all groups of youth.

Viewing friendships as being influenced by urban environmental factors, most particularly cultural and social, and as being grounded within a geographical context (place and space) have dictated the importance of local forces in shaping a multidimensional view of this youth asset and influencing how best to structure interventions to reach this sphere of influence. This chapter will pay close attention to how urban context or social ecology becomes such a powerful force in shaping community practice focused on youth and their friendship network and why it provides both rewards and challenges for the field.

Urban Context

It seems as if everyone in the United States has an image of a city. The mere mention of cities conjures up a wide variety of very vivid images, and unfortunately most of them are not positive. Urban riots (or civil disturbances, if you wish), such as those in Ferguson, Missouri, and Baltimore, Maryland, for example, are embedded in everyone's memory. For those of us old enough to have witnessed the riots of the 1960s and 1970s, these images will forever be emblazoned in our memories. Although cities mean much more than contested spaces, rarely will one find a narrative and set of images that convey a community coming together and caring and supporting each other or making an effort to stop unrest. Cities usually are thought of as buildings and concrete and being highly impersonal, almost totally devoid of any social fabric—mere "concrete jungles." Interestingly, rural areas have more in common with jungles than do cities, but they are never referred to as "rural jungles" or considered contested places.

Cities can also be considered a nation's crown jewels, although rarely referred to in this manner. A nation simply could not survive as a nation without them. They also constitute a vibrant social fabric that serves as a backdrop to understanding how relationships are formed, maintained (as in the case of friendships), and interact with the built environment (Broberg, Kyttä, & Fagerholm, 2013; Sampson, 2012). Having public places that are accessible and safe, such as parks, plazas, and playgrounds, provide opportunities to continue friendships as well as establish new ones.

A nation's cities evolve, change in composition, grow and contract, and react to social and global forces in ways that make the changes resulting from these forces highly visible, with profound social implications for a nation. Some of these changes can be positive. For example, social capital is increased when there is stability in urban community composition (Paranagamage, Austin, Price, & Khandokar, 2010), and this has tremendous implications for friendship and peer network development for youth. The breakdown of these relationships plays a major role in creating a lack of social cohesion that is essential in making communities function and thrive. As the composition of cities has changed and they have become increasingly of color and segregated, which translates into poor schooling, increased police vigilance (including incarceration), and concentration of corresponding social problems, social justice issues emerge.

The concept of social justice has been applied to cities for good reason (Marcuse et al., 2009) and results in the need for theory and practice that can be considered radical or critical to address issues of injustice (Brenner, Marcuse, & Mayer, 2011; Marcuse, 2009). Cities also become the focus of and vehicle for the unfolding of social values that can be affirming, empowering, and embracing of new groups or a target for the perpetration of social injustices.

Urban community social work practice, simply put, is about context, context, and even more context, in similar fashion to real estate being about location, location, location. Community practice is first and foremost about practice within a community, focusing on its social fabric but not disregarding structures or the built environment (Gamble & Weil, 2010; Payne, 2013; Popple & Stepney, 2008). However, distrust of the inner city is compounded by a historical distrust of cities overall (Hofstadter, 1972; Walklate, Hope, & Sparks, 2012), as addressed in greater depth in Chapter 4. Consequently, urban-focused practice signifies a philosophical set of values and practice stance that influences all aspects related to social interventions, and nowhere is this more prevalent than when it is urban- and youth-focused (Ogbu, 2013).

All community practitioners have a favorite context in which they feel most comfortable and effective, and that is quite natural. As a lifelong urban practitioner and one formally educated in urban universities, I know that community practice does transpire in suburban and rural areas of the country and that important work is being accomplished there (Areas, 2012; Flora & Flora, 2014; Luloff & Wilkinson, 2014). However, the concentration of youth and people of color in the nation's urban centers and, too, the social forces marginalizing these groups, makes social justice/critical urban community social work practice highly viable.

Population density makes these communities easier to monitor by enforcement authorities and the media "darlings" of national news coverage. The riots that followed the death of Mr. Freddie Gray in Baltimore, and other deaths and resulting riots across the country, highlight how urban centers represent social injustice zones that have captured large segments of the youth population and destined them to dismal futures, as addressed in Chapter 4. Increased media attention, or what is sometimes cynically referred to as "driveby media" that only appears when an "incident" occurs and goes away when attention to sustainable change requires continual media attention, typifies mainstream media coverage in this nation.

Social workers are very cognizant of the role of the environment in shaping behaviors and the outcomes of those behaviors, and our grounding in socioecological models has helped prepare us for this understanding. Browning and Soller (2014, p. 2) note that important advances have occurred regarding the influence of how urban neighborhoods shape youth outcomes, with implications for how youth engage in friendships and other relationships:

> The image of urban children growing up in economically deprived neighborhoods has spurred more than two centuries of reform and intervention aimed at ameliorating conditions thought to be harmful to youth. Alongside these initiatives, social scientists, policymakers, and health researchers have been engaged in a longstanding project to illuminate the mechanisms through which residential environments shape developmental outcomes.... These efforts have yielded important advances in uncovering the processes that account for variation across urban contexts in the experiences of youth.

How ecological forces positively or negatively shape urban youth friendships have nevertheless generally been overlooked by social scientists, thus limiting the development of interventions specifically focused on enhancing friendships while still seeking to accomplish other goals.

There is little disputing that scholarship on the intervening variables that enable marginalized and oppressed individuals to achieve a state of well-being have generally relied on an individual level of analysis. However, the emergence of a new scholarship emphasizes the importance of context in the lives of individuals and offers much promise for community practice (Case & Hunter, 2012; Duke, Borowsky, & Pettingell, 2012; Wexler & Eglinton, 2015).

The bringing together of the concepts of youth of color friendships and cities makes for an exciting context for all forms of youth community practice and for the introduction of innovation that expands the bounds of what has constituted community practice in the past (Green, 2013; Lekies, Yost, & Rode, 2015). For example, outdoor or wilderness programs can hold great appeal to urban youth (Norton & Watt, 2014; Passarelli, Hall, & Anderson, 2010; Thurber, Scanlin, Scheuler, & Henderson, 2007; Whittington & Mack, 2010), and youth programming can incorporate both outdoor and nature activities (Visscher, 2015). Libraries, too, are community institutions that can be tapped to reach urban adolescents and are places where youth development can transpire through collaborations between librarians and community practitioners (Agosto & Hughes-Hassell, 2010; Delgado, 2002).

It is essential to capture youths' entire network of affiliations (parents, friends, acquaintances, and romantic partners) in order to understand fully the significance of friendships within this constellation, rather than examine them in isolation (Lornado et al., 2009). However, adult practitioners and academics must guard against imposing adult norms and social expectations on youth (including romantic and cross-gender friendships) without making any effort to tap youth views on these and other subjects of great importance in their lives (Erni & Fung, 2010).

Leisure is an important concept across all groups regardless of their demographics, and it can provide an opportunity for youth to engage in positive or negative behaviors (Caldwell & Smith, 2013). However, leisure is precious among low-income youth and the limited amount of time they have for engagement in organized activities. Youth have limited amounts of time in their daily lives that is not controlled by adults, and this time is spent in carrying out their priorities in terms of relationships, with friends (of different levels) being a significant part of these relationships.

If policies and interventions targeting peer networks (those who youth spend time with or hangout with) are to increase the likelihood of success, they cannot ignore friendships and how they are formed and fostered (Halliday & Kwak, 2012; McDonald, Malti, Killen, & Rubin, 2014). Urban neighborhood contexts, particularly those that are highly dense and highly segregated—and as a result undervalued and stigmatizing—cannot be fully understood and appreciated by eschewing the presence and role of friendships, particularly the role they play in helping youth deal with the consequences associated with a wide range of stresses and trauma (Belgrave & Brevard, 2015; Overstreet & Mathews, 2011; Wade, Shea, Rubin, & Wood, 2014). It is not unusual for urban youth to experience trauma that may result in poor agreement between them and caregivers regarding their experiences and feelings (Oransky, Hahn, & Stover, 2013). These situations only make their friendship networks that much more important in their lives. Reinforcing these types of friendships reverberates throughout their social network.

The history of segregation in the United States and the deleterious consequences that have resulted are well understood and reinforced in an embrace of the social justice change agenda. Frey (2015, p. 167): "One of the most intimate settings of American life—one that has especially important role in shaping community race relations—is the neighborhood. Neighborhoods are where Americans socialize, shop, and attend school and where civic matters have the most impact. Most directly . . . the racial makeup of a neighborhood can either foster or prevent interactions with other groups." When neighborhoods are under siege (contested spaces), it dramatically alters all forms of social relationships within their borders, including friendships.

Furthermore, the segregation and stigmatization of youth in inner cities limits their ability to reach outside of the geographical confines of these neighborhoods to tap resources (formal and informal) to help them socially navigate their existence and fulfil their potential as members of society, including the development of friendships from different ethnic and racial backgrounds (Baysu, Phalet, & Brown, 2014; Schaefer, Rodriguez, & Decker, 2014; Schunk & Mullen, 2012; Skelton & Gough, 2013). Even more importantly, these geographical confines limit the reach of their dreams. A circumspect life is a life with compromised chances unless one is rich—and white, non-Latino, heterosexual, and male for that matter.

Geographic proximity is widely considered a significant determining factor in friendships. More specifically, the role and importance of propinquity (geographical proximity), including frequency of contact, is well understood in the professional literature and, when combined with homophily (common demographic resemblance), makes geographically focused intervention particularly attractive, as in the case of urban communities (Amichai-Hamburger, Kingsbury, & Schneider, 2013; Preciado, Snijders, Burk, Stattin, & Kerr, 2012). Understanding the power of proximity, however, goes beyond geographical distance and can include how common interests and beliefs generate connectedness in profound and very strong ways (Wang, Chin, & Wang, 2011).

DiMaggio and Garip (2012, p. 93) address how environmental circumstances and factors ameliorate or exacerbate inequality within neighborhoods (and critical urban space) and the role of social networks, with implications for community social interventions. Tendencies within neighborhoods to foster relationships among similar backgrounds and like-minded individuals has its benefits and liabilities. Homophily will be addressed again in the following chapter because of its influence on friendships and peer networks.

The framing of friendships as a critical source of multifaceted support for urban youth brings this resource forward as important in their lives and worthy of a community practice book devoted to this subject and of urban practitioners and scholars paying serious attention to it. Friendships among street youth, for example, is a severely neglected topic that takes on great significance because of the role such friendships play in helping youth socially navigate demanding ecological circumstances through reliance on cooperation, mutuality, and exchange (Aptekar & Stoecklin, 2013; Mizen & Ofosu-Kusi, 2010; Tyler & Melander, 2011). The unforgiving environment of living in the street often necessitates the creation of a strong ethos of friends helping friends, with friendships being developed that focus on aspects of daily living that are considered essential for survival (Dang, 2014; Mizen & Ofosu-Kusi, 2010).

Community social work practice has addressed a number of social issues and transpired in a wide array of arenas relating to undervalued population groups and geographical settings, with particular attention paid to urban settings and marginalized groups (Delgado, 2013, 2015; 2016b). However, the subject of friendship has escaped the attention it deserves in community practice, even though it represents a natural dimension or extension of any community asset–based paradigm, one that offers the potential for highly innovative forms of interventions that have development and enhancement of urban youth friendship as a central element and, in the process, enhance neighborhood quality of life.

Dolcini et al. (Dolcini, Harper, Watson, Catania, & Ellen, 2005) advocate for social interventions, in this case health promotion, to target youth friends within and outside of schools to increase their well-being and academic performance. Youth with disabilities, like their counterparts without disabilities, desire friends, and friendships are tied to feelings of well-being (Foley et al., 2012). Community-focused interventions, however, allow a broader range of activities because the community is where youth spend the greatest amount of unstructured time and it offers the greatest opportunity for innovative practice.

Culture is an integral part of urban context, and it shapes how interventions must unfold by taking into account ecological considerations and the cultural values of youth (Kim, 2014; Rodríguez, Baumann, & Schwartz, 2011; Scharf, 2014). However, understanding the role of culture and ethnicity necessitates that we view these constructs as not being static. In fact, they have been referred to as "fuzzy," "contextual," and "fluid" for very good reasons and with important implications for research and evaluation (Azmitia, Ittel, & Break, 2006).

Key Values

No social work practice book, particularly one focused on urban community practice, can eschew addressing how values explicitly or implicitly shape and guide interventions (Boehm & Cohen, 2013; Hardina, 2012, 2013; Slavin, Mizrahi, & Morrison, 2013). As Hardcastle, Powers, and Wenocur (2011, p. 20) note:

> Values have a greater emotional charging than do ethics. They motivate ethics and behaviors. Values direct the nature of social work's mission—the relationships, obligations, and duties social workers have for clients, colleagues, and the broader community. Social work's basic value configuration is the result of the many forces and orientations that the profession has been subjected to and embraced over the years. Some authorities hold that social work's value base distinguishes it from other professions.

Values can be thought of as the DNA of practice, with all of the same power and determination in shaping human beings. DNA, however, interacts with the environment, giving the outcome that is most responsive to local circumstances.

Social workers are well versed on how values underpin all aspect of our work, and never more so than when they are dealing with a difficult issue or a population group that is severely stigmatized. The embrace of an explicit set of values shaped the beginning of the profession (which, it should be noted, also started in urban communities) and continues to do so, and values are particularly pronounced when considering youth assets and community capacity enhancement (CCE). For example, a strong youth ethnic identity has been found to serve as a valuable coping mechanism against the forces of discrimination and can be considered a cultural asset that communities can build upon to construct a stronger social fabric (Stevenson & Arrington, 2009; Williams, Aiyer, Durkee, & Tolan, 2014). Way and

Rogers (2014) point out the importance of context in the shaping of racial identity and how empirical research over multiple decades has generally eschewed how the environment shapes it.

Maintaining fidelity to the implementation standards delineated by youth/ community development planners is always a challenge (Fagan, Hanson, Hawkins, & Arthur, 2008): simply put, to plan is human but to implement is divine. Translating theory and research findings into practice remains a challenge, and so does educating practitioners in carrying out the ideals of community practice (Graham & Langa, 2015). Nevertheless, having a clear set of values to guide these efforts helps ensure that fidelity is achieved.

What are the key values when working with urban youth? Identifying and prioritizing them is certainly open to debate, but most youth community practitioners and scholars will place the following in their top-ten list: (1) social justice, (2) assets-first, (3) empowerment, (4) reliance on indigenous knowledge, (5) local leadership development, (6) participatory democracy, and (7) adultism. Most of these values will be familiar to the reader, particular those with interests in social justice youth community practice in urban centers.

Each of these values is closely interrelated while also representing a particular practice stance. When practitioners bring these values to their work and they are reinforced by the organizations they work for, the job of community practitioner becomes easier to carry out. The consequences of a values lacunae between practitioner and organization will result in tension and possible conflict, compromising practice and ultimately failing youth and their communities.

How these values are rank-ordered is also open to debate. However, each of these values is significant on its own. When combined, there is a synergistic effect that creates a practice stance and vision that makes it uniquely youth- and community-focused. Each of these values will be discussed as a central goal in regards to urban marginalized youth, although these values obviously can reach other marginalized groups and be manifested differently based on the unique set of circumstances faced by these groups.

Finally, the reader may ask what ever happened to cultural competency/ humility? Cultural competence/humility is at the central core of the social work profession and for very good reason (Minkler, 2012; Reamer, 2013; Weil, Reisch, & Ohmer, 2012). However, this concept takes on even greater importance when viewed from a community or neighborhood perspective. This value permeates all seven other values, influencing how each gets operationalized in urban youth community practice. Its importance is such that it cannot be a standalone value but one deeply ingrained throughout all community interactional dimensions.

SOCIAL JUSTICE

I simply cannot imagine a list of critical values guiding urban youth community social work practice that would not include a firm embrace of social justice. Any practitioner or academic interested in reaching urban undervalued groups in this society must be guided by a vision and strong embrace of social justice because major social and economic forces have undermined youth abilities to succeed (Cummins, 2015; Staples, 2012).

The social work profession, as one example, has always been profoundly shaped by the extent of social justice's influence on various forms of practice (Ferguson, 2007). Its influence is particularly profound in community practice overall but more so when focused on youth (Delgado, 2016a). This is not to say that the embrace of social justice is universal within this or, one can certainly argue, any other profession.

The field of youth studies, too, is founded on a solid grasp of social justice as it relates to youth as a group (Côté, 2014). When intersectionality is introduced, social justice issues manifest themselves in different ways to take into account the multiple types of oppression that youth must contend with. The concept of Two-Spirit, for example, has emerged to facilitate Indigenous lesbian, gay, bisexual, transsexual, and questioning (LGBTQ) youth and adults to signal their Indigeneity and their queerness as they socially navigate their way through multiple oppressions (Wesley, 2015). Rogers, Scott, and Way (2015), in turn, introduce the concept of intersectionality and its close relationship with racial and gender identity, in this case involving black adolescent males, and its importance in shaping this identity.

Hardcastle, Powers, and Wenocur (2011, p. 341) address the role of values in social work: "social justice is a *sine qua non* of social work's advocacy obligations locally and globally. . . . Social work has chosen a side. Our values compel us to work to end or at least alleviate acute, chronic, and seemingly unfixable." Urban youth community practice is undeniably and profoundly shaped by social justice values, and its embrace of youth is a manifestation of this value in action (Atkinson, 2012; Hage & Kenny, 2009). There is good reason why this value is so prominent in community practice and so closely tied to human rights (Fraser, 2009; Harvey, 2010; Ife, 2012; Reisch, Ife & Weil, 2012), but youth rights have not received the same level and seriousness of attention that other forms of human rights have received worldwide (Delgado, 2016b).

Wearing (2011) argues that an embrace of a rights perspective (and we could substitute/add social justice) results in an inclusive practice approach that translates into increasing marginalized youth self-confidence and resilience and enhancing competencies. Social identity has been found to be shaped by numerous factors in youth lives (White & Wyn, 2008). Social justice campaigns bring multiple obvious and less obvious benefits for youth, including playing a role in shaping their social identity based on a solid grasp of race and ethnicity (Suyemoto, Day, & Schwartz, 2014).

Social justice can easily find a place in youth development efforts that use social action as a vehicle for achieving the goals usually associated with this practice perspective (Schusler & Krasny, 2010). Community-based organizations are ideal settings for undertaking social justice projects. Urban recreational centers ("just spaces"), for example, are often singled out as ideal settings for social justice–informed youth development (Pryor & Outley, 2014; Shiller, 2013).

Christens and Dolan (2011, p. 529) identified four key aspects of urban youth development that, when combined with social justice and social action, shape their expectations and outcomes:

> Compared to other models for youth community engagement, there are at least four distinguishing characteristics of youth organizing initiatives. First, youth organizing initiatives concentrate on the conditions faced by young people, the systematic nature of these conditions, and the role of power in creating and maintaining these conditions . . . . Second, youth involved in organizing learn strategies for collaboratively harnessing their collective social power to challenge powerful people and institutions to make community-level change . . . . Third, youth involved in organizing are choosing the issues that are most important to them through a collective decision-making process rather than working with a group whose issues have been predetermined . . . . Fourth, adults support youth involved in organizing, but youth often take the lead in decision-making processes around issue selection and strategies for achieving community-level change.

Christens and Dolan integrate many key values in advocating for youth social change efforts that benefit youth, their community, and society, and stress the awareness of how these values shape behaviors.

ASSETS-FIRST

A value that embraces assets-first may be new to most readers, and that is understandable. Assets-first draws on practice and literature about people with disabilities. Regardless of abilities and the labels we use, the focus is on the person first and then on the form of disabilities. Assets-first and communities translates into a stance that forces practitioners and academics to first identify assets before focusing on problems, issues, and deficits. This stance goes beyond rhetoric and has some very real pragmatic implications. This value brings forth a new worldview and language to support it when addressing urban communities and marginalized groups within these communities.

An assets-first value helps to counter oppressive forces, and that includes marginalized youth and their respective communities. An assets-first values does not mean, however, that needs, issues, and problems are totally or simply ignored. No community, regardless of its level of affluence, is totally devoid of needs. In similar fashion, no community, no matter how "socially disorganized," "marginalized," or "problem-infested," is totally devoid of assets. An assets-first value does not mean that youth cannot address community problems, and this does not take away from the values articulated in this section. Ife (2010, p. 68) addresses this very point in the following:

There can be some value in community development that is focused on a problem that has been defined by the community itself, and indeed this can help to bring a community together and to inspire local activism, for example when a community comes together to work on an environmental issue, to advocate for improved services, or to stop a private sector development which will have a negative impact on community life. However this is not the case with "capacity building." It would be rare for a community itself to define its problem as a "lack of capacity"; the very language suggests that the definition of the problem has been made by a bureaucrat, a manager, a policy-maker, or some other external actor implicitly claiming superior wisdom.

Communities, it should be emphasized, can mobilize assets not just to address internal problems but also to enhance qualities that are particularly attractive and that they want to emphasize in their future.

An assets-first value means that, before practitioners and academics focus on engaging a community, they must first pause and seek to identify what is right about a community. This is never simple because undervalued communities become adept at identifying the multitude of problems that the outside world attributes to them. News media coverage of marginalized urban communities will invariably be deficit- or problem-focused, further feeding into a negative image that can find its way into how a community thinks of itself. Asking what is right about their community can cause great consternation as residents try to identify their assets.

It has been my experience that I can collect a wealth of information on the problems of a community in a 1-hour conversation with a resident but will require 3 hours of conversation to uncover a small number of assets. The question of what is right about a community must be asked in many different ways to get at the answer. This requires patience on the part of the interviewer and creativity in drafting questions that eventually discover how local circumstances dictate community assets (Delgado & Humm-Delgado, 2013; Marsh, Chaney, & Jones, 2012).

EMPOWERMENT

The value of empowerment is certainly not restricted to community practice, but it is one that permeates all forms of social work practice and other professions, too (DuBois & Miley, 2013; Hur, 2006; Watson & West, 2006). It is a value that appeals to both the political left and right. However, the devil is in the details in how political ideology influences its operationalization (Christens & Peterson, 2012). Nevertheless, the roots of empowerment and marginalized communities has a long and distinguished history within the profession, and its evolution has been dramatic since the 1970s (Gutierrez, 1990; Lee, 2013; Solomon, 1976). No scholarly article or book on urban practice can be written without empowerment being an integral part of the publication.

Empowerment and social justice go hand in hand with many of the helping professions, but it has special meaning for social work (Adams, 2008). Wagaman (2011) argues that empowerment is not possible without social empathy, and social justice is a key component of this form of empathy.

Empowerment has been theorized as a construct with influential emotional, behavioral, and cognitive components (Christens, 2012). These three components become operationalized within a context, and age, documented status, and urban environment will wield considerable influence in how it manifests itself. The importance of sociopolitical control is such that it is considered a key element in discussing youth empowerment, which should not come as any great surprise when empowerment is grounded within a social justice context (Peterson, Peterson, Agre, Christens, & Morton, 2011).

Community-based organizational settings, in turn, can foster the empowerment of the organization's members and those they seek to serve (Maton, 2008), and none more so than those who serve youth (Deutsch & Hirsch, 2002). These settings have a special responsibility to embrace this value since youth are rarely part of institutions that actively seek to empower them even though youth involvement in decision-making is widely considered a key element in successful youth development programs (Bruening, Dover, & Clark, 2009).

Providing youth with an opportunity to assume decision-making roles and with the needed support (training and consultation) makes empowerment possible and translates into an organizational investment in youth. Organizational ability to tap the concept of youth self-knowledge has gained saliency when discussing youth social relationships, and it has become an attractive way of ensuring that youth empowerment transpires. Not surprisingly, empowerment is also closely tied to life satisfaction.

Jennings et al. (Jennings, Parra-Medina, Hilfinger-Messias, & McLoughlin, 2006, p. 31) studied four youth empowerment models and identified six key dimensions of critical youth empowerment: (1) an environment that offered safety and is welcoming, (2) youth can engage in meaningful engagement and activities, (3) there is equitable power-sharing between youth and adults, (4) critical reflection is encouraged and focused on interpersonal and sociopolitical processes, (5) youth can engage in meaningful sociopolitical processes to affect change, and (6) individual- and community-level empowerment coexist. Youth empowerment is multidimensional, dynamic, and closely related to critical social theory and praxis (Quijada Cerecer, Cahill, & Bradley, 2013). Thus, youth empowerment is also closely tied to community empowerment.

Critical consciousness-raising among marginalized youth has been found to translate into increased perceived capacity to achieve social change (self-efficacy) and undertake social justice–inspired action (Diemer & Li, 2011). The subject of youth empowerment, particularly as it relates to self-esteem and self-efficacy, is still to be validated, however (Morton & Montgomery, 2013). Nevertheless, its importance necessitates that a continued search to achieve empowerment must not be deterred and that we develop a more nuanced understanding of how empowerment practices can take into consideration local circumstances and youth backgrounds (Delgado, Jones, & Rohani, 2005).

RELIANCE ON INDIGENOUS KNOWLEDGE

The subject of knowledge and how it is conceived, researched, interpreted, and turned into practice is worthy of multiple books, and there certainly have been numerous volumes published on the subject. Society cannot advance without placing tremendous emphasis on knowledge acquisition for its citizenship and on translating this knowledge into interventions that are based on sound information. When this knowledge targets developing social interventions focused on a highly marginalized or stigmatized group, how it is obtained takes on great importance.

Not unexpectedly, there are many different forms and sources of knowledge. Creswell (2013) philosophically divided knowledge into four categories: (1) *ontological knowledge* places an emphasis on the nature of reality, (2) *axiological knowledge* explores how values influence the research process, (3) *methodological knowledge* explores the language and process of research, and (4) *epistemological knowledge* asks what can be considered knowledge. These topics may come across as erudite and relegated to those who are paid to think about them. Prior (2013), in turn, concretized Crewell's philosophical assumptions by posing five questions: (1) What to know? (2) What is known? (3) What is knowing? (4) Who knows what? And (5) How to know? Prior's five key questions bring these erudite questions to life for community practitioners and will be addressed again in Chapter 6 when discussing youth-led and -involved research approaches to urban friendship networks and the role of informal knowledge.

A definition of informal knowledge will share a great deal with other forms of indigenous knowledge. Informal learning can be defined as "learning resulting from daily life activities related to work, family or leisure. It is not structured (in terms of learning objectives, learning time or learning support) and typically does not lead to certification. Informal learning may be intentional but in most cases it is non-intentional" (Omerzel & Širca, 2009, p. 107).

Informal knowledge or self-knowledge in the context of youth work has been referred to as an art form rather than a technique or scientific method (Batsleer, 2008). This form of knowledge is empowering because it defines youth, as in the case of this book, as experts on their own lives. To have this stance taken by adults is rare in youth lives, and self-, experiential, or informal knowledge says to them that they have knowledge that is worthy of tapping, recording, and using in shaping community practice programs.

As a result, informal or experiential knowledge is not restricted to any particular setting, and it can reside in formal and informal or noninstitutional places (Delgado, 2006; Zanoni, 2013). This perspective, as a result, opens up the local community as a center of knowledge and learning. This is exciting from a community practice point of view and opens up the door for employing research methods that are collaborative and community-centered in approach and that take local circumstances into account in dictating the most appropriate research method.

LOCAL LEADERSHIP DEVELOPMENT

Youth-focused interventions that also seek to create a cadre of youth leaders are attractive from a community practice/youth development perspective because they represent an investment in the community and its residents (Kirshner, 2015; Kuttner, 2015; Yoshida, Craypo, & Samuels, 2011). The value of identifying potential youth leaders and supporting them benefits the present and the future as these youth assume leadership positions as adults (Iwasaki, 2015).

However, as noted by Delgado and Staples (2008, p. 115) "leadership" and "youth" rarely go together in society with notable exceptions: "The concept of leadership receives a tremendous amount of attention in society, which is not restricted to any particular age group, although youth generally seem to be missing when the term is used unless the reference is to gang leaders." Leadership is synonymous with adults, particularly males.

This value builds on a long tradition in community practice of actively engaging local residents and helping them develop leadership knowledge and skills that can enhance local capacity. Youth leadership development, it is important to emphasize, does not conform to the traditional view of a "leader" who must fulfill all of the aspects and functions associated with this position. Instead, this value provides a range of competencies or skill-sets. Thus, no one individual, be they youth or adult, should be expected to fulfill all of the functions associated with leadership. Some academics would go so far as to argue that all youth can be considered leaders (Linden & Feldman, 1998) and can exercise various leadership qualities depending on local circumstances.

We certainly would not be at a serious loss in thinking about the different ways of categorizing leadership. Libby, Sedonaen, and Bliss (2006), for example, differentiate between internal and external youth leadership that introduces formal and informal context into defining leadership. The former specifically addresses youth leadership within formal institutions; the latter focuses on youth leadership in the community and nonformal institutional settings. Some youth can embrace both, and some may be restricted to one or the other. This distinction is important when community practice seeks to identify current and potential youth leaders and where they exercise the greatest influence.

The subject of youth leadership development has gained saliency within youth community practice. Helping youth in roles as team sports captains develop leadership qualities can be a part of positive youth development (PYD; Gould, Voelker, & Griffes, 2013). The same principle can be applied to other forms of programming, with or without labeling those youth as "leaders" in the traditional sense.

PARTICIPATORY DEMOCRACY

Citizen or civic participation and democracy are synonymous, and this relationship can transpire in a wide variety of ways, both formal and informal, to foster engagement in society (Shaw, Brady, McGrath, Brennan, & Dolan, 2014). An almost exclusive focus on the former provides a very limited picture, particularly when communities provide ample informal ways for engaging in activities. Furthermore, there is a call to view youth participation in a more nuanced and less formulaic fashion, one that takes into account the interplay of numerous personal and environmental factors (Lawson & Lawson, 2013). Broadening our understanding of informal participation provides a more comprehensive picture of a community and its youth, although it makes the job of assessing level of participation that much more arduous for community practitioners.

Thomas (2013, p. 1) addresses the importance of youth being given an opportunity to participate because, in fact, they want to, have much to contribute, and can enhance their assets within their community: "When given opportunities to participate, they want to be involved in making changes to improve the neighborhood. Youth expressed having passion for their community, being acutely aware of neighborhood needs, and having creative solutions to community problems. In order to become assets to their community, youth need adults and institutions to operate in ways that promote their strengths and embrace youth as both resources and leaders in the community."

Our understanding of youth civic participation has been skewed because of the prevalence of a deficit perspective. I am always very fond of saying that it is so much easier to obtain statistics on crime, dropouts, and other negative issues than it is to gather statistics on the number of urban youth who help neighbors, other youth, and the enhancement of community well-being. Those statistics, unfortunately, must be generated because existing data sources do not record them for policy and programmatic decisions, which is often a limitation of using secondary datasets, as discussed in Chapter 6.

As the saying goes, "If it is about us, without us, it ain't for us." Active participation helps ensure that decisions impacting residents have the input of those most impacted by the actions. In the case of youth, participation brings added meaning for the present and the future, including accepting responsibility for outcomes. Community practice, be it with youth or any other group, will have participation as a central tenet, although it can be conceptualized in a variety of ways (Fisher, Busch-Rossnagel, Jopp, & Brown, 2012; Wearing, 2011).

Active and meaningful youth participation has certainly received its share of attention, particularly when discussing civic engagement and the benefits that it provides to both youth in their development and their communities (Ballard, Malin, Porter, Colby, & Damon, 2015; Head, 2011; Richards-Schuster, 2015; Roholt, Baizerman, & Hildreth, 2014). The concept of "authentic" participation has emerged to capture this position (Furman, 2012). There is little disputing the long-term benefits of civic engagement for youth in general and more so for youth of color (Chan, Ou, & Reynolds, 2014).

Youth civic engagement is probably one of the most prominent ways that youth participation has been conceptualized as unfolding in community practice, and this approach has been brought to the youth development and youth-led fields (Checkoway & Aldana, 2013; Flanagan & Christens, 2011; Watts & Flanagan, 2007). Ballard (2014) argues that an understanding of what motivates youth civic involvement is essential in the creation of programming. Not unexpectedly, there must be meaning before one can get youth enthusiastically involved.

Youth civic engagement, identity, and PYD, for example, have been found to be highly correlated (Crocetti, Erentaitė, & Žukauskienė, 2014; Soap, 2014). Civic engagement of urban youth, as in the case of African American/black, has also been found to be viable when civic education acknowledges systemic inequity (Hope & Jagers, 2014). However, engagement must be predicated upon meaningful activities in the case of urban youth of color and must eschew taking a charity paradigm or a debilitating view (Costandius, Rosochacki, & le Roux, 2014; Delgado, 2016b).

Verjee (2010, p. 7) addresses the typical activities that can be associated with a charity paradigm, and this can give the impression that civic engagement is fulfilling highly valued objectives, in this case involving students and service-learning:

> The charity paradigm of service-learning, therefore, promotes a view of citizenship that involves the transfer or reallocation of resources such as money, food, shelter, knowledge, labor, time, etc. to individuals or groups who have fewer resources. Food is donated, shelters constructed, urban community gardens built, re-cycling programs developed, and neighbourhood playgrounds are designed for children living in poverty. Students also tutor, paint buildings, serve in soup kitchens, build databases and other such things, and much of the research on service-learning is focused on the impact these experiences have on student grades, attitudes and sensitivities.

All of these activities can easily fall within a youth participation perspective, but they will not address the underlying social justice issues in urban lives and therefore will not be attractive to youth who are dealing with the deleterious ramifications of oppression in their lives and communities (Mitra, Serriere, & Kirshner, 2014).

Civic engagement provides youth with a chance to help make a difference in their community and the organizations in which they are involved (Pabst, 2014). However, "doing with" as opposed to "doing for" provides a dramatically different stance on participation (Verjee, 2010). "Doing for" can be considered politically conservative and charity-based, with the results being immediate or very limited in scope and producing apolitical outcomes. Youth personal transformation will not be possible with a charity paradigm that defines a provider and a recipient of service. Participation is widely considered a transformative experience because it is a practice stance that requires living versus being (Springett, 2010). Youth civic engagement involves mobilizing youth capital and generating community capital in the process of volunteering (Morimoto & Friedland, 2013).

Callina et al. (Callina, Johnson, Buckingham, & Lerner, 2014) identify trust and hope as two key elements in any form of meaningful civic engagement involving adolescents. It is no mistake that trust, as the reader will see in the next chapter, is a critical element in fostering meaningful friendship development and plays an essential role in any successful youth-focused social intervention.

Hope, in turn, can be a metaphor for dreaming, aspiring, and believing that there is a future worth living for in a world where life expectancy is short. Hope can play a significant role in helping youth address stressors in their lives resulting from contested spaces (Kirschman, Roberts, Shadlow, & Pelley, 2010; Stoddard, McMorris, & Sieving, 2011). The power of purpose, which is closely related to hope, has been advanced for marginalized youth to resist engaging in behaviors detrimental to their future well-being (Machell, Disabato, & Kashdan, 2015).

The value and concept of participation has provided a viable avenue for youth to take an active role in shaping community practice in a wide variety of ways to meet their specific needs within an environmental context that can be quite demanding. The concept of youth participation or engagement must be modified when one of the goals of youth development is to bring in youth with disabilities (Coster et al., 2012; Lal, Jarus, & Suto, 2012; Schuh, Sundar, & Hagner, 2015). These youth want to be a part of social interventions that include a wide range of youth, including those without disabilities, particularly if one of the central goals is to create possibilities for new friendships that open up new vistas in their lives.

Integrating these youth advances the fate of those youth and all other youths in a program. Hart (2013), a leading advocate for youth participation, sees youth playing important roles now and in the future as they age into adulthood in major social movements, such as the environmental justice movement. There is a close and natural alliance between youth participation and community practice, so it is not a major conceptual leap for this to transpire, and no more so than when social justice goals inform these actions (Checkoway & Gutierrez, 2006).

Youth participation in social justice campaigns, for example, brings a new and exciting element to the participatory literature by embracing social justice themes (Arches & Fleming, 2006; Delgado, 2016b; Lewis-Charp, Yu, & Soukamneuth, 2006). Youth empowerment, too, can transpire through social justice–informed civic engagement that opens up endless options for community-based organizations to increase youth participation (Elaine, Holosko, & Lo, 2008; Gant et al., 2009). Youth technological skills, for example, can allow them to play assisting roles in helping others without these skill sets (Wells, Vraga, Thorson, Edgerly, & Bode, 2015). These situations not only cast youth as experts but can also introduce co-learning as a key concept.

A number of frameworks have been proposed to conceptualize different levels and types of youth participation in community services. Wong, Zimmerman, and Parker (2010), for example, developed a five-part framework that can serve a heuristic purpose using a common language that includes terms such as (1) vessel, (2) symbolic, (3) pluralistic, (4) independent, and (5) autonomous. Delgado and Staples (2008), in turn, offer a four-stage framework that stresses youth power: (1) adult-led with youth participation (the more conventional view of youth participation), (2) adult-led with youth as limited partners or collaborators, (3) youth–adult collaborators or co-partners, and (4) youth-led with adult allies. These and other frameworks help practitioners understand how each stage brings certain rewards and challenges in balancing analytical (theory) and interactional (political) demands.

Youth participation is certainly not without its conceptual and practical challenges, however, and this is to be expected (Malone & Hartung, 2010; Percy-Smith & Thomas, 2009). Participation is a concept that can have many different meanings, including tokenism and giving the illusion of participation. Checkoway (2011, p. 340), a leading scholar and proponent of youth participation, notes that:

> Youth participation strengthens personal and social development, provides expertise for children and youth programs and services, and promotes a more democratic society, but questions arise about its most fundamental phenomena. Lacking agreement on its basic content, however, youth participation as a field of practice and subject of study will be limited.

A lack of consensus on the meaning of "participation" has not stopped this concept from gaining currency and its perceived value from gaining this currency in the field of youth community practice, and this attests to the importance of youth participation regardless of conceptualization.

ADULTISM

Children and youth have no history of playing an active role in socially constructing their lives. In fact, modern-day conceptualizations of children, with some exceptions, have not changed much since the 15th to 18th centuries, when they originated in European Puritanical views of children as evil and of society's role being to control and surveil them (Freeman & Mathison, 2009). This social history can only be rectified through new paradigms that influence research and scholarship, such as peer research methodologies (McCarthy, 2010; Schäefer, 2012a).

The concept of adultism has been around for almost 40 years and was first introduced by Flasher (1978) and popularized by Bell (1995). Fighting against adultism is the one value that specifically targets youth and is perpetrated by adults, sometimes consciously and most times unconsciously. Regardless of intent, adultism permeates the entire world that youth navigate on a daily basis, and it is perpetrated simply because of their age and has nothing to do with their acts.

Adult-centrism has traditionally dominated childhood and youth research (Pattman, 2015). The insidiousness and pervasiveness of adultism seriously limits our understanding of what youth can achieve if provided with an opportunity to exercise their freedom. The same insidiousness and pervasiveness can be applied to racism and sexism and how these forces limited the potential contributions to society of people of color and women, for example.

Checkoway's (1996, p. 13) definition of adultism resonates with the theme of this book: "all of the behaviors and attitudes that flow from the assumption that adults are better than young people and are entitled to act upon young people in many ways without their agreement." The relationship between power and adultism results in disempowerment of youth and makes adults supreme experts over the lives of all youth.

As the reader can no doubt discern from the seven values discussed in this section, each value is important in its own right but, in combination with the other values, makes each that much more significant. I can certainly argue that all seven must be present for urban youth community practice to succeed. In other words, we cannot pick and choose depending upon our circumstances. These values are woven together in such a way as to make them a "package deal," so to speak. Again, this does not mean that we cannot prioritize them differently to take into account local circumstances, however.

Community Practice and Capacity Enhancement

For community practice to be effective, it must be grounded conceptually, contextually, and within an explicit set of values, and trusting relationships are essential in achieving engagement and success. Furthermore, as commonly understood, trusting relationships are considered a foundation for any form of youth work (Ezaki, 2014), and tapping youth voices (values and perspectives) and having them play a decision-making role is one key element that helps ensure that these relationship evolve (Murnaghan, Laurence, Bell, & Munro-Bernard, 2014). Developing youth advisory structures is one way of helping to ensure that youth voices are heard by adults (Barnett & Brennan, 2006; Roholt & Mueller, 2013).

However, it is important that these structures are not intended to channel and control youth voices and decision-making powers under the guise of obtaining youth "input." This section will provide a detailed grounding in and understanding of how CCE as a paradigm and intervention can incorporate goals related to urban youth friendships and shape community practice.

Community practice and youth development enjoys a worldwide reputation and following (Banks, Butcher, Orton, & Robertson, 2013; Van Baren, Meelen, & Meijs, 2014) and will continue to do so as long as it is imaginative and participatory. Theory, rewards, and challenges will be outlined here to set an interventional foundation for the case illustration section that follows in Chapters 5 and 6. Community social work practice can be defined as "practice skills to alter the behavioral patterns of community groups, organizations and institutions or people's relationships and interactions with the community structure" (Hardcastle et al., 2011, p. 1). Capacity enhancement, in turn, is highly contextualized community practice embracing and mobilizing community assets in service to the community (Delgado, 1999; Ozanne & Anderson, 2010), thus countering a prevailing deficit or charity mindset.

Ife (2010, p. 68) makes some critical observations about how a deficit paradigm influences the language and approach to communities and how capacity development (enhancement) differs in its assumptions, philosophy, and values as well:

> The idea of capacity building conveys the idea of potential; if a community has "capacity" it presumably has some potential to do, achieve or accomplish something, though what that something is will often be left undefined. The community is presumed to be operating at a less than optimal level; it needs some sort of outside help to enable it to achieve its potential, and hence building capacity enables a community to achieve more. The assumption, therefore, is that there is a deficit; the community in question is seen as lacking something, vaguely labelled as "capacity," which needs to be "built." This deficit approach negates an important principle of community development. Starting with an assumed deficit is not an ideal way to begin working with communities, as community development works best when it is able to develop on the basis of a community's strengths rather than compensate for its weaknesses. Capacity building, in this sense, is little different from a pathology view of community development, where a "problem" is diagnosed and a "treatment" is prescribed. The community (or communities in general) is seen as "having" a "problem," and this has significant impacts on any developmental process. When community development starts with a problem it is a sure recipe for disempowerment, as it leads people in that community to see themselves as somehow lacking or deficient. This is even more significant when that "problem" is defined externally.

The differences between a deficit and an asset paradigm are not relegated to academics debating some obscure philosophical or methodological point that only academics could come up with. Ife strikes at the heart of these fundamentally different approaches toward communities and those who are marginalized.

Positive Youth Development

The field of youth development has caused tremendous excitement and a dramatic shift in how community practitioners view and interact with youth from all sociodemographic and geographical backgrounds (Hamilton, Hamilton, & Pittman, 2004; Lerner, Lerner, Bowers, & Geldhof, 2015; Peterson & Park, 2009; Rauner, 2013; Shinn & Yoshikawa, 2008). Noble and McGrath (2012) advance the notion that, over the past decade, there has been a gradual but persistent conceptual shift away from the concept of youth welfare, with its corresponding focus on problems, toward viewing youth well-being and resilience.

The popularity of PYD has much to do with a craving for a fresh and positive view of youth as a countervailing force against a pathology or deficit stance that permeates the fields of human development and services (Spencer & Swanson, 2013). A "blaming the victim" premise has caused considerable damage. The increased prominence of cultural contextualization represents an explicit effort to counter a deficit perspective. Praxis, in turn, provides youth with insight into the forces that shape their existence and the steps that they can take to alter their social circumstances.

The United Nations, in its global conversation on its post-2015 development agenda, has elevated a youth agenda and done so from an assets/strengths perspective (Bersaglio, Enns, & Kepe, 2015). The benefits youth derive from participating in youth development programs is impressive. Bundick (2011) found that youth engagement in positive development resulted in positive participation in student leadership and civic engagement. In essence, advances in one area translate into advances in other spheres.

Boyes-Watson (2013), in a Celsea, Massachusetts, urban youth program that I have written about (Delgado, Jones, & Rohani, 2005), discusses the use of peace circles in urban-focused PYD. Peace is not just the absence of conflict but also the presence of social justice and reduced policing of youth. One program staff member stated it quite eloquently (p. 30): "It is really easy to get into a place where you think of young people needing policing. Young people don't need policing; they need relationships." Friendship is such a relationship.

Youth development has taken on added significance when addressing different marginalized youth groups (Mueller et al., 2011). Poteat et al. (2015), for example, have found PYD to be effective with LGBTQ youth, serving as a bridge between these youth and straight youth in collaborative alliances and coalitions. Urban youth of color from low-income/low-wealth backgrounds, too, have been attracted to PYD when these programs attend to their operative reality (Ginwright & James, 2002; Silbereisen & Lerner, 2007); otherwise, they are not (Fredricks & Simpkins, 2013). They express a willingness to embrace social justice, and they seek to change oppressive circumstances in their lives.

There is a recognized need to understand and promote PYD with attention to contextual influences (Urban et al., 2009). Dawes and Larson (2011) found that youth must not only physically attend youth programming, they must also develop a psychological commitment that necessitates embracing three personal goals that must be present for them to psychologically engage: (1) learning for the future, (2) developing competence, and (3) pursuing a purpose. These three goals will be influenced by contextual factors and are all predicated on youth believing that there is a future worth working toward, as already noted in the discussion on hopes and dreams.

Youth development and community social work practice are congruent and therefore supportive of each other. This is not to say that the field of youth development has not enjoyed universal acceptance or eschewed conceptual tensions (Delgado & Staples, 2008, 2013). Tensions related to any form of practice are inevitable, particularly in a field that is increasing its presence in the field of human services and displaying a willingness to address structural oppression.

Stewart and Liddicoat (2014, p. 27) provide a historical account of how the field of youth development evolved and responded to social challenges over the past four decades:

> Within the past 40 years, the field of youth development has undergone several major paradigm shifts in an effort to better understand—and provide—what young people need to become happy, healthy, and successful adults . . . . Early strategies that simply forward on minimizing the problematic behaviors that got youth into trouble evolved into later strategies that focused instead on developing the beneficial behaviors that helped youth succeed. Today, the theory of positive youth development broadly represents a social science framework that identifies the external supports, structures, and opportunities that young people need to become successful contributing adults in society . . . . Effective youth development programs can therefore provide positive behaviors that intrinsically reduce negative outcomes.

Stewart and Liddicoat's historical summary captures the early tensions that led to the creation of PYD, and these tensions are still present. The emergence of social justice youth development is in response to this identified need in PYD (Iwasaki, 2015).

An emerging key area of major disagreement between PYD and those favoring youth-led development has been the degree of power that youth have in shaping their expectations and experiences within programs, the role of adults as allies, and the role and importance of social justice in guiding their intervention goals (Delgado, 2006; Delgado & Zhou, 2008; Ginwright, Cammarota, & Noguera, 2005).

An introduction of social justice values and corresponding actions into urban youth development programming enhances urban youths' awareness of their personal potential, community responsibility, and broader humanity (Cammarota, 2011). Spencer and Spencer (2014, p. 1027), in an introduction to a special journal issue on PYD, acknowledge a central criticism of PYD: "The inadequate sampling and follow-up of youth from families which continue to face persistent social inequality and having the most to gain from a positive youth development conceptual strategy was a major shortcoming." Any effort to reach out to marginalized youth cannot be undertaken without embracing social justice values and principles.

PYD is usually associated with latency and adolescent youth. However, there is no "magical" age when we can turn on the faucet and say that it is "appropriate" to engage in youth development (Mitra & Serriere, 2012). Nevertheless, youth development has historically targeted adolescents. Friendships, as addressed in the following chapter, evolve over the lifespan. Youth development, too, must be conceptualized in this manner.

PYD is best conceptualized as a resilience-based paradigm that consists of various internally focused constructs that actively seek to emphasize positive traits in youth (Lee, Cheung, & Kwong, 2012; Lopez, Yoder, Brisson, Lechuga-Pena, & Jenson, 2015). Kia-Keating and colleagues (Kia-Keating, Dowdy, Morgan, & Noam, 2011) draw attention to the potential of resiliency and PYD coming together:

> Resilience and positive youth development have substantial overlap and offer complementary perspectives on fostering healthy youth development. However, these two areas have not yet been fully integrated into a unified approach, one that has the potential to build on the interconnectedness of risk, protection, and assets within the ecological systems affecting adolescent development.

PYD has multiple ways of being manifested, and structuring leisure time to maximize it for PYD becomes an important goal of PYD (Barber, Abbott, & Neira, 2014).

Grounding a construct such as resilience is essential in order to understand what youth mean by "doing well," "making it," or "getting by" (Unger, 2012; Wright, Masten, & Narayan, 2013). These and other terms such "surviving," "head barely above water," and "hanging in there," for example, can mean different things in different contexts. Resilience, in addition, must take a historical as well as present-day perspective. Immigrant youth who left their homeland and traveled countless number of miles to get to the United States invariably encountered significant obstacles along the way. Episodes of extreme challenges take on great significance, and surmounting them can be thought of as resiliency. One British study tied together friendship and resilience and found a significant positive association between perceived friendship quality and resilience (Graber, Turner, & Madill, 2016).

The concept of forgiveness will emerge in the course of engaging with youth. Klatt and Enright (2009) note that PYD is increasingly addressing the concept of forgiveness. This bodes well for youth establishing friendships because, as already noted, no friend is perfect and there will be transgressions that can compromise a relationship and cannot be repaired without forgiveness entering into the social exchange.

Diprose (2014) does raise a flag of caution concerning the use of concepts and constructs that are to serve as a shield against life's tribulations, and we should not consider resiliency as a panacea, seeing this construct as playing a role of "business as usual." As a result, seeing resilience as a "bounce-back-ability bandwagon" and yet encouraging youth to be prepared to engage in contentious politics forms an incongruous alliance. Immense social forces require immense social responses. It would be unfair and a travesty to assume that an all-out assault on youth of color can be countered with an embrace of resiliency while ignoring these social forces or making passing reference to them as if they were a minor bump in the highway of life.

Traits associated with PYD fall into domains commonly referred to as the 5C's: Competency (musical, academic, and social), Confidence, Connection, Character, and Caring. Lerner et al. (2015) discussed Hamilton's (1999) concept of PYD from three interrelated but nevertheless different perspectives: (1) as a developmental process that emphasizes a strengths perspective, (2) as a philosophical stance or approach to youth programming, and (3) as examples of youth programming and organizational focus on fostering healthy or positive development. Contextualizing these domains is essential in taking into account local circumstances (Lam, McHale, & Crouter, 2014).

Bringing PYD and CCE within community social work practice helps ensure that youth strengths and assets are not viewed in isolation from those of the community of which they are a part. In essence, these two worldviews are complementary of each other and, when conceptually combined, further enhance each other's reach and influence in the lives of urban youth. Introducing a social justice value and the other seven values discussed earlier in this chapter in turn increases the relevance of PYD and CCE for reaching marginalized urban youth and their communities.

The use of collaboration as a central tenet in youth social interventions can bring these two worlds together. For example, community collaborative interventions have shown much promise in addressing infectious diseases such as HIV in marginalized communities, and in helping ensure that cultural factors and considerations shape these interventions (Belgrave, Abrams, Javier, & Maxwell, 2014; McKay & Paikoff, 2012; Reed, Miller, & Adolescent Medicine Trials Network, 2014). Youth peer-led interventions, as a result, represent one dimension of this form of collaboration.

Maticka-Tyndale and Barnett (2010), for example, report on a literature review of HIV peer youth interventions, which represent a growing trend that taps into active peer and friendship networks as a means of entry into a community by minimizing issues of trust and reducing communication barriers. The authors found this approach to be highly effective in producing change in knowledge, increasing condom use, and attitudes and norms. Peer-led research and interventions are themes that will be addressed again in the next chapter's discussion of youth-led research.

Youth community practice can embrace a multitude of approaches. Urban youth and poetry, for example, is an innovative way of engaging youth in an activity that is rarely associated with urban youth. Poetry serves to affirm youth voices through a writing and learning process as well as by helping to shape identity (Jocson, 2006). Bringing a social justice focus to this poetry, in similar fashion to hip-hop, will undoubtedly increase its influence and attractiveness for youth surrounded by social injustices and seeking to find a method to exercise their voices and affirm their identities (Aitken, 2014).

Slam poetry is an excellent example of how poetry, social justice, and youth development can come together in a manner that is appealing to marginalized youth by encouraging them to use their own words, symbols, emotionality, and rules to share their narrative (Pellegrino, Zenkov, & Aponte-Martinez, 2014; Sutton-Spence & de Quadros, 2014). Bean and Brennan identify other benefits to youth slam poetry (2014, p. 31): "Performance poetry is a strong vehicle for education, deepening literacy, creativity, and communication skills, while preparing students to become civic and social leaders." Exercising agency and their rights is empowering for youth (Fields, Snapp, Russell, Licona, & Tilley, 2014; Garcia, 2014). The audience for slam poetry is also very unique and differs from that found at a conventional poetry reading (Lovell, 2014).

Music, too, can be a vehicle for integrating PYD with urban youth, and more so when we are willing to introduce types that are indigenous to the communities these youth come from (Barrett & Bond, 2015). The prefix of "urban" to hip-hop is unnecessary for good reason: the two are one and the same. Rap-centered music provides an alternative to conventional youth development programming; it taps into a deep-seated desire to create music, and it also allows youth to explore the viability of a career in this highly competitive field (Foster, 2014).

Hip-hop's popularity has, in large part, to do with its message of injustice; this theme is central to the narrative being told in the language and symbols that relate to urban youth and their social world (Balakrishnan, 2014; Chang, 2007; Love, 2012, 2014; Rose, 2013). The social justice message has, not surprisingly, caused great concern on the part of adults, with its often central message of police brutality, although the recent killings of young African-American/black men attests to veracity of the lyrics (Anderson et al., 2015; Clay, 2012).

Hip-hop, protest, and social media are closely tied together, thus helping make this art form reach the level of popularity it enjoys today. Love and Bradley (2015) refer to the marriage between hip-hop and social media as "organic and messy." Hip-hop and urban are inseparable (Irby, 2015), and themes related to racism and classism resonate with urban youth (Jeffries, 2011). Butler (2010), in a book titled *Let's Get Free: A Hip-Hop Theory of Justice*, provides an erudite connection between hip-hop's central messages and key scholarly work on social justice. A similar discussion can be made concerning the integration of art as an activity in youth programming (Wright, Alaggia, & Krygsman, 2014; Yonas et al., 2009).

Finally, any form of technology can have positive or negative consequences. If we view technology from a negative perspective, we would emphasize topics such as sexual predators, cyberbullying, cyber stalking, video games addiction, cyber spying, and invasion of privacy, for example (Bers, 2012). The term "cyber addiction" has emerged to focus on a specific type of youth (Li, Garland, & Howard,

2014; Wallace, 2014). Even the subject of social media, in which youth are the undisputed rulers in navigating this world, has not gone unchallenged by adults. Rising concern about increasing youth use of social media has been led by adults and has ignored youth voices, views, and agency (Dinsmore, 2014).

Adachi and Willoughby (2013) posit that too much attention has been paid to youth playing video games and without exploring the use of video games to promote PYD, thereby missing a golden opportunity to engage youth who would otherwise not participate in youth development. In essence, technology can be an attractive tool for empowering youth (Mallan, Singh, & Giardina, 2010; Shank & Cotten, 2014). Developing activities, hobbies, and career aspirations related to technology can tap youth interests and bring them into contact with other youth who share similar proclivities (Alper, 2013).

Bers's (2012) book *Designing Digital Experiences for Positive Youth Development: From Playpen to Playground* recognizes and taps into technological advances in society and applies it to PYD. Digital landscapes bring a new area for youth engagement, one that has been labeled "positive technological development." A positive perspective facilitates the use of technology as an innovation and expansion of the field of PYD.

PYD can be conceptualized as a critical social justice intervention for African-American youth, and this approach is enhanced when it raises cultural awareness (Grills et al., 2015). Evans et al. (2012), too, address PYD and African-American youth and the potential for increasing this paradigm's effectiveness through greater attention to the role of families and, we can add, friendships.

The emergence of the concept of racial socialization has implications for urban youth community practice. Although most notably applied to African-American/black youth, it has applicability to other ethnic and racial groups (Elmore & Gaylord-Harden, 2013). Youth must be socialized to function in society. However, when introducing race, youth of color do not have the benefit of socialization to acquire competencies that can help white, non-Latino youth because they face different challenges (Hughes, 2003).

A number of scholars (Coard & Sellers, 2005; Gaylord-Harden, Burrow, & Cunningham, 2012; Neblett, Smith, Ford, Nguyen, & Sellers., 2009) conceive of racial socialization as a protective factor, introducing a different view of youth of color strengths or assets. Racial socialization has generally been conceived of as consisting of three separate elements: (1) the mainstream or dominant experiences (values and beliefs of US culture), (2) "minority status" experience (social injustice), and (3) cultural experiences (unique cultural experiences of an ethnic or a racial group). These three realms come together to create an experience unique to youth of color and, when reinforced, can further enhance race/ethnicity as a protective force in the lives of youth.

PYD has not explicitly eschewed the power and influence of friends and peers as a significant social arena. Nevertheless, neither has it singled out the significance of friendships within a peer network, as advocated for in this book.

Spirituality, too, has not been tapped to any great degree in PYD, and this requires further attention. The association of spirituality with the youth development/youth-led field can seem puzzling at first sight since we usually do not associate it with the 5Cs.

Rossiter (2011) reviews the literature on youth spirituality and notes that there has been a considerable shift in thinking about how youth construct spirituality to a more individualistic, subjective, eclectic, and secular spirituality. Thus, upon closer examination, its presence is not out of the ordinary and provides an important backdrop or context for understanding the motivation/engagement of urban youth in social justice change efforts. Caring, an essential C among the 5Cs, can be tied spiritual beliefs as well as to cultural values. Thus, although the subject of spirituality as a cultural asset for youth of color may seem out of place in discussing youth development and friendships, this is far from the case (Yeh, Borrero, & Shea, 2011). Spirituality can be closely associated with meaning-making, cultural identity, and social relationships.

Youth–Adult Relationships: The Potential of Mentoring

It is would be irresponsible to end this chapter on youth community practice without paying attention to youth–adult relationships (Brown, Redelfs, Taylor, & Messer, 2015). Although this book is about urban youth friendships, these friendships do not have to be age-specific to other youth. True, friendships are facilitated when there are minimal demographic differences between friends, which increases the intensity of the relationship, and age clearly is a key consideration; however, it does not mean that youth cannot make and sustain adult friendships within and outside of formal settings.

Friendships are a form of social relationship that can result from other forms of formal relationships. Mentoring stresses the importance of a social process that builds in many of the key elements associated with friendships, such as trust, mutually enjoyable activities, fun, advice, and support, to list but several expressive, instrumental, and informational benefits. Consequently, it is not surprising that mentoring relationships often cross the line and enter the realm of friendships.

The potential of mentoring with the specific purpose of helping urban youth expand their social network to include more friends is yet to be fully exploited. In addition, youth who are considered as having a greater likelihood of leaving school before completion and getting into trouble with the legal system bring their own unique set of needs. Thus, introducing programming that stresses mentoring highlights the importance of social relationships, which, it can be argued, is at the center of any form successful mentoring.

Youth who are at an increased likelihood of leaving school prematurely have a greater chance of engaging in behavior that can bring them into contact with legal authorities. Mentoring these youth and providing them with an opportunity to enhance their social skills through the establishment of positive relationships makes community programs focused on these areas highly attractive, with both short- and long-term implications in their lives.

Furthermore, successful mentoring experiences can translate into youth learning social skills that can create successful relationships with other youth, and these can then be converted into friendships, hopefully ones that can be long lasting (Karcher & Hansen, 2013). As a result, friendships provide what is widely accepted as a context or venue for youth to develop critical social skills that will help them negotiate difficult as well as life-enhancing situations (Glick & Rose, 2011).

Mentoring as an activity brings an important dimension to PYD and has been found to be an integral part of youth development, increasing the likelihood of youth achieving meaningful gains, including hope for a future (Ginwright, 2011; Kelly, 2013; Kuperminc, Thomason, DiMeo, & Broomfield-Massey, 2011; Vasechko, 2015). Mentoring programs must embrace an inclusive philosophy, reach out to all marginalized groups, and be keenly aware of the characteristics of those mentored in order to maximize this resource (Randle, Miller, Ciarrochi, & Dolnicar, 2014).

The youth development and youth community practice fields have recognized the use of mentoring as an attractive and viable tool in reaching urban youth. Use of mentoring programs to help strengthen friendships can play an influential role in helping urban youth expand their peer network (Liang, Bogat, & Duffy, 2014). However, mentoring programs must be inclusive of all youth and not discriminate intentionally or unintentionally, as in the case of LGBTQ youth, for example (Mallor, Sears, Hasenbush, & Susman, 2014). LGBTQ youth, too, can benefit from friendships, particularly in social circumstances where they are targeted for abuse and neglect by the systems that are supposed to serve and protect them, such as schools, community centers, and other community-based organizations.

Unfortunately, LGBTQ youth have not enjoyed the same access to mentoring programs that their non-LGBTQ peers have (Mallory et al., 2014), and the same can be said about youth with disabilities. The introduction of new approaches toward mentoring youth with disabilities are desperately needed (Shpigelman & Gill, 2013). Hopefully, these new models will seek to integrate these youth with nondisabled youth rather than treat them as separate entities.

Caring becomes an essential element in bringing youth and adults together in pursuit of a common goal or adventure. It certainly is understandable that caring is an essential element in PYD, and the concept of caring seems to permeate any activity targeting youth, as it does any effort to operationalize friendship. It takes on even greater importance when urban youth perceive and experience uncaring relationships with adults in authority (Fry et al., 2012). Creating a caring—and one may also add respectful—atmosphere that brings with it trust becomes an essential goal for youth development staff (Deutsch & Jones, 2008).

Not surprisingly, youth–adult relationships are critical in engaging youth, and this engagement has been found to relate to three relational strategies staff can use for minimizing relational distance, promoting active inclusion, and paying attention to proximal relational ties (Jones & Deutsch, 2011). Youth development programs provide youth with an opportunity to learn about and manage their emotions (Larson, 2011; Rusk et al., 2013). Bronk (2011) researched youth having a noble purpose, an essential element in PYD, and found that mentors and similar-minded peers play an influential role in helping youth develop and maintain such a purpose. College students, for example, can be effective mentors with youth of color (Black et al., 2012).

Mentoring relationships are not all alike, and they include distinctive patterns of interpersonal tones (Pryce & Keller, 2013). Matching interpersonal tones with youth comfort levels and expectations, as in friendships, cannot be left to chance. Youth development mentoring can cover short and intense time limits as well as extended and less intensive time periods. Youth helping other youth, in the case of Makhoul, Alameddine, and Afifi (2012) those in refugee camps, or youth mentoring youth brings a different dimension to mentoring and casts these youth as community assets. Mentoring, it should be noted, can also apply to community practitioners and academics mentoring other practitioners and academics, although this aspect is beyond the scope of this book (Cooper, 2014).

When youth engage in community practice programming, staff must be able to know youth well, including their close family and friends, because in many ways they, too, join in the experience of engagement because they may be called upon to support these efforts as well as benefit directly or indirectly from youth engagement (Boyes-Watson, 2013). Youth development programming must also seek to help transition to careers those youth who do not want to attend higher education in the near future (Hynes & Hirsch, 2012). This transition is facilitated when youth and adult staff members have a positive relationship and staff know youth participants.

It is incredibly important not to neglect staff needs in any discussion of youth–adult relationships. Thompson and Shockley (2013) identify the challenges that staff face and stress the importance of organizations putting in place supports and possible career advancements to retain staff. This support and career ladder takes on even greater importance in cases where staff are indigenous to the community being served and do not have extensive formal education. PYD's success is maximized when everyone (administrators, staff consultants, and board/advisory committee members) involved in these ventures is understood to be an essential part of the mission, and this does not apply only to youth participants. When discussions turn to empowering youth, staff, too, must be empowered.

Conclusion

Urban-focused youth community social work practice is not at a loss for a sound theoretical grounding and direction, including an understanding of oppositional resistance and resilience (Bottrell, 2009; Delgado, 2016*b*). Urban community practice with youth cannot be separated from a national propensity to view anything urban negatively, and this view is compounded by racism, classism, and ageism. Community social workers will no doubt encounter other helping professions subscribing to youth development and community practice, and our ability to include other professions and community residents, particularly youth, will determine the degree of success we can achieve. The potential is unlimited.

Values underpin all forms of practice, and any exercise or deliberative attempt to identify them and how they influence worldviews and programs is time well invested on the part of practitioners, academics, and, most importantly, youth. In the case of youth community practice, there are a set of values that lay the foundation and point to a clear direction for how this practice must unfold when it is focused on urban youth. These values, in essence, can be conceptualized as a form DNA that helps shape how a program unfolds when taking into account local circumstances.

This chapter has identified seven key values with an overarching cultural competency/humility perspective. These values are explicit and can be articulated and discussed in a manner inclusive of community. These values and the principles emanating from them will be found throughout this book. The following chapter on friendships provides a conceptual grounding and comprehensive view of different aspects related to friendships and why these social relationships are critically important for individuals, communities, and the nation.

3

Friendships

Introduction

The topic of friendship, fortunately, is not relegated to the outskirts or confines of academia. It is a topic that all individuals, regardless of formal educational achievement, age, and other demographic backgrounds can relate to, bringing universality to the subject and therefore ease in discussing it. A life without meaningful friendships can be considered a life that is incomplete (Blatterer, 2014), and friendships are often associated with love (Helm, 2010). Everyone has an opinion on what friendship means to them, including youth.

A trip down memory lane for those of us who are adults, regardless of life stage, cannot be completed without pausing and remembering a close friend who was there during a celebratory or sad period in our lives. This individual could even be classified as a natural mentor. As we age, the demands of time (family, career, public responsibilities) make it more arduous to make and maintain friendships, thus increasing the value of the friends we have even more so. However, the significance of former friends is never lost, particularly during challenging times in our lives. Memory narratives will be discussed later in this book.

Social interactions can be considered complex outcomes of contextual conditions, individual characteristics, and personal preferences (Derlega & Winstead, 2012; Knifsend & Juvonen, 2014; Petermann & Schönwälder, 2014). One cannot help but marvel at the dynamics and complexity of friendships, and no more so then when discussing urban youth of color, a population group that has suffered from scholarly neglect. When this group is addressed, it is often done so from a deficit paradigm, resulting in deleterious consequences (Ponting & Voyageur, 2001; Valencia, 2012; Weiner, 2006). Youth community social work practice, however, has the potential to stem this tide and to do so in an affirming and empowering manner by having youth play an instrumental role in shaping interventions to take into account local circumstances and their own definitions of what constitutes a friend, particularly ones who are considered "close."

Community practice interventions, whether positive youth development (PYD) or otherwise, are enhanced when they actively encourage youth to develop positive social relationships in their lives (Murnaghan, Laurence, Bell, & Munro-Bernard, 2014). Urban youth friendships, as a result, are best understood against a backdrop of friendships in general and the factors and parameters of the forces that typically shape this social phenomena (Edling & Rydgren, 2012). A backdrop grounds social relationships, including friendships, and allows for an in-depth examination of their significance. No youth subgroup is devoid of needing friendships. For example, friendship takes on an influential role within punk and hardcore culture and can be considered the most important personal relationship in this scene when placed within a broader theoretical work on friendship (Rohrer, 2013, 2014).

Friendships, however, are not a panacea for all of life's ills. Manen (2015), in a Finnish study of friendship as a protective factor in outcomes of victimized adolescents, found that having high levels of positive friendship quality and low levels of conflict do not necessarily result in friendships serving a protective function (Olson & Gillman, 2013). This chapter, as a result, provides readers with a multifaceted, multidisciplinary, multilayered, and nuanced perspective on friendships, and as a result, it is lengthier than the typical chapter in this book. Reviewing this context introduces new contents or perspectives on friendships that can expand the reader's understanding of the dynamic nature of this form of relationship, and what makes them significant in people's lives for positive as well as negative reasons, including viewing these connections as potential urban assets.

This chapter will not provide a definitive picture of friendships because it is a picture that is still evolving, one with many different shades that complicate a clear vision. Nevertheless, this chapter should provide a clear grounding in the concept of friendships and its use in youth community youth practice.

Definition of Friendship

Although we provided a simple definition of friendship in the introductory chapter as a means of introducing the subject, in reality, defining what we mean by "friendship" is far from simple. It might be wise to pause and devote considerably more attention to the range of definitions (there are even religious definitions for those wishing to take this perspective on the subject [see Hunt, 2014]) that highlight the complexity of fully comprehending this concept from a variety of academic disciplines, with implications for urban youth of color and how community practice can be implemented (Berndt, 2002; Smith, 2014; Tillmann-Healy, 2003).

Among the countless definitions of friendships, Flora (2014, p. 30) notes that the most frequently cited was advanced by Hays: "In the scientific literature, many scholars have settled on a definition for friendship that was coined by psychologist Robert Hays of the University of California, San Francisco. He described the bond as 'a voluntary interdependence between two persons over time that is intended to facilitate socioemotional goals of the participants and may involve varying types and degrees of companionship, intimacy, affection and mutual assistance.'"

Providing multiple definitions is not intended to overwhelm or confuse the reader but rather to expand our understanding and reach on this rich contextual and highly complex topic. Serious conceptual and ethical questions have been raised about the utility of promoting a single notion of friendship since it is a socially developed construct subject to all the influences of major cultural interpretations. Furthermore, this narrow focus takes on even more deleterious consequences when done from an adult and/or Eurocentric viewpoint.

Why devote a considerable amount of time and space to naming an elusive concept such as friendship? The naming process, it should be emphasized, informs measurement, guidance, implementation decisions, and the eventual evaluation of interventions (Tilton-Weaver, Marshall, & Darling, 2014). Consequently, what may appear as a pedantic or academic exercise is actually based on the consequences of not devoting serious attention to defining friendships, with the result of having an elusive concept that means anything and everything.

Digeser (2013, p. 34) puts forth a well understood challenge in defining friendship: "One of the great challenges of proceeding with any study of friendship—be it philosophical, historical, sociological, anthropological or psychological—is having an adequate account of the object of study. One can hardly proceed without providing some answer to the question 'what is friendship?' The challenge, however, is that any thoughtful exploration of friendship will soon face the reality of its extraordinary diversity." This "extraordinary" diversity makes an exciting concept even more exciting from a practice perspective and thus transforms a liability into an asset.

Allan (2008, p. 2) compares and contrasts familial and friendship relationships from a sociological point of view and in the process introduces the importance of how friendships are defined:

> In comparison to family relationships, ties of friendship are inherently more open to individual negotiation. How friends define their relationship, what they do with each other, and what expectations they have are matters that are for them to determine. In most regards, these matters are not seen as legitimate concerns of those outside the relationship. Thus, while issues of equality and reciprocity tend to loom large in these ties, friendships nonetheless have flexibility built into their content in a way that marks them off as different from other types of relationship.
>
> As we have seen, this does not mean that friendships are unaffected by the social and economic contexts in which they are enacted, but it does mean that friendships tend to be understood as individualized and personal. Indeed where these circumstances are for some reason problematic, as for example with sociable contacts restricted to a particular setting such as a workplace,

there is often a degree of uncertainty as to whether they really match the category of friendship.

Allan highlights how an individualized and, one might add, culturally based definition of friendships makes it challenging to develop a widely accepted and practical definition. This challenge, however, reinforces the importance of localized definitions of friendships.

Definitions in the social sciences are notorious for creating heated debates over the slightest detail, and arriving at a definition of friendship is no different. Differentiating between different levels and types of peer social relationships is essential when trying to arrive at a definition of friendship. However, any effort to form a conceptual definition of friendship that enjoys wide acceptance will result in frustration for practitioners and academics alike, and this should not come as any great surprise, particularly when contextual grounding is essential in any definition put forth. Nonacademics, too, do not have a universal definition and understanding of the meaning of friendship (Kempner, 2008). Thus, there is simply no canonized definition of friendship (Kunt, 2013), and this is even more true when addressing urban youth of color.

Matthews (1983), well over 30 years ago, found 147 different definitions of friendships. Needless to say, this number has increased considerably since then, attesting to friendship's importance and elusiveness (Bagwell & Schmidt, 2013, p. 9): "The importance of friendship is acknowledged across a number of disciplines, and each emphasizes different aspects of the relationship consistent with the overarching concerns, questions, and levels of analysis of the particular field of study." Several academic disciplines stand out because of the emphasis placed on defining and understanding friendships, however.

Anthropology, with some notable exceptions, has generally ignored the subject of friendship and instead has focused attention on kinship and political and economic relations (Rohrer, 2014), even though this academic discipline has much to contribute to our understanding on this subject. Sociology, too, has not escaped being criticized for neglecting friendships in the past, viewing these relationships as personal choices rather than choices associated with public matters (Holmes & Greco, 2011).

Bowker and Ramsay (2012, p. 1060) provide a very nice summary definition of friendships and why they are of such importance for adolescents:

> Friendships are close dyadic reciprocal relationships, with a shared history, a sense of commitment, and a general enjoyment of each other's company. Adolescent friendships are one of the central social relationships of this developmental period, perhaps the most important relationship to study during adolescence. In contrast to parent–adolescent relationships, friendships are voluntary, based on equality and reciprocity.

The potential centrality of friendships in youth social relationships is enhanced because these relationships are voluntary, as noted earlier, and thus it is within the power of youth to define and choose them. This power to select whom they call a friend will remain with them throughout the life cycle.

Thompson (2012, p. 63), in turn, presents an adolescent definition of a quality friendship: "an open ear to listen to me, don't judge me, different perspective on me, gives me no slack, gives me the power to talk about anything, something to smile at, give me hope, strength, courage, trust, self-confidence." Clearly, this nonscholarly definition from an adolescent perspective shows how much youth potentially expect from a friend and the importance of taking their perspective and words into account in any definition or community practice intervention that targets youth friendships. This important point will be reinforced throughout this book.

Not surprisingly, the popularity and importance of friendship, with its multitude of definitions, raises challenges when trying to arrive at a consensus definition that will have the necessary broad reach across cultures, academic disciplines, and professions (Zhao & Gao, 2014). The quest for this type of consensus will help ensure that partnerships or collaborations across disciplines and youth can transpire to maximize intervention benefits.

Di Nicola (2002, p. 71) offers a short but eloquent definition: "A friend is a person to whom you can show your dreams, delusions, fears and certainties, strengths and weaknesses." Demir, Özen, and Procsal (2014, p. 2359) also provide a simple but encompassing definition of friendship that introduces many key elements that will be addressed in this book: "Friendship is a voluntary interdependence between two individuals that includes the experience and satisfaction of various provisions (intimacy, support, self-validation) to varying degrees."

The various levels of friendships are best conceptualized as representing a series of concentric circles around an inner core, with each circle bringing certain benefits and challenges in categorization. Each of these circles may vary in size and is interconnected to represent a constellation or a network of friendships. As children age and enter adolescence, their ability to differentiate between different levels and types of friendships emerges, and this is due in large part because their world expands and they are granted greater freedom by parents or guardians (Bagwell & Schmidt, 2011). Thus, the meaning of friendship is evolutionary and can best be appreciated from a life cycle perspective.

Classification of Friendships Types

Why differentiate between types of friendships? It is acknowledged that enduring friendships represent a critical part of happiness and well-being among youth, and the meaning ascribed to friendships differs across the life cycle to take into account different developmental needs (Stephanou & Balkamou, 2011). Bagwell, Kochel, and Schmidt (2015) argue that even though there has been considerable research on the role of close relationships in adult happiness, friendship has generally escaped being thought of as an antecedent or consequence of adolescents' experiences with their friends.

Webb and Zimmer-Gembeck (2015) discuss the futility of thinking about friendships as static and unidimensional, with adolescents reporting multiple "best" or "close" friends, with many youth reporting no friendship stability, and with an extensive network not necessarily being seen as positive. Adults may have difficulty appreciating the concept of multiple "best" friends, particularly those adults embracing an individualistic versus a collectivistic value stance.

The dynamic nature of friendships allows for this social relationship to respond to changing circumstances and explains why this type of relationship can be so enduring over an entire life span, ebbing and flowing depending on needs and social circumstances. The concept of friendship exclusion, which lends itself to feminist and young peoples' geographies, has emerged to capture the situation in which youth are socially isolated; having a friend, particularly one who can be classified as "close," then has immense social and psychological benefits (Gutierrez & Hopkins, 2015).

Supportive and enduring friendships of high quality bring stability and endurance along with the requisite emotional and cognitive supports, thus enhancing the importance of understanding their social makeup (Bagwell & Schmidt, 2011). These types of relationships can even help keep friends from harming themselves (Buckley, Chapman, Sheehan, & Cunningham, 2012; Galloway, 2014; Rowe et al., 2014). For example, friendship has been found to be a positive influence with young (17–24) drivers by mediating risks undertaken while driving (Guggenheim & Taubman–Ben-Ari, 2015).

Rath and Harter (2010) address the multiple health benefits of friendships:

> There is something about having close friendships in general that is good for our physiological health. Relationships serve as a buffer during tough times, which in turn improves our cardiovascular functioning and decreases stress levels. On the other hand, people with very few social ties have nearly twice the risk of dying from heart disease and are twice as likely to catch colds— even though they are less likely to have the exposure to germs that comes from frequent social contact.

The health benefits of friendships, as a result, represent but the latest frontier in our understanding of the value and benefits of this form of social relationship.

Expressions such as "intimate," "genuine," "close," "buddy," "like family," "trusted," "bosom," "soulmate," "best," "special," "firm," "pal," and "BFF" (best friend forever), for example, are often used to identify friendship's inner circle and its particular significance (Beder, 2009; Dickie, 2009; Morrison & Nolan, 2009; Rumens, 2010). A lack of effort in establishing a close friendship, too, has found its way into this area.

Campbell, Holderness, and Riggs (2015) discuss "friendship chemistry" (an instant connection between two individuals that appears as easy and natural) resulting in an effortless relationship that evolves into a friendship. Other terms are used to signify those friends who are outside of the inner circle, such as those identified by site specificity, such as "work friends," "school friends," and "playground friends," for example, that signifies geographical distance from neighborhood, limitations, or conditions to a friendship (Hall, 2009; Markiewicz, Devine, & Kausilas, 2000).

Rawlins (1992, p. 271), in turn, defined a close friend as "somebody to talk to, to depend on and rely on for help, support, and caring, and to have fun and enjoy doing things with," in an effort to differentiate the levels and intensity of a friendship. Closeness can be both a subjective and objective measure. Harding (2008), for example, use a 5-point scale to provide a behavioral/objective measure: (1) visited friend's home in the past 7 days, (2) met friend after school to hang out in the past 7 days, (3) spent time with friend over the past weekend, (4) spoke with a friend about a personal problem over the past 7 days, and (5) spoke with friend over the telephone in the past 7 days. The reader may take issue with some or all of these measures, but they are presented as a means of helping to concretize how to judge the significance of a friend.

Individuals falling outside the inner circle or who cross settings and geography may also be referred to as "causal" or "distant." Fisher (1982), more than 30 years ago, drew a distinction between "friends" and "close friends," with close friends encompassing intimacy, willingness to discuss personal matters, and involving material exchanges. Strong friendships, for example, have been compared to having strong sibling relations because of how they can potentially mediate against peer victimization, particularly when the friends and siblings also embrace prosocial behaviors (Lamarche et al., 2006). Couples and their friendships, however, bring a different set of rewards and challenges to this subject because both need to embrace and be embraced as friends (Greif & Deal, 2012).

Classifying Types of Friendships

Readers wishing to engage in the process of classifying the various types of friends have an abundance of options available to do so. Classification, it must be noted, is much more than an academic exercise: it fulfills an important role in informing practice because a "one size fits all" approach is detrimental to interventions, and a classification system allows practitioners to determine the most appropriate intervention.

The more specific the type of friendship, the more focused an intervention can be, allowing practitioners to save effort, time, and money. As Hiatt and colleagues note (Hiatt, Laursen, Mooney, & Rubin, 2015, p. 149): "Friendships are critically important to adolescent development, providing validation and camaraderie, insight and emotional support, instrumental assistance and social skills . . . . But not all friendships are created equal." Being able to clearly differentiate between various types of friendships will become a lifelong skill for youth, one that will serve them well in adulthood.

Community practitioners need to assess the quality of a youth's friendship in order to determine where to classify them, which in turn will dictate the most appropriate friendship to reinforce or help develop. Friendship quality plays an influential role in shaping child and youth social adjustment and well-being. Bagwell and Schmidt (2011) address friendship quality by seeking answers to three key questions: (1) What determines the quality of a friendship? (2) What are the correlates of friendship quality? And (3), how does friendship affect development outcomes? The answers to these three questions, when grounded within an urban context and guided by an ecological framework, are very relevant to urban youth of color. This process is not without its challenges, however.

The existence of a "friendship paradox" in the sociological literature seeks to capture the observation that self-assessment of popularity is generally self-aggrandizing (Fotouhi, Momeni, & Rabbat, 2014). Simply put, I may consider you my friend, but you do not consider me your friend; or, I may designate you as a very close friend, but you only consider me as a distant friend. This paradox complicates our understanding of friendship when viewed from a singular rather than dual perspective, and it has research and practice implications.

Finally, Pahl and Spencer's (2004) friendship typology presents friendships on a continuum that ranges from those that can be classified as "very simple" ("fun" or "event–focused") and centered on participation in common activities, to "highly complex," "very close," or "soulmates" and involving an intense intersubjective relationship. Emotions are integral to friendships and, as a result, are interwoven throughout the very essence of friendships (Arter, 2014; Cronin, 2014).

There is general agreement in the field of childhood friendship studies that friends have an important role to play in helping children, particularly during early adolescence, become socialized in expressing emotions, and this desire to form close friendships increases as they age (Legerski, Biggs, Greenhoot, & Sampilo, 2015). Thus, the intensity and range of emotions, both positive and negative, will help separate various levels or types of friendships (Kimbriel, 2014).

Blackman (2007) brings a sociological view, which has been slow in evolving, to emotions and field-based research with a reflective direction for facilitating qualitative research and field-based projects. Flam and Kleres (2015) point out that it is impossible to research and fully understand urban youth friendships without attempting to tap the role of emotions in the establishment and maintenance of this form of relationship.

Life Satisfaction as a Backdrop to Friendship

Friendship and happiness are closely tied together, and decades of research have shown that friendship experiences are an essential element and predictor of happiness (Demir, Özen, Doğan, Bilyk, & Tyrell, 2011; Greco, Holmes, & McKenzie, 2015). There is a relationship between perceived life satisfaction and youth developmental assets as well (Valois, Zullig, Huebner, & Drane, 2009). "Well-being," as a result, is finding increasing saliency for capturing a broader appreciation of physical, mental, social, material, and civic health (Cahill, 2015). Including friendship development as part of a life skills development intervention, for example, ties friendship relationships to life well-being, and this is conceptually sound (Hodge, Danish, & Martin, 2013).

As addressed in the introductory chapter, friendship is socially and culturally constructed and is a significant scholarly subject unto itself within any well-informed discussion related to quality of life, life satisfaction, or well-being (Keller, Semmer, Samuel, & Bergman, 2014). Thus, a number of constructs exist that can include friendship as part of their conceptualization. For example, as already noted, constructs such as well-being and life satisfaction are natural extensions of health. The emphases placed on friendships will vary, but they all involve a social dimension, and friendships, after all, are an integral part of that domain. Quality of life, in similar fashion to life satisfaction and well-being, is an elusive concept that can incorporate friendships; when it does, it is made more meaningful (Andelman, Attkisson, & Rosenblatt, 2014).

Seligman (2012) posits that life satisfaction essentially measures cheerful mood and that well-being is a construct that consists of various measurable elements, with no one element defining well-being. Friendships, too, can fall within these two constructs (Wilson, Harris, & Vazire, 2015). However, when friendship is placed within a life satisfaction construct (subjective experiences of individuals) it increases our understanding and appreciation of why friends are significant in the lives of youth and why community practitioners are on firm ground in addressing them within social interventions.

Suldo and Huebner's (2004) define life satisfaction by bringing friendships into this construct. Life satisfaction, however, is not absolute and, as a result, does not enjoy a consensus definition that facilitates operationalization in research and practice across population groups (Góngora & Castro Solano, 2014; Huebner & Diener, 2008).

Life satisfaction is a construct that refers to an individual's cognitive/subjective view of the overall quality of his or her life. (Mohamad, Mohamad, & Ali, 2014). Consequently, life satisfaction is a highly subjective construct and relies on a strong social and cultural context to give it meaning (Diener & Diener, 2009; Keyes, 2014; Pavot & Diener, 2008; Sirgy, 2012). This makes it challenging for community practitioners because there is no universal definition and operationalization, but it does allow and encourage local contextualization.

Finally, an aspect of life satisfaction tying friendships to the workplace brings an added and significant dimension to any understanding of well-being. There is increasing recognition of the role and important function that business or work friendships play in advancing careers, particularly when viewing the instrumental benefits that are derived through these friendships and how they influence well-being (Ingram & Zou, 2008; Mavin, Williams, Bryans, Patterson, & Mavin, n.d.). These friendships not only bring potential instrumental benefits but also make the workplace a more enjoyable place, thereby increasing productivity.

Commercial friendships, however, are different and capture relationships between workers/staff and customers that bring intrinsic and extrinsic value (Rosenbaum, 2009). Socially supportive workplaces help reduce stress, burnout, and turnover, and work friendships can play an instrumental role in fostering a positive work environment (Ptacek, 2014). Affiliation needs can be a key motivator on the part of some workers in addressing life satisfaction. Staff/workers who can convey the qualities associated with friendship may derive a great deal more satisfaction from their employment than their counterparts who do not possess these qualities, with considerable impact on organizational climate.

Headey (2014) addresses bottom-up theories of life satisfaction (or subjective well-being) based on the idea that overall life satisfaction is the sum of its parts. Friendships, as a result, constitute a part of life satisfaction.

Evans and Prilleltensky (2007) argue quite convincingly that the well-being of any one individual is contingent upon the well-being of their close relationships and that of the community in which they live. Self-reports of life satisfaction represent the sum of different elements, one of which relates to friendships. Any effort to operationalize life satisfaction among youth cannot rely solely on concrete instrumental elements and must include social elements, too, to obtain a comprehensive understanding from the perspective of youth, rather than an adult point of view.

For the purposes of this book, life satisfaction, quality of life, and well-being are merged. Friendships, as a result, are an integral part of any social dimension of life satisfaction. Nevertheless, these conceptual challenges should not dissuade us from viewing friendship within the parameters typically associated with this well-accepted construct. This grounding allows us to develop social interventions focused on friendships that have the potential to influence other aspects of life satisfaction. In essence, friends exert influence on many different social aspects of life.

It can certainly be argued that youth life satisfaction has not received the same attention that adults have received, further reflecting an adult bias toward youth and limiting our comprehensive understanding of how this construct applies to this group (Saha, Huebner, Hills, Malone, & Valois, 2014). Life satisfaction scholarship among youth of color has generally been invisible. Furthermore, life satisfaction does not just "kick-in" when we become adults. Proctor, Linley, and Maltby (2009, p. 605) undertook a youth life satisfaction review of 141 empirical studies and concluded that:

> Specifically, the literature demonstrates the need for research among children and adolescents across cultures. The majority of past research in this area has

occurred within America, with most assessment measures being created and validated among American samples . . . . Future research should look to assess the ability of LS measures to transcend cultures and specific groups. More specifically, further research is required to differentiate between individual-istic and collective cultures and whether additional measures are required in order to overcome these differences.

Ethnic and racial backgrounds have generally escaped attention in the life satisfaction literature (Kirmanoğlu & Başlevent, 2014). Poor life satisfaction, unsurprisingly, is widely considered to be an important consequence of inequalities, thus bringing an important perspective on urban youth who are segregated and marginalized within the broader society (Knies, Nandi, & Platt, 2014).

Antaramian, Huebner, and Valois (2008) argue quite convincingly that it is necessary to distinguish between life satisfaction general measures that mask important life distinctions made by adolescents and multidimensional measures of life satisfaction that seek to capture critical nuances that are ecologically based. The emergence of a youth developmental assets paradigm ("relationships, social experiences, social environments, patterns of interaction, norms, and competencies over which a community of people has considerable control") is increasingly finding prominence in the youth development literature (Douglass & Duffy, 2015; Tolan, 2014; Valois, 2014).

The Search Institute's research on PYD and developmental assets (internal and external) has expanded our understanding of how youth can have these assets enhanced by including friendships as part of their external assets (Benson, 2007; Scales & Leffert, 2004). An ability to engage in social relationships (social skills) such as friendships, for example, would fall into the internal assets category. Friendships, however, cross boundaries between internal and external assets, thus attesting to their importance, and the unique role they can play in the life of youth.

Oberle and colleagues (Oberle, Schonert-Reichl, & Zumbo, 2011) view youth life satisfaction within an ecological and youth development context that includes life, optimism, and ecological assets in the school (connectedness), neighborhood (perceived neighborhood support), family (perceived parental support), and peer group (positive peer/friendship relationships), making this conceptualization of life satisfaction more attractive to community practitioners and facilitating the inclusion of peers and friends within multiple spheres.

Elements of Friendships

Any understanding of the role and importance of friendships necessitates identifying the key elements that make friendships functional and rewarding (De Goede, Branje, & Meeus, 2009; Desai & Killick, 2013). A number of scholars have devoted considerable attention to identifying the key factors operating to make friendships important when regarding perception of support: companionship, reliable alliance, guidance, affection, enhancement of worth, intimate disclosure, mutual respect, mutual reliance, help and security, and emotional support (Chow & Buhrmester, 2011; Furman & Buhmester, 1985; Hendrick & Hendrick, 2006; Mayo, 2007; Papapolydorou, 2014; Schall, Wallace, & Chhuon, 2014; Schmidt & Bagwell, 2007; Turnbull, Blue-Banning, & Pereira, 2000).

Digeser (2013, p. 34) argues that friendship can be understood through an embrace of a family resemblance concept: "How should we understand friendship given the extraordinary diverse forms that it can take? Building on the idea that friendship is a family resemblance concept . . . friendship can be understood as a set of social practices in which certain norms and expectations govern not only the actions, but also the motivations of the friends." In essence, Digesar posits that different understandings of friendship bear no more than a family resemblance to one another, thus necessitating the use of a set of rule-governed social practices to help us understand friendships.

Feelings and displays of gratitude have a special role in friendships, although they have been understudied (Lyons, David-Barrett, & Jokela, 2014). Rose and colleagues (2012) view friendships as providing youth with an opportunity to share personal concerns and problems and build trust and intimacy in the process. This form of disclosure provides youth in need with an opportunity to receive needed support, helping them currently and as they transition into adulthood (Davies, Tropp, Aron, Pettigrew, & Wright, 2011). It also provides them with the requisite tools to reciprocate. Girls, it should be noted, have been found to be more willing to engage in self-disclosure to friends when compared to boys.

Friendships play an influential role in shaping how prosocial behaviors can evolve in youth, including their willingness to extend help to others, with trust and sympathy playing a critical part in this exchange (Carlo, Randall, Rotenberg, & Armenta, 2010). Those with more extensive prosocial friends are also more likely to exhibit trust and sympathy, which has implications beyond race and ethnicity and long-term implications for a community, state, and nation.

Lundby (2013) addresses the point of whether friendships can be bought and, if so, the consequences for youth and their internalization of the value of goods and money in shaping their friendship network. Growing up, I remember a Spanish saying in my family that was very cynical of friendships: "A friend is like a dollar in your pocket. Once the dollar is gone, there goes the friend." The transitory nature of friendships is highlighted in that saying. The reader may argue that such a friend is not really a friend, however.

Mains (2013), in turn, brings a different dimension to discuss the similarities between friendship and love among young men in Jimma, Ethiopia, which often involve affection and reciprocal exchange of goods. Some friendships even "blossom" and transform into romantic relationships. The label "passionate relationships" has been advanced and seeks to capture the blurring of lines between friendships and romantic relationships (Glover, Galliher, & Crowell, 2015).

Drawing parallels between friendship and love further complicates an already complex social relationship. Trust is an essential element in any form of relationship, but it takes on added significance among urban youth, and nowhere is this more important than in romantic friendships (Laborde, vanDommelen-Gonzalez, & Minnis, 2014). Trust in this instance goes beyond fidelity and also refers to feelings of vulnerability and emotional intimacy. A Canadian study (Stolle & Harell, 2013) of social capital, trust, and ethnic and racial diversity found promising results regarding youth who have racial and ethnic diversity in their social networks; these youth are more likely than adults to show higher levels of generalized trust.

Temperament, however, plays a role in the development of youth social relationships (Chen, Wang, & De Sousa, 2006; Coplan & Bullock, 2012). Some youth are naturally outgoing, and others can be quite reserved. Shyness-inhibition limits youth opportunities to reach out and engage new experiences and friendships as well as their willingness to join in activities that bring forth this social potential. It is widely recognized that activity involvement has been associated with youths' social adjustment and various social characteristics and parental roles (Doey, Coplan, & Kingsbury, 2014; Miller, 2012).

Finally, as if our understanding of friendship was not confusing enough, the subject of genetics and their influence on friendships has entered deliberations on the subject, with the genotype of one person in a friendship being predictive of the genotype of their friend (Boardman, Domingue, & Fletcher, 2012). Fowler, Settle, and Christakis (2011) discuss how genetic properties of friendship groups might confer fitness advantages to individuals who seek to belong in these groups.

These and other key factors to be addressed are, not surprisingly, multifaceted and nuanced and must be contextualized to give them meaning and to assess their degree of importance. A cultural grounding of friendship brings a perspective that adds to the richness of the concept (Schneider, Lee, & Alvarez-Valdivia, 2011). In this book, this contextualization or grounding is urban, youth-focused, and of color, highlighting those who are marginalized in society. Bukowski and Adams (2006) rightly argue that there is an underlying assumption that peer relationships unfold in the same manner in all places and among all youth. This is obviously not the case with youth across a range of contexts and sociodemographic profiles, and it certainly is not the case when discussing marginalized youth.

This universal premise of the evolution of peer relationships can be too sterile and simplistic if contextualization is ignored or minimized. The importance of a sociocultural-ecological understanding or grounding of youth friendship is a counter to this universal view. Bowlby (2011), for example, urges a closer examination of how geographies (social context and spaces) impact friendships. The contextualization of friendship introduces key environmental forces and sociocultural influences on how friendship is defined, operationalized, and evolved over time, thus setting the foundation for targeted social interventions, particularly in urban contested spaces.

There may be core elements that cross demographic groups and geographic context, such as agentic (status and power) and communal (closeness and affiliation) goals, for example (Ojanen, Sijtsema, & Rambaran, 2013). Jesuvadian and Wright (2014) discuss the role of ethnicity, friendships, and research and how children are cognizant of how power is associated with race and daily interactions in deciding friendships. When power serves to suppress and oppress, it takes on significant meaning among children who are the focus of these forces, influencing their worldviews and creating suspicion of those with the racial characteristics of those in power.

However, the emphasis placed on key elements may differ, as well as on how they are conceptualized in general and how they are brought to life among urban youth of color in particular (Knox & Pinch, 2014). Daily activities, for example, have been found to provide a window through which to understand how youth friendships are initiated and maintained across networks and different evolutionary stages (Yang & Wu, 2013). When these activities are circumscribed, it limits who these youth come into contact with; when they do make contact, the conditions to make friendships may not be conducive to establishing these forms of relationships.

Benefits of Friendships

Friendships persist in society because they meet certain human needs and bring certain benefits in the process for all groups. Friendship has even been conceptualized as providing a haven or refuge from the stressors inherent in society (Jusdanis, 2014). In the case of youth with unresponsive or unsupported homes, this sanctuary takes on even greater importance. There certainly is no age group that cannot benefit from having a place, time, or person that can provide an affirming experience. The questions of when we begin developing close friendships and how these close friendships are defined take on great importance.

As noted earlier, there is general agreement that development of close friendships increases gradually during middle childhood and adolescence (Berndt, 2004). Adolescence as a developmental stage, as a result, can be thought of as providing the strongest opportunity for youth to increase their taking on of positive responsibility or increased risks (Bowers et al., 2011). The social consequences of urban youth taking increased risks can alter their lives forever because of this nation's criminal justice system.

Determining when someone is classified as a friend and differentiating between different types or classes of friendship complicates our understanding of what friendship means. The definition of friendship changes as we go through life and so does what we expect of friends. Local circumstances wield influence on what can be considered the benefits of friendships. Way (2006), for example, found that among low-income youth of color, exchange of money (borrowing and lending) is closely tied to friendship and trust, and this has not been found in other youth groups. These youth may be in unbanked families, and the exchange of money may simply represent a typical experience when placed within the local context. Low-income and/or newcomer families may be fearful of banks, and this fear can be carried over among youth (Delgado, 2011).

The subject of drugs, youth, and friends, particularly those of color and urban-based, has received a great deal of attention, and some academics and practitioners would argue, as do I, that it has come at the expense of the positive influences of friends. Belackova and Vaccaro's (2013) study of marijuana users found that the use of the term "friend" can be applied to drug dealers. However, Foster and Spencer (2013) concluded, based on their research in Canada, that drug use can be intricately woven into friendship, more specifically affective relationships of trust, intimacy, belonging, and sharing.

The influence of peer/friends on drug use has gained greater clarity as more research has focused on this phenomenon. Shadur and Hussong's (2014) study of adolescent friendship intimacy, close friend drug use, and self-medication in adolescence found that greater negative affect and lower friendship intimacy served as a predictive factor of greater substance use, with friendship intimacy and close friend drug use interacting to predict substance use overall, although not for self-medication.

La Haye and colleagues (le Haye, Green, Kennedy, Pollard, & Tucker, 2013) argue that it is widely accepted that friends can play major influential roles in shaping adolescent marijuana use, yet there are relatively few studies that have examined the role of drugs in friendship selection. The authors found evidence for friend selection based on similar lifetime and current marijuana use. However, there was minimal evidence that peer influences were moderated by personal, school, or family risk factors. Nevertheless, Ramirez and colleagues (Ramirez, Hinman, Sterling, Weisner, & Campbell, 2012) found peer/friendships playing a significant role. Friendships, however, have been found to play a protective role for substance use and aggression (Foster et al., 2015).

Seffrin's (2012) research on African-American/black and white, non-Latino adolescents' alcohol use found that African-American values can be viewed from a protective or strengths viewpoint in influencing lower alcohol use and in effect acting as a strong deterrent or buffer for engaging in drinking. These research findings counter the stereotypical view of African-American/black youth by stressing how positive cultural values can be present and active in their lives.

However, if alcohol consumption is considered an important peer-related activity in early adolescence, it serves an increasingly influential role in friendship selection in same-alcohol-use status relationships as youth progress developmentally (Light, Greenan, Rusby, Nies, & Snijders, 2013). Rees, Freng, and Winfree Jr. (2014) found that alcohol use did not prove detrimental to Native American youth social relationships with parents, friends, peers, and romantic partners. Nevertheless, the complexity of viewing the role of friendships in the initiation of alcohol and other drug use is significant but well worth the struggles in untangling this social issue because of the health and social consequences associated with this problem (Gilliard-Matthews, Stevens, Nilsen, & Dunaev, 2015).

Not unexpectedly, the topic of adolescents' smoking and friendship networks also has received considerable attention in the professional literature, and it has been established that friend selection and peer influence are associated with smoking frequency (DeLay, Laursen, Kiuru, Salmela-Aro, & Nurmi, 2013; Schaefer, Haas, & Bishop, 2012). Youth, for example, are more likely to share similar smoking levels as their friends who are smokers rather than nonsmokers and are more likely to be named as friends. This shared activity increases bonding and is an important element in fostering and maintaining these friendships. Lakon et al. (2015) found that the presence of reciprocity, or choosing a friend of a friend as a friend, and smoking similarity positively influenced friendship selection, as did parental support.

However, in a Belgian study of adolescent smoking, parental smoking behavior (particularly maternal) influenced youth smoking behavior and selection of smoking friends, raising implications for a broader outreach to parents and peers (Mercken, Sleddens, de Vries, & Steglich, 2013). Jeon and Goodson (2015) argue for attention being paid to the structural features of friendship networks (denser and smaller networks) and characteristics of adolescents (i.e., age and gender) in engendering social intervention programs with the goals of reducing adolescents' risky behaviors.

Fitzgerald, Fitzgerald, and Aherne (2012) undertook a meta-analysis of the literature on peer and/or friends' influence on physical activity among American adolescents and concluded that there was a positive relationship, one manifested through six processes: (1) peer and/or friend support, (2) presence of peers and friends, (3) peer norms (4) friendship quality and acceptance, (5) peer crowds, and (6) peer victimization. Each of these six processes brings a much needed nuanced perspective on friendship influences.

Maturo and Cunningham's (2013) meta-review of datasets on the influence of friends on children's physical activity also found positive associations, with friends encouraging such activities. Tapping these friendships early in childhood health promotion programs, as a result, can facilitate the promotion of lifelong healthy habits with important implications for overweight and obesity-related illnesses. High-quality prosocial friendships do make a substantial difference in these youths' lives (Reitz-Krueger, Nagel, Guarnera, & Reppucci, 2015). Finally, in turning to sexual relations, the presence of both family and peer/friendship influences are operative in influencing the sexual intention of Latina and African-American females (Barman-Adhikari, Cederbaum, Sathoff, & Toro, 2014).

Policarpo (2015) differentiates between a "good friend" and an "intimate friend." The meaning of friendship, as a result, is influenced by age, gender/sexual identity, and level of formal education, and is heavily dependent on contextualization, including culture. Those who are younger and more formally educated will emphasize the importance of trust and self-disclosure. Friendships among older adults and those less formally educated emphasize kinship ties.

Gendered pathways, for example, must receive extra consideration in arriving at any in-depth understanding of youth friendships, with particular attention paid to the role of self-disclosure, shared activities, and closeness (Baines & Blatchford, 2009; Martinussen, 2014; Radmacher & Azmitia, 2006). This knowledge takes on great significance in gender-specific community practice programming, as does ethnicity/race and other demographic factors. Furthermore, it has implications for the staffing of these programs to minimize differences that can interfere with establishing relationships based on mutual trust.

Clearly, there is no absolute definition of how to classify "close" or "special" friendships, making generalizations arduous to accomplish and necessitating contextualization to make the definitions meaningful (Way, Gingold, Rotenberg, & Kuriakose, 2005). This conclusion should not come as a great surprise to any academic or practitioner with extensive work in urban centers and with diverse youth population groups. Terms such as "close" and "best" do not have absolute meanings and, as a result, need to be locally grounded to take into account situational and cultural backgrounds that bring forth different degrees of significance (Jeffs & Smith, 2010).

Friendships Gone Bad

Although community practitioners are primarily interested in helping youth establish and maintain friendships as a means of fostering youth strengths/assets, it is still necessary for practitioners to understand what causes friendships to deteriorate and disappear in order to help youth to possibly repair them when this happens. No friendship is perfect, and conflicts can be expected over the course of a relationship (Jones, Vaterlaus, Jackson, & Morrill, 2014). Helping youth prepare for such bumps in the road and "normalizing" them helps youth better accept them.

We may rightly argue that some of the most significant friendships have survived crises and major disagreements and emerged even stronger as a result. The great Mahatma Gandhi stated it well when he said that true friendship involves negotiating differences: "Friendship that insists upon agreement on all matters is not worth the name. Friendship to be real must ever sustain the weight of honest differences, however sharp they be." Interestingly, although Gandhi was primarily known for his quest to achieve social justice, his point on friendship strikes an important chord.

It is not a question of whether friendships can go bad but rather when because not all friendships, close or otherwise, persist and thrive. In other words, friendships can certainly disappoint (MacEvoy & Asher, 2012). Forgeron (2011) and Fales et al. (Fales, Forgeron, Gulak, & Bennett, 2014) provide such an example in discussing how chronic pain impacts all aspects of an adolescents' life, including close friendships. Friendships needs, however, may not meet the new expectations (knowledge and skills), severely compromising and possibly terminating these relationships.

Meaningful youth friendships are predicated on basic elements of social competence or the ability to positively socialize across social arenas. The nature of friendship is such that the question of "trading up" when someone "better" comes along raises important questions of morals and ethics, which is always a landmine in any discussions of social relations (Helm, 2010). Is trading up a concept that only applies to adults, or can it also apply to children and youth? If so, are the motivations similar?

Friendship cutoffs can approximate the pain and sorrow associated with family cutoffs (Bruun & Michael, 2014), and some would argue that friendship cutoffs are even more painful because of the voluntary nature of these relationships. The sense of betrayal we experience when someone we consider a close friend commits an act that undermines the foundation of the friendship remains vivid in our memory and undoubtedly tests our ability to trust again (Deutz, Lansu, & Cillessen, 2015; French, Case, & Gosling, 2009; Smart, Davies, Heaphy, & Mason, 2012; Way, 1996).

Running across old friends, however, can prove problematic, particularly since they may have been friends during a period in our lives that we would rather forget, and thus introducing a time and situational perspective that is not easy to ignore (Smart et al., 2012). "Outgrowing" these friendships introduces a strategic decision-making process. Few friends can be considered lifelong; those who are, are particularly significant or special. But making time-situational or transitory friends is still important in people's lives.

In 2009, the Oxford English Dictionary awarded "unfriending" the word of the year because of its online popularity. A friendship can be terminated simply in this medium (Leib, 2011): a click and that is the end. Befriending, on the other hand, has also been conceptualized as an intervention method for isolated individuals or ones who lack social support (Balaam, 2015).

Friendships, as a result, are not permanent social relationships; they can and do change in response to varying circumstance. When the change is dramatic and friends stop being friends, a transformation has occurred that has deteriorated the relationship to the point where it was terminated. The length of time this process takes, and the nature of the termination, will have dramatic impact on the former or ex-friends. The saying that it is better to have loved and lost than not to have loved at all also can be applied to friendship: is it better to have been friended and lost than not to have been friended at all?

Smart and colleagues (2012, p. 92) argue that "friendship, like kinship, cannot be a static relationship and movement in and out of friendship, just like degrees of closeness with kin, entails negotiation. In turn this involves emotional work in relation to the other and the self. At certain times the emotional burden of this negotiation is heavier than at other times. Hence we are concerned here with understanding more about these processes of negotiation within ongoing friendships and concerning the departure from friendship." Relational transitions of any kind can be challenging, and this certainly applies to dealing with feelings of loss when losing a close friend. The mourning period that follows remains to be more fully explored and understood.

Friendships that have changed for the worse are certainly not rare. Sometimes this occurs over an extended period of time; at other times it is in reaction to a major social infraction that was viewed as unforgivable. Friendships "gone bad," so to speak, have not been ignored in the professional literature, and they go by a variety of labels, such as "difficult," "critical," and "antipathetic." Each of these terms share much in common but each emphasizes particular aspects or consequences in the change in friendship status.

Difficult friendships can be defined as "those that were kept going, at least for some years if not forever, notwithstanding irritations, disappointments, boredom and even some antagonisms. In a way these are the most surprising sorts of friendships. In truth rather a lot of people in the Directive responded to the idea of difficult friends by simply saying that they would drop someone once they were no longer fun or as soon as the relationship became tiresome or uneven in some ways" (Smart et al., 2012, p. 95). Interestingly, this definition highlights the importance of maintaining a delicate balance in a relationship and also highlights the dynamic nature of this form of relationship.

Heaphy and Davies (2012), too, address critical friendships and the need to have a balanced view of this phenomenon when a friendship changes from positive to negative because friendships are a value resource to which people turn when in need of social, emotional, and material support. A friend lost is a friendship lost, and, in the lives of those with few friendships, this loss can be significantly magnified and deter them from reaching out to find a substitute.

Friendships that have dissolved can also be referred to as "antipathetic." Jealousy, incompatibility, intimacy-rule violations, and even aggression can be themes in the transformation of a relationship from one considered productive to counterproductive (Casper & Card, 2010). These relationships are referred to as "broken" (Blumberg et al., 2012), "tainted" (Chang, 2013; Smart et al., 2012), "dropped" (Cotterell, 2007, 2013), "friendships that turn," (Johnson et al., 2004), "fading," or "damaged," signifying a shift in relations (Gartzke & Weisiger, 2013). Last, the emergence of the concept of "frienemies" ("friend" and "enemy") also illustrates the permeability of boundaries and how the loss of a friendship can be construed in the most negative of ways (Kazovsky, 2013).

Smart et al. (2012, p. 91) discuss the importance of youth friendships and eschew dealing with the debate on whether or not friendships are more or less important than other relationships. They focus on when friendships turn negative: "we analyze how friendship, when it goes wrong, can challenge one's sense of self and even produce ontological insecurity. Friendship, it is argued, is tied into the process of self-identification and so staying true to friends, even when the relationships becomes uneven or tiresome, can be a sign of ethical standing." Breakups are never easy, be they friendship or love. However, unlike in love where there is often an understanding that it is important to quickly to find another love to replace the one that was lost, friendships are not easily replaced.

Leib's (2011) book *Friend v. Friend: The Transformation of Friendship—and What the Law Has to Do with It*, introduces readers to a legal perspective on friendships when they transcend conventional disagreements and escalate to violate the law and why more attention needs to be placed on this social institution. The following example illustrates this point (Leib, 2011, p. 1): "You loan a friend $25,000. You don't write up any formal paperwork because the transaction seems to be predicated on trust, and you think it wouldn't make sense to formalize the loan because of the friendship. In any case, she loaned that much a few years back. She fails to pay you back even though she seems to have the money. Are you precluded from suing in a court to get your money back?"

The Leib case scenario involving money may not seem out of the ordinary because we may have often found ourselves both lending and receiving money from friends. Trust and a desire to help are essential elements in this transaction, and, as the reader will see, trust and reciprocity are essential in friendships that can be classified as close. Leib sees the importance of friendships as a public policy concern, one essential in maintaining a cohesive society. Friendship is thus worthy of attention by society and, we can add, the helping professions such as community practice.

Needs Met Through Friendship and Frameworks

Why is friendship considered so important in society, even to the point of being considered an essential element of the social fabric? Friendships obviously meet a wide range of needs (Padilla-Walkerm, Fraser, Black, & Bean, 2015). Friendships develop, grow, and even die out in what some would call slow painful deaths because of how they address or fail to address needs. One common perspective for understanding friendships is to focus on the multifaceted needs that they address explicitly or implicitly.

Adolescent loneliness, as manifested by a lack of friendships and perceived loneliness, can be countered by helping them develop friendships and a positive attitude (Martin, Wood, Houghton, Carroll, & Hattie, 2014). Cordelli (2015) brings an important dimension to our view of friendships by stressing how the benefits of friendships are influenced by sociodemographic factors: "Friendship distributes critical benefits across society and does so unequally. Income, levels of education and health vary dramatically according to the quality of individuals' friendships. Further, friendships shape the motivations and aspirations of their participants." As a result, understanding benefits requires a multidimensional view, one tying benefits to motivations for engaging in friendships (Ojanen, Stratman, Card, & Little, 2013).

Motivations for engaging in friendships are varied and ultimately impact the tenor and scope of the relationship (Digeser, 2013). The immense popularity of materialism, too, has certainly found its way into friendships. The concept of "friends with money" translates into being part of a friendship network that can involve money or access to material goods or gives access to information that can generate financial rewards (Engelberg, Gao, & Parsons, 2012). Friendships originate, persist, evolve, and may even be significantly transformative because they meet a wide range of instrumental, expressive, and informational needs. Sorting out these needs is not simple but is an essential exercise from academics and practitioners.

The emergence of "friends with benefits" (FWBRs), for example, introduces a "benefit" for adolescents and adults that challenges us in determining the meaning, level, and intensity of a friendship (Williams & Adams, 2013). These types of "friendships" make it difficult to sort out the various "other" needs (such as sexual) met through these relationships. Do sexual needs drive these relationship, and is friendship only a pretense? How do these relationships evolve? How and when do these friendships cross the line and turn "counterproductive?" Because FWBRs do not necessarily engage in sexual relations and can involve the exchange of mating advice (DelPriore, Butterfield, & Hill, 2013), these and countless other questions illustrate the complexities of sorting out relationships that have been formalized with a label.

Lasting and "meaningful" friendships persist because they bring a unique combination of elements that meet all needs, including intimacy and reciprocity, and a history of a shared relationship that can be thought of as the "glue" that keeps these elements together (Salmon, 2013). Happiness, too, is greatly influenced by friendships (Argyle, 2001; Demir & Urberg, 2004). Demir and Weitekamp (2007) address the strong relationship between friendship experiences and happiness and conclude that the close association between happiness and friendships is greatly fostered by promoting individuals' feelings of uniqueness, an aspect rarely mentioned in the literature and one with particular significance for urban youth who often feel uniquely underappreciated and misunderstood because of their marginalization.

There are virtually no social arenas where friendship cannot be influential. Youth friendships have been found to play influential roles in assisting them in making transitions to elementary school (Kingery, Erdley, & Marshall, 2011; Valdez, Lambert, & Ialongo, 2011), junior high school (Aikins, Bierman, & Parker, 2005), high school (Benner, 2011a; George, 2007; Newman, Lohman, Newman, Myers, & Smith, 2000; Parker, Lüdtke, Trautwein, & Roberts, 2012), and college (Oswald & Clark, 2003), and can involve academic achievement (Crosnoe, Cavanagh, & Elder, 2003; Roberts, 2011).

Cooper and Cooper (2008), for example, in a Canadian study of "ethno-racial" youth in their struggles to combat racial discrimination, found that youth with close friends demonstrated higher academic performance, lower rates of criminal involvement, and lower school drop-out rates. Having close friendships served as a buffer against racial discrimination, provided social support, and acted as a motivator to fit in. Having friends with similar experiences also provides an opportunity to share strategies and tactics that can help youth navigate these "difficult" situations.

The role of peer/friendship relationships in student academic and extracurricular engagement is considered significant, making interventions focused on broadening and shaping these relationships of great importance (Juvonen, Espinoza, & Knifsend, 2012). Friendships and the supportive role they can play in transitions across the life span and during particularly critical developmental periods provide community practitioners with identifiable periods on which to focus interventions (Haavind, 2014; Schuh, Sundar, & Hagner, 2014).

Introducing diversity into a definition makes the concept that much more relevant to disenfranchised groups. City streets and other public places are spaces where youth encounter a wide diversity of people, including those who are homeless (Witten, Kearns, & Carroll, 2015). Neighborhood diversity, as in the case of Houston and its Latino community, which is primarily Mexican/Mexican American, increases the likelihood of friendships crossing racial and ethnic groups, thus widening peer networks that can be strategically tapped in helping youth of color socially navigate unhealthy situations (Britton, 2014).

Friendships across racial and ethnic groups have been found to help decrease racial prejudice, a key element in an increasingly diverse society and in urban areas with histories of attracting newcomers, by serving as a social bridge, containing intergroup conflicts, and reducing inequalities (de Souza Briggs, 2007). In addition, cross-ethnic and -racial friendships can serve as a social bonding glue in communities undergoing rapid racial demographic transformations. These types of transformations invariably bring tensions, and any opportunity to minimize these tensions is welcomed.

Creating opportunities for youth of color to meet and interact with white, non-Latino youth can bring important individual, community, and societal benefits (Meyer, 2011; Nebbitt, Lombe, Cryer-Coupet, & Stephens, 2015; Poulin, Kiesner, Pedersen, & Dishion, 2011; Stanton-Salazar & Spina, 2005). In the case of newcomers, there are many benefits to having them welcomed in a community, beyond creating social and cultural bridges. For example, urban communities with increasing immigration have been found to foster greater economic (capital) innovations (Lee, 2015). These innovations, in turn, can expand social relationship and civic engagement opportunities. Communities with newcomers, too, will find that these new residents are interested in giving back to their newly adopted communities (Weng & Lee, 2016).

The categorization of friendship has advanced considerably in an effort to understand various benefits and types of friendships. Fredricks and Simpkins (2013), for example, organize the peer relations literature into three distinct categories: (1) peer groups, (2) peer relationships, and (3) peer interactions. Turnbull, Blue-Banning, and Pereira (2000), in a study of friendships of Latino youth with disabilities, propose a framework consisting of three domains related to relationships (companionship, instrumental support, and emotional support) and intensity levels (acquaintance, casual, and intimate). Although this framework has been applied to a particular population group, it has the potential for a broader reach to other groups, too.

Youth with disabilities and chronic health conditions also benefit from friendships in dealing with the challenges associated with their conditions (Devine, Holmbeck, Gayes, & Purnell, 2012; La Greca, Bearman, & Moore, 2002; Rose et al., 2011; Rossetti, 2015), including returning to school to facilitate recovery and reintegration into daily life (Danby, Thompson, Theobald, & Thorpe, 2012). The life satisfaction literature, it should be noted, is very limited in this regard (Proctor, Linley, & Maltby, 2009). Furthermore, friendships can help youth cope with stress and other personal and ecological challenges (Abaied & Rudolph, 2011; Chow & Buhrmester, 2011).

Contextualization of Friendship

Youth friendships require both a normative (nomothetic) and individualized (idiographic) context in order to avoid in engaging in stereotypes when discussing them (Bagwell & Schmidt, 2013). Urban youth friendships cannot be understood, appreciated, and addressed successfully without taking into account cultural and geographical backgrounds such as age, gender, race/ethnicity, immigrant status, acculturation levels, physical and intellectual abilities, neighborhood, and socio-economic class, for example, thus bringing a cultural and highly nuanced dimension to this concept (Bauer, Loomis, & Akkari, 2013; Holter & Guilfoyle, 2013; Van Zantvliet & Kalmijn, 2013; Way, 2006; Way & Greene, 2006).

Failure to contextualize friendships translates into failure to understand and possibly generalize findings, a key element in program design. Grounding friendships socially; culturally; geographically; or based on intellectual, physical, or emotional abilities makes the work of social scientists that much more arduous and expensive. Providing practitioners with frameworks, or guides, however, facilitates the translation of research into practice, which, when evaluated, advances knowledge on urban youth friendships.

Numerous perspectives, frameworks, and typologies have been offered that reflect various academic viewpoints based on different disciplines and helping profession backgrounds, including feminist views, for example (Whitaker, 2011). It is important to emphasize, however, that efforts to categorize friendships (or any other concept) represent an attempt to capture the "quality" of the relationship, which is not an apolitical or value-free exercise but rather one that brings a subjective perspective that it is necessary to acknowledge. Making the values of these guides explicit is one way of counteracting unintended sociopolitical conse-quences. The following guides are but several examples that illustrate the richness of this area as well as the challenges inherent in any form of classification.

French, Pidada, and Victor (2005) propose a four-part framework for under-standing the role and value of friendships across cultural dimensions, making it particularly attractive for use in neighborhoods that are increasingly diverse in composition: (1) similarity across cultures, (2) dimensions of friendships that vary across cultures, (3) the utility of the individualism/collectivism dimension for explaining cultural differences in friendship, and (4) methodological issues in the study of culture and friendship.

The ability to differentiate within and between groups along multiple dimen-sions, including social and demographic factors and considerations, allows interventions to be specifically targeted to maximize often limited resources. For example, the term "associate" has emerged in the literature on young urban African-American/black youth and men and signifies a differentiation between a "friend" and someone who is known or with whom one engages in illicit activities but does not get too close to (Edwin & Rosenblatt, 2015). Clearly, an associate will not be confused with being a friend.

Youth lead much more circumspect lives when compared to adults, bringing a geographical perspective and influence that cannot be ignored. A geographic view of friendships (Bunnell, Years, Peake, Skelton, & Smith, 2012) provides a dif-ferent window for increasing our understanding of the role of mobility in defining friendships: (1) geographies of affect/emotion and the ontological construction of the human, (2) children's and young people's geographies and the (re)produc-tion of social ordering, and (3) geographies of mobility and transnationalism in a world of increased human spatial movement and social relations at a distance. Bunnell and colleagues highlight both the rewards and challenges of developing an understanding of friendship in a world that increasingly has gotten easier to traverse electronically rather than physically because of the advent of social media.

Way (2006, p. 403) points out that of our knowledge and understanding of youth friendships has been shaped by a biased and limited contextual understand-ing, limiting our abilities to undertake a comprehensive set of interventions that can enhance these forms of relationships:

> Researchers, particularly in the American context, have tended to concep-tualize friendships as a universal rather than a culturally situated set of rela-tionships. This universal conceptualization is evident in the large body of research on the friendships of American, middle-class, White youth and the almost nonexistent body of research on the friendships of those who are not American, middle-class, and White. The implicit and explicit assumption in the research on the American, middle class, White youth is that the findings derived from these youth generalizes to all youth, and thus there is little rea-son to explore the friendships of other groups.

Way's disturbing conclusion has a profound impact on the development of our understanding of urban communities, youth, and interrelations, of which friendship is but one dimension, albeit a very critical one.

Furthermore, when attention is paid to youth-of-color friendships, and particularly to those friends who can be labeled as close, it invariably focuses on the negative impact friendship has on behavior, feelings, and future outlooks. Relational aggression between friends is considered an understudied topic for both boys and girls, one that has implications for their well-being (Waasdorp, Bagdi, & Bradshaw, 2009), but it can have a profound impact on youth under intense scrutiny by authorities, particularly law enforcement. As a result, youth relational aggression can result in a number of consequences, including sadness, isolation, being disliked (Rose, Swenson, & Carlson, 2004; Sullivan, Helms, Kliewer, & Goodman, 2010), suspension from school, and possible incarceration, particularly in the case of low-income/low-wealth youth of color who become legally involved.

Friendships can have other negative ramifications, such as compromising life chances, victimization, suicide ideation, diminishing self-esteem, and avoidance of engaging other youth who are different from themselves (limiting exposure and potential growth), to list a few (Bunnell et al., 2012; Fujimoto & Valente, 2012; Knecht, Snijders, Baerveldt, Steglich, & Raub, 2010; Winterrowd, Canetto, & Chavez, 2011). Understanding the potential negative consequences associated with friendship is necessary for a balanced and comprehensive appreciation of the various types and roles of friendships that are possible (Boman IV, Krohn, Gibson, & Stogner, 2012; Osgood et al., 2013; Wei & Jonson-Reid, 2011).

A focus on understanding how youth perceive and reach out to potential friends engaged in negative activities, or when positive relationships cross the line into negative relationships, is critical in maximizing the potential benefits of positive friendships in developing social interventions grounded within youth operative reality. The concept of "forbidden friendship" surely comes to the mind of parents (Keijsers et al., 2012). These types of friendships are viewed by parents as negatively influencing their children to engage in antisocial activities and are not condoned.

It is also necessary to differentiate between dyadic friendships and affiliations with peer groups, although friends can rightly be considered part of a peer network within which they occupy a special place (Brown & Klute, 2003). Peers bring transitory and superficial elements to relationships, whereas friends bring depth and permanency, including increased expectations. Casual affiliations or relationships can sometimes be confused with friendships, but they are based on superficiality, which can be mistaken for friendship. Membership in gangs illustrates this key point. Belonging to a gang introduces peer affiliation but not necessarily friendship (Hallsworth & Brotherton, 2011).

A social capital perspective provides a widely accepted lens for appreciating how gangs and other group memberships connect members in meaningful ways (Moule Jr., Decker, & Pyrooz, 2013). Bonding as opposed to bridging social capital reinforces peer relationships but also can limit youth from reaching out to other racial/ethnic groups to form new friendships that can be positive influences in their lives and introduce new perspectives or worldviews.

There certainly is a tendency to view social capital among marginalized youth as either "bad" or "good," and this is a too simplistic view of such a critical and influential construct, as in the case of gang membership of urban youth of color, for example. Billett (2014) introduces the potential of this construct to be tapped in understanding resilience and identity construction, which, incidentally, are key elements associated with friendships and invariably are part of social interventions focused on urban youth. Broadening our views and understanding of youth social capital as a coping mechanism (strength or asset) provides practitioners with a popular construct that can be enhanced in youth practice when specifically targeted (Collins, Neal, & Neal, 2014; Hunter, Neiger, & West, 2011).

However, Billett (2012) points out that using adult indicators of social capital and then imposing them on youth leads to imperfect research and serious misunderstandings. Taking concepts developed by adults for adults and then applying them to children and youth is rarely questioned, so Billett's conclusion is correct. Empowerment is another example of how youth differ from their adult counterparts in how they think and act on this concept (Delgado, 2002).

The topic of gangs and friendships has been addressed in the literature. Chu et al. (2015) found that gang-affiliated youth often noted establishing and maintaining friendships as their primary reason for joining. Expanding our understanding of the role of friendships as a key motivator for joining and staying in gangs will go a long way toward helping to counteract gang influence on urban youth (Baskin, Quintana, & Slaten, 2014; McDaniel, 2012; Mendoza-Denton, 2014; Morch & Andersen, 2012).

Friendship Groups

Friendship groups have historically suffered from a lack of scholarly attention when compared to friendship dyads, and they continue to do so (Rohrer, 2014). Any discussion of friendships must entail attention being paid to youth friendship groups since groups play such an important role in youth lives. Friendships are usually conceptualized as dyads and the literature favors such a view. However, friendships can also transpire in groups (Hiatt et al., 2015).

Learning, a topic addressed later in this chapter, occurs in friendship groups, and it has been argued that the group context facilitates learning through discussions, explanations, and applications to real-life situations (Senior & Howard, 2014). Goins (2011) introduces a racial (black) and gender (women) perspective on creating a safe ("home place") environment that facilitated group members to freely express culturally based truths without concerns about marginalization.

Friendship groups bring different dimensions, including peer influences, both positive and negative (Karlsson & Evaldsson, 2011). Webb and Zimmer-Gembeck (2015) discuss friendship groups and the various contexts in which they are embedded. A collectivist orientation, as opposed to one that is individualistic, as in the case of youth of color, will make friendship groups that much more important to understand in the effort to develop interventions that are group-sensitive and friendly Azmitia, Ittel, & Break, 2006; Hofstede, 1980; Sharabany, 2006; Triandis, 1990).

It stands to reason that a friendship group context has a different set of expectations and dynamics than a dyadic relationship. Groups have the potential to exert influence in a manner different from a one-to-one interaction. Friendship groups, however, can also provide a group context for bullying and other negative behavior (Faris & Ennett, 2012; Maunder & Marks, 2014; Percy, Wilson, McCartan, & McCrystal, 2011). Much needs to be learned about urban youth group friendships that goes beyond membership in gangs.

Demographic Influences

Although friendship is a universal concept, how it materializes and evolves must take into consideration demographic factors and, in turn, how they interact with environmental forces. Thus, the nature and importance of friendship is influenced by demographic factors such as gender, age, ethnicity/race, abilities, socioeconomic status (SES), community dynamics, and intersectionality, to list but several key factors and considerations (Bogat & Liang, 2005; Hall, 2011; Kahn, 2014; Miche, Huxhold, & Stevens, 2013; Way, 2013).

Furthermore, as the United States has become increasingly more ethnically and racially diverse, other influential friendship factors have begun to capture the attention of scholars (Aberson, Shoemaker, & Tomolillo, 2004; Holoien, Bergsieker, Shelton, & Alegre, 2015). The increasing number of newcomer youth living in urban areas of the country, for example, requires special attention within any discussion of diversity and in the interest of creating a positive social life (Evans & Holt, 2011). Newcomer youth also bring assets that can be tapped in the development of youth-focused community interventions (Wray-Lake, Rote, Gupta, Godfrey, & Sirin, 2015).

Tassara (2014) sums up the lack of knowledge on unauthorized Latina/o youth friendships in the results of a study on Latino newcomer youth, which revealed of our lack of understanding on the subject even though they are important in providing advice, helping youth socially navigating their new surroundings, and helping them feel a part of a group, with trust is a critical ingredient of these friendships. A tremendous amount of important influence is presented in Tassara's discussion of newcomer friendship networks and the roles they play, including how parental concerns about friendship influence is weighed by these youth.

Discussion of friendship among newcomer youth must take into account acculturation factors in addition to documented status and neighborhood segregation because acculturation levels influence English language competencies, cultural values, and subsequent views of the world (Schlueter, 2012; Teja & Schonert-Reichl, 2013). Roche et al. (Roche, Ghazarian, & Fernandez-Esquer, 2012) addressed the role of acculturation among Mexican-origin youth and found that higher levels of acculturation not only translated into higher educational achievement, but also into a higher chance that such youth associated with peers and friends from similar backgrounds that reinforced cultural values and heritage.

Kathiravelu (2013) addresses the increased diversity in cities and the increasing importance of friendship as a subject for research:

> The study of diverse and multicultural cities has gained considerable interest, reflecting a growing concern with migrant populations and the implications of "strangers" . . . one of the key considerations centers around understanding how ethnically, linguistically and culturally diverse peoples "rub along" and live together in tight and dense metropolises. One strand of this research is interested in the everyday encounter—ranging from the fleeting non-verbal to more sustained engagements over longer periods of time. Despite growing interest in the mundane and quotidian, friendship as a form of social relation and interaction has been largely unexamined.

Cities have sections that are highly segregated according to ethnicity, race, and socioeconomic class. Nevertheless, there are public places where all segments encounter each other, be it at a park, public square, library, or some other geographical setting that is accessible geographically, psychologically (perceived as safe), operationally (acceptance), or logistically (hours and days).

It can certainly be argued that proximity to ones' own ethnic and racial group members may be the source of critical cultural, social, or emotional resources that are linked to higher levels of well-being in an increasingly challenging world (Knies et al., 2014). However, fostering diverse friendships has been found to reduce prejudices and result in greater appreciation of diversity values and in diverse friendships (Bahns & Springer, 2015). Not surprisingly, when diverse friendships are formed early in childhood, it becomes easier to make these types of friendships later in adolescence (Al Ramiah, Hewstone, Voci, Cairns, & Hughes, 2013).

Kathiravelu goes on to argue that it is impossible to fully appreciate and understand cities without understanding friendships (networks and ties built on trust, respect, and reciprocity) and their role in the politics of co-existence within a confined geographical area (social and spatial configurations of friendships) that help to make strangers into friends. Lack of knowledge is a prodigious impediment to creating opportunities (time and space) that foster connectedness outside of homogenous groups, particularly in the case of ethnicity and race (Fainstein, 2005; Koopmans, Lancee, & Schaeffer, 2014).

The introduction of language preference, too, enters into factors tied to demographics and makes for exciting conclusions and challenges for developing an understanding of youth friendships because the ability to communicate in the language of preference is an essential element in establishing and maintaining friendships and shaping identity (Bucholtz, 2010a, 2010b; Paris, 2010; Rampton, 2014). In the case of newcomer youth, language preference takes on even greater significance (Brinegar, 2010; Salehi, 2010).

Social isolation due to language and cultural factors can have serious interpersonal and academic manifestations. Benner (2011b) in a longitudinal study of Mexican/Mexican-American male and female adolescents in high school highlighted the academic consequences caused by loneliness and identified three loneliness trajectory classes: (1) consistently low, (2) chronically high, and (3) low but increasing. Friends can serve as role models for attitudes and behavior, directly or indirectly, and can share histories that can be of use in present and future situations (McMillan, 2013); this can result in positive academic outcomes for Latino youth when these friends also share similar outlooks to education.

Key Factors in Friendships

As noted in the introductory chapter, friendship is a complex interpersonal bond that consists of multiple factors and layers that are equally complex, further compounding our understanding and potential use of friendships as a critical goal and component of social interventions (Bellotti, 2007; Helve & Bynner, 2007; Schneider et al., 2011). This complexity should not dissuade us from embracing youth friendships as goal in community practice.

Many different aspects of friendships have generally escaped serious attention by scholars. Roberts (2009), for example, reports on how friendships foster mutual learning, a dimension of friendship that has generally escaped attention in the professional literature even though learning is an essential element in life. An intellectual friendship brings a different dimension to learning, as discussed by Cohassey's (2014) coverage of the relationship between Ernest Hemingway and Ezra Pound, for example, and can exist among youth friendships.

Upon closer examination, friends learn from each other through openness, patience, and a willingness to share in an atmosphere that is nonjudgmental and conducive to both teaching and learning (DeLay et al., 2014; Nicholson, 2009; Senior & Howard, 2014). The concept of "friend-based learning" has emerged to capture this form of interaction (Borrero & Yeh, 2010) and can be applied to youth community practice.

Respect as a key factor also has generally escaped serious attention (Du Plessis & Corney, 2011). Empathy, too, can easily be associated with many of these elements and has not received its deserved attention (Schonert-Reichl, Smith, Zaidman-Zait, & Hertzman, 2012; Zalk et al, 2010). However, other aspects of friendships have received considerable attention in the literature and are worthy of focus in this book. Hall (2012) identified six factors of expectations (i.e., symmetrical reciprocity, agency, enjoyment, instrumental aid, similarity, and communion) that constitute the "ideal" standards of friendship.

As noted in Figure 3.1, nine elements will be focused on in this section. They were selected because of their prominence in the friendship literature and because they lend themselves to being a focus of the social interventions proposed in this book: (1) reciprocity, (2) intimacy, (3) self-disclosure, (4) humor, (5) advice, (6) trust, (7) homophily (common demographic resemblance), (8) availability/access, and (9) fun. These elements are highly interrelated; they are addressed in no particular order of importance and in varying degrees of depth.

Each practitioner may place these elements in his or her own order of importance and even include other elements not covered in this section because there certainly is no consensus as to what key elements must or cannot be a part of friendships. Furthermore, these factors are highly correlated or interrelated even though they will be treated as separate entities in this section; there will be

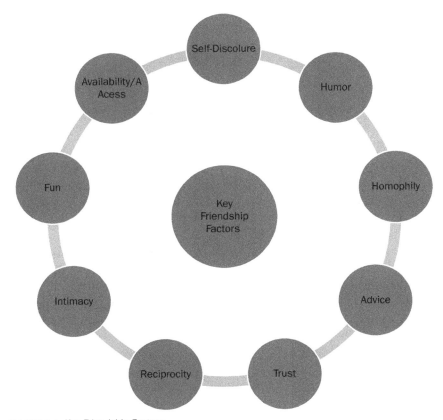

FIGURE 3.1 Key Friendship Factors

instances where quotes are used bring several different factors together to illustrate their close interrelationships.

RECIPROCITY

Reciprocity is a concept that is familiar to all age groups and captures the importance of both receiving and giving emotional or instrumental assistance (Ciairano, Rabaglietti, Roggero, Bonino, & Beyers, 2007; Helm, 2010). Willingness to both receive and give assistance, regardless of how it is conceptualized, introduces an element or bond to a relationship that lends itself to being researched and well understood. Friendship is often thought of as a human instance of mutual cooperation within a dyadic relation (Ohtsubo et al., 2014). This cooperation can be extended into both receiving and giving, with significant implications for friendship development and maintenance (Maqubela, 2013).

How is the need for assistance conveyed, and how do friends give and receive assistance? Reciprocity is a key element in any form of relationship, but it takes on even greater significance in friendships. Leib (2011, p. 21) provides a succinct description of friendship reciprocity:

> Friends engage in mutual regard and make an effort to reciprocate in the realms of caring, emotional support, and goodwill: they have concern for one another's well-being. In addition, friends wish their counterparts well *for their own sake*, rather than solely for any benefit that might accrue to a friend on account of the other's well-being. Each party to a friendship self-consciously engages in reciprocity and is aware of her counterpart's goodwill. Unlike a romantic interest, which can be unrequited, friendship must be shared with an awareness of mutual regard.

The influence of friendship reciprocity has been found to be a critical source of social support beyond the number of friends reported by youth (Rude & Herda, 2010; Vaquera & Kao, 2008). Thus, quality of assistance is far greater in importance than the quantity, which should not be surprising.

Assistance can be thought of as falling into instrumental (concrete), expressive (emotional), and informational exchanges. Each of these forms of assistance brings different levels of commitment and social exchanges between the friend providing and the friend receiving help. Expressive assistance is probably the most important and difficult to develop and sustain in a friendship. Instrumental and informational assistance can be time limited, and these do not carry the emotional burden of expressive assistance. However, it is not unusual to find all three forms of benefits in a friendships. In fact, it can be argued that friends who excel in providing all three will be more likely considered a special or close friend.

Block (2015), for example, identifies the interactions of reciprocity and transitivity as key elements in any understanding of friendship; he asks whether friendships that exist outside of social groups have more or less probability of being reciprocal than those embedded in a group. This question necessitates a nuanced understanding that must be answered for marginalized population groups.

Bukowaski, Motezons, and Meyer (2009), too, argue that any measure of friendship must tap the level of reciprocity and closeness (intimacy), key dimensions of quality between two individuals, although this poses challenges in arriving at a definition and measurement. A friendship that becomes "one-sided" by having one individual provide assistance but never receive or require "payback" is a relationship that may not last. However, one youth study of friendship found that a mild degree of internalizing distress may serve to enhance, as opposed to harm, a friendship (Hill & Swenson, 2014). Reciprocity, similar to any social construct, has a strong cultural dimension that influences how it is defined and unfolds, and that includes youth culture.

INTIMACY

Understanding how intimate relations are established and evolve helps social scientists and practitioners understand social relationships such as friendships (Derlega, 2013). Maslow's hierarchy of human needs places love and belonging, which includes friendship and intimacy, at the third of five stages (McLeod, 2007). Level of intimacy and intensity are the aspects that differentiate relationships of "best" friend, which is more intense, intimate, and rewarding, from acquaintanceships, at the opposite end of the continuum, that are considerably less intense, less intimate, and less rewarding (Coleman, 2013; Rybak & McAndrew, 2006).

Intimacy, not unexpectedly, is a complex and multifaceted social construct that incorporates differences in quantity and quality. It also incorporate at least eight themes, many of which touch on other elements covered in this section (Sharabany, 2006): (1) *frankness and spontaneity* (involving self-disclosure and honest feedback), (2) *sensitivity* and *knowing* (self-disclosure and honest feedback), (3) *attachment* (considered a dimension of closeness and bonding), (4) *exclusiveness* (unique qualities that are a part of the relationship), (5) *giving* and *sharing* (material goods and giving and receiving advice), (6) *imposition* (willingness to receive help from friend and being in debt as a result), (7) *common activities* (mutually enjoying sharing time and activities together), and (8) *trust* and *loyalty* (assurance that the friend is there when you need him). These eight themes bring unique qualities, but these qualities are also highly interrelated, thus complicating our understanding of intimacy.

The topic of friendship intimacy has received attention in the social sciences over the past several decades because of an understanding that the ability to establish close and intimate relationships early in life is a harbinger of the ability to do so later in life (Buhrmester, 1990). In fact, intimacy may be considered the most important construct that serves to distinguish between different levels of close friendships, although that is certainly subject to debate (Shulman, Laursen, Kalman, & Karpovsky, 1997).

The discussion of whether women or men experience greater intimacy is certainly bound to generate its share of discussion and cannot be separated from gender stereotypes in our society. However, there is general agreement that women are more capable of intimacy and possess better emotional regulation skills that can lead to better positive interactions with friends (Ruiz-Aranda & Zaccagnini, 2013). Thus, if we accept this position, it has implications for how gender influences how close friendships are defined and what is expected from these types of relationships.

David (2014) notes that at intimacy's core, friends share mutual respect and trust, and each partner feels prized by the other. Similarly to other elements associated with friendship, in best friend relationships there is a propensity toward self-disclosure that contributes to intimacy (Bauminger, Finzi-Dottan, Chason, & Har-Even, 2008). Intimacy can best be conceptualized as "the quality of close connection between people and the process of building this quality" (Jamieson, 2012, p. 137). Jamieson not only defines intimacy but also helps practitioners and researchers operationalize it for the enhancement of relationships in general and more specifically friendships.

SELF-DISCLOSURE

The concept of self-disclosure is often associated with any definition of friendship that transcends the ordinary. In fact, we can certainly argue that having someone to self-disclose to is one of the primary benefits of having a friend. The subject of self-disclosure and youth friends is certainly not new. Rivernbark (1971), almost 45 years ago, addressed self-disclosure patterns among adolescents. Self-disclosure is also closely associated with intimacy and closeness (Martinez & Howe, 2013), and separating intimacy from self-disclosure is difficult if not impossible (Bauminger et al., 2008).

If having a best friend is conceptualized as a strength or asset, as in the case of LGBTQ youth for example, then it can facilitate self-disclosure and resulting personal growth (Baiocco, Laghi, Di Pomponio, & Nigito, 2012). Gay youth and men who have not come out find dissonance in their existence and identity. Gay friends who are cognizant of this dilemma can help in reducing the deleterious consequences associated with a compromised or soiled identity, which impacts behavior (Kocet, 2014).

Friendship disclosure provides youth with an opportunity to practice sharing and responding to possible painful feelings and experiences (Rose et al., 2012). Self-disclosure takes on even greater importance among LGBTQ youth of color, for example, because of how isolated they may be within their respective families and community and the impact of intersectionality in marginalizing them.

Tilton-Weaver, Marshall, and Darling (2014, p. 553) have arguably done the most informative work in this area involving youth, and they have identified four key disclosure characteristics: "First, the person who is self-disclosing is deliberately and voluntarily revealing information; it is not revealed accidentally or through coercion . . . . Second, the information is private and not self-evident. Third, the speaker is divulging information that he or she believes the partner would not know if it had not been disclosed to them. Fourth, self-disclosure involves revealing more information than is required for the situation." Disclosure is an intimate act undertaken with an explicit or implicit understanding that the information will not be shared beyond the two parties and that the information being shared needs to be shared in order to obtain relief and/or assistance. In essence, sharing brings with it an expectation of help.

The scholarly literature on adolescence differentiates between two types of disclosure (Martinez & Howe, 2013; Tilton-Weaver et al., 2014): (1) sharing with parents/adult authorities and (2) sharing with friends and peers. The former (routine disclosure) entails sharing with parents and adult authority figures and involves disclosure of information pertaining to whereabouts and is of a nonsensitive nature; the latter (self-disclosure) is voluntary and provides an opportunity for expression of thoughts, feelings, and enhancement of intimacy and best approximates what is commonly thought of as disclosure.

Von Salisch, Lüpschen, and Kanevski (2012) address the immediate and potential long-term consequences of a loss of a friendship and the resulting loss of an ability to self-disclose, which can impact on behavior and friendships by intensifying reliance on physical and relational aggressive behavior and thoughts about revenge. In essence, losing a friend can have deep emotional consequences. Disclosure is clearly not a routine activity, and it is reserved for special friends and special moments and situations.

HUMOR

The reader may be surprised at the inclusion of humor as an important element of friendship. Nevertheless, if one stops and thinks about how humor plays a facilitative role in establishing and maintaining relationships, it should not come as any great surprise that humor will find its way into friendships. A sense of humor can be viewed as a strength in individuals (Müller & Ruch, 2011), and it is correlated with individuals who are socially warm; possessing a sense of humor facilitates social interactions and can be considered a desirable social skill in friendship development.

Humor can facilitate and enhance friendships in many different ways (Treger, Sprecher, & Erber, 2013; Way, Santos, & Cordero, 2012; Woodbury-Fariña & Antongiorgi, 2014). Positive humor is acknowledged to help in handling stress and making friendships (Jackson, 2011). Humor has also been found to be a strong stress reducer in the workplace, and this can be reinforced through the establishment of work friends who also share a sense of humor (Dyck & Holtzman, 2013; Ptacek, 2014). Humor can also be a stress reducer in schools, although this topic is yet to be researched in any serious manner. Gordon (2013, 2014) examines the relationship between humor (different from joking and laughter) and friendship and how humor can enhance intimacy in friendships. Humor is considered a prominent predictor of emotional closeness in friendships (Curry & Dunbar, 2013). Humor and friendship have been found to facilitate socioemotional development in middle childhood, and affiliative spontaneous conversational humor also contributes to positive friendship quality (Wimsatt, 2014).

ADVICE

Where would be if we did not have someone close to turn to for friendly advice? The ability to both give and receive advice brings a dimension to friendship that should not surprise any reader. Advice giving, not surprisingly, does not stand alone within the constellation of other elements covered in this section. The giving of advice is closely related to reciprocity, although it brings added dimensions and nuances to a friendship. Reciprocity, as noted earlier, can involve instrumental (concrete), expressive (emotional), and informational exchanges in any combination or permutation. Providing and willingly accepting advice is based upon mutual respect and openness.

Advice and truth often go hand in hand in a friendship and have significant meaning. The statement that "truth hurts" applies to friends. However, a friend possesses the insights and abilities to give advice in a manner that is tailored to the most receptive style of the person seeking help. The words and sentence structure are just right, including the requisite pauses. Only someone who knows the individual well and for an extended period of time knows just how to say it. However, how advice evolves over the course a friendship is understudied (MacGeorge, Guntzville, Hanasono, & Feng, 2013).

Chentsova-Dutton and Vaughn (2012) specifically focus on the role of advice in friendships and introduce the influence of culture in shaping this element in both receiving and giving advice. The introduction of culture brings a much nuanced appreciation of advice between friends and its influence on what can be shared and how it is received.

TRUST

Trust is one of those factors that will be on everyone's list or at the top of essential factors in establishing and shaping friendships regardless of sociodemographic background. Way emphasizes its importance (2006, p. 416): "the practice of friendships among ethnically diverse, low-income, urban youth in the United States involves a multidimensional experience of trust, becomes more emotionally laden and complex over time, is embedded in a context of peers, and deteriorates over time with respect to perceptions of peers in general."

Trust and distrust influence the quality of economic, political, and social life by facilitating communication and cooperation; distrust, in turn, serves as a self-protective barrier against those individuals we should be concerned about (Davis, 2008). Unfortunately, there is no unified and standardized definition of trust (Mühl, 2014). There is no denying that there is an influential context to understanding trust, which includes social class (Du Plessis & Corney, 2011). I remember the 1960s and the saying that "you cannot trust anyone over the age of twenty-five." That age divide was generational and very symbolic of tensions in this society and how youth (anyone under the age of 25 years) were misunderstood by the older generation.

Trust takes on even greater significance in the case of marginalized urban youth of color who live in high-crime areas because trusting the wrong person can result in physical harm or even premature death. In fact, it can be argued that an ability to determine when to trust and distrust is integrally related to daily social navigation in urban life. Some readers may even go so far as to argue that trust is the most important element in any friendship and that all the other elements are not possible without mutual trust being present and openly exercised (Irjana Ule, 2013; Whitmore & Dunsmore, 2014).

Davis (2008, p. 4) provides a workable definition of trust: "Despite this complexity, some consensus does exist. Scholars appear to agree that trust involves some degree of risk because the trusting individual (hereafter, the trustor) lacks complete knowledge and control over the current and future actions of others .... By trusting others, we are able to act despite such risk. Trust enables individuals to engage in the tasks of today and approach those of tomorrow." The social consequences of trust are quite profound in helping youth navigate establishing and maintaining friendships.

HOMOPHILY

Although the concept of homophily may be new to most readers, the meaning and consequences are certainly not because it resonates in our daily life. The concept of homophiliy as we understand it today can be traced back to the early 1950s and the scholarship of Lazarsfeld and Merton (1954). De Guzman (2007) addresses peer influence and similarities between adolescent friends:

> [P]eer influence is not a simple process where youth are passive recipients of influence from others. In fact, peers who become friends tend to already have a lot of things in common. Peers with similar interests, similar academic standing, and enjoy doing the same things tend to gravitate towards each other. So while it seems that teens and their friends become very similar to each other through peer influence, much of that similarity was present to begin with.

The saying that opposites attract is seriously called into question when addressing friendships. Similar backgrounds help to break down potential language and cultural barriers, help increase trust, and help decrease the misunderstandings inherent in differing language and culture during initial encounters.

Strohmeier defines friendship homophily (2012, p. 99) as "a preference principle referring to the tendency that friendships between similar people occur at a higher rate than among dissimilar ones. Same cultural or ethnic background is one aspect of similarity on which friendship choices are based. Friendship homophily is often measured with the percentage of same ethnic friends out of all friends." The propensity to seek friends with similar backgrounds and interests should not be surprising.

Vanhoutte and Hooghe (2012) discuss the choice-constraint approach, which is predicated upon how the choice of one's friends will be determined by individual choices and the constraints associated with their interactional context. When homophily is introduced, it further limits outgroup friendships and becomes a factor when discussing urban youth of color friendships and their willingness or abilities to reach out to other groups (Muttarak, 2014). Salmon (2013) addresses adolescents with disabilities and raises the possibility of self-exclusion as a strategy for developing and maintaining sustainable friendships, bringing a different perspective on homophily that must be taken into account when discussing youth of color with disabilities.

Sharing a common background, including racial and ethnic background, can facilitate communication and the establishment of friendships. Ethnic/racial identity is also closely associated with friendship homophily through selection and socialization (Syed & Juan, 2012). Kiang et al. (Kiang, Peterson, & Thompson, 2011) also discuss the topic of ethnic and racial youth homophily:

> Growing diversity and evidence that diverse friendships enhance psychosocial success highlight the importance of understanding adolescents' ethnic peer preferences . . . . Adolescents with same- and mixed-ethnic friends reported significantly greater ethnic centrality than those with mostly different-ethnic friends. Adolescents with same-ethnic friends reported significantly higher perceived discrimination and lower English proficiency than those with mixed- and different-ethnic friends . . . provid[ing] further insight into specific influences on peer preferences (e.g., shared traditions, homophily [and] . . . speak to the importance of cultural experiences in structuring the friendships and everyday lives of adolescents.

The role and importance of similarities is undeniable and speaks to the challenges in helping youth develop a willingness and opportunity to broaden their everyday friendship networks.

Other dimensions to homophily go beyond youth ethnicity and race. Homophily, as in the case of young children with internalized problems, brings commonality, and this can be a successfully coping mechanism (Stone et al., 2013). Such similarity can also translate into individuals with depressive symptoms seeking out similar individuals with which to form friendships (Zalk et al., 2010). Having similarities in personal characteristics and social circumstances increases the likelihood of friendships developing because it minimizes differences in communication and expectations of what constitutes friendships (Neal, Neal, & Cappella, 2014).

However, homophily can hinder the establishment of friendships outside of one's own comfort level group, thus limiting the potential to grow emotionally, culturally, and socially through exposure to new perspectives and understandings. Few people will have friends who are very dissimilar to them (Chen, 2013). This is not necessarily a conscious choice: sharing similar backgrounds, be it racial/ethnic, socioeconomic class, language competencies, neighborhood, or school, makes communication, sharing, and constructing meaning easier (McIntyre, 2000).

AVAILABILITY/ACCESS

At first glance, to make and have friends readily available when one wants or needs them makes intuitive sense because contact is necessary to bring all the other elements into play. An often overlooked benefit can be had by having a friend live nearby. One study found that having a friend live within a mile can have a positive influence on well-being when compared to a friend living several miles away (Rath & Harter, 2010). This "on-demand" quality takes on added meaning when one is in a state of crisis. Consequently, availability and access are integral to making and maintaining friendships.

Physical accessibility is still the preferred method for engaging friends (Salisch, Zeman, Luepschen, & Kanevski, 2014). However, accessibility does not have to be physical and no longer applies with social media and the Internet. In the "old days," writing could be a form of communication when telephone and in-person contact were not feasible. Needless to say, these methods of maintaining contact did not enhance friendships but did sustain friendships until a physical rendezvous could transpire. Transnational friendships, for example, defy conventional wisdom on the subject of friendships and friendship networks because of the immense distance between friends (Shik, 2015).

Finally, Mason (2014) introduces an often overlooked aspect of friendship distance by discussing the concept of *distal networks* (three degrees of separation— the friend of your friend's friend), their influence on youth behaviors, and their importance for research and practice. Distal networks ground youth friendships within a broader constellation and more integrally into a community context, thus helping community practitioners more fully grasp the significance and influence of these friendships.

FUN

The concept of fun, similar to play, is one that everyone can relate to, but there is no universal agreement of what it entails and its significance in establishing and maintaining youth friendships. Having someone to have "fun" with takes on greater significance than having fun alone, and that statement certainly applies to youth and adults of all ages. Sharing the moment, so to speak, brings a youthful perspective on friendship that technically knows no age limit. When fun is closely associated with friendship, it takes on added meaning for both parties, making the activity that much more worthwhile and memorable.

Furthermore, fun can involve any number of activities and can range from having conversations to engaging in structured interactions. Not surprisingly, fun is invariably associated with youth friendships (Walker, 2011). It is important to note, however, that the definition of "fun" is not universal and will vary based upon youth demographics (gender identity, SES, age, and race/ethnicity), culture, and context. A conventional sense of play diminishes or, some would argue, changes over the life cycle, resulting in a diminishment of instrumentality (activity) and an increase in intimacy needs, thus bringing an added dimension to discussions of play and fun.

Playing video games with friends is an activity invariably associated with fun, but it can also have important sociopersonal benefits for youth, particularly for boys because of the higher percentage who engage in this activity when compared to girls (Ferguson & Olson, 2013). For those readers who had a summer camp experience away from home, fun and friendships are closely tied together in dictating whether that experience was memorable in a positive or negative way (Garst, Browne, & Bialeschki, 2011).

Play, fun, and friendship are often interchangeable in young children, and this illustrates how friendship can be closely tied to activities that are considered pleasurable, serving to reinforce a relationship (Howes, 2009). These activities do not have to be costly. Fun can entail engagement in pro-social or anti-social activities. Fun can entail drinking together to the point of excess and having stories to share about the consequences of doing so with someone who was a close friend (MacLean, 2015; Tutenges & Sandberg, 2013).

Example of Gaps in Knowledge

An endless number of friendship aspects remain to be explored in depth; the following are but a few to illustrate this point. Voorend and colleagues (2013) focused their research on female adolescent best friends' food choices and dietary practices and how they influences overweight/obesity to address the question of how eating and foods reinforce friendships.

What are the friendship networks of gifted and talented youth, particularly those who are of color (Eddles-Hirsch, Vialle, McCormick, & Rogers, 2012; Kaul, Johnsen, Witte, & Saxon, 2015)? Are there networks, and is the nature of their friendships different from those who are not gifted or talented?

Although "hanging-out" (unstructured and unsupervised socializing) with friends is often reported to be a favorite youth activity, to what extent does it contribute to or hinder engagement in positive or negative behaviors (Siennick & Osgood, 2012)?

Much needs to be learned about how youth friendships are manifested and mediated in residential settings (Emond, 2014), and for that matter, total institutions such as prisons. Friendships within these institutions are closely related to quality of life (Duvdevany & Arar, 2004; Narendorf, Fedoravicius, McMillen, McNelly, & Robinson, 2012).

Natural disasters disrupt relationships in profound ways, and that includes youth friendships. To what extent do environmental events such as hurricanes impact youth of color and their friendships (Banks & Weems, 2014)?

Finally, mentoring has a wide following as an attractive and effective method for engaging and helping youth and other age groups. However, there is a strong possibility that mentoring relationships can morph into friendships (Sanfey, Hollands, & Gantt, 2013; Sudak & Arbuckle, 2013). How do these friendships evolve, and how are they maintained in the case of urban youth?

Interestingly, the concept of gratitude has generally escaped scrutiny regarding youth friendships (Froh et al., 2011), even though one cannot help but be grateful for a close friendship. To what extent does gratitude reinforce close friendships?

Community Practice and Friendships: Community Capacity

ENHANCEMENT

The reader may ask how youth friendships can be a focus of a social intervention when they are supposed to be natural occurrences. I would pose a different question. Are there any urban youth interventions that cannot address friendships as part of peer relationship networks or other focus? Social work, for example, has certainly understood the value of friendships and why they should be fostered among consumers of their services (Furman, Collins, Garner, Monanaro, & Weber, 2009). Thus, youth friendships may be considered too important to ignore but also too amorphous to focus on in a program.

My practice and scholarly experience has taught me that urban youth friendships can be both implicitly or explicitly addressed as part of a broader social intervention within and outside of schools. Urban youth development, for example, has peer, and indirectly, friendship relationships as an important aspect of programming, along with other notable goals (Jones, Dunn, Holt, Sullivan, & Bloom, 2011; Schonert-Reichl et al., 2012). However, we rarely gather baseline data on how friendships evolved within and outside of programs, thus limiting our comprehension of this peer relationship. As a consequence, important information on program participants is simply lost.

In *Community Practice and Urban Youth: Social Justice Service-Learning and Civic Engagement* (2016), I addressed the importance of an asset-based and participatory approach to urban youth- and community-focused interventions, particularly when based on social justice values. However, the subject of friendship among urban youth did not take center stage, although it played a role in getting and maintaining youth in community service-learning and civic engagement. In the process of conducting research for that book, community interventions that integrated friendship goals were identified, and these are tapped for inclusion in later chapters in this book, most notably in Chapters 5, 6, and 7.

Caring and its various manifestations can be a direct result of friendships within a youth development paradigm (Bowers et al., 2010; Lerner, Alberts, Jelicic, & Smith, 2006; Lerner, Phelps, Forman, & Bowers, 2009; Rauner, 2013; Zeldin, Christens, & Powers, 2013). Noddings (1995), as quoted in Cohen et al. (Cohen, Silber, Sangiorgio, & Iadeluca, 2012, p.188), identified four key benefits of caring as it relates to teaching but with equal applicability to youth community practice and social and friendship development:

> (1) It expands children's cultural literacy, (2) it helps children perceive transfers across standard school subjects, (3) it addresses existential questions, such as how one should live and the meaning of life, and (4) it helps children connect with one another and demonstrate respect for all human talent.

Community practitioners willing and able to share that they care about youth participants will increase the likelihood of having youth be more willing to commit to the program and develop trusting and respectful relationships with adults.

Thus, it is best to conceptualize interventions seeking to enhance youth friendships within a broader spectrum rather than to develop a specific intervention (Poteet & Simmons, 2014). Once conceptualized in this manner, friendship broadens options for social interventions across all youth-focused settings (Agnihotri, Lynn Keightley, Colantonio, Cameron, & Polatajko, 2010). Friendships are a form of community assets (Lenzi et al., 2012) and can be a key aspect of asset assessments and interventions (Delgado & Humm-Delgado, 2013).

Youth peers have been found to be a key predicator of whether or not they elect to join youth programs (Perkins et al., 2007). Caring staff and friends, in turn, increase the likelihood of youth staying in programs (Gillard & Witt, 2008). It stands to reason, therefore, that having peer/friendship relationships play a more prominent role in these programs can facilitate recruitment and retention, and have these skills transfer over into other spheres in youth lives. A willingness and ability to make friends from different backgrounds can be a goal for these types of interventions, whether this goal is explicitly or implicitly introduced into activities (Thurber, Scanlin, Scheuler, & Henderson, 2007).

Community practitioners have numerous settings and opportunities in which to foster urban youth friendships (Garst et al., 2011; Walker, 2011; Watkins, Larson, & Sullivan, 2007), particularly when potential settings for practice are conceptualized formally and informally, as in the case of nontraditional settings (Delgado, 1998). Formally, community organizations such as schools and neighborhood agencies can provide urban youth with opportunities to both form and repair friendships within the context of their own neighborhoods (Rodríguez &

Conchas, 2009). In these situations, opportunities to form new friendships outside of their neighborhoods is limited, however.

After-school settings, in turn, offer endless possibilities for community practitioners to create neighborhood-specific interventions in an atmosphere that encourages innovation in programming activities (Hanlon, Simon, O'Grady, Carswell, & Callaman, 2009; Intrator & Siegel, 2014; Woodland, 2014). PYD has been found to be particularly attractive and viable in these types of settings, which are not burdened by the school regulations applicable during regular school hours and often involve personnel from outside of school who are more likely to be well-versed in youth development and to embrace innovation (Durlak, Weissberg, & Pachan, 2010).

Hirsch, Deutsch, and DuBois (2011) developed a series of case studies highlighting successful and unsuccessful after-school centers using youth development, and they propose an "integrative strategy" for ensuring that the principles of youth development are fulfilled:

(1) Have a strong, explicit focus on promoting positive youth development; (2) Conduct regular reviews of youth progress, including intensive case conferences; (3) Encourage collaborative mentoring; (4) Use training resources as a means of promoting reflective dialogue about best practices; (5) Have staff observe good after-school programs to learn more about best practices; (6) Form youth councils to make sure youth voice is heard; (7) Schedule regular external review and site visits; and (8) Require leadership to engage in regular supervision and coaching.

These principles are invaluable in helping to shape programs that specifically seek to enhance youth friendships as part of their goals.

Strobel and colleagues (Strobel, Kirschner, O'Donoghue, & Wallin McLaughlin, 2008) see after-school settings as critical arenas for the development or fostering of friendships and as ideal settings for social interventions, including positive youth–adult relationships. Bullying prevention programs in schools and other settings are another example of how youth-focused community practice focused on friendship development can have far-reaching implications (DeRosier & Marcus, 2005).

Youth development interventions in these settings can embrace friendship development goals (Ahn et al., 2014; Hirsch, Deutsch, & DuBois, 2011). Community practice involving mentoring programs offers practitioners an established venue for influencing urban youth friendship. Mentorship programs focused on youth with increased challenges take on even greater importance, as evidenced in the Colorado case illustration in Chapter 5.

Houses of worship, too, are community settings that can create opportunities for urban youth to establish friendships within and outside of their communities (Brown, 2011; Holland, 2016; Windzio & Wingens, 2014). Faith communities, as in the case of one Latina/o youth study, have the potential for youth members to engage in prosocial behaviors, and the friendships in these communities can be conceptualized as assets in fostering this goal by tapping spirituality as a vehicle (Antrop-González, Garrett, & Vélez, 2015).

Practitioners can facilitate and support youth interethnic and interracial friendships in faith communities through the creation and fostering of activities that can pair youth across demographic factors or use other ways to help bridge differences in backgrounds (Chen & Graham, 2015; Pica-Smith & Poynton, 2014). This can be accomplished in an atmosphere of acceptance, validation, and celebration of differences. This, of course, is based on an organizational climate that is psychologically safe for youth participants.

Shared experiences can be one of the many benefits of special events, and participation in programming can help create friendships that can last a lifetime (Boyes-Watson, 2013). Mentorship relationships, too, can eventually transform into lasting friendships (Thomson & Zand, 2010). Sharing similar histories of oppression and challenges provides a critical context that helps mitigate differences in demographics while creating a profound sense of willingness to trust and share, key elements in the creation of meaningful and long-lasting friendships (Toy, 2011).

Capturing these factors or forces in the case of urban youth of color will introduce a significant missing perspective that can be tapped in forming urban-focused community interventions. For example, how does humor play a role in initiating and fostering friendships? Humor has been found to play an important role among youth with developmental disabilities, for example (Rossetti, 2015), but the role of humor among youth of color and its influence in determining and shaping friendships remains unexplored.

Gang membership, as noted earlier, introduces friendship goals as a critical, if not primary reason, for joining a gang, including the role of group dynamics in shaping and sustaining friendships in collectivistic manner (Wood, 2014). Youth community practice, as a result, can play an influential role in altering the course of how gangs and the search for friendship can be countered in urban communities with high gang affiliations (Lachman, Roman, & Cahill, 2013).

Providing attractive alternatives to gangs is essential in these communities. These alternatives, however, must go beyond conventional programming and introduce innovative activities that increase their attractiveness as a counterbalance to gangs. Introducing stipends for participation bring an economic motive to help counter the economics of gang membership, although providing money for participation can introduce ethical dilemmas that must not be ignored.

A community capacity enhancement paradigm provides a conceptual base that incorporates requisite values (empowerment, participatory democracy, indigenous knowledge, community assets, and leadership development), an emphasis on local collaboration, and the tapping of local assets that can be mobilized toward achieving goals central to a community (Delgado, 1998, 1999, 2016). Fostering a positive social fabric can be an explicit or implicit goal in community practice.

Efforts to reach hidden or difficult to engage groups can be facilitated through the use of friendship networks. Friendship networks, for example, can be tapped in outreach and intervention programs, facilitating the engagement of difficult to engage population groups within urban areas (Boyer et al., 2013). In addition, community practice interventions can assist urban youth of color in developing coping strategies and positive influences in their lives, as through friendships, and in addressing localized stressors (Cooley-Strickland, Griffin, Damey, Otte, & Ko, 2011; Sanchez, Lambert, & Cooley-Strickland, 2013).

The initial question posed at the beginning of this section asked why community practitioners should bother to study and understand youth friendships and friendship networks. These types of relationships are natural occurrences in the course of life. There may be a universal need for friends, but this does not necessarily translate into having this expressive and instrumental need met. In essence, the knowledge we gain on how urban youth interact and socialize is important in disease control, urban planning, education, and increasing the quality of life now and in their future, and that is just the tip of the iceberg (Sekara & Lehmann, 2014).

Better preparing urban youth to think of friendships as a potential and conscious source of support will serve them well in receiving and giving a wide range of assistance and developing greater insights into how they define friendships and what they seek in these relationships. In other words, knowing how to initiate and support friendships is a skill that can be taught and learned; learning how to handle difficult friendships or the breaking up of friendships also is important to know.

Staff–Program Participant Friendships

The subject of friendship between staff and program participants is one that deserves much more attention, and this is particularly the case in a book advocating for urban youth community practice that fosters friendships. Activities are very important in youth community practice, but relationships are at the core of any social intervention, with many of the key factors addressed earlier in this chapter being present to foster engagement and development of meaningful social friendships.

The field of qualitative research, and more specifically ethnography, has addressed the role and ethical challenges of researcher and researched friendship development (Robards, 2013; Taylor, 2011), and this will be discussed again in Chapter 6. The literature on mentoring, too, has explored the role, rewards, and challenges of friendships between mentor and mentee involving marginalized youth (Coller & Kuo, 2014; Gettings & Wilson, 2014; Quinn, 2014; Thomson & Zand, 2010), with implications for youth community practice.

Reimer (2014) brings friendship into the practice realm by stressing the value it plays in professional relationships that eventually evolve into friendships.

Reimer's central thesis has tremendous implications for youth development and community practice staff and scholars interested in this field, and it brings a very practical as opposed to theoretical dimension to the subject, which is essential in the world of practice.

Faking friendships, however, introduces ethical issues in carrying out research or interventions (Duncombe & Jessop, 2002; Nairn & Clarke, 2012). Furthermore, "false" friendships are very disconcerting, and they reinforce power imbalances between adults and youth. Youth have a distinct ability to identify adults who are falsely trying to establish a relationship when their heart is not in it and the reason they are doing it is simply to fulfill their job responsibilities.

Youth community practice staff genuinely have the potential to form positive and friendly relationships with youth participants if they are willing to share more about who they are and why they do the work that they do. This sharing not only increases staff satisfaction with their work but also puts them in a unique position of role modeling positive relationships, particularly when they have faced major challenges in life that are similar to those of participants. This relationship can be enhanced when the age gap between staff and participant is not so great that they would have great difficult sharing commonalities or even language (slang).

Conclusion

The importance of friendship is only matched by the challenges we encounter in trying to understand why this form of social relationship has continued to be of such importance in our lives. This importance only increases in the lives of select youth who increasingly find themselves on the margins of society. Friendships persist, simply stated, because of the multidimensional needs they meet, and that is certainly the case in urban youth.

This chapter has provided a multifaceted grounding in friendships as a general topic. The deconstruction of this construct is essential if we, as community practitioners, are going to embrace enhancing this form of social relations in the lives of urban youth who are in effect segregated and limited in their travels. Some aspects of friendships will appeal to the readers while others may not. That is to be expected. However, we do not have the luxury of not addressing this topic in a comprehensive manner. Friendship is a relationship that everyone can understand but very few have actually taken the time and made the effort to really comprehend its complexity in the lives of youth. Furthermore, it is a concept that is still evolving within the social sciences and helping professions, so one can think of it as an expanding universe.

A foundation has been established that allows us to focus specifically on the interaction of geographical setting (urban) and youth ethnic/racial subgroups. Contextualizing the meaning, roles, and definition of friendship is very much dependent on who is doing the contextualization and how it is socially and ecologically grounded. Possessing a social justice framework will uncover answers that others without such an approach would miss because it influences the type of questions we ask and our willingness to hear unanticipated answers. The following chapter will take on greater specificity regarding urban youth and how friendships evolve and are maintained. Chapter 4 will also provide a detailed demographic foundation to ground youth of color as a demographic group.

4

Urban Youth of Color Friendships

Introduction

Crosnoe's (2000, p. 388) observation, as quoted by Bagwell and Schmidt (2011), is a wonderful way to start this chapter focused specifically on urban youth of color friendships: "We must view friendships as dynamic, as reactive and evocative; as predictor, outcome, and process; as links between individual lives and the larger world; as components of development and socialization throughout life." This all-encompassing statement is both eloquent and strikes fear in the hearts of scholars. Why? Because it highlights the dynamic qualities associated with youth friendships and why it is so important that scholars and practitioners get it right when discussing urban youth of color who are marginalized in society.

This chapter builds on much of the material covered in the previous chapter with a particular focus on three youth of color groups (African American/black, Asian, and Latino). Unfortunately, Native American youth will receive minimal coverage, but material on them will be integrated whenever possible. Native Americans are not heavily concentrated in the nation's urban areas with one notable exception: Minneapolis has the highest concentration of urban-based Native Americans and is rich resource on Native youth within an urban context. Unfortunately, the professional literature is very deficient when addressing Native youth (Kenyon & Carter, 2011), and no more so than when they reside in the nations' cities. Case 2 in Chapter 5, based in Minneapolis/St. Paul, Minnesota, has Native American youth as part of a photovoice project.

Although adolescent friendships have suffered from "benign neglect" (Hirsh & Renders, 2014), we can certainly argue that urban youth of color friendships have suffered from "insidious neglect," a term that captures well the state of knowledge on this topic. Their friendships have not been viewed from a normalized or positive psychological perspective. Instead, we have had a tendency to classify these relationships as influencing antisocial behaviors and as being ones that practitioners must arduously work to dissolve or protect youth from.

No youth group of color has benefitted from scholarship that has been affirming and focused on ordinary or normalized behavior. There is general agreement, for example, that there has been a paucity of research and scholarship on African-American youth peers and friendships (Belgrave & Brevard, 2015). One can include other ethnic and racial groups in this declarative statement and more specifically, friendships, such as those among Native youth (Willeto, 2015). The United States is not alone in this gap in knowledge about urban ethnic and racial youth. Canada for example, needs more research and scholarship on youth of color friendships (Daniel, 2013; Daniel & Hakim-Larson, 2013).

The subject of race and ethnicity brings a more nuanced perspective on youth of color outgroup friendships against a backdrop of marginalization and intersectionality. Unfortunately, we have a tendency to lump together all African-American/black, Asian, Latino, and Native youth under the label of "youth of color," and I am also guilty of this. This "grouping" or "lumping" together, if you wish, is often done under the guise of facilitating discourse since these youth groups often occupy the same neighborhoods and face many of the same oppressive forces.

Living in the same neighborhood and attending the same schools and many of the same community organizations, for example, creates similarity in facing social forces and sharing a worldview, and it makes it arduous for these youth to expand their contacts and make new friendships that do not share similar experiences. Increased ethnic and racial outgroup births, however, have introduced the need to view youth, their peer networks, and friendships from a bi- or multiracial perspective, as will be addressed later in this chapter (Bonilla-Silva, 2004). Bi-raciality can serve to facilitate friendship development across racial and cross-ethnic groups because of a shared commonality that is increasing in this country (Buckholz, 2014).

It is undisputable that youth in each of these groups bring histories, cultures, and current life experiences and trajectories (pathways) that can share commonalities, but they also exhibit significant differences in a variety of spheres, including friendship networks. For example, South Asian Muslim youth bring a different set of social challenges in making friendships with other youth of color post September 11, and they face challenges that other youth of color simply do not share (Maira, 2004). In a Canadian study, South Asian youth in more Westernized contexts showed greater willingness to engage in activities that parents did not consider culturally appropriate, with friends playing a greater influential role in supporting these actions (Dhariwal & Connolly, 2013).

Chinese American youth are another case in point because, on the surface, they may appear as a homogenous group to the outside world, but, in reality, within-group differences can be quite significant and can manifest themselves in social relationships (Fuligni, Yip, & Tseng, 2002; Qin, Way, & Mukherjee, 2008; Rivas-Drake, Hughes, & Way, 2008). Cambodian youth are another example of a group that have generally gone unnoticed or been combined with other Asian groups, thus limiting our understanding of their peer and friendship networks and how the history and process of migration has impacted how they view their social environment (Chhuon, 2014).

The concept of intersectionality brings an added dimension to any serious discussion of urban youth of color, further challenging practitioners and academics in creating policies and programming that take into account multiple sources of oppression. Undocumented youth face challenges that their documented/authorized or citizen counterparts do not, even when sharing the same ethnic or racial backgrounds. Gender introduces the potential role of sexism; males, particularly African-American/black, also face added surveillance and a higher likelihood of being harassed or killed by the police, thus creating an atmosphere of distrust and feelings of persecution (Kennedy, 2015).

Youth who have obvious disabilities, in turn, face the challenges posed by society but also those found within their own families and communities, influencing their life chances at success and having a robust social network, including close friends who share or do not share their disabilities. For these youth, rejection is one of the most salient concerns, but an overprotective home can also translate into challenges in having new experiences and establishing and maintaining new friendships, thus limiting disabled youths' development of the requisite social skills to engage in social relationships outside of a very limited social circle.

Marginalization can have various manifestations and can occur in multiple arenas, including in one's own backyard, which makes it considerably painful. Issues of race, ethnicity, and sexual identity, for example, makes certain youth anything but "typical" and increases the challenges of developing friendships sensitive to their unique and vulnerable position in society and in their community.

Every effort must be made to capture commonalities while also acknowledging within- and between-group differences, particularly in the case of friendships (Denscombe, Szulc, Patrick, & Wood, 2014; Graham, Munniksma, & Juvonen, 2014). Davies et al. (Davies, Tropp, Aron, Pettigrew, & Wright, 2011) undertook a cross-group friendships and intergroup attitudes meta-analytic literature review and concluded that although there has been increased research and scholarship on the subject, use of varied assessment approaches have left the field without clarity on how different operationalizations affect relationships between friendships and attitudes. A unified and consensus definition of friendships across groups and within groups may be an "impossible dream," but we must acknowledge that it is a goal worth striving for.

For community outsiders who are white and non-Latino, it is relatively easy to say that youth of color have a tendency to hang out together and display minimal interest in broadening their friendships and social peer networks beyond their own ethnic or racial group. However, as Kao and Joyner (2006) point out based on their research, Latino and Asian adolescents display an overwhelming preference for same-ethnic peer relationships over same-race relationships (different-ethnic) and different-race peers. The power of ethnicity is well recognized by urban community practitioners because of how powerfully it shapes social and political interactions at the local level, including development of local institutions and the sharing of culture.

Kao and Vaquera (2006), in turn, studied Latino youth friendships and found, too, that ethnicity is a stronger predictor of youth preferences when compared to race. This translates into Puerto Rican youth preferring other Puerto Rican youth as friends when compared to having Dominican friends, for example. It can even go so far as to have Puerto Rican youth born and raised in the United States preferring other Puerto Ricans born in the States over those born in Puerto Rico, thus bringing an often overlooked dimension of how culture is enforced by environment.

Introducing gender, life cycle stage, type of friendship (close or general), and income level provides a more in-depth and nuanced understanding of youth racial and ethnic preferences (Way & Chen, 2000). Obviously, more research is warranted to do justice to how ethnicity and race influence friendship preferences. However, this type of research must actively endeavor, as noted in Chapter 6, to engage youth in shaping the research methods used and questions being asked, their active participation, and interpretation of the findings and implications for practice. Youth possess knowledge that adults simply do not possess because of the power of age and youth culture.

Anti-Urban Sentiments

It is impossible to discuss urban youth of color and their friendship networks without pausing to discuss anti-urban sentiments in this country as a contextual grounding for a focus on youth. The militarization of city police forces and the treating of social demonstrators as the "enemy" are but two examples of this anti-urban attitude. In fact, I would argue that it is impossible to separate out youth of color from urban and this strong military force. Furthermore, it is also impossible to separate physical environment from the transcendent and aspirational qualities that are closely associated with a geographical entity such as a city. In essence, "urban" is a state of mind, being and becoming ingrained with ethnicity and race.

Historical anti-urban or counter-urban attitudes have shaped negative views of urban communities and their inhabitants for centuries in this country, sentiments fueled by European history of cities (Hadden & Barton, 1973; Văetişi, 2013; Volti, 2014). Conn (2014), in an interview, defines anti-urbanism as (Onion, 2014): "On the one hand, it's the deep, deep fear of the messiness of urban life, and particularly the social messiness . . . . In the 20th century as American society became more and more socially mixed, [anti-urbanism acquired] a flavor of xenophobia. It's a sense of 'I want to be closer to my kind, I'm either scared of or angry at these people who are different than I am.'" Separating urban structures and spaces from inhabitants is simply artificial since both are interrelated from an ecological perspective.

Anti-urban sentiments are not restricted to one political ideology either, with liberals as well as conservatives sharing this perspective, making this stance that much more pernicious and consequential (Onion, 2014):

> But a new history shows that anti-urban feelings have cut a wide swath through American history and politics. Conservatives have described the city as a hotbed of vice and crime, with an alienating level of diversity and too much government regulation. Over time, plenty of liberals have crusaded against city living as well, arguing for smaller-scale, decentralized towns where people could form what they saw as more authentic communities.

Surprisingly, liberals have not eschewed exploiting tales of urban decline to justify policies and programs targeting cities; conservatives, in turn, have blamed these very programs for the deterioration of cities and for groups and communities failing to take responsibilities for their actions (Moroz, 2010), including serving as "magnets" for attracting the undocumented or unauthorized.

Some scholars trace this nation's anti-city attitudes to the popularizing of the virtues of Jeffersonian small-town ideals (Gandy, 2006; C. Yang, 2014). The early members of Congress were anti-urban (Wells, 2015); Thomas Jefferson was quite clear in his anti-urban stance, as quoted by Speck (2013, p. 58) and considered cities as the "pestilential to the morals, the health, and the liberties of man." Furthermore, in discussing urban density: "when we get piled up upon one another in large cities, as in Europe, we shall become as in Europe, and go to eating one another as they do there." It is almost as if this ant-urban bias is part of the nation's DNA, making it very difficult to address because it is so deeply woven into the nation's social fabric.

Conn (2014), one of the latest historians to focus attention on this country's love-hate affair with its urban centers, traces 20th-century anti-urban feelings to the convergence of several major social and political forces, most notably an aversion to high urban density and how it impacts well-being and the political perception that cities are the cause of "big government." Big government can easily be code for "big cities" and the people who inhabit these geographical settings.

The following statement by Lyman Abbott, made in the early 20th century and quoted in Conn (2014, p. 16) summarizes this love-hate relationship very eloquently, and this assessment is still as relevant today as it was well over a century ago:

> On the one hand, the city stands for all that is evil—a city that is full of devils, foul and corrupting; and, one of the glory of God, and shining with a clear and brilliant light. But, if we think a little more carefully, we shall see that the city has in all ages of the world represented both these aspects. It has been the worst, and it has been the best. Every city has been a Babylon, and every city has been a New Jerusalem; and it has always been a Jerusalem or the New Jerusalem would extirpate the Babylon. It has been so in the past. It is so in the

present. The greatest corruptions, the greatest vice, the greatest philanthropy, the greatest purity, the most aggressive and noble courage, are to be found in the great city. San Francisco, St. Louis, Chicago, Cincinnati, Philadelphia, New York, Boston, and Brooklyn are full of devils—and also full of the glory of God.

Abbott's assessment of the city well over a century ago captures this country's ambivalence toward its urban centers, which has only gotten more intense since that initial observation. The terms generally used with cities invariably tend to be negative in language or stance: "urban poverty," "urban slum," "urban crime," "urban drug abuse," "urban decay," "urban ghetto," "urban riots," "urban unemployment," "urban inequality," "urban crisis," "urban slime," "urban myth," "urban pollution," "urban density," "urban doom," "urban jungle," "urban diseases," " urban decadence," "urban warfare," and "urban apocalypse," for example. Yet, how often do we hear "urban oasis," "urban culture," "urban dream," "urban renascence," "urban lifestyle," or some other positive term related to cities (Moroz, 2010):

We have forgotten that the story of our cities is actually a great story of American progress: new kinds of housing, new social services, new forms of mass transit, new regulations of employment conditions and many other innovations that boosted living standards for the vast majority of Americans over the past century or so all began as urban experiments. Cities are laboratories of progressive change where government plays an outsized role in improving our daily lives. Despite this record of accomplishments, American cities have been framed in negative terms across the political spectrum. Even as cities evolved into economic juggernauts and diverse cultural centers, their inner cores were racialized and slandered by both parties as poverty-ridden, crime-infested and ungovernable.

Apocalyptic rhetoric feeds into historic anti-urban fears and lends itself to media terms that resonate with society, thus further reinforcing these sentiments (Angotti, 2006; Conn, 2014; Cunningham & Warwick, 2013). This anti-urban perspective can be traced back to classism, anti-immigrant bias, racism, and anti-Semitism. This subject matter will be addressed again in the Conclusion of this book because of its significance in shaping urban youth context.

Glaeser (2010) identifies some of the major present-day national anti-urban policies that illustrate the pervasiveness and consequences of this attitude toward cities:

The billions of dollars being spent on infrastructure across the nation provide an opportunity to plan for a better America, but politics-as-usual favors sprawl over city. This anti-urban bias of national policies must end. Over the past 60 years, cities have been hit by a painful policy trifecta: subsidization of highways, subsidization of homeownership, and a school system that creates strong incentives for many parents to leave city borders.

A pro-urban ethos will not only counteract a bias against cities, it also will generate innovative thinking and responses specifically focused on urban neighborhoods and the people who populate these geographical entities. Cities and their residents are simply one and the same and can be thought of as a living organism.

Urban Youth as a Focus

Youth of color and urban centers are inseparable, although youth certainly do live in non-urban areas of the country. Horschelmann and Van Blerk (2013) make the argument that cities are much more than context when discussing youth. Anyone who has lived in a large city can certainly attest to this observation. A focus on the built environment without regard to the people who make urban culture is simplistic thinking, making for flawed social policies.

The importance of neighborhood context in shaping urban youth of color outcomes, particularly the role and constant threat of violence in their lives, is finding increasing recognition in understanding social relationships (Rendón, 2014, 2015). Developing social relations or friendships with older youth can be a strategic approach toward warding off violence by obtaining physical and symbolic protection and respect.

Kang and Bodenhausen (2015), in turn, address the increasing need for a nuanced understanding of the process of categorization, which has increasingly played such a critical role in society and how youth socially navigate daily life, to help social scientists understand social daily interactions.

Undoubtedly, the world is getting more complex and interconnected, and we as academics and practitioners must be prepared to accept the role of categorization—but not without embracing a nuanced appreciation of how categories are changing as society and communities change. Simplistic thinking never leads to comprehensive social policies and programs.

Friendships are obviously not the exclusive domain of any one age group, and youth certainly constitute a significant age group, although they can span a wide number of years. Furthermore, few social scientists and practitioners would take issue with friendships playing an irreplaceable role in youth social development (Liuliu & Jianwen, 2014). However, the design of social interventions that specifically target friendship development is still arguably in its infancy.

Contextual influences on youth of color pathways to success (Allison & Obeidallah, 2014; Wright, 2011) will invariably involve a friendship network playing an active and supportive role in shaping the decision-making process. This statement is not intended to diminish the role and importance of kinships, however. Furthermore, friendship network influence is not limited to youth ethnicity and race. It is widely understood that friendship experiences for transgender individuals are complex and unique (Galupo, Krum, Hagen, Gonzalez, & Bauerband, 2014), and this uniqueness takes on even more significance when discussing transgendered youth of color and why contextualization is essential to understanding how this grounding influences perceptions, behaviors, and social supports.

Callahan and Obenchain (2012) identify the unique position that immigrant youth occupy in this society: "Immigrant youth, by definition, are neither from the dominant culture, nor from that of their parents' home country; yet they are both. The space in which immigrant adolescents reside . . . presents an intriguing area of inquiry." Immigrant youth of color friendships can be expected to help them navigate two different sets of social terrains or social worlds, yet our understanding of the composition and role of these friendships is severely compromised, thereby limiting our potential to maximize such friendships through programming.

When we place these youth within urban neighborhoods, the interplay of immigration status, race/ethnicity, "negative social mirroring" (Suárez-Orozco, Suárez-Orozco, & Qin-Hillard, 2014), and environment creates a unique social situation with implications for all forms of community practice. Understanding newcomer youth peer and friendship networks will require new social relations conceptualizations. Racially segmented assimilation in primary group relation (peer and friendship networks) has necessitated a nuanced understanding of inter-ethnic/racial youth social relationships (Quillian & Campbell, 2003).

Youth friendship types are best understood within the constellation of friendships in general and when grounded within an encompassing construct such as life satisfaction, for example. Human beings do not exist on friendships alone, yet friendship significance can increase or decrease based on the unique social circumstances a youth possesses, including environmental factors. Community practitioners, as a result, must have a comprehensive assessment of an individual's range of friends and how are they particularly helping.

A youth with extensive family support, including relatives of similar ages and an array of other significant adults, may have a diminished need for friendships. However, in those circumstances where positive adults and family are not available, friendships take up the "slack," so to speak, and gain in significance as a result. As already stressed, peer acceptance and their ability to form and maintain friendships are considered significant in the lives of children and youth with immediate and long-term implications (Gifford-Smith & Brownell, 2003).

Parental and cultural influences on adolescent social relationships take on even greater significance in the case of newcomer youth. Updegraff et al.'s (Updegraff, Kim, Killoren, & Thayer, 2010) study of Mexican-American parents' involvement in their adolescent children's peer relationships found that gender influenced (mothers, but not fathers) restrictions on relationships. Findings further revealed some evidence that parent and adolescent gender moderated these patterns, with mothers' (but not fathers) placing greater restrictions on the peer relationships of daughters than of sons.

Cherng, Turney, and Kao (2014) found that adolescents of color, and first and second-generation adolescents, have a tendency to be less engaged in friendships when compared to white, non-Latino, third-generation counterparts. This calls for more attention within and outside of schools to facilitate these forms of relationships, with teachers, school personnel with student contact, and community practitioners needing a heightened awareness of the nature and extent of friendships in their students and program participants.

Community practitioners and educators are in excellent positions to foster youth social relationships, particularly in cases of youth who have special circumstances that limit their abilities and opportunities to develop friendships outside of schools and community-based organizations (Rossetti, 2012). Quane and Rankin (2006) stress the importance of neighborhood-based organizations in providing a space for youth to come together and feel safe and welcomed, prerequisites for establishing social relationships and obtaining or enhancing new competencies.

When these places and spaces provide ideal conditions for creating new friendships, these friendships can be even more important than those formed within school (Anderson, Sabatelli, & Kosutic, 2007). Sporting and performance events also create activities that facilitate sharing, interactions, and celebrations (Cheadle & Schwadel, 2012; De La Haye, Robins, Mohr, & Wilson, 2011; Smith, 2003; Stark & Newton, 2014; Weiss & Smith, 1999, 2002). Providing adults with the requisite skills to help create these types of settings that foster youth friendships must be a part of any educational and social work curriculum, to list two prominent professions.

Akom, Cammarota, and Ginwright (2008) provide a succinct summary of the historical focus of social science research on urban youth and why our knowledge base is limited by our reliance on a problem focus (crime and safety) and a social disorganization school of thought (disregard for authority, educational indifference, unwillingness to engage in socially sanctioned employment). The authors paint a dismal but realistic picture of the state of our knowledge of urban youth and how different schools of thought address environmental forces

The field of critical youth studies has emerged to respond to this dearth of knowledge with a focus that is not deficit-focused and apolitical in examining the contextual forces operating to marginalize youth (Akom et al., 2008; Baldridge, Lamont Hill, & Davis, 2011). Critical youth studies have embraced social justice as a central lens through which to increase our understanding of social factors and how they shape adult perceptions and responses to youth and their needs. This has included acknowledging a paucity of research on youth of color peer and friendship networks and how this has compromised our understanding of this group (Pagano & Hirsch, 2007). Again, when youth of color peers and friendships are addressed, they eschew efforts at identifying positive peer and friendship networks. Part of the reason for this proclivity may be that research funders are only interested in identifying and addressing problem areas.

Graham, Taylor, and Ho (2009) undertook a specific journal article literature review of PsycInfo covering the 1986–2006 period for childhood and adolescents using "peer relations," "peer networks," "peer nominations," or "sociometrics" as search terms. They found 1,495 journal articles. A similar search was conducted focused on "race" and "ethnicity," specific racial/ethnic groups, and other terms such as "racial relations" and "racial and ethnic attitudes" and found 111 journal articles (7%). Although a content analysis of these 111 articles was not reported, it would not be much of a stretch to conclude that negative or deficit themes would predominate.

Rodriguez and Morrobel (2004), in turn, undertook a review of the literature on Latino youth development in six youth development journals and two Latino-focused journals and found a dismal state of affairs regarding Latino youth, with a heavily deficit-oriented focus. Unfortunately, an update of this study using current results will not in all likelihood reveal significant progress. Similar studies regarding Asian-American and Native American youth could not be located, and this is a sad admission on the state of affairs regarding these two groups.

Azmitia, Ittel, and Break (2006, pp. 435–436), in a rare article specifically focused on Latino adolescent friendships, concluded that what little literature on the subject existed has primarily focused on three areas: "(1) the coordination and developmental significance of relationships with family and friends, (2) the role of friends in individual educational and deviant pathways, and (3) the quality of Latino-heritage adolescents' friendships relative to the qualities that have been used to characterize European-heritage adolescents' friendships."

The social impact of the neighborhood on children and youth will vary, with parents, as is to be expected, playing a more mediating role. Urban youth, in turn, have more freedom of movement and opportunity to interact with strangers as they age. However, this freedom does come with an increased set of risks or challenges in negotiating city streets and their inhabitants, as addressed in the following section.

Youth Living a Challenging Existence

I remember an acquaintance saying that "life is a hassle and then you die." This quote may appear harsh and the reader may argue that hassles are a part of life that make the joys encountered along the way that much more meaningful. However, there is no denying the applicability of this dismal declarative statement to millions of urban youth of color with life expectancies that are lower than those found in the harshest environments of emerging nations and who are relegated to the margins of society where the message is that they are to blame for poor schools, substandard health care, violence, imprisonment, and an extensive list of other societal ills (Thomas, 2013).

Thomas (2013) discusses how marginalized youth of color are quick to be blamed but not quick to be credited when deserving to be so. In essence, urban youth of color have become convenient scapegoats for society. Yet, some still manage to make it and even thrive. Urban youth's ability to survive and thrive should never be underestimated!

Chen and Brooks-Gunn (2015) sum up the close interrelationship between neighborhoods and individual well-being, which has significant implications for urban youth of color and how youth community practice unfolds:

> Research on neighborhoods and individual well-being has produced a sub-stantive body of knowledge over the past quarter century. Neighborhood conditions—especially socioeconomic status (SES), which is based on income and education and to a lesser extent on residential stability—are predictive of cognitive development. The strongest evidence controls for individual and family- level characteristics or examines individuals clustered within neighborhoods in order to obtain estimates of within- and between-neighborhood variance.

A focus on individual well-being without paying attention to environment is counter to urban community practice for very good reasons since this form of practice is predicated on a socioecological paradigm.

Zolkoski and Bullock (2012) undertook a review of the literature on children and youth resilience in an effort to increase our understanding how youth facing incredible odds against success still manage to persevere and even thrive in the harshest of environments. The authors concluded that community assets can play influential roles in helping children and youth surmount adverse life situations but that risks do differ according to the group being targeted, context, and outcomes.

Leipert (2013) addressed resilience through the use of photovoice as a means of concretizing this construct and illustrating the potential viability of visual methodologies regarding this construct. To eschew development of indicators that have no or minimal applicability when discussing urban youth, resiliency must not be grounded within a Eurocentric definition (Ungar, 2013).

The use of pathways as a concept for understanding different youth outcomes offers much promise. Schoon (2015, p. 115) discusses youth pathways to adulthood and how they differ according to social circumstances:

> Social change has affected all young people—but not all in the same way. While the transition to adulthood has generally been extended, not all young people are delaying the step into paid employment, independent living, and family formation, especially those from less privileged family background. Existing templates for the transition to adulthood are, however, dominated by the assumption of a standard trajectory generally involving pathways through post-compulsory education, without taking into account the resources available to young people nor the complexities and variations of the demands they have to negotiate in making the transition to independent adulthood.

Children born to mothers with a college education will follow a far more predicable path than those born to mothers without, who are destined to a less attractive path (McLanahan & Jacobsen, 2015). Those born to single mothers have increased odds of facing a different future than those born into intact households (Cohen, 2015).

Needless to say, the beginning of the pathways of those youth who go from birth to prison will look dramatically different from those who go from birth to an Ivy League university (Black, 2010; Cramer, Gonzalez, & Pellegrini-Lafont, 2014). Thus, pathways are much more than an intellectual concept because they represent real-life social consequences in the case of low-income/low-wealth urban youth of color. These highways of life, so to speak, dictate destinations for multiple generations.

Youth with criminal justice experiences are often treated as damaged goods and permanently tainted, further isolating them from society and even their own communities (Price, 2015). They experience a "social death" by restricting who they can associate with and even who they can consider friends. This profound social marginalization further pushes them into a social abyss, making a broadening of social relationships arduous, if not impossible. Knight and Carlo's (2012) call for increased research on prosocial development (actions to benefit others) among Mexican-American youth comes in response to the urgent need for positive developmental pathways for youth of color and an effort to address the consequences of social death.

Pathways are another way of conceptualizing the chances of contracting life-altering illnesses. Targeting youth with high probabilities of contracting life-altering diseases is labor intensive, and when these youth are highly marginalized, must use nonstigmatizing methods. Health inequalities are one of the consequences of communities being marginalized and becoming the subject of intervention strategies to address these injustices (Belgrave, Abrams, Javier, & Maxwell, 2014). The popularity of prevention programs makes these types of programs viable for developing youth friendships while addressing a life-altering diseases or social situations.

Although prevention programs are problem-focused, that does not mean that they cannot incorporate typical social relationships. Harper et al. (Harper, Dolcini, Benhorin, Watson, & Boyer, 2012), for example, report on an innovative and highly successful program that incorporated urban African-American youth friendships into an HIV/STI prevention initiative:

> Results demonstrate high acceptability of the intervention. Both males and females revealed multiple benefits of attending the intervention with friends including feeling more comfortable, experiencing general satisfaction with the program, experiencing greater ease in talking and expressing self, being able to reveal sensitive information, and being able to relate to each other's experiences .... These results suggest that delivering HIV/STI and other prevention interventions within adolescents' friendship networks may offer unique benefits not found with traditional programs that include random groupings of youth who are not familiar with each other.

Social interventions focused on highly stigmatizing diseases and illnesses can be successful in urban communities and when targeting youth of color if carefully planned and integrated into social networks, such as those consisting of friendships (Fergus & Zimmerman, 2005).

Photovoice as a research and intervention method has a broad reach and can address a wide variety of topics that are either sensitive and stigmatizing or of everyday occurrence (Cushing, Love, & van Vliet, 2012). Keeping with the theme of HIV prevention, Prado, Lightfoot, and Brown (2013) call for a broadening of HIV prevention initiatives to address both macro- and individual-focused issues. Youth community practice is in a strategically advantageous position to address development of social interventions that target macro-, meso-, and microsystems and alter the pathways of urban youth.

Blackburn and McCready (2009) discuss the importance of understanding and addressing the intersection of multiple social and cultural issues inherent in sexual and gender identities, and we can certainly add ethnic and racial for those youth who are also of color. Singh's (2013) study of transgendered youth of color and how resilience influences daily lived experiences highlights how youth development domains shape these young people's ability to fight against racism and trans-prejudice and why a social justice focus is needed. The importance of transgendered youth of color developing a positive and affirming social peer and friendship network is integrated throughout these domains, shaping expectations and outcomes.

Drones (1993), as quoted in Freeman and Mathison (2009, p. 1) states it well when stressing that there is no one single childhood: "There is not one childhood, but many, formed at the intersection of different cultural, social and economic systems, natural and man-made physical environments. Different positions in society produce different experiences." Multiple pathways through childhood translates into multiple potential outcomes and opportunities for social interventions that are tailored to specific circumstances, rewards, and challenges. A pathway does not automatically result in a particular outcome; it does, however, increase the likelihood, and I can certainly attest to this statement.

France and Roberts (2015), in turn, advocate for the use of a social generation paradigm to both acknowledge and take into account the complexities and challenges facing youth today, which can include making and maintaining friendships. The introduction of power dynamics and forces and how they impinge on youth and their relationships introduces a dynamic process that can easily incorporate social justice issues and values into our understanding of peer and friendship networks.

Urban youth hopelessness has a strong etiology in communities that have suffered from decades of disinvestments; have a high percentage of residents, particularly men, involved with the criminal justice system (probation, parole, incarceration, and ex-inmate); experience high levels of personal violence and crime; and suffer from poor quality education and health inequities (Bolland et al.,

2007; Bolland, Lian, & Formichella, 2005; Brown & Grumet, 2009; Harley, 2015). The rise of suicides among African-American/black children aged 5–11, for example, may be an indicator of a shift in thinking among these youths, one with dire consequences for them, their families, and their communities (Tavernise, 2015).

A life without hope is essentially a life without dreams. When hope is present and then destroyed, it takes on particularly tragic proportions. However, an assets- or strength-based perspective on urban violence, for example, would purposefully seek to identify the role and importance of family, teachers, religious leaders, and friends in helping youth negotiate the stressors associated with violence (Benhorin & McMahon, 2008; Elsaesser & Voisin, 2015). Few studies can be found that specifically focus on the moderating impact of close friendships on community violence and aggression (Veits, 2014). A comprehensive understanding of youth social networks facilitates identifying areas of strengths and areas amenable to interventions to bolster their social contributions to youth well-being.

Anderson (2013) advances the concept of "streetwise" to capture both an urban attitude and a skill-set that helps youth and adults of color socially navigate (how to behave in public and keep safe), including who they can trust and who they have to be worried about. Needless to say, this worldview and skill-set translates well into selecting and maintaining close friendships because these friendships can mean the difference between life and death. Being trusted with "secrets" is one indicator of a close friendship (Way, 2006). This level of trust is considered essential for urban youth to bring someone into their inner circle of social relationships because of the potential deleterious consequences of breaching this trust.

The impact of violence, as in the case of homicide of urban youth of color, is undeniable since homicide is considered the leading cause of death of African-American youth in the United States (Johnson, 2014). Not unexpectedly, the loss of their friends to murder brings forth social and psychological consequences that reach into peer and friendship networks and identity formation, as in the case of adolescent girls, for example. This has been short-term and long-term consequences for social development and establishing friendships in the future.

Furthermore, the presence of secondary trauma brings a sad but vivid picture of psychological loss in young lives: the question of how many friends have you lost to violence can bring forth numbers, lists of names, and many stories (Post et al., 2014; Thomason et al., 2015; Wade, Shea, Rubin, & Wood, 2014). The same question asked in a middle- or upper-middle class community will most likely bring only a look of puzzlement. When one's friends also have lost friends, it creates an atmosphere that reinforces the "shortness" of life.

Maturo and Cunningham (2013) specifically addressed the role and influence of friends on children's physical activity in their review of the literature on this subject during 2000–13 and found friendships to wield significant influence; these researchers called for greater attention to using friendships in the promotion of positive health behaviors and health promotion programs. Engagement of urban youth in youth development programming brings benefits to participants, and they may be well cognizant of how they can benefit because of the lack of viable alternatives. However, urban youth engagement in after-school programming can be severely limited in some cases because of familial and work responsibilities (Serido, Bordem, & Wiggs, 2014). Positive youth development (PYD) lends itself to being integrated into many different arenas, including the world of sports (Camiré, Fomeris, Trudel, & Bernard, 2011; Vierimaa, Erickson, Côté, & Gilbert., 2012) and physical activity–related programs (Weiss, Bolter, & Kipp, 2014; Witt & Caldwell, 2010).

However, affirming and beneficial social integration is not without its challenges for urban youth. Coakley (2011), for example, raises a concern about the role of sports in fostering youth development and the lack of data substantiating the benefits of these claims. Sports, it is important to emphasize, must be part of an extensive menu that consists of many different activities because not all youth can be expected to engage in sports as their primary extracurricular activity.

Organized youth activities such as sports have a tendency to encourage friends to engage together. One study found that 70% of participants had friends with them and that having friends in activities is associated with lower problem behavior and better academic functioning (Poulin & Denault, 2013). However, team versus individual sporting activities can produce different outcomes, with friends in individual sports being more academically oriented when compared to friends in team sports, which, in turn, are more supportive. Team sports, however, may be more conducive to developing friendship networks consisting of youth from differing backgrounds, however.

Sports are often considered "safe" ways of enhancing youth skills, and Coakley (2011) grounds this attitude within a conservative political stance. Sports have certainly entered the youth development world (Holt & Neely, 2011, p. 310): "Various frameworks of PYD from developmental psychology have been adopted in the sport psychology literature with varying degrees of success. Some of the key issues that once require consideration once the roles of coaches, parents, and peers in creating a social context in sport settings that provides ideal conditions for the promotion of PYD." PYD projected outcomes must not only take into account youth expectations but also that of their parents, as in the case of sports activities (Riley & Anderson-Butcher, 2012).

Youth of color are more likely to join organized sports activities if they already have friends involved (Stodolska, Sharaievska, Tainsky, & Ryan, 2014; Yan, Voorhees, Beck, & Wang, 2014). Wright and Li (2009), in this instance involving youth of color, advocate for the integration of PYD within all aspects of schooling, including the classroom. Urban sports activities, however, can go beyond the conventional basketball and football games (Delgado, 2000; Mohan, 2014). They can also include soccer (Joassart-Marcelli, 2010), swimming (Irwin, Irwin, Ryan, & Drayer, 2009), tennis (Fry & Gano-Overway, 2010), and lacrosse/field hockey (Fultz & Chen, 2012), for example, which are sports usually not associated with urban youth.

Plante et al. (Plante, Moreau, Jaimes, & Turbide, 2014) identified five factors or considerations in the engagement of youth in organized sports, which translates into four programming strategies:

> Five factors influencing recruitment emerged: (1) socialization/belonging; (2) training/physical aspects; (3) 'extraordinary' dimension; (4) practicality of the program; and (5) social influences. Four key elements thus appear important to consider when promoting the recruitment of youths in voluntary community programs: (1) favoring social interactions; (2) insisting on the specific and beneficial elements of the program; (3) allowing youths to experiment a trial period; and (4) including testimonies of former participants in the information session.

Although this framework focuses on sports, it breaks down engagement and programming in a manner that facilitates data-gathering, analysis, and discussions of potential challenges in using other activities not related to sports.

The use of rope courses, for example, represents an often overlooked activity that is not competitive and may be appealing for youth who eschew win–lose activities. Thor (2014) undertook a meta-analysis of the effects of rope courses as an intervention for "at-risk youth" and concluded that this activity had a significant impact on personal growth and interpersonal relations and also served to increase their self-confidence and belief in themselves to succeed in challenging situations; these are all key dimensions necessary for maintaining friendships. These types of activities can be modified to take into account various physical challenges, too, and lend themselves to creating group bonding experiences that can foster youth friendships.

Demographic Characteristics

Cities are undergoing dramatic changes in composition, and this will be reflected in the age and race/ethnic groups living in these geographical areas. It can certainly be argued that cities are constantly undergoing transformation and that the current changes are just a continuation of this historical trend or evolution. It is estimated that more than 50% of the world's children live in cities, and this percentage is only expected to rise in the foreseeable future (Horschelmann & Van Blerk, 2013). The increase in the world's population residing in cities is also applicable to the United States. This nation's cities, with some notable exceptions, have continued to experience population increases.

The nation's cities are witnessing unprecedented shifts in ethnic/racial compositions. Urban population growth is largely attributed to the increase of Latinos and Asians, particularly in the central cities. Suburbia, too, has undergone demographic shifts with the inclusion of Latinos, Asians, and African-American/blacks moving out of the cities. Nevertheless, at least in the case of Latinos and Asians, those who move out are quickly being replaced at a far greater pace than their out-city migration (Delgado, 2007; Frey, 2015; Short & Mussman, 2014).

According to a 2012 US Bureau of the Census report (2012a), the United States' urban population increased by 12.1% from 2000 to 2010, significantly outpacing the nation's overall population growth rate of 9.7% for the same time period. A focus on the nation's 486 urbanized areas will show that they increased by 14.3% from 2000 to 2010.

Latinos accounted for more than 50% of the nation's growth between 2000 and 2010 (US Bureau of the Census, 2011), which is why they have received so much media attention (Riffe, Turner, & Rojas-Guyler, 2008). In 2014, Latinos numbered 55.4 million, or 17.4% of the country's total population (Krostad & Lopez, 2015). It is estimated, for example, that 50,000 Latino youth citizens turn 18 years of age (voting age) every month in the United States (Suddock, 2012). That translates into 6 million potential new voters. These Latino youth are not evenly distributed throughout the United States, as already noted. Thus, their potential politically transformative power has not received the attention it deserves.

An examination of the distribution of the nation's top 10 most densely populated urbanized areas will reveal that nine are located in the West, with seven of those in California. The New York–Newark region is the nation's most populous urbanized area with 18,351,295 residents. Los Angeles–Long Beach–Anaheim is the second most populous (12,150,996), followed by the Chicago area (8,608,208). These areas have the distinction of holding these top three positions since the 1950 Census (US Census Bureau, 2012a). It is no mistake that these areas are also home to large concentrations of people of color, most notably Latinos, African-American/blacks, and Asians.

From a regional perspective, the West is the nation's most urbanized section with almost 90% (89.8%) of its population living in cities, which may surprise the reader, followed by the Northeast with 85%. Although the difference is minor (less than 5%), the trend is significant. In turning to the least urbanized regions, the Midwest (75.9%) and South (75.8%) have the lowest urban-based percentages of population.

An examination of the nation's top five cities with youth under the age of 14 years will reinforce the statistics just presented on urbanized regions of the country (Kotkin, 2014): (1) Salt Lake City, Utah (24.7%); (2) Houston, Texas (23.0%); (3) Dallas–Fort Worth, Texas (22.9%); (4) Riverside–San Bernardino, California (22/8%); and (5) San Antonio, Texas (21.7%). Three of these cities are located in Texas, and all five are located in the southwestern and western parts of the United States.

Demographics and Youth of Color

The United States passed a demographic milestone in 2011, the year when the number of babies of color born surpassed white, non-Latino births, with Latinos constituting the largest group, representing 25% of all births (Frey, 2015). In some parts of the country, that milestone had been passed much earlier, as in Southern California, for example. According to the US Bureau of the Census, 2011, the nation's population younger than 5 years was 49.7% of color, an increase from 49.0% in 2010.

The nation's demographic trends highlight a country that is increasingly getting grayer (boomers and older adults) and browner (people of color), making the nation as a whole as well as specific regions and cities more racially and ethnically diverse from a browning perspective. Youth of color represent a significant group that will only increase in representation in the near future, making it important to examine a demographic profile, particularly when viewed within a cities and national context (Cauce, Cruz, Corona, & Conger, 2011).

Figure 4.1 provides a stark visual representation of how the United States demographic profile has changed. In 2012, there were an estimated 82,500,000 youth under the age of 20 years in the United States, of which 38.8 million are of color, representing 47% of this age group. Latinos accounted for almost 20 million (24%), or the largest group of color. They were followed by African-American/black with 11.55 million (14%), and Asians with 3.3 million (4%). Others accounted for 4.125 million (5%).

The 2012 figure reflects a continued increase in youth of color representation in the United States. In 1990, for example, they represented 32% of the under-20s. However, in 2000, that percentage increased to 39%: a short period of 12 years witnessed their percentage representation increasing to 47% (Johnson, Schaefer, Lichter, & Rogers, 2014).

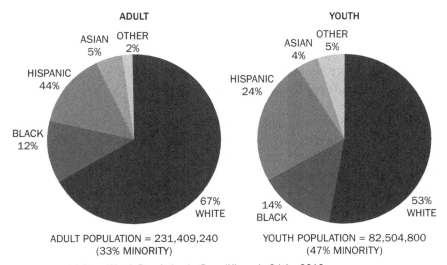

FIGURE 4.1. Adult and Youth Population by Race/Hispanic Origin, 2012

Source: US Census Bureau Reports (2012b). Growth in Urban Population Outpaces Rest of Nation, Census Bureau Reports. Washington, DC.

Not surprisingly, the percentage of adults over the age of 20 followed a distribution similar to their ethnic and racial youth counterparts. Latinos accounted for 32.4 million (14%), followed by African-American/blacks with 27.8 million (12%), Asians with 11.6 million (5%), and other with 4.6 million (2%).

Distribution

In 2001, according to the US Census Bureau (2012*b*), there were five majority-minority states or equivalents; not surprisingly, Hawaii (77.1% minority) led the nation in the percentage of its population being of color, followed by the District of Columbia (64.7%), California (60.3%), New Mexico (59.8%), and Texas (55.2%).

The state of California had the largest Hispanic population of any state with 14.4 million, as well as the largest numerical increase within the Latino population since April 1, 2010 (346,000). New Mexico, however, had the highest percentage of Latinos in the country with 46.7% (US Census Bureau, 2012*b*). African Americans were the second largest group of color in the United States, at 43.9 million in 2011 (up 1.6% from 2010).

The State of New York had the largest African-American/black population of any state or state equivalent in 2011 with 3.7 million. Texas, however, had the largest numerical increase since 2010 (84,000), and the District of Columbia had the highest concentration with 52.2%, followed by Mississippi (38.0%). Asians, in turn, numbered 18.2 million and were considered the second fastest growing group of color, increasing by 3.0% since 2010. California had both the largest Asian population of any state with 5.8 million, and the state experienced the largest numerical increase since 2010 (131,000).

Hawaii is the nation's only majority-Asian state, where they represent 57.1% of the total state population. Its proximity to Asia has no doubt played an influential role in shaping its composition. Los Angeles had the largest Asian population of any county (1.6 million) in 2011 and also the largest numerical increase (16,000) since 2010. Honolulu, with 61.2%, had the highest percentage of Asians in the nation.

The nation's American Indian and Alaska Native (AIAN) population was an estimated at 6.3 million in 2011, an increase of 2.1% from 2010. California, not surprisingly, had the largest AIAN population of any state with 1,050,000 and also the largest numerical increase relative to initial population size since 2010 with 23,000. Alaska had the highest percentage of AIAN (19.6%) of any state. Los Angeles had the largest AIAN population of any county with 231,000, and also the largest numerical increase (9,000) since 2010, with Shannon County, South Dakota (located within the Pine Ridge Indian Reservation) having the highest concentration of AIAN (93.6%).

Finally, the nation's Native Hawaiian and Other Pacific Islander (NHPI) population was 1.4 million in 2011 and increased by 2.9% since 2010. Hawaii, not surprisingly, had the largest numerical state population of NHPIs of any state, with 359,000 in 2011. California, however, had the largest numerical increase since 2010, with 9,000. Hawaii had the highest percentage of NHPIs, representing almost a quarter of its population (26.1%). Honolulu had the largest population of NHPIs of any county (235,000), and Los Angeles County had the largest numerical increase since 2010 (2,700). Hawaii County had the nation's highest percentage of NHPIs (34.0%).

Ethnic and racial groups, as the reader can see, are not evenly distributed across the nation, and this certainly applies in the case of youth of color, who are heavily represented in cities across the nation. Thus, the subject of urban youth friendships takes on greater significance in certain sections of the United States. Schools of social work and community-based organizations in these areas, as a result, are in a more propitious position to undertake friendship community practice projects as compared to areas that have historically attracted older adults.

Figure 4.2 shows a graphic representation of how the country's youth population is distributed, including how certain ethnic/racial groups cluster and why certain major cities stand out in importance because of how city and state compositions are closely related.

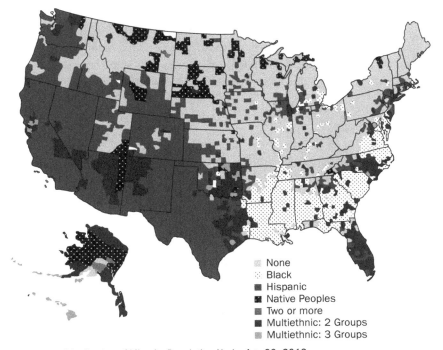

FIGURE 4.2. Distribution of Minority Population Under Age 20, 2012

Source: US Census Bureau Reports (2012*a*). Most Children Younger than Age 1 are Minorities. Washington, DC.

This youth of color distribution is the result of historical trends, in which people of color settle in particular areas of the country, with both coasts reflecting these historical patterns and new demographic trends reflecting greater dispersal across areas and regions historically not known to attract people of color (Johnson et al., 2014). It is almost as if the United States is the result of the amalgamation of two countries, one white, non-Latino and the other of color. The part that is predominately white, non-Latino, however, will increasingly experience an influx of people of color, and the part that is predominantly of color will only increase its concentration of people of color if current projected trends continue unabated.

There are distinct patterns, with African-American/black youth heavily represented in southern states and Latinos represented in the southwest and the northeast. Dispersal patterns, however, have introduced a new set of population dynamics. Johnson et al. (2014, p. 6) specifically address the population composition of inner cities:

> In large urban cores, where minority populations have traditionally clustered, 66 percent of the 24.5 million children and youth are minorities. The population of minority children has grown by more than 1.8 million in these areas since 2000.
>
> Population declines among blacks and whites have been offset by this large Hispanic population gain.

Large population declines of African Americans, as in the case of Detroit, for example, bring forth new social, political, and economic challenges for major urban areas, including the dislocation of social networks within these communities (Sugrue, 2014), which has significant implications for friendship networks.

Future Projections

Projecting demographics into the future is not an exact science, and no self-respecting demographer would argue this point (Kearney & Levine, 2015; Lee, 2011). Demographics are influenced by three distinctive yet interrelated trends: (1) birth rates, (2) death rates, and (3) in- and out-migration (Colby & Ortman 2015; McDonald, Mojarro, Sutton, & Ventura, 2015; Tilley & Barnett, 2015). Johnson et al. (2014), for example, summed up the birth rate forces operating to change the demographic profile of the United States: "American diversity is fueled by differing fertility rates among racial and ethnic groups, changes in the racial composition of women of childbearing age, and immigration."

One trend that is rarely discussed but worth addressing here is the emergence of multiracial groups. The Pew Research Center (2015, p. 1) notes that the emergence of multiracial individuals further clouds an already challenging scene regarding ethnicity and race:

While multiracial adults share some things in common, they cannot be easily categorized. Their experiences and attitudes differ significantly depending on the races that make up their background and how the world sees them. For example, multiracial adults with a black background—69% of whom say most people would view them as black or African American—have a set of experiences, attitudes and social interactions that are much more closely aligned with the black community. A different pattern emerges among multiracial Asian adults; biracial white and Asian adults feel more closely connected to whites than to Asians. Among biracial adults who are white and American Indian—the largest group of multiracial adults—ties to their Native American heritage are often faint: Only 22 percent say they have a lot in common with people in the U.S. who are American Indian, whereas 61 percent say they have a lot in common with whites.

The Pew Center's findings necessitate that multiracial individuals play an active role in providing a definition of what this identity status means to them, rather than having the definition imposed on them.

By 2060, taking birth–death rates and immigration factors into considerations, Latinos are projected to account for 29% or one in four residents of the United States (Colby & Ortman, 2015). In 2014, they became the largest racial and ethnic group in California (Pew Research Center, 2015). A projection 60 years from now can find Latinos constituting more than 50% of the State of California, making that state a Latino majority state. In 2014, California's Latinos officially surpassed white, non-Latinos, with 14.99 million compared to 14.92 million (Panzar, 2015).

Yanez (2015) sums up quite poignantly what Latino youth will mean for the future of the country: "With a recent rise in Hispanics across the United States, most Americans are realizing that it is not simply children who are our future, but instead it is Hispanic children. With the recent cultural accomplishments made by these Hispanic children, the support from Americans of various ethnicities will propel the United States into a better future." Yanez's statement has profound implications for cities, states, and regions of the country with high percentages of Latino children and youth and for the school systems and community-based organizations that seek to educate and serve them.

National debates about undocumented residents are an example of the dynamic nature of demographic projections (Donato & Sisk, 2015). Passel (2011) focuses on the nation's newcomer youth and notes that they account for 25% of the nation's 75 million children and are projected to account for one-third of the nation's 100 million youth in 2050. Population trends, in turn, can be dramatically impacted by major global trends and natural disasters, introducing a degree of unpredictability. Does this mean that we should totally disregard population projections? No, but it does mean that we should be cautious about the level of validity given to them.

Two distinct but converging demographic trends are projected to occur in the United States in the next 15 years—the numbers of both older adults (64 and older) and youths (20 years and younger) will continue to increase in representation (Astone et al., 2015). Furthermore, a demographic transition is projected to occur resulting in groups of color ascending to occupy a majority demographic position and white, non-Latinos becoming a minority (Lichter, 2013). William Frey's (2015) book, *Diversity Explosion: How New Racial Demographics are Remaking America*, provides a comprehensive assessment of how the country will experience profound transformation, with no segment of the country escaping its impact.

According to the US Bureau of the Census, the next 25 years will bring a series of demographic milestones that will result in the browning of this country. The first milestone will be reached in 2018 when the majority of youth under the age of 18 will be of color. In 2027, the majority of 18- to 29-year-olds will be of color; within 6 years of that, in 2033, the majority of 30- to 39-year-olds will be of color; and 8 years after that (in 2041), the majority of 40- to 49-year-olds will be of color.

The prediction by United for a Fair Economy of what the United States' racial composition will be in the year 2042 paints a graphic picture (Sullivan, Mwangi, Miller, Muhammad, & Harris, 2012, p. i):

> A major demographic shift is underway in the United States. According to the 2010 Census, White babies now make up a little less than 50% of all babies in the country. By 2030, the majority of US residents under 18 will be youth of color. And by 2042, Blacks, Latinos, Asians, Native Americans, Pacific Islanders, and other non-Whites will collectively comprise the majority of the US population. For the first time since Colonial days, the United States will be a majority-minority country.

It is projected that in the next 40 years the number of Latinos, Asians, and multiracial groups will double in representation (Frey, 2015).

In 2025, it is projected that half of the nation's youth of color will live in nine states, with profound implications for youth services within the cities in those states (Collins, Grimes, & Franklin, 2014). Key educational and youth community-based institutions in these communities also will experience profound transformations, providing policy-makers and community practitioners with ample opportunities to focus on youth and develop models for the rest of the country.

The reader should not be surprised with this final prediction of how the country will eventually become a majority-minority country and how this impacts cities. How well the nation and its cities address these profound social, cultural, economic, and political changes will have a great deal to say to the world about how a democracy can evolve and respond to major social-demographic trends that transform the ethnic and racial makeup of a country.

Gangs and Friendships

My initial impetus in writing this book was to avoid writing about urban gangs. My concern was that introducing gangs would shift the focus from positive to negative peer and friendship network behaviors, and this is a conceptual trap that is so easy to fall into because of the preponderances of the literature on deficits. Nevertheless, after some thought, and upon the recommendation of an external reviewer, I came to the conclusion that it was important to address the subject of gangs, and it was appropriate to do so in this chapter. The topic of US gangs is one that is closely associated with youth and urban communities, particularly youth of color, and there is a need to share some insight on the role of friendships in motivating youth to join, stay, and exit gangs in cases where these groups no longer meet their needs. There are certainly lessons to be learned from this understanding that can have applicability in other situations.

Urban youth relationships and friendships are complex, and that is to be expected based on the themes raised in the discussion of critical place theory in the introductory chapter. Space, as already noted, does not just exist: it shapes behaviors and expectations based on how urban physical structures and social forces influence attitudes within and outside of relationships. One of the key forces is the presence of gangs and how they dictate movement, communication patterns, and expectations of relationships within urban communities. How gangs are conceptualized and viewed within and outside of the communities where they exist introduces a much needed and often overlooked critical theory perspective on the interrelations and actions that occur between space and the presence of gangs.

If one were to ask anyone on the street about their opinions on gangs in the United States, it would be a rare person who would say that the answer is complex and contingent upon a host of social-ecological factors. The overwhelming typical response will be that gangs are negative and counterproductive to urban life. Uunfortunately, a deficit paradigm extends to gang-related research and scholarship, and, as a result, typical assessment methods of gang-involved youth often overlook the presence of positive peer ties and the role they can play in fostering prosocial behaviors (van Dommelen-Gonzalez, Deardorff, Herd, & Minnis, 2015). The predominance of the scholarly literature one can draw upon is negative in tone and content, with some notable exceptions. This is no doubt the result of how funders of this research emphasize a particular school of thought that emphasizes problems. Brotherton (2015), as a result, advocates for an alternative narrative on gangs by using a critical analysis and studies approach, interpreting these groups as a manifestation of resistance.

If public opinion is based on the amount of attention given to gangs in the public media, then one can easily believe that gangs are overrunning numerous neighborhoods across the nation's cities. Howell (2013, p. 7) makes a persuasive argument for gang membership prevention and places gangs within a historical and current-day perspective:

> Youth gangs are not a new social problem in the United States. They have been a serious problem since the early 19th century—and they remain a persistent problem. Overall, one-third (34%) of cities, towns and rural counties in this country reported gang problems in 2010. Recent data indicate that nearly half of high school students report that there are students at their school who consider themselves to be part of a gang, and 1 in 5 students in grades 6–12 report that gangs are present in their school. Other data have found that nearly 1 in 12 youth said they belonged to a gang at some point during their teenage years.

The reach of gangs within communities makes them a significant force in the lives of youth and a part of the social fabric of these communities.

It is estimated, however, that only between 1% and 2% of youth are actively involved in gangs, representing a very small portion of a community's youth, with African-American and Latino groups being overrepresented and increasing the significance of gangs in these neighborhoods and among these two racial and ethnic groups (Huey, McDaniel, Smith, Pearson, & Griffin, 2014). Research suggests that 6% to 30% of youth from economically disadvantaged neighborhoods actually affiliate with or join a gang during their lifetime (Guerra, Dierkhising, & Payne, 2013). Nevertheless, this small percentage has shaped public opinions based on major news coverage of cities such as Chicago, Detroit, Miami, New York, and Los Angeles, to select but five. Unfortunately, these are major media markets and will attract national if not international coverage.

This section, however, is only intended to provide an overview of the topic since most urban youth are not in gangs—although based on the prevailing view, one can easily get the impression that all urban youth are in gangs. Furthermore, a focus on youth friendships as assets necessitates attention being paid to how urban youth engage in resistance and thereby avoid joining gangs (Pitts, 2014; Pyrooz, Decker, & Webb, 2010; Sweeten, Pyrooz, & Piquero, 2013). Toy (2011) specifically addressed urban gang violence and notes how facing this violence creates friendships and links that frequently survive through to early adolescence.

Gang membership is best conceptualized along a continuum and in similar fashion to membership in any organization. Studies have shown that the gang-joining process is similar to how most of us join an organization (Howell, 2013). Learning that a gang or organization exists is the first stage; if one has a friend or relative in the organization, the chances of continuing along the path toward joining is greatly increased. Visiting and participating on a limited or trial level follows. This step does not require commitment. Eventually, a commitment is made to join once an invitation is extended. Each of these stages will be influenced by the level of personal connections (i.e., friendships) youth have, and each level lends itself to an intervention strategy.

Barrett, Kuperminc, and Lewis (2013), for example, studied gang involvement among US-born and immigrant Latino youth to understand the role of environmental stressors (e.g., discrimination and acculturative stress in the case of immigrant youth) and found that gang membership works differently between these two groups. Developing friendships that are not gang-involved increases the likelihood that Latino youth eschew gang membership. It has been found that gang members spend greater amounts of time with friends when compared to time spent with family, which is the opposite of non-gang members and thus illustrates the power of friendships (Taylor & Smith, 2013). Again, this represents a different paradigm, one that has not received the attention it deserves from policy-makers and academics, not to mention community practitioners. Shifting paradigms toward assets facilitates the integration of a cultural and more nuanced understanding of gang membership and desistance.

It should be noted, however, that our understanding of gang memberships and relationships is complicated by the fact that there are definitional challenges about what constitutes a gang and gang membership (Shelden, Tracy, & Brown, 2012). Gangs, it should be emphasized, are not a homogenous group—contrary to how they tend to be portrayed in the popular media—and motivation and participation experiences, as a result, will differ across members and demographic characteristics (O'Brien, Daffern, Chu, & Thomas, 2013; Pyrooz, Sweeten, & Piquero, 2013; Trevatt, 2014). Furthermore, gang member friendships can extend beyond the gang itself, so these groups are not totally insular in relationships (Gormally, 2004).

There are numerous long-term benefits as well as negative consequences for those adolescents with social ties to positive-influencing peers and "risky" friendships, with those in the latter category possibly engaging in gangs (Baskin, Quintana, & Slaten, 2014; Sletten, 2011; Wood & Giles, 2014) and the role of peers and friends in disengaging from the group once their needs change (Owen & Greeff, 2015). Gangs, as a result, open up possibilities for establishing friendships with those of similar ages.

Gang memberships for females, for example, can result in developing friendships that lead to increased risky sexual behaviors (Piquette, 2013). Gang membership for these youth facilitates developing friendships that may reinforce propensities existing prior to gang membership. The interrelationship between positive and negative influencing peers will alter over an extended period of time, with one group taking on greater influence and the other fading into the background. Friendships play an influential role in helping to shape identity, and gangs do provide a reference point, thus bringing a unique perspective on identity formation (Taylor & Smith, 2013).

Vigil (2010), in a book titled *Gang redux: A Balanced Anti-Gang Strategy*, posits that male bonds created out of mutual trust and friendship growing up together in the "hood" are powerful forces to encourage gang membership and instill loyalty and a "comrade-in-arms" mindset, thus making gang membership strong and immutable. Girls, in turn, generally join gangs as a way of obtaining friendship, care, and love, and as an alternative to problems at home (Vigil, 2008; Wolf & Gutierrez, 2012). Friendships, as a result, may serve different motivations for join-ing and staying in gangs, with demographics and life circumstances helping to shape joining motivations and expectations. As a result, programs that foster the potential of friendships outside of a gang can be an effective strategy that taps the power of friendship (Gormally, 2015).

The study of youth gangs has generally been viewed from an antisocial behavior perspective, and, as a result, criminologists have wielded considerable influence in shaping popular and scholarly knowledge on the subject. Antisocial behavior, in turn, has generally fallen into three categories: *aggression, social rejec-tion,* and *delinquency* (Martinez, Tost, Hilgert, & Woodard-Meyers, 2013; Pyrooz et al., 2013). Although these categories have been conceptualized as independent of each other, peer network influence can cut across them. Focusing on friendships (special and voluntary close relationships), however, introduces a perspective that facilitates our understanding of friendship's role in gang membership (Densley, 2014; Deptula & Cohen, 2004; Way, 2013).

Gang recruitment is primarily done through two organizational meth-ods: fraternity and coercion (Durán, 2010). Both of these methods have gotten a fair amount of attention in the professional literature. Gang membership may be spurred through a search for protection, fun, respect, money, or because a friend was in the gang (Hoffman, Weathers, & Sanders, 2014). Weerman, Lovegrove, and Thornberry (2015), in a study of US and European membership transitions in joining and leaving gangs, found friendships playing influential roles in both stages. Gangs have been found to promote insular friendships as a key mechanism in maintaining control (Kissner & Pyrooz, 2009).

It has been found that gang members with low levels of embeddedness (rela-tional and structural components), of which friendship is but one element, are more likely to leave a gang earlier than those with high levels (Pyrooz et al., 2012). Conceptually, embeddedness reflects adhesion to the gang as manifested through varying degrees of engagement, identification, and status among gang members. In similar fashion to peer and friendship relationships, these degrees of participa-tion will vary according to age. Group peer and friendship relationships repre-sent a dimension that could benefit from greater attention (Wood & Giles, 2014). A society that values individualism has a difficult time conceptualizing a collectiv-ist perspective on group friendships and the appeal that gangs can have because of this dimension.

Practitioners and academics must not ignore or underestimate the role of gangs in urban youth community practice. Human service professionals can reach and assist gang members to meet basic health needs, for example, and in the pro-cess establish linkages that can identify and assist members wishing a different lifestyle (Morris, 2012). Of course, not all helping professionals have the ability to establish these forms of relationships, and that includes youth practitioners.

Unfortunately, there is no "magic bullet" for preventing youth from joining gangs. However, friendships within highly confined or segregated communities limit options for urban youth to the immediate geographical setting. Program participants may have close family and friends in gangs, and these individuals can wield strong influence on program youth. Successful community youth programs will not escape the attention of gangs, and these programs can be allowed to operate without interference when the activities are deemed as social justice–focused and meeting the needs of the community. In essence, they are fulfilling a worthy rather than a social control purpose.

It is fitting to end this section on gangs with a warning about how community practitioners, researchers, and policy-makers must approach the subject: (Taylor & Smith, 2013, p. 27): "It is very important that local decision-makers who determine which gang-prevention strategies are implemented—and the practitioners who actually implement them—have solid information regarding what gang attractions are at play in their community. A one-size-fits-all approach to tackling the issues of gang attraction and recruitment will not work when constructing local, state, or federal policy. The ability to understand exactly what young people are facing—in their respective cities, communities and neighborhoods—is key."

Conclusion

Youth exist within contexts, and this ecology influences virtually all visible and invisible aspects of their lives. In communities where gangs wield significant influences, for example, an ability to socially navigate outside the gravitational pull of this group takes on great significance in the daily lives of youth. For those who cannot avoid the gravitational pull, which can be the result of many different factors, the presence or absence of friendships will wield great influence in whether they stay or leave.

The demographic picture of urban youth of color shows a clear and indisputable portrait of the United States at the present and not too distant future, including perspectives on the distribution of youth of color across the country. This demographic profile provides a clear road map of how youth will increase their representation across the nation's cities, with some regions witnessing tremendous increases.

Youth community practice will only increase in importance in the immediate future as urban youth continue to increase their demographic presence; certain sections of the country will be in a more propitious position to embrace youth community practice because of their increased numerical presence. This final section sets the stage for Section II that follows and the use of case illustrations.

SECTION II

Case Illustrations

5

Enhancement and Tapping of Friendships in Youth Development and Community-Based Interventions

Introduction

Newfound knowledge and insights on friendships in general and urban youth of color in particular are always noteworthy. However, what we as community practitioners do with this information takes on even more important. This chapter will highlight current programmatic efforts that seek to enhance friendships among urban youth of color as a primary or secondary goal in a variety of social situations, and using a variety of social intervention methods to illustrate the range of possibilities. Tapping youth friendship networks offers great potential in community-based interventions (Harper, Dolcini, Benhorin, Watson, & Boyer, 2014), particularly when they are geographically sensitive and grounded within a social-cultural context. Friendships can help recruit participants and retain them in programs.

Tapping these networks, as a result, can be an effective and efficient approach for community practitioners, helping to ensure that interventions are grounded within the community in a manner that is more organic rather than externally imposed and helping to increase the likelihood of success. Every effort was made to select case examples/illustrations that sought to capture regional differences and different ways that friendship has been emphasized, including the rewards and challenges of identifying and engaging them in social interventions (Hancock & Algozzine, 2006).

Four case illustrations will be covered in this chapter. Two case illustrations have been devoted to photovoice. This method of engagement offers tremendous potential for engaging youth in pursuit of activities that lend themselves to social relationship building without putting pressure on them. I had personal contact with the project leaders of these two programs and thus had access to them.

The first case illustration is based in Minneapolis/St. Paul, Minnesota; the second photovoice case illustration is based in Miami, Florida. Photovoice as a research-focused method will be addressed again in the following chapter. One remaining case illustration involves the use of technology with refugee youth, and the other case focuses on social action and development of peer and friendships across ethnic and racial youth. It is no mistake that three out of the four cases involve technology in some form or shape because of youth's fascination with this method of communication.

These cases will provide brief yet important glimpses into how youth of color friendships are identified, defined, and addressed through a variety of activities, programs, and staff interactions. In addition, each of the cases covered will consist of six sections: (1) Overview; (2) Brief Review of Literature (grounding the intervention within the broader youth community practice field); (3) Description of the Youth Group and Organizational Setting; (4) How the Intervention Is Focused on Youth Friendship; (5) Research/Evaluation Implications; and (6) Important Results and Lessons Learned. Each section provides enough information for the reader to develop an appreciation of the content to make an informed judgment on the merits of the case and how friendships were targeted and enhanced.

The case illustrations from Georgia and Minnesota have youth friendships and social relationships as the primary goals. The case examples from Miami and an unidentified Midwestern city have friendships/social relationships as secondary goals. Each case values friendships in a unique and affirming manner and shows the potential for inclusion in a variety of forms. The following chapter on cross-cutting themes will provide the reader with insights into how these practice experiences are interwoven with the scholarly literature on the subject.

Case 1: Camp CAMERA (Minneapolis/St. Paul, Minnesota)

OVERVIEW

The opportunity to use an innovative approach in youth community practice must not be overlooked because it can serve to attract participants and funding, and lead to new insights into youth programming. It is appropriate to start this chapter on case illustrations with an example of such an innovative method: the use of photovoice. The case of Camp CAMERA is different from the second case illustration, which also used this method in Miami, both in duration of project and goals.

However, as the reader will see, the Miami case example fostered youth-to-youth social relationships and friendships whereas the case of Camp CAMERA focused on youth relationships with each other and college students from Macalester College whom they partnered with. In the latter case, social relationships were central with photovoice being the mechanism through which these relationships would be fostered. Interestingly, both cases involved partnerships with local universities.

BRIEF REVIEW OF THE LITERATURE

The literature on photovoice has exploded over the past decade, all signs indicate that it will continue this amazing expansion, and the number of articles devoted to analyzing this literature attests to its popularity and importance (Harley, Hunn, Elliott, & Canfield, 2015; Hannes & Parylo, 2014). It seems as if no part of the world has not ventured into using this method to address a wide range of research and social intervention goals (Oliveira & Vearey, 2015; Saimon, Choo, & Bulgiba, 2015; Wickenden & Kembhavi-Tam, 2014).

Youth as a group have been particularly receptive to using photography to share their stories and concerns (Harley, 2015; Imasiku, 2014; Madrigal et al., 2014; Stegenga & Burks, 2013). Very young children, too, can master use of cameras and can engage in various types of visual research, including photovoice (Änggård, 2015). This method also can be used with children and youth with various types of physical, emotional, and intellectual challenges if modified accordingly (Lal, Jarus, & Suto, 2012). It is a method that lends itself to being used in collaborative situations, as in the case of Camp CAMERA, for example, thus opening possibilities for establishing friendships with peers and adults participating in the program (Delgado, 2015).

This brief review of the literature will focus on outlining the various approaches to implementing this tool as a social intervention method. The literature that follows in the Overtown, Miami, case illustration will focus on implementation of a photovoice youth project in an effort to avoid duplication, with friendship and peer relationships playing a secondary role. For those readers interested in pursuing further reading on this subject, there is an abundance of literature to select from many different disciplines.

DESCRIPTION OF THE YOUTH GROUP AND ORGANIZATIONAL SETTING

Camp CAMERA represents a collaboration between a university (Macalester) and three community organizations (YouthCARE, Open World Learning Community School, and the Al Lenzmeier West Side Boys & Girls Club). It should be noted that YouthCare's mission is to develop youth leadership and employment skills while building multicultural friendships among youth through positive after-school and weekend activities. Macalester College provided space, volunteers, and support. This form of collaboration is a recurring theme throughout this book, one that brings university resources to bear in creating community-based programs that can foster a wide variety of social goals, including social relationship building and enhancement.

Camp CAMERA is best thought of as an after-school program structured to be both a "fun" interactive photography program for high school students and a service learning and leadership development program for college students. Camp CAMERA involved girls from a variety of ethnic and racial backgrounds. Each semester, high school youth (approximately 11) come to campus and participate with Macalester student volunteers (ranging from 4 to 7) in an experience of self-exploration and photography. The racial and ethnic breakdown of the youth participants was as follows: African American (49%), Asian American (10%), Caucasian (20%), Latino (10%), Native American (3%), and multiracial (8%).

HOW THE INTERVENTION FOCUSED ON YOUTH FRIENDSHIP

Camp CAMERA focused on utilizing positive youth development (PYD), greatly influenced by the work undertaken at the Search Institute and the building of positive relationships between high school and college students through affirming collaboration, creativity, and mutual respect. It is important to emphasize that social relationship enhancement was a primary goal of Camp CAMERA, and photovoice was the mechanism or activity that fostered friendship and peer relationships.

Friendships, incidentally, played an important role in recruiting and maintaining youth in the program since the program sought to have youth expand their social relationships. Friendships developed while participating in the program carried over into other spheres, which should be a goal of any youth intervention that stresses social relationship development. Breaking down barriers that emerge from different backgrounds and living in different neighborhoods expands social capital and highlights the importance of bridging social capital.

Camp CAMERA embraces a curriculum that addresses technical aspects related to photography, artistic principles, and communication/interpersonal relationship building. This emphasis on social relationships played an instrumental role in fostering expanding peer networks but also in the establishment of friendships within the participant group and also between participants and Macalester student volunteers.

Activities became the mechanism through which social relationships emerged and maintained high attendance levels. Each session began with a 30-minute icebreaker exercise that required youth participants and college students to share aspects of themselves; this sharing highlighted commonalities as well as differences. Having both youth participants and student volunteers together and sharing helped each group learn from the other. The label "mentor" was never used in the program because this label often stresses a power differentiation between mentee and mentor. Everyone in the program was there to learn from each other.

The friendships developed within the program transferred over to outside the program. For example, even though many youth participants attended the same high school, separate grades meant that they had minimal contact with each other. However, as a result of participation in Camp CAMERA, older participants would connect with younger participants in the high school and were in a position to help guide younger participants through the high school experience. Participants living in the same community were able to look out for each other because of their connections in the program.

There are a distinct set of values and principles guiding Camp CAMERA's conceptualization. The values embraced are very similar to those identified in Chapter 2: embrace of diversity, experiential and incidental learning, community investment, leadership development, utilization of local and self-knowledge, cultural competency/cultural humility, and social justice. The focus on these values facilitated youth taking chances and seeking new relationships beyond the program.

Camp CAMERA provided an opportunity to establish positive relationships with older youth. These youth got to know college students as well as making friends with many of their peers through weekly team building, icebreakers, and workshop activities on campus. Youth were able to step out of their comfort zone and join a community of trust centered on photographic activities. Leaving their comfort zones resulted in painful and tension-producing experiences. This can be thought of as part of a learning experience, which will hopefully better prepare them for future encounters that expose them to new relationship experiences.

One Camp CAMERA participant with interests in becoming a marine biologist addressed the importance of friendships in helping her achieve this goal in a photograph she took: "As a student who has a dream to become a marine biologist, a lot of people tell me. 'It's not about what you know, but who you know.' This photo exemplifies that the relationships that one makes can benefit them in the long run. It could be as simple as making wise choices among the group of friends one chooses to be around, or it can be as easy as introducing yourself to different people. Having a relationship and connection with positive people will benefit the individual in his/her future. This photo focuses on the web of people holding each other up. Connections and positive relations will build a better, healthier community." Social capital is often looked on as a key ingredient in expanding possibilities beyond local communities, and this student is cognizant of how social capital brings forth instrumental and expressive benefits.

The exhibition of photographs provided youth participants with an opportunity to invite key members of their social network to attend, including friends from their neighborhood. This format allowed them to celebrate with those members of their social network that they valued and represented a fitting end to their unique experience. In addition, it showcased how this group became a collective through sharing and taking chances, key elements in any friendship development process.

RESEARCH/EVALUATION IMPLICATIONS

Researchers and evaluators seeking to capture the importance of relationships and friendships in Camp CAMERA will quickly see the power of the group in shaping these relationships and the need to capture how a collectivistic view of friendship development, introducing the use of social capital in a manner that goes beyond one-to-one, opens up possibilities for joining other groups over the course of a lifetime. There are many different levels of social capital.

The sharing of personal information that provided insights into why photographs were taken and how the photos provided a window into who the photographer was represented a new way of capturing motivation and sentiments that require nuanced understanding. In addition, how youth change over the course of program participation, and more specifically how they have changed in attitudes toward others from different neighborhoods and racial and ethnic backgrounds, is critical for researchers and evaluators. In essence, transformation occurs over an extended period of time; it is necessary to see this transformation through a development frame in order to fully understand how it has changed the individual in seeking to establish new friendships.

Youth–adult relationships introduce a key emerging theme in the field of youth community practice, and research and evaluators must actively seek to shed light on how and why the relationship between a program leader and youth participants carries over into viewing adults as potential friends and allies rather than as authority figures. Breaking down perception barriers like this is essential in broadening relationships across age groups to include adults.

IMPORTANT RESULTS AND LESSONS LEARNED

The social interactions and the need to share oneself are hallmarks of a photovoice project such as Camp CAMERA. The selection of photographs and the reasons why they were selected allow participants to both listen and share. These experiences can be quite emotional, providing participants with an opportunity to develop and enhance skills conducive to the development of social relationships.

Activities such as icebreakers can play an influential role in breaking down stereotypes and helping youth to see commonalities where only differences existed prior to the program experience. Validating and offering advice based on personal experiences, for example, are common skills that help build social relationships. Common themes emerge through this process, and a group bonding experienced can manifest itself in relationships outside of program hours and activities.

Food also facilitated the development of social relationships, including helping to cement new friendships in Camp CAMERA. Youth shopped for food together, thus introducing an activity that is nonthreatening and that facilitates the sharing of thoughts and experiences regarding meals. They also cooked and cleaned up together, again providing an opportunity to engage in a non–highly charged context that facilitated individual and group relationship building. Finally, the process of eating or sharing bread together provided a conducive climate and a moment to engage with each other in a safe space and helped break down barriers between youth and adults.

Careful attention to the staff–participant ratio is essential. A low ratio helps ensure that relationship building can transpire and facilitates the sharing of expectations and communication. However, making sure that there is no separation where youth are there to be taught and staff/volunteers are there to teach should be avoided at all cost. Sharing across age, racial/ethnic, social class groups is rare. Having everyone involved with a program share and learn, equalizes potential power differences.

One youth reflected on the Camp CAMERA experience by saying, "I feel like by the end of the program I was close with everyone." Another student wrote, "It made me realize that even our smallest interactions with people can have such a profound impact." Activities in which youth pair up can begin with friends pairing up; however, as a program unfolds, every effort must be made to encourage new pairings based on strategic decisions that facilitate an expansion of a participants' social network and even friendships.

One activity used in the last session at Camp CAMERA captures these sentiments very well. Each participant, both youth and college volunteers, put her name on a paper plate, strung a cord through a hole in the plate, and put it around her neck, with the plate on her back. As they interacted with the group, each member would write something affirming about the individual on the person's paper plate. These statements could be signed or anonymous. At end of the session, the plates would be removed and everyone had an opportunity to read their plates and share the information with others. These plates, not surprising, became mementos of their experience in learning and sharing while in the program and of the new relationships they developed.

The close similarity in ages between youth participants and student volunteers was minimized because the student volunteers were primarily providing technical assistance with photography, making it easier for Camp CAMERA youth to accept this assistance. Although the technical interactions led the way in the relationships, this also opened up the door for social relationships to evolve and even flourish.

Case 2: "Photovoice in Overtown," Miami, Florida

OVERVIEW

As noted in the brief review of the literature involving Camp CAMERA, photovoice lends itself to addressing a wide variety of themes and issues of particular relevance to urban youth of color. In this case, the theme of identifying assets for the children and youth of Overtown, Miami, involved developing a community assets map (Delgado & Humm-Delgado, 2013) and presenting it to their community as a gift. However, the youth participants in this project, through purposefully carrying out activities sometimes in pairs, developed social relationships and friendships that carried over into their community.

Photovoice provides a visual representation of community assets, although not all assets lend themselves to being portrayed in a visual manner. Lightfoot et al. (2012), for example, describe the importance of using youth friendship groups within a black churches photovoice HIV prevention project and how these resources can facilitate the introduction of an intervention that has historically been difficult to introduce in such a setting.

An assets approach to community offers endless potential for grounding youth in a positive view of their community without losing sight of the issues of social justice in their lives (Kovacic, Stigler, Smith, Kidd, & Vaughn, 2014). Furthermore, an assets approach broadens social networks beyond a narrow confine, opening up the potential for establishing new friendships based on a positive set of assumptions. The relationships that youth develop, both within a program and outside in the community, can be considered direct benefits of an asset-focused project such as the one undertaken in Overtown, Miami (Richardson, 2011).

BRIEF REVIEW OF THE LITERATURE

The goals of a photovoice project can focus on a perceived need or issue as well as on assets or an affirming purpose (Delgado & Humm-Delgado, 2013; Sutton-Brown, 2014). This flexibility makes this form of research particularly attractive in responding to local issues and needs. This method also can easily focus on friendships and the elements that make them special and the places where these relationships can be formed and fostered.

Using photovoice to identify African-American youth/community assets is viable and attractive. However, assets are dynamic and interact with other assets, thus raising challenges in isolating, measuring, and mobilizing them (Elias Rodas, 2011). Teixeira (2015) found in a youth photovoice study of neighborhood vacant lots that their perceptions of neighborhood features may alter outcomes related to anxiety and hopelessness, thus highlighting the multiple instrumental and expressive benefits for engaging youth in assessing and intervening in their community.

Skovdal and Ogutu (2012) report on the establishment of friendship clubs with the explicit purpose of helping HIV-infected Kenyan youth develop these social relationships as a means of helping them develop social capital and using photovoice as a mechanism to facilitate this goal. Skovdal and Ogutu do a wonderful job of highlighting how youth friendships, social capital, and, in this case, challenges related HIV status, raise the potential of friendships to aid in periods of great stress, and they use photovoice as a mechanism to help these youth share their narratives.

In the case of Overtown, Miami, youth participatory action research helped youth enhance their competencies but also helped them make unanticipated social connections (social capital) with each other. Having a defined purpose and support facilitates relationship building and addressing topics that may be very difficult to capture with a visual representation, as in the case of attitudes and cultural competencies, for example (Johansen & Le, 2014).

Photovoice projects are group projects, and these groups can accommodate different numbers of participants. Photovoice projects usually consist of six phases or stages: (1) assessment (needs and assets) of goals; (2) planning, scheduling, and implementation; (3) selection of images/narratives; (4) cultural final portrait/exhibition; (5) project evaluation; and (6) social change action. Each of these stages presents an opportunity for youth to bond with the group and enhance their social relationships with others in the group.

Photovoice is an instrument for bringing forth social change. Sanon, Evans-Agnew and Boutain (2014) undertook a meta-review of social justice intent in photovoice research studies (2008–13) and found that these studies emphasized awareness (13 out of 30) over amelioration ($n = 11$) or transformation ($n = 3$), thus raising the need for social action to be a guiding principle. Thus, photovoice and community asset assessment can reinforce social network expansion and relationship building for youth participants and set the stage for social action, as in the case of Overtown, Miami.

DESCRIPTION OF THE YOUTH GROUP AND ORGANIZATIONAL SETTING

Overtown, Miami, is a neighborhood primarily composed of African Americans and so were the youth who participated in this project, although representing different geographical areas of the Overtown community. Overtown is considered one of the oldest neighborhoods within the original boundaries of the City of Miami (Fields, 2015). It is geographically adjacent to downtown Miami.

It has a history of being segregated by custom and laws and was home to blacks who built and maintained the railroad, streets, and hotels. Fields (2015, p. 1) comments on the role and influence of newcomers to this community: "Over time, immigrants arrived from Cuba, Haiti, Jamaica, Trinidad and Tobago, Barbados and other countries throughout the Western Hemisphere. Their common heritage was their slave fore-parents, forced from Africa and left as cargo in various ports throughout America. Different cultures developed in the various ports and some languages changed, but the common ground for all was race. These skilled migrants and immigrants arrived with a determination to improve economic conditions for their families. In turn they helped build Miami and Miami Beach, a tourist mecca for others to enjoy."

"Photovoice in Overtown" is a collaborative undertaking by the Overtown Community, the Overtown Children and Youth Coalition, and Barry University's School of Social Work, and it illustrates the potential of bringing university resources to benefit communities while advancing a scholarly agenda. Two showings were undertaken, one based at a community center and the second at Barry University, thus bringing together two worlds that can often coexist as if they were in different dimensions. The presentation was part of an informal community gathering and facilitated youth having their family and friends attending.

Urgent, Inc. reached out to Dr. McGhee at Barry University School of Social Work with the idea of a photovoice project focused on Overtown's community assets. Urgent, Inc. had undertaken a previous photovoice project and was particularly interested in a follow-up. Urgent, Inc. was an ideal community organization to carry out this project: "URGENT, Inc. is a 501(c)(3) Miami, FL based youth and community development organization dedicated to empowering young minds to transform their communities. Guided by the principles of innovation, growth and transformation URGENT sees young people as the drivers of change and works to provide empowering opportunities to create the next generation of social change agents."

Its mission, vision, and goals set the stage for a community asset photovoice project: "MISSION – To empower young minds to help transform their communities VISION – All people have the social, economic and educational resources to thrive CORE VALUES – Compassion, Innovation, Patience, Learning, Reciprocity, Responsibility, Teamwork." These core values are found throughout the literature on friendships covered in this book and thus facilitated social relationship development.

HOW THE INTERVENTION FOCUSED ON YOUTH FRIENDSHIP

The name of the project was "What Are the Assets of and for the Children of Overtown." It was only fitting that youth played an influential role in having their voices heard on this topic and shaping how it unfolded. A similar project that focused on older adults, for example, would present a very different portrait of Overtown, maybe to the point that an outsider would be hard pressed to think we were talking about the same community.

Dr. John Hope Franklin, the nationally known historian, as quoted by Fields (2015, p. 1), summed up well the importance of Overtown and its community assets to the City of Miami: "This is a very historical area . . . . The very history of Miami is incomplete without the history of Overtown." Miami's changing demographics regarding Latinos has produced a national identity of it being a Latino city. Consequently, the history of African-Americans/blacks in this city has largely been overshadowed by the influx of Latinos and has largely disappeared on the national scene, thus undermining the historical contributions of African-Americans/blacks in the city. Having its youth capture this history is fitting because they will help carry it on to future generations.

The youth made a presentation of "Overtown Voices: Photovoice Exhibition" that showcased a participatory research project with aims to "elevate the voices of Overtown stakeholders and foster community-level and community-engaged transformation through the use of photography, reflection, and informed action." This was a low-pressure presentation, it should be noted.

Community asset assessments cannot achieve their lofty goals without positive social relationships taking place in the process, and that is certainly the case in Overtown, Miami. Numerous group gatherings and activities provided ample opportunities for youth to share collectively and develop group bonding. Individual relationships, however, were formed through pairings and small group activities. When youth are able to engage in activities that are meaningful to them, and they are paired, it reinforces the value of their work and helps them form relationships with others who share similar sentiments and values.

RESEARCH/EVALUATION IMPLICATIONS

Drawing program participants from different communities opens up the potential for establishing friendships that cross traditional geographical boundaries, which is often an important goal in helping to expand the horizons of youth who are often restricted in crossing neighborhood boundaries. Expanding these options can be a central goal of social research/evaluation.

Friendships may begin while participating in a program, but much happens outside of a program to further enhance these relationships. Consequently, researchers and evaluators have to gain greater insight into how free time is shaped to reach out and establish and maintain friendships. It would be foolhardy to think that friendships developed during program participation can be maintained after participation occurs. Much can transpire outside of the program.

Communities with long and distinguished histories bring added challenges for researchers and evaluators to capture how these histories shape current relationships, including friendships that cross racial and ethnic lines within and between neighborhoods. These communities, too, had reputations that either attracted or repelled visitors. It is not unusual to have friendships develop within these neighborhoods and have them span an extended period of time simply because residents do not leave.

Researching youth friendships, as a result, can benefit from a multifaceted approach that allows youth to play central roles in shaping the research undertakings in order to capture nuances that often exist in communities with long and well-known histories.

IMPORTANT RESULTS AND LESSONS LEARNED

The activities that formed the basis for the project were instrumental helping youth to engage with an enthusiasm that is rare in their lives. Being part of a community conversation in which their voices were actively sought and held a prominent place created an affirming and inclusive climate. Even though youth were from the Overtown community, many lived in different parts and did not know each other. Although friendships served to bring some of the youth into the project, new friendships developed through pairings that facilitated new social relationships based on shared goals and activities. These pairings involved both males and females, bringing a cross-gendered opportunity to establishing social relationships and possible friendships.

Five key themes emerged from the photovoice asset mapping approach: awareness; education; empowerment; past, present, future; and potential.

One youth participant summed up the importance of the social interconnectedness of Overtown youth: "In Overtown, if it is not for the children we have no Overtown. We have no future. They are the sustainers. We say that the elders are the anchors. The parents and young adults are the coaches, and the children are the drivers of change. So without the children there is no change. And behind every decision we make, we make sure that we have a kid's face, so we are making the right decision for the children."

This conceptualization illustrates the importance of taking a holistic perspective on a community, with every age group playing an important role in sustaining and enhancing a community's well-being and interconnectedness. The role of youth as agents of social change is not new to youth and taps into the importance of social justice values guiding their actions (Delgado, 2016a, 2016b). This role is predicated on having a strong understanding of a community's history and its strengths and challenges.

Intergenerational connections were found to be of great importance for these youth: "It is a great thing to know that the current Ms. Overtown knows the old Ms Overtown because some of our youth do not know what our ancestors did to pave the way for us to be where we are now." Social relationships, including friendships, can span significant age groups, and intergenerational friendships can bring their own set of rewards as they help ground youth within a cultural and historical context. In the case of older adults, it helps connect them with a younger generation that is often depicted as dangerous and to be avoided, thus causing a great age divide in some communities.

Not surprisingly, youth participants developed relationship with the two adult participants. The adult participant from Urgent, Inc. possessed interpersonal qualities that made it easy for youth to connect and develop friendships with. This social relationship can be expected to bear fruit in enlisting future youth participants to Urgent, Inc. programs because of the role friends play in recruiting their friends into after-school activities.

One youth participant captured the sentiments of the group: "We need to have more programs like this; it needs to be expanded. More enrichment programs in general." Enrichment not only referred to new knowledge and skill acquisition, but also to relationship and friendships. Another participant specifically targeted the role of activities in creating an affirming and empowering experience. "When you involve kids in art, education, and transformative experiences, community pride increases and more people engage in community activities." When activities are carefully planned and youth partner with other youth they do not know, it enhances the opportunity for new social relationships.

Case 3: Digital Storytelling and Newcomer Youth in Georgia

OVERVIEW

Newcomer youth and the challenges they face in this country is worthy of attention. The case illustration that follows brings together the use of digital storytelling and technology and a newcomer youth group (Burmese and Thai Karen people). Digital technology has been found to be an effective method for engaging newcomer youth (Gilhooly & Lee, 2014; Prinsen, de Haan, & Leander, 2015).

Storytelling can involve a variety of methods such as cartoons, movies, music narratives, photographs, and videos allowing youth to use their preferred artistic means for expressing themselves and taking into account cultural beliefs, values, and expectations. This flexibility is particularly attractive for newcomer youth with limited language and social skills and who are contending with acculturation challenges. This case illustration brings together newcomer youth, technology, and the importance of social relationships such as friends in their lives.

BRIEF REVIEW OF THE LITERATURE

Although friendships are important to all youth regardless of their ethnic and racial backgrounds, they take on greater significance among newcomer youth because of the challenges associated with adjusting to a new homeland (McGovern & Devine, 2016). The importance of technology and social media among youth of all backgrounds has been addressed earlier in this book and will also be addressed in Chapter 6 in a discussion of innovative youth-friendly research methods and in the Conclusion. Oh (2012), for example, specifically addresses the use of photovoice in fostering social relationships, including friendships with refugee youth in Thailand.

It is appropriate to highlight a case example involving technology, and, in this case it addresses the use of digital storytelling and social skill development because of its potential to reach out across youth groups, particularly to those who may be socially isolated because of their social circumstances. Digital storytelling brings a new and, what many including this author consider, potentially significant method for integrating youth narratives and technology; when conceptualized as creative arts, creative writing, theatre, and autobiography programming it introduces a natural medium for youth to share with their peer and friendship networks (Alrutz, 2014; Warschauer & Matuchniak, 2010).

The sharing of personal narratives provides a bridge within a classroom or program for friendships to be examined and understood and for them to occur under a very protected environment that allows youth to take the necessary risks often associated with sharing personal stories (Blummer, 2008; London, Pastor, Servon, Rosner, & Wallace, 2006, 2010; Lovell & Baker, 2009). Hewitt and Lee (2012) discuss how Canadian First Nation youth were able to develop meaningful friendships with non-First Nation youth through narrative exchanges. Opportunities to undertake these types of exchanges between white, non-Latinos and youth of color, however, are rare.

Youth community practice is becoming an integral part of programming because of its attractiveness as a recruitment method and as a vehicle for programming activities.

The increasing use of technology in developing and maintaining social relationships, including friendships, makes digital storytelling a youth-friendly method for expanding this network (Buskirk-Cohen, 2015; Collin & Burns, 2009; Hopkins & Ryan, 2014). Lambert (2013, p. 4) describes the attractiveness of digital storytelling:

> Many people, and communities, are waking up to the power of their own voice in the media, and finding the means to express themselves, for themselves and their communities through the new media. Change is constant, from iPhone apps to produce and edit digital stories, to intensely creative social media projects like cowbird (www.cowbird.com), we can imagine a thousand new ways to lure us into sharing our stories. We are just beginning to see how our shared creativity will become our main ways of entertaining each other.

Digital technology's potential is greatest with a generation that knows no other world than the digital world and is comfortable using this technology to produce the story they wish to share with others.

Digital storytelling can be viewed as both a research method and an intervention. The former provides a window into friendship narratives and how they are conceived, including their rewards and challenges, thus setting the stage for the development of an intervention. In the latter, friendship storytelling can be thought of as a means for creating and expanding the friendship networks of program participants.

The sharing of personal narratives provides a bridge within a classroom or program for friendships to be examined and understood and for them to occur (Blummer, 2008; London et al., 2006, 2010; Lovell & Baker, 2009). Youth community practice can help bridge potential barriers between parents and youth, as in the case of Latino parents and their children (Fuller, Lizárraga, & Gray, 2015).

DESCRIPTION OF THE YOUTH GROUP AND ORGANIZATIONAL SETTING

The Karen people from Myanmar, formerly known as Burma, are an ethnic group that has sought asylum in the United States as a result of a long history of political upheaval in that country. This case study is based on two brothers aged 15 (arrived in the United States at age 12 years) and 17 years (arrived at age 15 years) who were resettled in Georgia. Resettlement in Georgia represented a serious challenge in connecting with other Karen youth.

Schools, as noted through this book, are ideal settings to help youth connect with other youth and develop friendships. When this is not possible because of social climate or circumstances, information technology provides an accessible way to do so within and outside of a school setting.

HOW THE INTERVENTION FOCUSED ON YOUTH FRIENDSHIPS

Friendship networks can involve in-person and online friends, with technology allowing immigrant youth to cross geography and time zones (Gilhooly & Lee, 2014, p. 389): "Language, therefore, is viewed not simply as a set of skills to be mastered but as an ever-reoccurring part of the social experience of life. For the brothers, their online worlds are their primary sites for socialization and information gathering and, therefore, their literate lives. Their participation in online spaces provides access to social worlds otherwise denied to them because of their second-language limitations, rural isolation, and outsider status at school and within the host community."

Technology, when accessible and mastered, expands the world of resettled refugee youth and helps transition them into their new surroundings. In essence, it can supplement existing relationships where some exist or completely develop them where none exist locally. Gilhooly and Lee (2014, p. 395) talk about the space that technology creates for social relationships to unfold in a very controlled manner:

> The Internet and other digital media provide new immigrant youths with a means to cope with and thrive in their new communities. Technology, in all its incarnations, can and does give marginalized students a place in a classroom and their community, and it positions them to socialize and build friendships that support their transnational lives. Moreover, it provides them with the creative license to express and explore self, their heritage culture, and the host culture.

This creative license increases in significance the more youth feel isolated, and newcomer youth fall into this category because of their cultural and language backgrounds, as in the case of Burmese newcomer youth. Facebook has opened up an avenue for isolated youth to reach out and connect with other youth outside of their immediate peer network and establish friendships, as evidenced in this case illustration.

RESEARCH/EVALUATION IMPLICATIONS

There are tremendous rewards and challenges in capturing how digital relationships transform into friendships and how these friendships are similar or dissimilar to those based on conventional place-based friendships. Are these relationships more significant for newcomer youth who are very limited in their mobility geographically and due to limited English proficiency? How can these friendships be supplemented locally in cases where these youth have local friendships but find them unsatisfactory?

As noted earlier throughout various sections of this book, social media has introduced new perspectives on relationships and more specifically on friendships. Youth who are newcomers to this country are no longer dependent on local relationships and can still maintain contact with friends in their country of origin. The days of letter writing to maintain contact with the "old country" are no longer viable. Understanding the benefits and limitations of such relationships can draw on knowledge gained in social media use in this country. However, our understanding of the transnational aspects of youth friendships is still in its infancy.

Ethnographic research, particularly participant observations, played an important role in increasing our understandings of newcomer youth. It introduces a research approach that holds much meaning for newcomer youth and taps into their interests in narratives pertaining to entering a new world and community. These forms of qualitative research, in turn, lend themselves to addressing goals that are modest as well as those that are ambitious, including corresponding budgets.

IMPORTANT RESULTS AND LESSONS LEARNED

Technology played an instrumental role in helping the brothers in broadening their friendship/peer social network and assisting them in acquiring language skills and developing a more in-depth understanding of their new country. Gilhooly and Lee (2014, p. 391) identified four key findings on how involvement in various online literacy spaces served the youth and family: "(1) maintaining and building coethnic friendships, (2) connecting to the broader Karen diaspora community, (3) sustaining and promoting ethnic solidarity, and (4) creating and disseminating digital productions."

Technology allows youth to move at a pace that suits their needs, personalities, and competencies, and it provides them with a tool, as in the case of digital storytelling, that best matches their comfort level in sharing their stories. This flexibility taps into the relative easy accessibility of technology and allows youth to both increase their technological competencies while reaching new contacts that can evolve into friendships. Technology, obviously, is not for every youth. Nevertheless, it can be considered a potentially viable option that can be part of a constellation of social relationship building activities.

Case 4: Youth Action, Midwestern City

OVERVIEW

No community intervention seeking to be integrated into the basic social fabric of an urban neighborhood can ignore the social relationships of youth participants.

Marginalized youth are separated from society, but they can also be separated from each other. Urban youth may share the same geographic confines and attend the same schools, but possessing racist views and living with stereotypes undermines their ability to form social relationships and friendships with diverse groups of youth.

Watkins, Larson, and Sullivan (2007) provide a unique youth development case study illustrating how relationships and friendships can be a part of an intervention that is social action–oriented, even though this are not the central focus of the intervention. This case involved youth developing relationships (changing attitudes and behaviors) across ethnic and racial lines while in the process of undertaking a social justice campaign focused on a particular disease. The case highlights the development of a critical understanding of the interpersonal and systemic processes that result in marginalization and injustice.

BRIEF REVIEW OF THE LITERATURE

Themes of oppression and its deleterious consequences for urban youth of color are well documented in this book and particularly in Chapter 4. One of the major criticisms of PYD is the need for this approach to embrace social justice to make interventions relevant for urban youth who face oppression on a daily basis. Youth social action has great saliency in urban communities of color because of how this method taps youth's sense of justice. However, these efforts can also serve as a mechanism for creating social relationships across ethnic and racial groups, including friendships.

The introduction of social justice values and the resulting social actions as activities is one way of making PYD relevant. Bringing youth from different racial and ethnic backgrounds together in pursuit of social justice goals, however, requires a conscious effort to address racism and stereotypes in order for them to work together effectively and expand their social networks in the process of seeking justice. One of the benefits of bringing diverse groups together is the creation of opportunities for social relationships and friendships to occur outside of one's own group.

Ardizzone (2007, p. 39) poses a series of questions that set the stage for why social change inspired by social justice creates a climate for the learning and change that results from youth social activism: "What makes learning to action? Why does social responsibility serve as an impetus for activism? What 'clicks' for these young people and how do their conscienziation come about?" One of the secondary benefits of youth social action is the social relationships that emerge through this process and the camaraderie it creates (Delgado & Staples, 2008, 2013).

Youth social activism is a legitimate form of democratic protest and represents a counter-narrative to prevailing views on this form of youth community practice activity (Costanza-Chock, 2012, p. 5): "Youth are often dismissed for a lack of civic engagement, or attacked for being disruptive. Yet disruption of oppressive laws, norms, and practices is a crucial aspect of all liberatory movements: think of the struggle to end slavery, or to gain suffrage for women." Youth engagement in social protest stands as testament to their willingness to become involved in creating a better world for themselves and others and is a far cry from their being seen as apathetic, which is counter to prevailing adult views.

Creating an atmosphere where youth feel comfortable and safe to exchange and learn is a fundamental part of critical literacy. Learning about race and ethnicity and why and how certain groups are marginalized and oppressed will lead to activities such as social action to bring change and, in the process, establish important social contacts and relationships. Bishop (2014), for example, addresses the role of critical literacy in shaping youth organizers:

> Youth organizing programming . . . can offer a generative, safe space within community-based organizations from which to engage young people in critical reflection upon their social and political contexts, to collectively envision and take action for positive change. As a space not congested by external measures of formal education, organizing projects provide an informal youth development platform through which critical literacy learning is more fully realized . . . [and] call for further creation of such safe spaces for ethical, intersubjective, social justice youth activism.

The case illustration of Youth Action brings together the concepts of critical literacy, social action, and praxis in a manner that enhances youth participant friendship development.

DESCRIPTION OF THE YOUTH GROUP AND ORGANIZATIONAL SETTING

This case illustration took place in an unidentified large Midwestern city. Youth Action is a community-based program that seeks to achieve positive social change with a central focus on schools (citywide summit, lobbied school board, organized rally against high-stakes testing, research on disproportionate suspensions and expulsions). The initiative involved 20–25 core members who were either Latino or African American drawn from various city high schools. The Youth Action mission was to empower youth through "building the leadership and power of young people to work for community and institutional change."

Ten members were selected to be part of the research and were interviewed with attention to gender (5 female and 5 male), age, length of participation, and ethnicity and race (6 Latino and 4 African American).

HOW THE INTERVENTION FOCUSED ON YOUTH FRIENDSHIP

Bridging differences was a central theme, and this was manifested through embracing a social change agenda that youth shared. Activities related to the change goal, in turn, allowed youth to work together and, through praxis, understand their commonalities regarding oppression even though they differed in terms of racial and ethnic backgrounds. Workshops on various ethnic and racial leaders against oppression, for example, created a climate that helped youth examine their biases toward other ethnic and racial groups and facilitated dialogue on a very sensitive subject.

The following quotes illustrate how youth participants harbored negative stereotypical views of youth outside of their group (Watkins et al., 2007, p. 388):

> I used to be a pretty big jerk to people that were different from me. I would make a bunch of like horrible racial slurs and stuff like that.

> Before I got involved in Youth Action, I was brainwashed [homophobic] by my friends' parents and my friends. [I used to be] like, "Oh, f—n' faggots and like queers" and just like talking mad shit.

> Before I got here, I ain't talked to nobody out of my race.

> I grew up in a Latino community. I really didn't think about different ethnic backgrounds. But you can't help but [develop] stereotypes, like the racism that you see in the community. Like if you were in a car or something and you passed a predominantly African-American community: "Lock your doors because they're gonna do something."

These quotes do a wonderful job of highlighting how youth sharing the same community may still be isolated from groups outside their own. Having an opportunity to go outside of one's own group, facilitated through social justice education and action, helps youth broaden their social peer networks, see the commonalities they share with others, and develop an appreciation of the differences as well.

RESEARCH/EVALUATION IMPLICATIONS

Bringing together youth from very disparate backgrounds and levels of acculturation may seem like a challenge, and it certainly is, but not as great a challenge as adults fear. The process of co-learning about cultures and histories is one that possesses rewards and challenges for researchers and evaluators, particularly in discovering the impact of parents and legal guardians on the development of these new friendships. Although it is tempting to develop an understanding of the process and hurdles that youth face in developing unconventional friendships when viewed from an ethnic and racial perspective, we must ask what roles adults in their lives play in fostering or hindering the continued growth of these friendships.

The introduction of a co-learning concept also facilitates the introduction of educational goals into programming that, on the surface, does not address education. Research and evaluation, as a result, need to not only focus on youth but also on how staff and other adults in their lives have been transformed. An individualistic approach toward evaluation translates into a focus on youth participants.

However, a collectivistic stance necessitates a broader reach in research and evaluation. This broadening of the goal of research and evaluation makes it more challenging from a cost and conceptual standpoint.

Research and evaluation methods that focus on co-learning strategies help break down adultist barriers, and it is important to capture how this transpires and its implications beyond the research undertaking. Qualitative methods, not unexpectedly, stand out as the most viable and attractive in such endeavors because youth can feel that they have a role to play in carrying out this type of research. Co-learning, it must be emphasized, must not restrict itself to cognitive subjects but must also seek to increase knowledge about how age, socioeconomic status, and other demographic factors influence the learning process both short- and long-term. This makes the research process more exciting for urban youth and facilitates the introduction of social justice themes.

IMPORTANT RESULTS AND LESSONS LEARNED

Mutual learning and the change that results is powerful in the lives of urban youth if given opportunity and a supportive environment. Social justice goals help identify commonalities regarding oppression; social change activities, in turn, provide a concrete mechanism through which to engage in dialogue.

These interactions lead to the formation of peer contacts and friendships that cross ethnicity and race and that help create a more sophisticated view of people, as noted by one youth (Watkins et al., 2007, p. 388): "You meet a whole bunch of different people. During the summer program. I met a lot of Arab people. I met people with different sexual preferences. I got to meet some socialists, which was kind of weird. I also met some Russians too, [which] was kinda cool." Another youth captured an important lesson (p. 389): "You know at school they're mostly black people, or white people. Latino, like that? Right here there's like Arabian, Chinese, I don't know, there is a lot of them, and we go out to places to eat once in a while. It's like we do things together." Youth learn about those who are different by using their own experiences to measure or judge others' beliefs and experiences. This highlights the importance of experiential learning as compared to conventional academic/book learning. There are many different forms of knowledge, as noted in Chapter 3, and youth can be made aware of this as a way of validating the knowledge that they possess but that did not originate in formal education.

Those working with urban youth, too, must be prepared to share their own narratives as a means of setting the tone and reinforcing how the process of learning can transpire. Sharing our stories represents a critical step in the journey of breaking down the stereotypes that youth and adults may have about each other, and the same can be said about ethnic/racial backgrounds and neighborhoods.

Opportunities (places and spaces) for urban youth to learn about their own histories and that of others are rare, and it would take an exceptionally socially secured youth to venture out on his or her own to accomplish these learning goals.

Youth community practice can create these opportunities while pursuing goals related to social justice. Activities that foster exchanges such as those in Youth Action can be integrated into programming. The social benefits derived can be considered as important as the social justice goals achieved, including lasting and meaningful friendships.

Conclusion

Case illustrations have a wonderful capacity to bring highly abstract concepts to life. This chapter sought to help the reader concretize the role and importance of developing friendships as either a primary or secondary goal. The four case illustrations in this chapter did not have the depth associated with traditional case studies and, as a result, do not have the richness of details associated with such in-depth studies. Nevertheless, the range of case illustrations provided the reader with examples of the varied ways that urban youth friendships can be conceptualized and carried out to take into account a range of budgets and program goals.

The cases generally involved use of technology in facilitating social exchanges; again, this should not be surprising based on youth fascination and competencies with social communication technology. This does not mean, however, that youth social skills and their abilities to establish and maintain friendships cannot be enhanced in the old fashioned way, through group activities, for example. Finally, as noted in the Youth Action case illustration, because youth bring biases concerning ethnic and racial groups, these must be addressed in an affirming and nonthreatening manner in order for them to be open to expanding their peer network and even establishing friendships outside of their own group, a key goal as cities grow more diverse.

6

Co-Production of Knowledge

URBAN YOUTH OF COLOR AS RESEARCHERS OF FRIENDSHIPS

Introduction

The subject of research is integrally related to community practice although it generally is covered in the professional literature as its own category and often is expected to be carried out by a different set of actors. Community practitioners are supposed to take this newfound knowledge and then apply it. "Good" community practitioners never have the luxury of relegating research to someone else. In fact, the more that staff can be involved in all facets of a program, the greater the chances of staff ownership of what happens as a result of an intervention, and the greater the insights on what findings mean. When youth actively participate in the research as co-researchers they are, in turn, in a better position to be involved in the programming and evaluation of their efforts (Bulanda, Tellis, & Tyson McCrea 2015; Delgado, 2006).

Youth community practitioners must be prepared to play an active and meaningful part in all segments of an urban-based intervention, including the role of advocates for greater youth participation in shaping local responses. This helps to ensure the integrity of the process. This is not to say that the production of knowledge generated through research and program implementation will not be challenging, because it will. Nevertheless, including youth as co-researchers is indispensable, and it brings joy and excitement, too, to all parties involved in this form of endeavor.

The dearth of knowledge on urban youth friendships must be addressed before community practice interventions can be developed based on a sound understanding of this form of peer relationship and its social implications. Researching youth friendships will help researchers and practitioners better ground our understanding of how youth handle crises and the everyday hassles associated with a lived urban experience, and importantly, what can be done to build on this asset to increase the likelihood of these youth achieving lifelong success (Sassi & Thomas, 2012).

Woodman and Wyn (2013) put forth a persuasive argument that innovative research and social interventions are needed to comprehensively understand the influence of social conditions on young people's lives. "Pushing the envelope" must be a part of urban community practitioners mindset when engaging youth.

However, it is rare to find field-based examples of how youth can research this topic and generate new insights or knowledge that can influence policy and community-centered programmatic interventions (Heath & Walker, 2012). Boocock & Scott (2005, p. 33) address adult ideological bias:

> While women and members of racial and ethnic minorities have fought for and (to a varying degrees) gained the right to define themselves rather than simply being objects of research by their social superiors, children rarely study themselves and just as rarely have any say in how they are studied. This tendency to obtain, analyze, and interpret data about children from the perspective of nonchildren has been termed the *adult ideological bias.*

This bias is formidable and often goes unrecognized and unchallenged by fellow adults, thus making addressing it that much more arduous. Making this bias visible is a critical step in addressing it.

Having youth give voice to their own experiences and views opens up the potential for exciting new insights and interpretations of their lived experience (Schaefer, 2012a). Fortunately, innovative approaches, including casting youth as researchers and knowledge producers, are emerging and have the potential to generate research findings that are sensitive and open to youth interpretations (Beebeejaun, Durose, Rees, Richardson, & Richardson, 2014; Liebenberg & Theron, 2015).

Youth-led research has been integrated into positive youth development (PYD), reinforcing the concepts of youth participation and empowerment (Alfonso, Bogues, Russo, & Brown, 2008). Nevertheless, there is a need for a non-adult view of this field, with youth–adult teams being one possible option (White, Shoffner, Johnson, Knowles, & Mills, 2012). This chapter lays out a conceptual and ethical argument for the need to approach urban youth friendships from a youth empowering and affirming perspective. This chapter will also highlight examples of youth researching the subject of friendships (Zenkov & Harmon, 2009, 2014). This research approach goes by many different names in the professional literature. However, four standout methods—collaborative, co-produced, youth participatory action research (YPAR), and peer research—and their engagement of youth as active members of the research process will be a central theme in this chapter.

Community Participatory Research

There are a variety of ways to frame this chapter to concisely stress highly relevant approaches to knowledge creation that meet the needs of the youth community practice field and offer great promise for increasing our understanding of urban youth friendships. The vibrancy associated with community-based participatory research (CBPR) is contagious and very relevant to this chapter. It serves as an excellent overarching framework that can help community practitioners categorize various research approaches to make an informed judgment on their viability for understanding youth in general and friendships in particular (Jacquez, Vaughn, & Wagner, 2013; Stoecker, 2013).

Community-based participatory research has continued to find a prominent place within the social sciences and helping professions, and it provides an umbrella with a sufficient number of spokes to bring together highly innovative approaches to youth friendships. There is no social phenomenon that cannot benefit from a CBPR approach, and this is particularly so when discussing highly marginalized groups.

Interestingly, community participatory research involving youth represents one of the latest evolutions of this approach and has the potential to engender friendships between youth and between adults and youth, thus bringing an added dimension and benefit to this activity (Childers-McKee, 2014; Verkuyten & Martinovic, 2006). This should not come as any great surprise because this research approach stresses the implications of inherent power imbalances, sharing, mutual trust, interactions, and the embrace of affirming goals, all of which can spill over into other community arenas and networks (Castleden, Mulrennan, & Godlewska, 2012; Peterson, Dolan, & Hanft, 2010).

Innovative and youth-friendly approaches, particularly those that have youth playing active and meaningful roles in shaping these approaches, address the power imbalance between adults and youth in research undertakings and thus seek to place adult researchers in a nonhierarchical relationship with youth. These relationships either border on or result in friendships, which raises ethical challenges for adult researchers (Abebe, 2009; Hallett, 2013; Taylor, 2011). For example, Mann, Liley, and Kellett (2014) raise the critical question of who is the ultimate judge on whether actions are ethical or unethical—children, adults, or both? The answer to this question goes beyond the academic and has profound consequences from a practical standpoint.

As noted earlier in this book, youth friendship networks are not restricted to their own age group, but age similarity is still a very strong factor in shaping youth friendship networks. Youth and their adult counterparts' relationships can evolve into friendships that do not compromise the outcomes of a research project, just as they do not undermine programming, and extend far beyond the scope and time period of the research undertaking.

In my book (Delgado, 2006) on youth co-production of research and knowledge written more than 10 years ago and titled *Designs and Methods for Youth-Led Research*, I argued then, and continue to do so now, that youth have a major contribution to make in conducting research on their own, with adult guidance as needed or as co-investigators with adults, and this partnership opens up the door for interventions that are youth-centered and can encompass topics that are out of the ordinary, as in the case of friendships. These relationships engender tensions and will encounter obstacles but also bring innovation, energy, excitement, and potential social change (Mosher, Anucha, Appiah, & Levesque, 2014). Tensions and advances are closely intertwined.

Shelton and McDermott (2015), for example, discuss *duoethnography* as a methodology for researching friendship, taking into account how the study of friendship shapes both the inquiry and also the friendship itself. There is an understanding that duoethnography brings with it an inherent source of energy that influences the research process (Norris & Greenlaw, 2012). It also brings inherent challenges regardless of the age of the researchers as well.

Digital storytelling, too, can be viewed as a research method and an intervention. The case illustration discussed in Chapter 5 uses this method as a form of intervention. Digital storytelling provides a window into friendship narratives and how they are conceived, including their rewards and challenges (Wexler, Gubrium, Griffin, & DiFulvio, 2013). Storytelling allows youth to construct their own narratives in a manner that facilitates the sharing of meaning through a variety of artistic means. Friendship storytelling can be thought of as a means for creating and expanding the friendship networks of program participants by bringing together groups of youth in pursuit of a common agenda. This approach is exciting and can draw on youth energy and interests.

Kaplan's (2013) *We Live in the Shadow: Inner-City Kids Tell Their Stories Through Photographs* is an excellent community-based example of how we can develop new insights into the role of friendships in the lives of urban youth, in this case African Americans living in South Central Los Angeles. Storytelling can transpire in many different ways, and photography is one method finding increased saliency. Photovoice is but one of the latest examples of how innovation, participatory democracy, and youth have come together to create a narrative and also serve as a basis for social action (Delgado, 2015).

These forms of research, and others not mentioned, can transpire within and outside of schools, with both settings bringing different rewards and limitations for how this research unfolds (Hacking & Barratt, 2009). There is, for example, an increasing recognition that, in qualitative research, researcher characteristics do wield an influence on data gathering and interactions with those who are the focus of the research, and we can certainly include age and racial/ethnicity as factors (Pezalla, Pettigrew, & Miller-Day, 2012). Acknowledging and minimizing these differences represents a positive step in the right direction.

Heron and Reason (2006) advocate for "co-operative inquiry," or the practice of research with rather than on or for people, which can also be referred to as co-production. This perspective on research resonates with community capacity enhancement and youth-led interventions because of how the power shifts. The values outlined earlier in Chapter 2 shape co-produced research because they inform how research should unfold from a participatory point of view.

It is fitting to end this section by addressing how participatory research can translate into new forms of practices. The impact of participatory research goes beyond the researcher and researchee, and it must also include understanding its impact on practictitioners and practice. Pascal and Bertram (2014, p. 279) identified multiple practice mechanisms that, incidentally, can be used with youth of various ages to address the topic of urban youth friendships: video stimulated dialogue, cultural circles, critical incident analysis, storytelling and naming your world, wishing trees, listening posts, map making, guided tours, focused observations, photography and film making. These activities can be modified to take into account varying goals, organizational settings, programs, and youth age groups.

Community-Based Research Challenges

Community-based research is certainly exiting, and no two days of conducting this form of research are ever the same, particularly when embracing participatory values. Those of us who thrive in these situations find this is exciting; for those of us who dread uncertainty must brace themselves for a ride. There is energy in urban and inner-city communities that cannot be found anywhere else, and this bodes well for youth community practice. It would be irresponsible, if not unethical, for youth-focused community-based research to ignore the life struggles that marginalized youth face in their day-to-day living.

Azmitia, Ittel, and Break (2006, p. 446) put forth a challenge for the development of policies that are based on the operative reality of urban youth and how they must be accounted for in setting policies and programs:

> A more realistic portrait of ethnicity and socio-economically diverse adolescents' friendships would also be useful toward developing policies that improve adolescents' experiences in school and the larger society. Given that so many ethnic minority and low-income adolescents live in poverty, more informed policies would result in a brighter, more hopeful future for them and our society.

The achievement of this goal necessitates the surmounting of numerous research methodological, political, and ethical obstacles and challenges. Making this goal explicit, in turn, increases the likelihood of success.

Before turning to a critique of youth friendship research approaches and methods, a commentary on where this community practice friendship-focused research must ideally transpire is in order. Countless researchers, myself included, extol the virtues of community-based research as the most appropriate approach to capture and elucidate the social forces operating to marginalize youth. Nevertheless, community-based research is really very arduous to undertake because the researcher, as in the case of the practitioner, will enter a world (community) that she does not control, and she is expected to engage a populace that may not trust her (Ferrera, 2015; Lucero, 2013; Mitchell, 2015).

Community-based research is a broad umbrella under which many different forms of research can be undertaken, including those that are participant-driven (Cammarota & Fine, 2010; Cutter-Mackenzie, Edwards, & Quinton, 2015; Miller, Clark, Flewitt, Hammersley, & Robb, et al., 2014; Nygreen, Ah Kwon, & Sánchez, 2006; Powers & Tiffany, 2006). Research with youth can also go by many different names, such as child-/youth-centered, YPAR, shoulder-to-shoulder, and youth-led, which are the most popular terms (Due, Riggs, & Augoustinos, 2014; Griffin, Lahman, & Opitz, 2016; Raffety, 2015). Having various labels compounds arriving at a comprehensive grasp of the field.

Pyne et al. (Pyne, Scott, O'Brien, Stevenson, & Musah, 2014) discuss the importance of preparing undergraduate researchers as mentors as opposed to mentees in YPAR; this stance helps them view the youth they are researching within an equal-power position, helping youth researchers mentor other youth and completing the cycle. Pyne et al. (2014, p. 51) also to identify a series of guiding values and principles that resonate with those articulated in Chapter 2 influencing how research unfolds:

> Although YPAR projects range widely in design and implementation, they generally embody a common set of values and principles that we characterize as: (1) a collective and collaborative team working on a shared problem; (2) a multivocal expression of experience, analysis, and interpretation; (3) critical perspective that recognizes structural inequalities; (4) an emancipatory orientation focused on future better worlds; and (5) an active agenda that includes both personal transformation and social change.

The emphasis of YPAR in seeking social justice lends itself to broadening youth social networks in pursuit of a common vision and change and has great applicability for the central theme of this book on urban youth friendships.

Childers-McKee (2014), based on a review of the literature on YPAR and intercultural relationships between youth of color, concluded that there is a potential for this method to achieve this goal:

> YPAR may provide a vehicle by which educators might explicitly engage students in conversations about the constructedness of their social worlds and reductionist thinking that attributes stereotypical labels to particular groups. Teaching youth to deconstruct racist narratives must involve the cultivation of a more critical literacy to give them tools to challenge representations of themselves and others and to see both the constructedness and commodification of youth identities.

It is important that the entire weight of improving intergroup relationships, possibly resulting in creating new friendships, not be put on YPAR. YPAR, however, can be part of a broader strategy that involves other activities.

Youth participatory research brings with it tremendous advantageous and challenges, some of which are ethical in character because of the importance of establishing social relationships based on mutual trust that can easily transcend into friendships between youth and their adult counterparts (Hooper & Gunn, 2014). These friendships can prove problematic in the conduct of this form of research and/or in the interpretation of findings.

The undertaking of peer-led research entails the creation of these positions as employment, with job descriptions, supervision, performance evaluation, and a pay scale. Creating these types of learning opportunities involving pay, however, does open up the potential for coercion (Delgado, 2006). In the case of internships or service-learning projects, the dropping of payment does not diminish the significance of the experience. In essence, this is meaningful and serious work. Bringing a "job" perspective or mindset to this research approach means that it does raise potential ethical conflicts, however (Delgado, 2006).

We should not eschew this form of research, because it has tremendous value when using a socioecological model. However, I would be irresponsible to advocate for community-based research in any of its various manifestations without issuing a warning about the pitfalls, tensions, and challenges it brings (Te Riele & Brooks, 2013). For example, the setting in which interviews take place brings an overlooked dimension in research focused on youth and proposed for understanding friendships. Generally, conducting research in homes places the researcher as a guest (Heath et al., 2009, p. 93):

> A particularly important issue when conducting interview-based research with young people is the question of where to hold interviews. This is important for two reasons. First, physical space is rarely neutral but instead has the potential to confer advantage on one or other party to the interview to the disadvantage of the other; and second, certain locations may place both the researcher and/ or the participant at risk. Bearing these points in mind, the ideal is often for interviews to be held in a public space of a young person's choosing in order to minimise any potential discomfort and to minimize the power differential between researchers and interviewees.

Nontraditional settings are places in a community where residents feel safe and can go to purchase a product or service or congregate, and these spaces bring an added perspective to the knowledge generated from interviews. Beauty parlors, barbershops, bars, and botanical shops are examples.

Coad et al. (2015) identified three phases to conducting interviews in the homes of children/youth: (1) planning entry to the child's home, (2) conducting the interviews, and (3) exiting the field. In planning entry, we include children/youth's engagement and issues of researcher gender. Each of these phases can be conceptualized as distinct for the purposes of the research process. Youth researchers must take into account factors related to the balance of power, the role and importance of building rapport, consent agreement, the necessity of maintaining a flexible interview structure, and how to exit the home with sensitivity.

It is impossible to actively undertake research on urban youth friendships without establishing a mutually trusting and respectful relationship, and this is always so much easier said than done. An effective research process translates into effective relationship building (Runk, 2014). A participatory relationship helps ensure that youth voices are not lost in the translation, so to speak. Holt and Pamment (2011), for example, discuss the use of assisted questionnaires as a means of overcoming challenges associated with young offenders but also applicable to research and youth of color friendships.

Finally, active engagement of youth in research endeavors translates into having goals beyond the generation of knowledge and also encompassing increasing youth human capital by providing them with research skills and experiences that can be transferred to other social spheres in their lives. Having youth consult on all aspects of a research project focused on them is one way of meaningfully involving them (Leadbeater et al., 2006), although the human capital development aspect is minimized (Calvert, Emery, & Kinsey, 2013; Delgado & Humm-Delgado, 2013).

Challenges and Limitations of Peer-Led Research

Peer-led research brings its share of challenges or limitations, and it would be irresponsible for me not to point them out. These challenges are not insurmountable, but they are significant and will not be crossed without considerable expenditure of time and energy (Bugos et al., 2014; Jardine & James, 2012). Ten challenges/limitations stand out because of their importance to the integrity of the process (Delgado, 2006):

1. Peer-led research is never to be conceived as a panacea. This form of research is an essential element in the seeking and discovery of solutions pertaining to social injustices, but it should not be conceived of as a solution unto itself.
2. Youth are not superhuman, and they bring their own set of social biases and temptations that all human beings have.
3. Youth, in similar fashion to their adult counterparts, display preferences for certain types of research and avoid other forms of research.
4. Youth are not formally educated in conducting research, and valuable time and resources must be invested in them, which would not be the case with adult researchers.
5. Parental permissions and concerns about safety bring an added layer to the research process.
6. Confidentiality may prove to be a challenge because youth understanding of this concept will in all likelihood differ from that of their adult counterparts.
7. Youth must be prepared to have their hard work challenged as to its scientific merits by the academic community and policy-makers who do not subscribe to this research approach.

8. Youth-initiated research will in all likelihood face challenges from adults in their own community because if the research is "serious," it should not be undertaken by youth.

9. Youth-led research or co-research may involve entering sections of a community where youth may be endangered, and their safety must shape the nature of the research endeavor, whereas adults may not face similar challenges.

10. How the results of the research are distributed when youth are decision-makers may not be the "preferred" approach that adult researchers would embrace, thus bringing tension to this phase of the research process.

The reader find several limitations on this list that are not "overwhelming" and others that are simply impossible to address. That is what makes limitations challenging. The limitations, however, do not overshadow the rewards and advantages of youth peer-led research, and it is well worth the time and effort devoted to moving this approach forward when addressing urban youth issues and concerns.

Furthermore, researchers may have their own limitations that they consider to be of equal if not greater importance, and I accept this possibility. What is important, however, is that practitioners question what they do and identify the positives as well as the negatives of their methodology since no research or social intervention is totally devoid of either. Last, an understanding of the values guiding these actions never stops being important, and the time and energy spent in identifying values is time and effort well spent.

Critique of Friendship Research Approaches and Methods

Numerous books have been written and many a scholarly career has been advanced by developing and critiquing children/youth research methods. Bagwell and Schmidt (2013), for example, devote an excellent chapter to the process of studying children/youth friendships. Boocock and Scott (2005), too, devote a chapter to reviewing the study of children and childhood research methodologies that grounds readers in the richness and breadth that have guided research in this field. Both these chapters highlight the importance of children and youth not being passive subjects but rather active participants and members of research undertakings.

This section, however, seeks to ground the reader in some of the major challenges in conducting research with youth, particularly those who are suspicious of research—and rightly so. It is safe to say that urban youth have generally seen very little direct benefits from research conducted among them and in their communities. This distrust, and the ethics associated with feelings and other dimensions, must be acknowledged and addressed before major headway is made in knowledge creation regarding friendship networks (Alderson, 2014; Bucknall, 2014).

It is important to remember that the field of childhood studies has a very recent history, with the 1980s considered the decade when the field became well defined (Clark, Flewitt, Hammersley, & Robb, 2014*a*), although research focused on children and youth can be traced back to the end of the 19th century (Fraser, Flewitt, & Hammersley, 2014). As the field of childhood studies gained currency in the 1980s, attracting increased funding and research, it coincided with the emergence of the youth development field, bringing these two influential fields together.

Youth research traditions have generally fallen into one of five approaches (Hopkins, 2013): (1) developmental psychology, (2) educational research, (3) cultural studies, (4) youth transitions, and (5) social and cultural geographies. Heath et al. (2009) broaden their conceptualization of youth research traditions beyond the five identified by Hopkins to include feminist youth research and "girl studies." Each of these youth research traditions brings advantages and disadvantages in developing a well-rounded understanding of urban youth friendships.

However, cultural studies and social and cultural geographies stand out because youth play a more meaning participatory role in the crafting of research focused on them and bring added meaning and significance to them. For example, the transition from youth to adulthood is undergoing revision to take into account major social structural changes that have occurred, particularly in relation to employment and familial living arrangements, including age-related distributive justice (Irwin, 2013).

Youth-focused research has been shaped in relation to problems and service delivery goals, and this results in a language that is pathologically driven, with deleterious corresponding consequences (Slater, 2013). It should not be surprising that marginalized youth friendships, too, have suffered from a pathology-focused scholarly stance. A critique of research on friendship approaches and methods cannot be separated from this foundation on pathology and deficits.

As already addressed in great detail, the subject of urban youth of color suffers from a lack of research attention, and, when addressed, it has been from a deficit perspective. Gillespie and colleagues (Gillespie, Lever, Frederick, & Royce, 2015), in turn, interject methodological factors and challenges in the conduct of research on friendship, particularly an overreliance on quantitative methods because of how they fail to pick up on important nuances and respond to unanticipated events in the field.

Case and Haines (2014) argue quite convincingly that the positivist method, with its premise of researcher independence, has avoided addressing the relationship between researcher–researched and has thereby overlooked one of the key elements of high-quality research, with implications for how data are interpreted and the actions that can result from the findings. Blackman and Commane (2012, pp. 235–236) speak to the benefits of friendships in field research:

> In field research the friendships built over time show how trust, respect and a sense of togetherness is vital to how the field is understood and then

conceptualized . . . . Understanding the dynamics of friendships shows how vital it is to negotiate consent through trusting and always respecting the decisions made about what can be included in the write-up. Significantly understanding friendships allows critique to shine a positive light onto the moral codes and achievements of groups, which is often absent from understandings of young people's culture.

The sharing of a common cause or purpose and an atmosphere of respect and trust creates a situation where friendships can evolve because sharing is facilitated. Commonality is engendered by emphasizing similarities rather than differences.

Researchers in the positivist tradition are taught about the virtues of being objective and not allowing their emotions to enter into the research decision-making process for fear that they will influence the outcomes of a study. Research as objectification loses its meaning and significance when focused on youth who are oppressed and are angry and distrustful as a result. An "independent" researcher who is totally free of bias is unrealistic, and this stance serves to build a wall between the researcher and those who are the focused of the study. Good research calls for breaking down walls rather than constructing or reinforcing them.

Understanding memory narratives of friendships, for example, is a dimension of friendships that is beginning to be recognized as important in the field of friendship studies and is helping us understand how memories shape expectations and hold significance in the lives of individuals (Tani, Smorti, & Peterson, 2015). These memory narratives have great applicability for adults, particularly those who are older, as they reflect on their life's journey. However, memory narratives of children and youth bring more and different challenges for researchers since their life spans may be very limited, yet their memories may well last a lifetime and be worthy of our attention.

On a different note, people consist of more than their problems and strengths, and, in the social sciences and particularly in human service-related fields, we have limited insights into the ordinary everyday occurrences of individuals, be they youth, adults, of color, or belonging to any other group (Coleman, 2013). By narrowing definitions, measurements, and what is worthy of being researched, we focus our attention on the extraordinary and simply ignore the ordinary. Knowledge of the ordinary, in turn, provides an important baseline or foundation from which to examine the out-of-ordinary experience. In the case of this book, urban youth friendships are ordinary.

Researching "ordinary" youth and their "ordinary" or everyday experiences represents a novel approach that is receiving increased attention in the social sciences. Woodman (2013), for example, advocates for youth researchers to pay greater attention to "ordinary" youth because they often represent a missing population group because of an overemphasis on youth who are vulnerable, out of the ordinary, or special:

[A] focus on ordinary young people that draws on the legacy of the sociology of generations, has affinity with conceptual critiques of youth research for marginalising the everyday experience of youth .... Young people can be ordinary, or in the "missing middle," in many aspects of their lives, while "excluded" or "spectacular: in others ways that happen to bring them to the attention of researchers, authorities or the popular media. From this perspective, the important call to focus on the ordinary experience of youth may have greater purchase if the "missing middle" is not seen primarily as a particular group of young people who have been neglected, whether defined more narrowly or widely.

The ordinary youth perspective is essential to understand more fully youth who fall outside the norm. However, understanding the "norm" or the "typical" also helps us respond to out-of-the-norm behavior, including friendship and peer networks.

Peer research, sometimes referred to as co-produced research, methodologies bring tremendous excitement and potential because they open up new approaches and arenas for research, but they are not without their share of tensions and challenges for all parties. However, not all agree on this point (Francis & Hemson, 2009, p. 223):

> We found striking advantages to using fieldworkers who are close in their characteristics to that of respondents: these included ready access to respondents, the immediate use of language appropriate to the respondents, and an ability to swiftly establish rapport. We also observed striking limitations: the peer researchers struggled with the wish of some respondents to establish supportive friendships with them, they lacked the authority of an academic researcher, and they sometimes resorted to false promises in attempts to get cooperation. The main conclusion drawn is that, in principle, using youths as peer researchers is neither better nor worse than using professional researchers, but each approach can produce its own challenges and possibilities.

I, for one, consider that no research process is perfect but that advantages can far outweigh the limitations, particularly when training youth to conduct research translates into engaging capacity enhancement by building their human capital and increasing our knowledge base in the process.

Before moving on to critique research approaches and methods, it is important to emphasize the need for quantitative and qualitative research on youth of color social identities and their impact on friendships (Azmitia et al., 2006). Social identity goes beyond race and ethnicity. Will we ever get to the point where a critique is not necessary (Bucknell, 2014)? The answer is no, and Lahman (2008, p. 283) provides an eloquent rationale as to why: "the moment we feel our research has captured an understanding of childhood we are on the shakiest ground. As long as we remain in a posture of questioning findings, reflexively considering the research process, acknowledging the power of our memories of childhood experiences over research interpretations, and respecting children, we are on firmer ground."

A critique of research approaches and methods on friendships can be classified as falling into seven categories that are highly interrelated yet distinctive enough to warrant their own designation: (1) age-specific, (2) race/ethnicity, (3) geographic, (4) gender/gender identity, (5) intellectual/physical abilities, (6) acculturation level of newcomers, and (7) socioeconomic class.

AGE-SPECIFIC

The evolutionary process associated with friendships corresponds to a life cycle perspective, meaning that the more age-sensitive the research is, the greater its relevance for community practice interventions with children and youth (DiDonato, 2014). Engaging youth of all ages in research allows their unique voices to be heard and shapes how research on youth friendships unfolds.

Not surprisingly, there is a call for development of friendship research methods for young children, specifically because they present researchers with unique challenges related to developmental stage (Van Hoogdalem, Singer, Eek, & Heesbeen, 2013), including the infancy/toddler stage (Malaguzzi, 2014). These early stages, in turn, necessitate turning to extraordinary methods to capture their voices. The use of drawings and photographs, for example, facilitates capturing insights without relying the conventional written question-and-answer formats, thus allowing those who are less verbal to share their knowledge and insights.

RACE/ETHNICITY

Youth participation in friendship-focused research opens up a portal into their daily world that can add much depth to our understanding on the subject and the role that race and ethnicity play in shaping their social interactions. The dearth of scholarly knowledge on friendships from a normalized perspective is well understood but certainly alarming, based on the demographics presented in Chapter 4.

This book emphasizes race and ethnicity, with an acknowledgment that this perspective is significant but can be moderated based how other social and contextual factors intersect. Youth are marginalized to begin with, and introducing race and ethnicity further focuses on the marginalized within marginalized youth groups (Griffin, 2013).

Youth have a culture and language that is an essential element within this construct. Examining language, particularly ethnolinguistics, and ethnicity among adolescents introduces yet another layer into our understanding of how they shape their interactions across and within groups (Rampton, 2014). Cultural values related to ethnicity and race, in turn, have received some scholarly attention, yet there is much more than must be explored and understood before community practice focused on urban youth friendships can transpire. Attention to how collectivistic values influence behavior and friendship expectations is essential in shaping research and program development by bringing cultural values into the discussion of race and ethnicity.

The emergence of multiracial youth, as noted in Chapter 4, introduces a new category related to race and ethnicity, one that will only increase in importance in the next generation. Researchers and community practitioners will need to rethink the categorization of youth based on this factor, further reinforcing the need for youth to define themselves along racial and ethnic lines.

GEOGRAPHIC

Context, context, context and youth friendships. Add "urban" and an important dimension is introduced to research on and by youth (Ozer, Newlan, Douglas, & Hubbard, 2013; Ozer & Douglas, 2013; Zaleski, Martin, & Messinger, 2015). There are dramatic differences among urban, suburban, ex-urban, and rural settings. The later three, for example, will have limited public transportation, and, as a result, cars will play a prominent role in shaping contact between youth outside of school. Urban centers, in turn, will in all likelihood have public transportation readily available, thus facilitating movement across different neighborhoods.

Geography becomes a facilitating or hindering force in social relationships since youth friendships are generally geographically centered in neighborhoods. The Miami case illustration in Chapter 5 illustrates how communities with strong identities shaped by historical events can effectively isolate youth in these communities from considering friendships with youth in other communities. Research undertakings can help break down these perceived and actual barriers.

Roberts and Jette (2016) report on the success of an urban Native American and Alaskan Native participatory research project and the importance of long-lasting social relationships that are built within the community. Concentration of groups within narrow geographical confines can be viewed from a positive as well as a negative point of view. Urban settings often exemplify this concentration.

Changing population composition introduces an emerging phenomena that is bound to impact youth social relationships, including friendships of various types. Urban centers losing population (e.g., Detroit) bring a different set of social dynamics when compared to urban centers that are gaining population. Friendship networks may be disrupted when neighborhoods start to break up and residents move to other parts of the city or even to new cities and geographical regions of the country. The out-migration of African Americans from Los Angeles and their replacement by undocumented Latinos, for example, will send shockwaves across communities resulting in disruptions of social networks.

GENDER, GENDER IDENTITY, AND LGBTQ

Youth gender; gender identity; and lesbian, gay, bisexual, transgender, and questioning (LGBTQ) youth friendship networks function to fulfill many different needs beyond the conventional thinking on the subject. LGBTQ youth face immense social challenges (Higa et al., 2014). Intersectionality increases the importance of obtaining knowledge on friendships among LGBTQ youth, which is only enhanced when they are playing active roles in shaping this research (Voisin, Bird, Shiu, & Krieger, 2013).

Fortunately, the literature on youth regarding gender and gender identity also has started to expand based on increased research attention, and this includes scholarship on friendship and peer networks (Crosnoe, Erickson, & Dornbusch, 2002; Fine, 2012). Intersectionality, however, has only now started to receive increased attention as it relates to urban youth of color (Munro et al., 2013; Walker, 2015). Their social networks, including friendships, are in much need of serious scholarly attention.

Enlisting the support of LGBTQ youth in conducting research on friendships and other social relationships will enhance our knowledge base because their insights will play a significant role in shaping interventions and enlisting their support or buy-in of these efforts (Wernick, 2015; Wernick, Woodford, & Kulick, 2014). Participatory action research brings the potential for LGBTQ youth to shape the questions and obtain the answers that can lead to social changes and interventions with meaning to their social and political circumstances (Mansfield, Welton, & Halx, 2012).

INTELLECTUAL/PHYSICAL ABILITIES

The subject of friendships among youth with various kinds of physical, emotional, and intellectual challenges has been integrated throughout this book. However, their unique social circumstances and challenges necessitate particular attention being paid to their social networks and friendships. Researching friendships and youth with disabilities, in this case those with intellectual, physical, and emotional disabilities, necessitates that informed consent and other ethical aspects associated with research be modified to increase youth participation and decision-making. This makes youth instrumental in debating outcomes rather than being subjects of outcomes, with particular keen attention paid to intersectionality (Chappell, Rule, Dlamini, & Nkala 2014; Snelgrove, 2005).

Youth with disabilities often have a central goal of making friends when working with practitioners. Gerhardt et al. (Gerhardt, McCallu, McDougall, Keenan, & Rigby, 2013) identified four themes that are integral to the friendship-making process, the first three of which lend themselves to research: (1) person factors influencing friend-making, (2) friend-making as a priority, (3) opportunities for friend-making and motivations to make friends, and (4) a little bit of luck in making friends, a theme occasionally identified. Youth with disabilities, as a result, can have friendship goals specific to their unique circumstances.

Youth with disabilities can take an active role in shaping and conducting research on friendships, a topic that holds great significance to them. Their motivations and insights must not be ignored by community practitioners (Salmon,

2013). Schuh, Sundar, and Hagner (2014) found that their use of a photovoice project on friendships played an important role in helping youth with disabilities make a successful transition to adulthood, and these researchers advocate for future research on the role of friendship networks in transition planning as a natural support. Jivraj et al. (Jivraj, Sacrey, Newton, Nicholas, & Zwaigenbaum, 2014, p. 782) address youth with disabilities as co-investigators, in this case involving autism but applicable across the board with necessary modifications:

> Participatory research aims to increase the relevance and broaden the implementation of health research by involving those affected by the outcomes of health studies. Few studies within the field of neurodevelopmental disorders, particularly autism spectrum disorders, have involved autistic individuals as partners .... A search of databases and review of gray literature identified seven studies that described participatory research partnerships between academic researchers and individuals with autism spectrum disorder or other neurodevelopmental disorders. A comparative analysis of the studies revealed two key themes: (1) variations in the participatory research design and (2) limitations during the reporting of the depth of the partner's involvement. Both themes potentially limit the application and generalizability of the findings.

Unfortunately, in all likelihood Jivraj et al.'s conclusions are not restricted to this disability and can be applied other forms of physical, emotional, and intellectual challenges.

ACCULTURATION LEVEL OF NEWCOMERS

The emergence of the concept of acculturation is widely embraced when addressing newcomer groups and more specifically youth (Strohmeier & Spiel, 2012). Acculturation brings an often missing element into discussions of Latino and Asian youth who are either immigrants or were born in this country to foreign-born parents (Azmitia et al., 2006; Delgado, 2007; Poteet & Simmons, 2015). The Georgia case illustration in Chapter 5 taps into the role of acculturation and the challenges newcomer youth face in reaching out to new groups for potential relationships, with social media opening up possibilities beyond geographical community.

Titzmann, Brenick, and Silbereisen (2015, p. 1318) speak to the importance of youth engaging in outgroup friendships involving newcomer youth. The social isolation often associated with newcomer status is particularly pronounced in the case of newcomer children and youth. Again, the Georgia case example in Chapter 5 illustrates how being creative in developing activities—in this case digital storytelling—can help newcomer youth in their transition.

Youth with low levels of acculturation will rely more heavily on their parents and families and are less likely to have a friendship network that extends beyond other newcomer youth. Thus, any research focused on newcomer youth and their

friendship network must take into account the role and influence of acculturation and generational status in the United States (Greenman, 2011). In the case of
those who are undocumented, their undocumented status will make the research
process that much more difficult to accomplish because of the political climate
regarding their presence in the United States. The 2016 Republican presidential
candidate Donald Trump's inflammatory statements on Mexicans who cross the
US border is but one glaring example.

Limited social access to friendships outside of newcomer or undocumented
status necessitates that any concerted effort to learn about the friendship process
of these youths will require entrance into the world of the undocumented. This
will require that researchers be sponsored by a trusted someone or organization
within this community. This will add an extra but unavoidable step to the research
process. Enlisting youth within this community to become co-investigators
thus brings an attractive dimension to knowledge co-production (Delgado &
Humm-Delgado, 2013).

SOCIOECONOMIC CLASS

The influence of social class on social relations is significant regardless of economic level and age group, and urban critical place theory helps in developing
a narrative to let understand its influence on social relationships, particularly on
peers and friendships. However, the impact of socioeconomic conditions on youth
friendships is undeniable because youth are limited in venturing outside of their
immediate surroundings because of the potential of increased surveillance and
possible arrests (Hollingworth, 2015; Papapolydorou, 2014).

In several instances throughout this book, the term "urban" has been a prefix
for low-income/low-wealth youth even though middle-class families of color do
reside in the nation's cities (Pattillo, 2013). These youth also face racism. However,
they do not have to contend with the intersectionality of economic class. The
growing inequality in income, as a result, cannot be ignored when controlling
for research on youth race and ethnicity (Gilbert, 2014; Healey & O'Brien, 2014;
Urciuoli, 2013).

There is a tendency in peer relations research to ignore socioeconomic class
and focus on race and ethnicity (Graham, Taylor, & Ho, 2009). In many cases,
the two are highly interrelated, as in the discussions of many Latino and African-
American/black youth.

Nevertheless, within-class categories must also be captured whenever possible in order to more fully grasp the impact of employment, type, and full- versus
part-time employment, thus bringing a nuanced understanding of how socioeconomic class is manifested in youth friendships. Urban youth who work with
other youth in fast-food establishments, for example, may have developed friendships that would not have been possible otherwise because of the unique setting.

Availability and type of employment, as a result, takes on added social significance in these situations.

Promising Emerging Methodologies

There are many different reasons for community practice to embrace youth empowering research and participatory approaches to make research relevant and appealing to youth. The four case illustrations presented in Chapter 5 provide an in-field backdrop to the discussion of promising emerging methodologies covered in this section.

Youth peer research has demonstrated its usefulness and attractiveness to youth for very good social and political reasons. These undertakings open up possibilities for social interactions of great depth and significance and bring the potential for establishing friendships. Heath et al. (2009, p. 45) address one of the principal reasons for advocating youth peer research that will resonate with practitioners and researchers alike because of how age gaps influence interactions:

> [D]espite the increasingly widespread use of peer-led youth research strategies . . . it remains the case that the vast majority of youth research is conducted by researchers who tend to be older than those they are researching. Sometimes this may only be a matter of a few years, but in many instances youth researchers are old enough to be the parents of the young people involved in their research, or even old enough to be their grandparents: an insistence on shared age would rule out most youth researchers from ever conducting empirical research in their chosen field again!

The same conclusion can be made about the ethnicity/race and urban background of adult researchers. The lacuna between researcher and "subject" can be minimized when youth are enlisted to conduct the research. This goal will increase the chances that the findings can be translated into actions of significant meaning to youth. Heath et al. (2009) identified six promising methods for youth research that have great applicability for research involving youth of color friendships. Each of these six approaches can be conceptualized with youth playing significant, if not leadership, roles: (1) qualitative interviewing, (2) ethnographic approaches, (3) visual methods, (4) surveys, (5) using secondary data, and (6) use of the Internet.

There certainly are other methods, such as research involving documents, archives, and artifacts (Clark, Flewitt, Hammersley, & Robb, 2014*b*; Hearn & Thomson, 2014); case studies (Clark, 2014); and participant observation (Montgomery, 2014; Hammersley, 2014), for example; although these are not as popular as the six approaches emphasized here, each has its rewards and challenges. Participant observation, for example, may appear as a simple and user-friendly research method, yet looks can be very deceiving. When conducted thoughtfully, it provides insights into youth relationships that may be difficult or outright impossible to achieve using other research methods (Bucknell, 2014). Competencies, however, have much to say about practitioner preferences.

Some of these methods may have more appeal to practitioners than other methods, and that is to be expected. Community-based organizations, too, have their favorites and the capacity to undertake some but not all. Local circumstances and goals also will play an influential role in rank ordering these six approaches. Expanding research approaches enables the research question to dictate the method rather than the method dictating the research question.

Community practice encompasses these methods; however, applying these research methods to youth friendships provides practitioners with an opportunity to introduce innovation to knowledge creation. Each of these methods will be addressed in varying details. However, a cross-cutting theme will be that of having youth play instrumental (co-production) roles in the planning and carrying out of the research.

Co-production of research translates into co-production of knowledge (Case & Haines, 2014; Weichselgartner & Truffer, 2015) and co-production of resulting social interventions (Wehrens, 2014).

Youth have a vested interest in crafting the questions that they want answered about friendships and peer relationships. As a result, there is a higher likelihood that the answers to those questions will have a better chance of being translated into actions to address the major issues in their lives and communities. In the case of friendships, the questions and answers may lead to discovering environmental changes that are needed to facilitate friendships. For example, having public places and activities that are conducive for social exchanges, such as parks, sporting activities, community-sponsored activities, and recreation centers, should serve as opportunities to maximize contact and the development of new friendships. The case example of Overtown, Miami, in Chapter 5, saw results from the photo-voice project presented at a local celebratory event as a means of increasing social interactions.

Griffin, Lahman, and Opitz (2016) address the methodological challenges of conducting research with children and advocate for the *walk-around* (a form of mobile interview) and the *shoulder-to-shoulder* methods as a way of overcoming inherent tensions and obstacles in reaching out to better understand a population group that may have difficulty in responding to conventional research methods that emphasize written forms of communication.

It is certainly possible, and some would argue also highly advisable, that community practitioners use more than one method (Watkins & Gioia, 2015). Davies and Heaphy (2011) advocate for a mixed-methodological research approach when trying to develop an understanding of personal relations such as friendships because of the nuances that must be captured at many different levels of detail. Use of multiple methods casts a wider net in knowledge creation and, in the process, creates a more holistic understanding of youth identities and those playing significant roles in their lives (Bagnoli, 2012).

QUALITATIVE INTERVIEWING

Qualitative interviewing opens up the field of research to gather information from a wide variety of sources and methods and provides youth with an opportunity to express their sentiments using their own words and symbols (Bucknall, 2014; Schelbe et al., 2015). There is little disputing the value of qualitative data in helping to describe and analyze social relationships such as friendships.

It is widely considered to be an empowering method from both the researcher and participant viewpoints. Interpretivist epistemology emphasizes the importance of subjective meaning and gives voice or opportunities to share stories in a manner that does not inhibit youth in telling them (Heath et al., 2009). This is vital, especially in light of the paucity of research focused on youth of color from an assets or strengths perspective.

Qualitative research, for example, has a long history of focusing on children and youth friendship and peer networks (Corsaro, 2006) and lends itself to research that can foster community practice in an empowering and affirming way. Qualitative interviewing also lends itself to undertaking program or project evaluation, thus increasing its relevance to youth-led research (Bulanda, Szarzynski, Siler, & McCrea,2013; Denison et al., 2012; Richards-Schuster, 2013; White et al., 2012).

Clarity concerning the anticipated outcomes sought in youth development is essential in order to properly evaluate any intervention (Law, Siu, & Shek, 2012; Shek, 2013). Clarity, however, is either difficult or impossible without meaningful input from youth who are expected to be the ultimate beneficiaries of a social intervention, such as youth development.

The importance of generating a greater and more nuanced understanding of the role of friendships among urban youth of color must be well understood by policy-makers, academics, and practitioners, and much research and scholarship is warranted. The "openness" of this field lends itself to the introduction of innovative research approaches, methodologies, and considerations (Dulai, 2014; McCormack, Adams, & Anderson, 2013).

Liebenberg and Theron (2015, p. 203) stress the need for culture to be integral to any effort at introducing innovative qualitative research in order to understand its influence on resiliency:

> To fully understand how culture and resilience are intertwined, the use of innovative qualitative research methods is imperative, irrespective of a study's design. However, more important is astute choice and use of innovative methods. Although many authors advocate the use of novel, interactive methods in

studies of marginalized youth, they seldom flag the importance of considering the cultural and contextual appropriateness of methodological choices, or how methodological choices advance understandings of the sophistication of pathways to resilience.

Qualitative methods lend themselves to bringing culture to bear by increasing the understanding of resiliency among youth of color.

Qualitative research can be structured (questions are highly structured and sequential), semi-structured (data shapes follow-up questions), or unstructured (resembling a talk or chat), thus bringing a high degree of flexibility to addressing a variety of research goals (Flewitt, 2014; Kristensen & Ravn, 2015). It can be conducted with a key informant, with focus groups, and in community forums, for example, all of which are methods most community practitioners are familiar with in conducing needs and asset assessments (Delgado & Humm-Delgado, 2013; Gomez, 2013; Gupta, 2011; Soriano, 2012).

Echetebu (2014), for example, describes a Champaign, Illinois, program, a highly innovative and locally responsive way to engage youth "lock-in" with a late-night basketball competition and talent show that would tap their perceptions and recommendations for initiatives related to increasing safety, recreational opportunities, and housing quality, while preserving and enhancing social peer networks and the "nostalgic aspects of the physical structure of the neighborhood."

ETHNOGRAPHIC APPROACHES

According to Goldthorpe (1997, p. 74), ethnography's greatest strength is "its capacity to tell not only 'what it is all about' but further 'to tell how it is' from the actors point of view.'" Ethnography lends itself to innovative and highly engaging participatory research approaches that do not have the negative associations usually found with social science research (Birmingham & Calabrese Barton, 2014; Goldstein, Gray, Salisbury, & Snell, 2014; Haynes & Tanner, 2015).

It is no mistake that the concept of "urban ethnography" has emerged to take into account geography as a context for better understanding individual beliefs, expectations, and behaviors (Black, 2014). This increases the attractiveness of youth-led research because it not only brings adventure (exploring new areas/ learning), but also the fun often associated with adventure. Ethnography and story or narrative are closely intertwined, and this makes ethnography attractive for individuals who normally do not share their lives with outsiders by encouraging them to do so in a manner that is affirming, nonthreatening, and, one could add, highly imaginative.

Ethnography brings unimaginable potential for uncovering new knowledge related to intersectionality and marginalized groups (Jones & Watt, 2010), with youth being a prime beneficiary of this approach (Bradford & Cullen, 2013). Brown (2014) advocates for the use of ethnographic methodology in children's research. This form of research produces rich and highly detailed knowledge that is best captured through the integration of the researcher into a child's world, where he gets to see this world through the child's eyes, so to speak.

Intersectional ethnography, as argued throughout this book, must be taken into account in the co-production of research and knowledge regarding friendship and is further challenged when discussing LGBTQ youth, for example. These youth face the label of being "at-risk" and in need of protection, and they are potentially engaging in "risky behavior," being dangerous to themselves, putting them in a precarious social situation, and bringing additional challenges to the generation of knowledge and understanding pertaining to their lived experiences and friendships (Taylor & Dwyer, 2014).

VISUAL METHODS

The quest for innovation is well answered with the introduction of visual research methods, and this qualitative approach is finding currency across academic disciplines and helping professions that are using it with a wide variety of topics and population groups, including children and youth (Clark-Ibanez, 2007; Karlsson, 2012; Rose, 2012; Yefimova, Neils, Newell, & Gomez, 2015). The two case illustrations in Chapter 5 attest to this point.

The photographs that youth took in Minneapolis/St. Paul and Overtown, Miami, involved more than just taking images. These images served as a focal point for sharing information and discussions that resulted in collective reflection, including reflexivity. Reflexivity is central to any visual work (Mitchell, 2011) and is a critical process to any social justice–inspired community practice intervention, making this method particularly appealing for urban youth who are confronting issues of oppression in their daily lives. In the Miami case illustration, youth captured community assets with historical significance, effectively serving to bridge different generations. Visual work allows the bridging of generations in a way that few methods can.

Schaefer (2012b, p. 159) brings an added dimension to youth motivation for engaging in research: "Analysing young people's motives for using or not using specific virtual methods provides an insight into young people's methodological sensitivity and might provide future youth research with valuable insights into young people's everyday life." Youth friendships certainly fall into everyday or ordinary life experiences.

Focusing on youth friendships, by the way, makes it easier to research than a focus on the typical problem areas we associate with urban youth, such as drugs, violence, crime, school drop-outs, and incarceration, to name a few of the most obvious (Greene, Burke, & McKenna, 2013). Friesem (2014), for example, used the methodology of portraiture and youth pairings in the development of a classroom video and notes how this process resulted in unleashing a mixture of emotions but also engendered strong social relationships in the process.

The field of community practice also has embraced this form of research (Delgado & Humm-Delgado, 2013; Goodnough, 2014). The emphasis placed on visual methods in this section, when compared to the other five approaches, is due to this excitement and my acknowledged bias toward this form of research. Participatory visual approaches can encompass a variety of types (Mitchell, 2011, p. 4): "'draw a scientist'; 'Take a photograph of where you feel safe and not so safe'; 'Produce a video documentary on an issue in your life'; 'Find and work with seven or eight pictures from your family photographs that you can construct into a narrative about gender and identity.'" This listing by Mitchell does a wonderful job of illustrating the range of potential projects that can fall under a participatory visual approach, and this is evidenced in the photographs youth took and displayed in the case illustrations in Chapter 5. We could easily substitute friendship into each of these activities to increase its relevance for community practice and urban youth friendships.

There is an increased use of images to obtain insights into meaning, opening up the potential of this medium and methodology for researching difficult topics such as the meaning of youth friendships (Asaba, Rudman, Mondaca, & Park et al., 2014; Delgado, 2015). Strachan used visual methods to gain insights into youth sporting experiences, for example. Davies (2015), in turn, reported on his experiences in using photovisual research methods, noting that they have a high potential for use with children and youth (Clark-Ibanez, 2007; Pink, 2007; Thomson, 2009), and lend themselves to a co-production approach because they introduce a "fun" tool that youth can relate to and also allow a sharing of power.

Rice, Primak, and Girvin (2013) provided an example of photo elicitation with youth in foster care and not unexpectedly found the need for family and friends to be a key need in their lives, particularly if they were to be engaged and empowered.

Youth in foster care can use virtual methods to help articulate their needs and desires in a way that facilitates reaching out to others in similar situations and possibly expanding their social networks, including friendships, in the process. This visual method also serves to highlight what aspects of friendships have particular saliency.

Cook and Hess's (2007) research on children and fun was greatly enhanced through the use of cameras and photographs, although their approach was not specifically photovoice. Thus, visual methods cover a wide range of options, and practitioners and academics must be careful in how they employ imagery. Photovoice, however, is probably the most widely form of visual research and particularly so when introducing ethnography to this method (Mitchell, 2011).

Use of photovoice, as illustrated in Chapter 5, is both a research method and a social intervention, and it lends itself to use by youth in researching the meaning of friendship in their lives (Delgado, 2015; Zenkov & Harmon, 2009; Johansen & Le, 2014; Skovdal & Ogutu, 2012; Wilson et al., 2007); an urban youth of color case example using this visual ethnographic method offers great promise for the field of community practice. Photovoice brings significant flexibility in how it is used and can be used as both a research and community intervention method (Bananuka & John, 2015).

SURVEYS

To obtain a broader conceptualization of friendships and other relationships, there certainly is a place for friendship-specific surveys or surveys that capture social relationships in general but with specific subsections focused on peers and friendship networks. Youth involvement in planning and conducting surveys is certainly not new, and their active participation can be traced back to the 1970s (Delgado, 1979).

Surveys have been found to be effective with youth of color from backgrounds that are usually associated with youth-led research, such as urban-based Native Americans (Roberts & Jette, 2015) and Cambodian-American youth (Sangalang, Ngouy, & Lau, 2015). Youth input on the questions and wording of the questions is essential to minimize or eliminate silent voices or unanswered questions (Alerby & Kostenius, 2011).

Surveys bring tremendous potential for gathering qualitative information, although this information may be limited in the depth of detail because many surveys cover a wide range of subjects (Checkoway & Richards-Schuster, 2003; Powers et al., 2007; Suleiman, Soleimanpour, & London, 2006). Surveys can accommodate a wide variety of goals and budgets, bringing important flexibility to youth-led knowledge creation. This knowledge, in turn, can serve as the basis for more in-depth efforts as outlined in this chapter. Surveys can be cross-sectional and capture information at one point in time or be longitudinal, gathering information over a prescribed period of time that can involve months or even years (Health et al., 2009).

Surveys are also flexible in how they are conducted, which takes into account varied goals, budgets, and time frames. In-person surveys allow researchers, in this case youth, to visit households within their communities or centers with large numbers of youth and ask a series of questions. Surveys can also require considerable investment in sample selection, question construction, training of interviewers, data analysis, and report writing and dissemination. Each approach brings advantages and disadvantages.

USING SECONDARY DATA

The reader may be surprised by the inclusion of secondary data, particularly when youth are involved in what many practitioners consider to be a less than exciting research approach relegated to an office and reams of data. I am not a big advocate of this approach because of the importance of researchers/practitioners building relationships with youth and communities. In addition, large datasets are founded on information that funders think is important to know. These data, however, may not answer the questions that youth think are important. Yet, it would be irresponsible not to include secondary data use in the roster of research approaches.

Secondary data can play an influential role in helping to inform qualitative data gathering, and this aspect does not get the attention it deserves. As a result, it can be part of a mixed methodology that depends on expertise in conducting this form of research. The availability of datasets, for example, means that these data do not have to be generated from scratch, thus making the method economically feasible. Nevertheless, secondary data reflect an inherent bias on what information is considered important, and its use does not lend itself to building relationships between researcher and the community.

There certainly is, nevertheless, enough room in the constellation of youth research methods for this form of data, and youth can still partner with experienced researchers in helping to develop an understanding of friendships. Secondary data analysis can either be a central or supplementing focus of youth friendship research. Relatively few authors address this topic. Health et al. (2009), however, devote a chapter to secondary data analysis in their book *Reaching Young People's Lives*, and the reader interested in a more in-depth treatment of this approach is referred to this work.

USE OF THE INTERNET

It is appropriate to end this section with a look at the Internet since this medium plays such a prominent place in youth lives and the debate on how it influences their well-being (Best, Manktelow, & Taylor, 2014). Online relationships, including friendships, have received considerable attention in the professional literature and raised provocative questions as to the meaning of social relationships and the need, or lack of, physical proximity to establish and maintain close friendships (Chan & Lo, 2014; Lenhart, Rainie, & Lewis, 2001; Skoog, Sorbring, & Bohlin, 2015).

The Georgia case illustration featuring Burmese youth in Chapter 5 illustrates the power and potential of the Internet to reach outside of one's community and cross borders and to do so in an inexpensive manner. Research focused on youth online friendship and social relationships was addressed earlier in this book. The Internet and social media have tremendous potential for research (Pattaro, 2015). For example, use of the Internet and social media resources among homeless youth brings a new and exciting dimension to this form of research (Rice & Barman-Adhikari, 2014).

Youth Competencies and Interests

One key theme in this book has been that urban youth are not powerless or apathetic. Youth have agency, yet adults have great difficulty in understanding this because of an inherently biased view. A shift in thinking to embrace youth assets and not just their issues and needs is necessary, and nowhere is this more apparent than in discussing the undertaking of research and the competencies that youth can develop or enhance in the process (Bucknall, 2014, p. 82): "Far from being vulnerable, incompetent and unreliable, children are now widely acknowledged to be competent and rights-bearing social actors whose voices increasingly appear in social research." Although sociodemographic differences between researchers and practitioners and youth are inevitable, adults can engage in a reflexive process that focuses on how these differences may impact the research outcomes (Taft, 2007).

This deliberative process helps increase the consciousness of the researcher to privilege and how it influences perceptions and interactions. There is no phase in this process that cannot benefit from an exchange between youth and adult researchers. For example, the post-research conclusion stage also presents an excellent opportunity for children and youth researchers to exchange with adult counterparts their reactions to various aspects of the research process and experience (Pinter & Zandian, 2015; Taiapa, Barnes, & McCreanor, 2013).

Youth have technological competencies that adults may not possess, and this asset can be tapped in research undertakings like those proposed in this volume and elsewhere (Santo, Ferguson, & Trippel, 2010). The case example of newcomer youth using the Internet in Chapter 5 shows the potential of this method to break down communication and cross cultural and geographical boundaries. However, youth grasp of youth culture, which is subject to the dynamic and ever present influence of sociocultural forces, gives them insights that adults simply cannot possess. In addition, socially navigating difficult urban situations brings an often missing perspective on what can constitute "normal" and "extreme" reactions to environmental stressors. These skills and interests influence social relationships, including friendship selection.

Last, youth enhance their social skills (social capital) in the process of conducting community-based research, and the acquisition of these new forms of relationship knowledge and skills stay with them after a project is completed and can be applied in new social situations as they traverse new organizations and experiences (Walsh, Casselman, Hickey, Lee, & Pliszka, 2015). Friendship development and maintenance is not possible without social skills. The more urban youth understand their own social skills, the better position they will be in for establishing and maintaining friendships.

Conclusion

The importance of research informing the field of community practice is undebatable, and this takes on greater importance when social interventions are urban-focused and specifically seek out highly marginalized youth. The dearth of information pertaining to a normalized development and interrelationship is glaring. The demographic predictions for urban youth of color necessitate that the field of community practice refocuses itself on urban youth and an embrace of a positive or assets-based paradigm.

Practice debates often center on the kind of research that informs practice and on who is doing the research. As this chapter has argued, there is a prominent place for research conducted by youth in advancing our knowledge of friendships, whether it is youth-led or co-produced with adults. This shifting of youth roles from subject to researcher offers much promise for research on youth friendships. Furthermore, when youth are enlisted to play prominent roles in research, their human capacity is increased in the process.

SECTION III

Reflections

7

Cross-Cutting Themes from Field Examples and Scholarly Literature

Introduction

This chapter, as the title indicates, synthesizes material obtained from field-based examples and the latest and most relevant literature on the subject of urban youth friendships. The subject of urban youth friendships is extremely complex and in much need of bridging between research literature and the practice field. Translation of research results is always a struggle, and when discussing urban youth friendships it is no exception. Research for the sake of research is not what community practitioners stand for because it does not immediately benefit communities.

This synthesis is important because it will provide strategies and activities that practitioners can embrace and adopt where necessary and possible to improve service delivery and social interventions. Furthermore, there is a need to contextualize this knowledge so that it is applicable at the local level. As noted throughout this book, the nation, its cities, and its youth are integrally related and one cannot be separated from the other.

A total of six major cross-cutting themes will be addressed in this chapter. These themes have been selected not only for their importance in the lives of urban youth of color but also because of how they impact how community practice can transpire in a manner that affirms the importance of friendships in the lives of youth. Each theme can easily stand alone in importance. However, when looked at as a group, they take on immense significance for community social work practice with urban youth and their friendship networks. In addition, each theme can easily consist of multiple smaller themes, bringing a certain richness and depth that is warranted in this type of community practice.

RECRUITMENT OF YOUTH DYADS

Recruitment of program participants is often a central topic in planning community-based programs, and it certainly is the case in this chapter. Historically, youth development and other community practice interventions have recruited youth and conceptualized their participation as individuals. In fact, it would be rare that any program form, intake, or baseline would collect data on their friendships even when youth clearly can enter a program with a friend(s). This focus on individuals come as no great surprise to any practitioner or researcher since this country is founded on individualistic beliefs and principles.

However, cultural values of youth of color, as already addressed earlier in this book, may emphasize collective rather than individualistic values, and this is particularly the case in programs reaching out to newcomer youth. Leisure settings, for example, have been found to provide excellent settings for newcomer youth's stories and maps, social learning, language skill development, and fostering friendship and peer connections (Campbell, 2014).

A shift in thinking about how recruitment can or should transpire for youth programming and research, and the structuring of activities to both reinforce old friendships and establish new ones, is bound to generate innovative approaches and activities, bringing rewards for youth, their friends, family, communities, and the field of practice. Gathering data is often not seen as a high priority by staff who may be more interested in carrying out activities rather than documenting the process and the results. These data will become essential in securing funding for future projects and substantiating programming for policy-makers.

How programs are advertised and the outreach conceived will require significant changes from conventional approaches that emphasize individual youth participation. For example, key informants are often a key source for obtaining referrals and spreading the word about programs and initiatives. These individuals, as a result, will no doubt have many questions as to why dyads are sought rather than the conventional individual and why friendship is a topic of concern from a programming perspective.

These meetings will often require considerable expenditure of additional time. However, it is important to re-emphasize that youth often join programs with accompanying friends or because friends in the program encourage them to join. Friendships and associations with youth programming is not new, but we have rarely formally recognized this relationship phenomenon; therefore we have undertaken activities without acknowledging how these relationships influence outcomes.

Concerns about how these friendship dyads may interfere with the making of new friendships within the program must be acknowledged. Nevertheless, this can be easily dealt with when there is an explicit recognition that the intent is not to break up friendships but to expand friendships through participation in a common and affirming experience. Probably the greatest challenge will be in new programs that stress or incorporate youth friendships. Once these programs are established and successful, graduates will be the best ambassadors of the program and bring their newfound knowledge and skill sets to the community, thereby enhancing community capacities in the process.

FRIENDSHIPS OUTSIDE OF PROGRAMMING

We must remember that youth have a social peer network, as do we all. This network exerts influence in their lives, and their friendships stand out. Planning activities can also include special outreach to friendships outside of the program. We often think of activities that seek to showcase youth accomplishments to family and significant adults in youth lives. These celebrations are intended for family. However, purposefully reaching out to their friends outside of the program will require flexibility in how key program components are conceptualized and modified as needed.

Community practitioners must contend with many of the issues raised in earlier chapters but particularly those raised in Chapter 3 and the case illustrations in Chapter 5. Thorny ethical, conceptual, and practical questions will emerge on what constitutes a friend and the meaning of this friendship. The concept is illusive under the best of circumstances, yet its potential to bring about significant changes in social networks makes it worthwhile to pursue. Having youth themselves play a prominent role in this form of research and practice helps increase the likelihood that the end result has significance for them.

DATA-GATHERING ON PEERS AND FRIENDSHIPS

Programming-specific data rarely seeks to gather information on how peer or friendship networks have changed or evolved as a result of youth participation and how these social relationships may have benefitted indirectly because of youth participants. Furthermore, programs rarely if ever gather data on youth attempting to capture collectivistic or individualistic perspectives. Youth who embrace collectivistic values view social relationships differently from those who subscribe to individualistic values.

A collectivist approach to youth represents a natural extension of community practice when based on an ecological model. Thus, a collectivist approach necessitates that data be gathered to reinforce this perspective. Nonparticipant friends of program participants can benefit from a program even though they are not directly involved. This can prove challenging from a data-gathering perspective because we rarely conceive of social interventions going beyond participants and their immediate family. However, this spread of benefits can be viewed as integral. Program participant friends can even be involved in data gathering by sharing their perspective on friendships with program participants.

A detailed account of peer and friendship networks to supplement data gathered on kinship networks provides a critical baseline from which to understand how these networks evolve while youth participate in programming. Developing an understanding of how these networks overlap or isolate youth is critical if community practitioners are going to be strategic in how interventions are planning and evaluated. These data can be expansive or limited, as dictated by budgets and program goals, which brings much needed flexibility.

FRIENDSHIP AS A PROGRAMMING TOPIC

As evidenced throughout this book in both theory and case illustrations, youth friendships are either explicitly or implicitly addressed through programming. In cases where friendship is explicit, there is an acknowledgment that advancements are not only possible but highly valued by youth and program staff, and programs specifically utilize activities that promote exchanges and learning as a central theme for all participants and staff. This is particularly the case in efforts to have youth broaden their social network outside of their ethnic or racial group (Tropp, O'Brien, & Migacheva, 2014).

The subject of friendship can either be a central or secondary goal in youth community practice. In the former, the subject is openly addressed; in the latter, it is integrated in various aspects of programming. This flexibility is essential because of how funding sources dictate program goals. The field, as already noted, still has to make significant strides in encompassing youth friendships. Flexibility in programming, as a result, allows local circumstances to dictate how and to what extent friendships can play a central role in program activities.

As addressed throughout the coverage of theory and case illustrations, youth friendships take on many different forms and levels of importance, and it becomes critical that community practitioners do not fixate on one definition or manifestation of friendship. Broadening our conception of friendship will increase the chances of programming success and, in the process, help create a new knowledge base that will prove invaluable for future programming efforts.

Activities or exercises that focus on how youth define friends, what makes friends special, and what it takes to break up a friendship can be constructed, including efforts to find out what it would take to expand a friendship network. When these activities are followed with time for reflection and dialogue, they bring deeper meaning and potentially more long-lasting change in the social skills necessary to establish and maintain meaningful friendships.

Youth conceptions of friendships, as noted, are subject to the influence of many different forces. Parental or legal guardian attitudes toward friendship wield considerable influence, particularly in the case of younger children. Consequently, programming staff must seek to capture these attitudes and expectations in order to more fully appreciate youth participant conceptions of friendships and to appreciate how these conceptions have evolved during their time in a program.

CONNECTIVE TECHNOLOGY/DIGITAL YOUTH

Technology permeates our entire lives, both personally and professionally. Today's youth live in a world where technology and its varied manifestations are integral to their everyday experience (Erstad, 2012). Thus, it should come as no great surprise that technology is a key theme in relation to friendship and peer networks. H.C. Yang (2014) addresses young people's friendship and love relationships and the use of connectivity technology to exert control over the extent of their investment of personal resources, time, and emotion in friendships.

Online friendships can supplement or substitute for in-person friendships in cases where urban youth are having difficulties establishing friendships in school or in their neighborhoods. Thus, any discussion of peer friendship networks will invariably involve a mixture, with each friend (online and in-person) possibly meeting different needs. This broadening of a friendship network makes assessment of the role of friendships that much more difficult. However, it also expands the options beyond a narrow geographical confine.

FUTURE RESEARCH AGENDA

Although the subject of research was addressed in great detail in the previous chapter, it remains a theme that must be addressed to move forward community practice with urban youth in the immediate future. The subject of knowledge ownership will re-emerge in the Conclusion. Knowledge serves as the foundation upon which progress can occur in the future, and research, regardless of how it is conceptualize, will prove to be the cement that new and bold initiatives will be based on (Cooper, 2014).

Youth community practitioners must assume a more active research role in this field in order to advance our knowledge of urban youth friendships (Dickson, Vigurs, & Newman, 2013). Gormally and Coburn (2014) discuss the importance for cross-disciplinarity between youth work and research practices to introduce and/or reinforce research-mindedness among youth workers who bring about necessary advancements in this field of practice, with implications for youth community practice in the United States. The authors identified five elements of youth work practice that can easily be aligned with research processes: (1) reflexivity, (2) positionality and bias, (3) insider cultural competence, (4) rapport and trust, and (5) power relationships. These themes were identified and addressed earlier in this book.

Bagwell and Schmidt (2013, pp. 261–262), in their charge to move forward the general field of children and youth friendships, identified six themes that also have particular implications for urban youth of color:

(1) [A]cknowledging the strengths and limitations of the individualism framework, (2) including alternative dimensions along which cultures differ,

(3) considering culture in terms other than national boundaries, (4) expanding the aspects of friendship that are studied, (5) incorporating multiple methodologies within individual studies, and (6) expanding the number and variety of cultures that are studied.

Bagwell and Schmidt's themes stress the importance both of research being highly focused and of contextualizing youth friendships along a variety of critical social-cultural dimensions.

The importance of youth friendships is too great to have one profession dominate this field. In fact, its importance is such that it requires a multidisciplinary approach, although that recommendation is made with an understanding of how difficult this is to accomplish. As noted earlier in this book, each profession conceptualizes friendship slightly differently, making collaboration based on an agreed-upon definition difficult. Embracing a community focus and the set of values outlined earlier will facilitate this collaboration. Furthermore, youth must be central players in this research if it is to have profound meaning in their lives.

Conclusion

The themes identified in this chapter will not be surprising to experienced community youth practitioners and academics. Yet there is no denying the excitement and potential contributions that youth friendships can have on changing participants and their community. The series of themes raised can easily have multiple books devoted to them to do justice to their significance for the field of urban youth community practice. That is the nature of knowledge. The more we learn about a topic, the more we realize that there is so much more to be learned. That is also the case when writing a book.

An author gets a book contract because he or she is judged worthy because of his or her reputation and knowledge on the book's subject. In the process of writing the book and seeing it through the various stages of production before it actually appears in print, the author quickly realizes the immensity of the pursuit and how limited his or her knowledge really is. In essence, welcome to the field of knowledge creation!

Conclusion

Introduction

There is no universal definition of what constitutes a conclusion. Ironically, there is no universal definition of friendship either. This lack of clarity allows each author to conceptualize conclusions to meet his or her own needs. In essence, a conclusion allows an author to present the ideas or themes that emerged in the course of writing the book and are of sufficient importance to make note of before completing it. Another way of putting it is that it encourages reflection. This reflection can be philosophical in nature, therapeutic, or even both, as the case in this book. The experience of concluding is very different from that of beginning a book: that period is dominated by periods of excitement and pure dread about the task that is ahead.

Much goes through my mind as this book comes to its logical conclusion. Urban youth community practice is an expanding universal concept, without an end in sight. This book stands as a testament to the potential of the field to reach out into uncharted territory. This is not to say that this expansion does not come with its share of challenges and pitfalls. For example, when do we say that a particular focus or goal is not within the purview of an expanding field of practice? In essence, what is *not* youth community practice? I have identified nine key points that left a profound impact on me in the course of writing this book. The concept of intersectionality, too, has expanded to take into account how urban youth of color have changed in composition and the consequences of these changes on their well-being. Intersectionality is dynamic, and it can be viewed from an evolutionary point of view. The accompanying evolution of our understanding will no doubt complicate how social interventions are conceptualized, funded, implemented, and evaluated in the future. The following themes, I believe, help capture some of the major forces at work that will shape youth community practice into the foreseeable future.

Youth of Color Are Not Monolithic

As the saying goes, life is complicated—and so is community practice when focused on urban youth of color. As noted in Chapter 4, "youth of color" is a catch-all phrase that is meant to bring all youth of color under one rather big umbrella, with each spoke representing one group of color. However, in reality, that umbrella requires countless numbers of spokes if it truly is going to be encompassing of all groups.

Major social forces are operating to make racial and ethnic groupings difficult to undertake. Out-group births are increasing, and the days when we looked at race and ethnicity as representing singular entities are long gone. Some would go so far as to argue that those days never existed in the first place. Nevertheless, there is no denying that race and ethnicity have become complicated as this nation has undergone dramatic changes and evolutions in composition of its populace.

When we add documented status, acculturation levels, religious/spiritual beliefs and practices, formal educational attainment, skin pigmentation, geographical context, gender identity, and abilities—to list but several factors—the argument that no two youth are alike takes on even greater significance. Thus, we should eschew groupings that do a disservice to youth for the sake of expediency. This is a tall order in a world that seeks to collapse categories to simplify discourse, but one worth pursuing whenever possible if we are to do justice to our calling as community practitioners with the goal of engaging oppression. How we gather and report data will be done in a manner that does justice to who we are talking about and how it should impact urban youth programming.

Youth Friendships Are an Understudied Area

Yes, urban youth of color are understudied. Yes, what little we know of these youth is adult biased and deficit driven. The subject of youth friendships in general, however, is vastly understudied, even though the topic of youth and friendships is universally understood to be inseparable. In addition, the concept of friendship is not static and never has been. It, too, is evolving and bringing into discussion new and never addressed aspects, particularly on intersectionality.

The extent of this dearth of information was surprising and quite disturbing. I fully expected the subject of youth community practice focused on addressing friendships to be limited in scope. Nevertheless, the topic of friendship, considering its importance within a youth peer network perspective, is simply nowhere near as represented in the literature compared to other forms of social relationships, and it pales in comparison with the literature on adults at all stages of life.

What does this mean for the field? It means that much basic and groundbreaking work will need to transpire before community practice can more fully maximize the potential of urban youth friendships in creating positive community change in the nations' cities. Establishing a sound foundation based on clarity of theory and empirical evidence will help practitioners, academics, and youth to collaborate on community ventures. This not only means increasing the amount and substance of scholarship and research; it also means that this new knowledge must find its way into the classroom and field placements.

Understanding the importance and power of friendship is not an alien concept to those of us in community practice. It isn't like drug abuse, child abuse, and some other social conditions that we have personally never experienced but still manage to have empathy for. Consequently, it is not a great leap to understand the role of friendships and why we should strive to enhance and create them in the lives of those who can best benefit from them. In essence, friendships are normalizing.

A Deficit/Problem Perspective Continues to Be Alive and Well

I marvel at the tenacity of a deficit or problem perspective. I have been writing about this worldview for more than 40 years, and I was very disturbed by its power while I was a graduate social work student in New York City. The cognitive side of me understands the power and attraction of problems and how research funding and careers are built on publishing articles and even books on problems and their potential solutions. However, the power and attraction of a deficit or blaming-the-victim perspective goes beyond money and careers.

The popularity of prevention necessitates that the fundamental premises that these initiatives are based on be open to scrutiny. Prevention initiatives are intended to prevent problems; prevention is still problem-focused although it can certainly embrace activities that are positive youth development (PYD) or youth-led in philosophy and process. I make this observation realizing that it will ruffle feathers and will be controversial. This is not to say that important work is not being undertaken in the prevention field. Nevertheless, preventing a problem from occurring results in a focus that minimizes or ignores "typical" or "normal" development, as in the case of youth friendships.

It seems as if the power of deficit thinking is so immense that makes it easier to undertake research and attract the attention of funders and policy makers. Problems are always easier document, making it easier for elected officials and policy-makers to bring attention to specific issues. It is also much easier to research and document a problem as opposed to documenting when a problem has been averted because of careful planning. Measuring the mitigation or elimination of problems also makes it easier to substantiate the funding of programs.

Values Are the DNA of Community Youth Practice

The importance of values must never be underestimated in shaping worldviews and how practice is conceptualized and implemented. The role and importance of the seven values addressed in Chapter 2 lie at the crux of youth community practice. Our ever-expanding universe of practice must follow physical laws, and values provide these laws. These values help those interested in youth community practice socially navigate difficult local circumstances. I am always very fond of saying that "to plan is human; to implement is divine."

Practitioners never have the luxury of thinking about values as "warm and fuzzy" because of the importance that values have in understanding the power they wield in influencing human reactions, professional and personal. Any practitioner or academic who has been in a situation where his or her values were being compromised will attest to the uneasiness and restless nights this causes. This is not to say that delving into values is easy, and the discovery process can make practitioners and academics uneasy.

Values lead the way to intervention development and use of practice principles, which then can be combined with theory to help guide how interventions and research can unfold within a changing urban context, including responding to the new population groups that are ushering in a new era in the United States. Discussing implicit values, however, can raise great tensions and challenges because of how powerful these hidden or implicit values are.

All interventions have a theoretical and political side. Unfortunately, we have a propensity to avoid discussing the politics of interventions and instead focus on theory and research findings as if they existed in a world without political considerations and reactions. Values, however, permeate both sides of this practice equation and help practitioners and academics acknowledge the interrelationship between theory and politics (Delgado, 1999).

Can We Be Friends?

We are certainly not at a loss in counting the numerous configurations that friendships can take. However, friendships between "professionals" and "clients" historically has been a topic that has received considerable attention in professional education, particularly on the challenges and pitfalls when this occurs. The subject of staff–youth friendships, as noted earlier in this book, does raise questions pertaining to objectivity and to maintaining a distance that is supposed to increase authority. I started my social work career as a clinical (or casework) practitioner, and I always had great difficulty in withholding personal information and showing the humanity in me for fear that such disclosure would compromise my "professional" relationships with "clients."

Friendship relationships between staff and youth can and often do occur. Staff get to know youth, their families, and friends outside of the program when programs are community-based and -centered. Staff become part of a community in programs that enjoy positive reputations. They may even be invited to attend major cultural ceremonies in youth participant lives, such as weddings, graduations, and baptisms. The most successful staff members will have the distinction of being considered part of the community.

Finally, it would be hypocritical of me not to turn my attention to educators and their friendships with students. Anyone who has been in the field of teaching over an extended period of time has had an opportunity to develop friendships with students. This topic is rarely, if ever, talked about. However, sharing similar interests on a topic or sharing similar sociodemographic backgrounds develops a special bond that can continue after graduation.

Anti-Urban Sentiments Are Alive and Well

One key theme raised in various chapters of this book dealt with a historical and prevailing anti-urban ethos in the United States. Interestingly, and I guess not unexpectedly, cities have continued their evolution as magnets for attracting individuals seeking better lives, as in the case of newcomers and lesbian, gay, bisexual, transgender, and questioning (LGBTQ) groups. Cities, in essence, have continued their role as havens for the marginalized. Cities, too, have continued to be havens for the well-off and even the nation's infamous "One Percent."

The deep historical roots of an anti-urban bias go back to the founding of the United States, and it would be foolhardy of me to think that this bias will be erased overnight since it has had such staying power. Nevertheless, it is impossible to separate the composition of cities—and, in the case of this book, one that is of color—from the physical structure of this geographical entity. Cities are living organisms and not static entities without life.

Identifying a bias is the first and most important step toward rectifying it. This new awareness does not come without pain and deep reflection. Acknowledging why this nation is fearful of cities is one dimension of this process of identification; another is to propose an alternative view, one that is positive. Urban centers have historically played a critical role in nation-building in this and other countries. A shift in thinking about cities from a deficit-based to an asset-based viewpoint is essential in shifting this nation's bias against cities. Bernstein (2000), for example, identified 10 urban assets that are generally overlooked in any discussion concerning this nation's cities but are worth noting:

1. Purchasing power (concentration of capital and markets)
2. Concentration of workforce (availability)
3. Mass transit systems (available and do not have to be created)
4. Accessibility (general geographical accessibility facilitates development)
5. Abandoned and underused land (open land and buildings are available for development)
6. Underutilized infrastructure (available for upgrading where needed)
7. In-place infrastructure and underutilized carrying capacity (ready availability of utilities)

8. Already assembled rights of way (incentives to establish new institutions and businesses)
9. Efficient resource use (concentrated facilities)
10. Biodiversity and natural capital (availability of uncultivated land)

Bernstein's list emphasizes physical capital. However, social capital in the form of human diversity and cultural assets also need to be considered as urban assets. A community practice addendum to Bernstein's list provides a balance between physical and social capital, for example.

Human cultural achievement would not have been possible without urban centers that concentrated people together to exchange ideas and learn from each other. This evolution, in turn, made nations possible. Where would the birth of the United States be without cities such as Boston, New York, Philadelphia, and Washington, DC? The American Revolution was not conceived in rural America but in the taverns of major cities.

The United States in 2050

If the United States can be expected to thrive over the course of the next 40 or 50 years and continue to be a major social and economic force in the world, it must evolve in a manner than is inclusive of all its residents and taps them as potential assets. The United States will have no difficulty in obtaining population replacement if we embrace our history as a nation of immigrants. This inclusive mindset has evaded the majority of European countries, for example, so that population replacement has become a major social issue. We, however, will not be faced with that challenge because of our history of accepting (with notable exceptions) immigrants.

Baby boomers and older adults will not have to worry about the Social Security system becoming insolvent because few younger people will be expected to support many older people. However, if demographics is destiny, as the saying goes, the United States will look dramatically different in the year 2050 when compared to today, and some states and cities already serve as role models for this profile today. Embracing demographic changes rather than resisting them will wield significant influence on how this nation is positioned to address the challenges the future will bring.

Youth/Young African-American/Black Men and Race Relations

Writing this book while witnessing racial riots across the nation because of the deaths of young African-American/blacks at the hands of police officers only reaffirmed the importance of social justice as a guiding theme in urban-focused community practice. The anger and distrust found in these and other communities is unmistakable. These "urban disturbances" were not just about race but also about socioeconomic class. Baltimore stands out because of the number of African-American/black police officers involved in the death of Freddie Gray.

A youth perspective on race relations cannot be limited to police–youth of color relations. The June 17, 2015, mass murder of nine African Americans at the historic Emanuel African Methodist Episcopal Church in Charleston, South Carolina, by a young white male (Corasani, Perez-Pena, & Alvarez, 2015) highlights the insidious and violent nature of racism in the United States and brings home the fact that no community or organization is safe: in this instance, the site of violence was a house of worship (Weisman, 2015).

Schools of social work located in these areas are called upon to respond to and help ensure that tensions do not escalate and that further harm is minimized. Bridging divides between universities and communities is never an easy accomplishment; nevertheless, universities, particularly those located in central cities, have an obligation to reach out and be an integral part of the community's life rather than just being in the community. Research and scholarship that is undertaken must have social justice goals guiding them to make them relevant to these communities.

Who Controls Knowledge Production?

The topic of self-, local, and experiential knowledge was addressed earlier in this book, and it is sufficiently important to identify as a key theme throughout this book. The answer to the question of who owns the production of knowledge has profound social, political, cultural, and economic implications. Knowledge shapes policies and the programs that emanate from them. If that knowledge is severely compromised, as in the case of urban youth of color, for example, then determining who controls it has some very real consequences.

The answer to the question of ownership may well depend upon who is asking the question in the first place and where it is that they sit. Those in positions of power—as manifested through elected office, academic appointments, or organizational position—will answer the answer in one manner; but if the knowledge is based on those telling their stories or narratives, such as youth of color, then their view of what knowledge is important takes center stage. This book has taken the latter position.

Nevertheless, it is possible that a co-ownership model of knowledge can be advanced by bringing together at the table those in power and those with self-knowledge, so to speak. This model is attractive from a "real-world" perspective as opposed to a strictly "academic" model. This model brings with it the tensions associated with power, but any community practice approach encounters this tension. The key is whether or not this power imbalance is recognized and addressed.

Community Practice Is an Expanding Universe

It is fitting to end this conclusion by paying attention to why community practice, particularly urban-based, has such prodigious potential for altering the life circumstances of millions of this nation's most marginalized youth of color. The topic of self-, local, and experiential knowledge was most particularly addressed in Chapter 6, in the discussion of peer-led research.

The roots of social work can be traced back to the 19th century and the Settlement House Movement, which acknowledged the importance of being community-centered in our practice. The profession of social work has evolved and taken many detours along the way since its origins. However, for many of us, it never left the community, and community practice has started to re-emerge as a field of practice with the potential to cast the profession in a central role in helping to craft policies and programs focused on the nation's inner cities. This is not to say that community practitioners are not swimming against the tide in answering this call to duty. Nevertheless, after you have done this for a while, is there any other way to swim?

I sincerely hope that many other books on previously unexplored ways of conceptualizing youth community social work practice are forthcoming in the next decade and that this, in turn, will spur funding and policy decisions to make urban community social work practice that much more prevalent. The scholarship resulting from these efforts, in turn, will serve to prepare youth community practitioners to take up the charge laid out in this book and do so with enthusiastic fervor.

Conclusion

This conclusion brings to an end this book and our journey. The reader has hopefully been inspired to venture into embracing urban youth friendships and including them in community practice interventions. The mysteries of urban youth friendships are far from being solved. No one book or series of books on the subject can do justice to this subject. The reader, nevertheless, is hopefully in a better position to help seek these answers and pose new and provocative questions in the process. The field of youth community practice will reap the benefits of these advances and help shape the lives of urban youth in the process, resulting in a brighter future for them, their communities, and society.

REFERENCES

Abaied, J. L., & Rudolph, K. D. (2011). Maternal influences on youth responses to peer stress. *Developmental Psychology, 47*(6), 1776.

Abebe, T. (2009). Multiple methods, complex dilemmas: Negotiating socio-ethical spaces in participatory research with disadvantaged children. *Children's Geographies, 7*(4), 451–465.

Aberson, C. L., Shoemaker, C., & Tomolillo, C. (2004). Implicit bias and contact: The role of interethnic friendships. *Journal of Social Psychology, 144*(3), 335–347.

Adachi, P. J., & Willoughby, T. (2013). Do video games promote positive youth development? *Journal of Adolescent Research, 28*(2), 155–165.

Adams, R. (2008). *Empowerment, participation and social work.* New York: Palgrave Macmillan.

Adams, R. G., & Allan, G. (Eds.). (1998). *Placing friendship in context* (Vol. 15). New York: Cambridge University Press.

Adler, J. (2013). *Soulmates from the pages of history: From mythical to contemporary, 75 examples of the power of friendship.* New York: Algora.

Agnihotri, S., Lynn Keightley, M., Colantonio, A., Cameron, D., & Polatajko, H. (2010). Community integration interventions for youth with acquired brain injuries: A review. *Developmental Neurorehabilitation, 13*(5), 369–382.

Agosto, D. E., & Hughes-Hassell, S. (Eds.). (2010). *Urban teens in the library: Research and practice.* Chicago: American Library Association.

Ahn, J., Subramaniam, M., Bonsignore, E., Pellicone, A., Waugh, A., & Yip, J. (2014). "I want to be a game designer or scientist": Connected learning and developing identities with urban, African-American youth. In *Proceedings of the 11th International Conference of the Learning Sciences* (ICLS 2014).

Aikins, J. W., Bierman, K. L., & Parker, J. G. (2005). Navigating the transition to junior high school: The influence of pre-transition friendship and self-system characteristics. *Social Development, 14*(1), 42–60.

Aitken, S. C. (2001). *Geographies of young people: The morally contested spaces of identity* (Vol. 14). Washington, DC: Psychology Press.

Aitken, S. C. (2014). *The ethnopoetics of space and transformation: Young people's engagement, activism and aesthetics.* Farnham, UK: Ashgate.

Aitken, S. C., Swanson, K., & Kennedy, E. G. (2014). Unaccompanied migrant children and youth: Navigating relational borderlands. *Children and Borders,* 214.

Akom, A. A., Cammarota, J., & Ginwright, S. (2008). Youthtopias: Towards a new paradigm of critical youth studies. *Youth Media Reporter, 2*(4), 1–30.

Alberly, E., & Kostenius, C. (2011). "Damned taxi cab"—how silent communication in questionnaires can be understood and used to give voice to children's experiences. *International Journal of Research and Methods in Education, 34*(2), 117–130.

Alderson, P. (2014). Ethics. In A. Clark, R. Flewitt, M. Hammerseley & M. Robb (Eds.), *Understanding research with children and young people* (p. 85). London: Sage.

Alfano, M. (2015). Friendship and the structure of trust. In A. Masala & J. Webber (Eds.), *From personality to virtue* (pp. 186–206). New York: Oxford University Press.

Alfonso, M. L., Bogues, K., Russo, M., & Brown, K. M. (2008). Participatory research and community youth development: VOICES in Sarasota County, Florida. *Journal of Community Engagement and Scholarship, 1*(1), 34–44.

Allan, G. (1998). Friendship, sociology and social structure. *Journal of Social and Personal Relationships, 15*(5), 685–702.

Allan, G. (2008). Flexibility, friendship, and family. *Personal Relationships, 15*(1), 1–16.

Allegra, M., Gualini, E., & Mourato, J. (2016). *Conflict in the city: Contested urban spaces and local democracy*. Berlin: Jovis.

Allison, K. W., & Obeidallah, D. (2014). Among inner-city African-American teens. *Pathways through adolescence: Individual development in relation to social contexts* (pp. 119–138). New York: Psychology Press.

Alper, M. (2013). New perspectives on youth participation with media. *Routledge international handbook of children, adolescents, and media* (p. 148). New York: Psycology Press.

Al Ramiah, A., Hewstone, M., Voci, A., Cairns, E., & Hughes, J. (2013). It's never too late for "us" to meet "them": Prior intergroup friendships moderate the impact of later intergroup friendships in educational settings. *British Journal of Educational Psychology, 83*(1), 57–75.

Alrutz, M. (2014). *Digital storytelling, applied theatre, & youth: Performing possibility*. New York: Routledge.

Al-Shaar, N. (2014). *Ethics in Islam: Friendship in the political thought of Al-Tawhidi and his contemporaries*. New York: Routledge.

Amichai-Hamburger, Y., Kingsbury, M., & Schneider, B. H. (2013). Friendship: An old concept with a new meaning? *Computers in Human Behavior, 29*(1), 33–39.

Anagnostaki, L. (2006). *"What do they tell their friends?" Intimacy and self- disclosure in young children's friendships* (Doctoral dissertation). London: School of Social Sciences, Brunel University.

Andelman, R. B., Attkisson, C. C., & Rosenblatt, A. B. (2014). Quality of life of children: Toward conceptual clarity. In M. E. Maurish (Ed.), *The use of psychological testing for treatment planning and outcomes assessment* (Vol. 2, pp. 477–510). New York: Taylor & Francis.

Anderson, E. (2013). *Streetwise: Race, class, and change in an urban community*. Chicago: University of Chicago Press.

Anderson, S. A., Sabatelli, R. M., & Kosutic, I. (2007). Families, urban neighborhood youth centers, and peers as contexts for development. *Family Relations, 56*(4), 346–357.

Anderson, V., McKenzie, M., Allan, S., Hill, T., McLean, S., Kayira, J., . . . Butcher, K. (2015). Participatory action research as pedagogy: Investigating social and ecological justice learning within a teacher education program. *Teaching Education, 26*(2), 179–195.

Änggård, E. (2015). Digital cameras: Agents in research with children. *Children's Geographies, 13*(1), 1–13.

Angotti, T. (2006). Apocalyptic anti-urbanism: Mike Davis and his planet of slums. *International Journal of Urban and Regional Research, 30*(4), 961–967.

Annas, J. (1977). Plato and Aristotle on friendship and altruism. *Mind, 86*(344), 532–554.

Antaramian, S. P., Huebner, E. S., & Valois, R. F. (2008). Adolescent life satisfaction. *Applied Psychology, 57*(s1), 112–126.

Anthony, A. K., & McCabe, J. (2015). Friendship talk as identity work: Defining the self through friend relationships. *Symbolic Interaction, 38*(1), 64–82.

Antrop-González, R., Garrett, T., & Vélez, W. (2015). The impact of family religiosity for Latina/o youth: Building a case for personal and academic enhancement through faith. In W. Jeynes & E. Martinez (Eds.), *Ministering spiritually to families* (pp. 165–179). New York: Springer International.

Aptekar, L., & Stoecklin, D. (2013). *Street children and homeless youth: A cross- cultural perspective*. New York: Springer Science & Business Media.

Archer, K. (2013). *The city: The basics*. New York: Routledge.

Arches, J., & Fleming, J. (2006). Young people and social action: Youth participation in the United Kingdom and United States. *New Directions for Youth Development, 2006*(111), 81–90.

Ardizzone, L. (2007). *Getting my word out: Voices of urban youth activists*. New York: State University of New York Press.

Areas, T. O. R. (2012). Rural community practice. In M. Weil, M. S. Reisch & M. L. Olmer (Eds.), *The handbook of community practice* (p. 461). Thousand Oaks, CA: Sage.

Argyle, M. (2001). *The psychology of happiness*. New York: Routledge.

Arter, J. (2014). *Evidence of conditional strategies in human friendship* (No. e347v1). PeerJ PrePrints. Retrieved from https://peerj.com/preprints/347v1.pdf

Asaba, E., Rudman, D. L., Mondaca, M., & Park, M. (2014). 11 visual methodologies. *Qualitative Research Methodologies for Occupational Science and Therapy*, 155.

Astone, N. M., Stolte, A., Martin, S., Hildner, K. F., Peters, H. E., Pendall, R., & Nichols, A. (2015). *Children and youth in an aging America* (Research Report). Urban Institute: Elevate the Debate. Retrieved from http://webarchive.urban.org/UploadedPDF/2000067-Children-and-Youth-in-an-Aging-America.pdf

Atkinson, K. N. (2012). *Education for liberation: A precursor to youth activism for social justice* (Doctoral dissertation). University of Illinois, Chicago

Azmitia, M., Ittel, A., & Break, C. (2006). Latino-heritage adolescents' friendships. In X. Chen, D. French & B. Schneider (Eds), *Peer relationships in cultural context* (p. 426). New York: Cambridge University Press.

Bagnoli, A. (2012). Making sense of mixed methods narratives: Young people's identities, life-plans, and time orientations. In S. Heath & C. Walker (Eds.), *Innovations in youth research* (p. 77). New York: Palgrave.

Bagwell, C. L., & Schmidt, M. E. (2011). The friendship quality of overtly and relationally victimized children. *Merrill-Palmer Quarterly, 57*(2), 158–185.

Bagwell, C. L., & Schmidt, M. E. (2013). *Friendship in childhood and adolescence*. New York: Guilford.

Bagwell, C. L., Kochel, K. P., & Schmidt, M. E. (2015). Friendship and happiness in adolescence. In *Friendship and happiness* (pp. 99–116). Rotterdam: Springer Netherlands.

Bahns, A. J., & Springer, L. S. (2015). Fostering diverse friendships: The role of beliefs about the value of diversity. *Group Processes & Intergroup Relations, 18*(4), 475–488.

Baines, E., & Blatchford, P. (2009). Sex differences in the structure and stability of children's playground social networks and their overlap with friendship relations. *British Journal of Developmental Psychology, 27*(3), 743–760.

Baiocco, R., Laghi, F., Di Pomponio, I., & Nigito, C. S. (2012). Self-disclosure to the best friend: Friendship quality and internalized sexual stigma in Italian lesbian and gay adolescents. *Journal of Adolescence, 35*(2), 381–387.

Baiocco, R., Santamaria, F., Lonigro, A., Ioverno, S., Baumgartner, E., & Laghi, F. (2014). Beyond similarities: Cross-gender and cross-orientation best friendship in a sample of sexual minority and heterosexual young adults. *Sex Roles, 70*(3–4), 110–121.

Balaam, M. C. (2015). A concept analysis of befriending. *Journal of Advanced Nursing, 71*(1), 24–34.

Balakrishnan, A. S. (2014). Children of Moses's experiment: Youth, mental health, and hip-hop in the South Bronx (Doctoral dissertation). Massachusetts Institute of Technology.

Baldridge, B. J., Lamont Hill, M., & Davis, J. E. (2011). New possibilities: (Re)engaging Black male youth within community-based educational spaces. *Race Ethnicity and Education, 14*(1), 121–136.

Ballard, P. J. (2014). What motivates youth civic involvement? *Journal of Adolescent Research, 29*(4), 439–463.

Ballard, P. J., Malin, H., Porter, T. J., Colby, A., & Damon, W. (2015). Motivations for civic participation among diverse youth: More similarities than differences. *Research in Human Development, 12*(1–2), 63–83.

Bananuka, T., & John, V. M. (2015). Picturing community development work in Uganda: Fostering dialogue through photovoice. *Community Development Journal, 50*(2), 196–212.

Banks, D. M., & Weems, C. F. (2014). Family and peer social support and their links to psychological distress among hurricane-exposed minority youth. *American Journal of Orthopsychiatry, 84*(4), 341.

Banks, S. (2012). *Ethical issues in youth work*. New York: Routledge.

Banks, S., Butcher, H., Orton, A., & Robertson, J. (Eds.). (2013). *Managing community practice: Principles, policies and programmes* (2nd ed.). Bristol, UK: Policy Press.

Barber, B. L., Abbott, B. D., & Neira, C. J. B. (2014). Meaningful activity participation and positive youth development. In M.J. Furlong, R. Gilman, & E. Scott (Eds.), *Handbook of positive psychology in schools* (p. 227). New York: Routledge.

Barman-Adhikari, A., Cederbaum, J., Sathoff, C., & Toro, R. (2014). Direct and indirect effects of maternal and peer influences on sexual intention among urban African American and Hispanic females. *Child and Adolescent Social Work Journal, 31*(6), 559–575.

Barnett, R. V., & Brennan, M. A. (2006). Integrating youth into community development: Implications for policy planning and program evaluation. *Journal of Youth Development, 1*(2), 2–16.

Barrett, A. N., Kuperminc, G. P., & Lewis, K. M. (2013). Acculturative stress and gang involvement among Latinos: US-born versus immigrant youth. *Hispanic Journal of Behavioral Sciences, 35*(3), 370–389.

Barrett, M. S., & Bond, N. (2015). Connecting through music: The contribution of a music programme to fostering positive youth development. *Research Studies in Music Education, 37*(1), 37–54.

Bartos, A. E. (2013). Friendship and environmental politics in childhood. *Space and Polity, 17*(1), 17–32.

Baskin, T. W., Quintana, S. M., & Slaten, C. D. (2014). Family belongingness, gang friendships, and psychological distress in adolescent achievement. *Journal of Counseling & Development, 92*(4), 398–405.

Batsleer, J. R. (2008). *Informal learning in youth work.* Thousand Oaks, CA: Sage.

Bauer, S., Loomis, C., & Akkari, A. (2013). Intercultural immigrant youth identities in contexts of family, friends, and school. *Journal of Youth Studies, 16*(1), 54–69.

Bauminger, N., Finzi-Dottan, R., Chason, S., & Har-Even, D. (2008). Intimacy in adolescent friendship: The roles of attachment, coherence, and self-disclosure. *Journal of Social and Personal Relationships, 25*(3), 409–428.

Baysu, G., Phalet, K., & Brown, R. (2014). Relative group size and minority school success: The role of intergroup friendship and discrimination experiences. *British Journal of Social Psychology, 53*(2), 328–349.

Bean, E., & Brennan, K. R. (2014). Youth voices: Performance poetry as a platform for literacy, creativity, and civic engagement. *Journal of Applied Research on Children: Informing Policy for Children at Risk, 5*(1), 23–31.

Becker, J. A., Johnson, A. J., Craig, E. A., Gilchrist, E. S., Haigh, M. M., & Lane, L. T. (2009). Friendships are flexible, not fragile: Turning points in geographically-close and long-distance friendships. *Journal of Social and Personal Relationships, 26*(4), 347–369.

Beder, J. (2009). It's about family: The death of a close family friend. *Families in Society: The Journal of Contemporary Social Services, 90*(2), 227–230.

Beebeejaun, Y., Durose, C., Rees, J., Richardson, J., & Richardson, L. (2014). "Beyond text": Exploring ethos and method in co-producing research with communities. *Community Development Journal, 49*(1), 37–53.

Belackova, V., & Vaccaro, C. A. (2013). "A friend with weed is a friend indeed": Understanding the relationship between friendship identity and market relations among marijuana users. *Journal of Drug Issues, 43*(3), 289–313.

Belgrave, F. Z., Abrams, J., Javier, S., & Maxwell, M. (2014). More than an African American facilitator and a prayer: Integrating culture and community into HIV prevention programs for African American girls. In B. Toni (Ed.), *New frontiers of multidisciplinary research in STEAM-H (Science, Technology, Engineering, Agriculture, Mathematics, and Health)* (pp. 147–160). Heidelberg: Springer International.

Belgrave, F. Z., & Brevard, J. K. (2015). Peers and peeps. In F.Z. Belgrave & J.K. Brevard (Eds.), *African American boys* (pp. 49–65). New York: Springer.

Bell, J. (1995). *Understanding adultism: A key to developing positive youth-adult relationships.* Olympia, WA: The Freechild Project.

Bellotti, E. (2007). Friendship as social support: Friendship networks of single youth. In *UK Social Network Conference 2007* (pp. 52–55), Academia. Retrieved from http://www.academia.edu/download/30588432/10.1.1.108.5345.pdf#page=53.

Benhorin, S., & McMahon, S. D. (2008). Exposure to violence and aggression: Protective roles of social support among urban African American youth. *Journal of Community Psychology, 36*(6), 723–743.

Benner, A. D. (2011*a*). The transition to high school: Current knowledge, future directions. *Educational Psychology Review, 23*(3), 299–328.

Benner, A. D. (2011*b*). Latino adolescents' loneliness, academic performance, and the buffering nature of friendships. *Journal of Youth and Adolescence, 40*(5), 556–567.

Benson, P. L. (2003). Developmental assets and asset-building community: Conceptual and empirical foundations. In *Developmental assets and asset-building communities* (pp. 19–43). New York: Springer US.

Benson, P. L. (2007). Developmental assets: An overview of theory, research, and practice. In R.K. Sibereise & R.M. Lerner (Eds.), *Approaches to positive youth development* (pp. 33–58). London: Sage.

Bernat, D. H., & Resnick, M. D. (2006). Healthy youth development: Science and strategies. *Journal of Public Health Management and Practice, 12*, S10–S16.

Berndt, T. J. (2002). Friendship quality and social development. *Current Directions in Psychological Science, 11*(1), 7–10.

Berndt, T. J. (2004). Children's friendships: Shifts over a half-century in perspectives on their development and their effects. *Merrill-Palmer Quarterly, 50*(3), 206–223.

Bernstein, S. (2000). *Using the hidden assets of America's communities and regions to ensure sustainable communities.* Symposium on the Future of Local Government in Midland, Michigan.

Bers, M. U. (2012). *Designing digital experiences for positive youth development: From playpen to playground.* New York: Oxford University Press.

Bersaglio, B., Enns, C., & Kepe, T. (2015). Youth under construction: The United Nations' representations of youth in the global conversation on the post-2015 development agenda. *Canadian Journal of Development Studies/Revue canadienne d'études du développement, 36*(1), 57–71.

Best, P., Manktelow, R., & Taylor, B. (2014). Online communication, social media and adolescent wellbeing: A systematic narrative review. *Children and Youth Services Review, 41*, 27–36.

Billett, P. (2012). Indicators of youth social capital: The case for not using adult indicators in the measurement of youth social capital. *Youth Studies Australia, 31*(2), 9–16.

Billett, P. (2014). Dark cloud or silver lining? The value of bonding networks during youth. *Journal of Youth Studies, 17*(7), 847–856.

Bird, J. M., & Markle, R. S. (2012). Subjective well-being in school environments: Promoting positive youth development through evidence-based assessment and intervention. *American Journal of Orthopsychiatry, 82*(1), 61–66.

Bird, K. (2011). Against all odds: Community and policy solutions to address the American youth crisis. *University of Pennsylvania Journal of Law and Social Change, 15*, 233.

Birmingham, D., & Calabrese Barton, A. (2014). Putting on a green carnival: Youth taking educated action on socioscientific issues. *Journal of Research in Science Teaching, 51*(3), 286–314.

Black, S. (2014). "Street music," urban ethnography and ghettoized communities. *International Journal of Urban and Regional Research, 38*(2), 700–705.

Black, T. (2010). *When a heart turns rock solid: The lives of three Puerto Rican brothers on and off the streets.* New York: Vintage.

Blackburn, M. V., & McCready, L. T. (2009). Voices of queer youth in urban schools: Possibilities and limitations. *Theory into Practice, 48*(3), 222–230.

Blackman, S. J. (2007). "Hidden ethnography": Crossing emotional borders in qualitative accounts of young people's lives. *Sociology, 41*(4), 699–716.

Blackman, S., & Commane, G. (2012). Double reflexivity: The politics of friendship, fieldwork and representation within ethnographic studies of young people. In S. Heath & C. Walker (Eds.), *Innovations in youth research* (pp. 229–247. New York: Palgrave.

Blatterer, H. (2014). *Everyday friendships: Intimacy as freedom in a complex world.* New York: Palgrave Macmillan.

Block, P. (2015). Reciprocity, transitivity, and the mysterious three-cycle. *Social Networks, 40,* 163–173.

Blumberg, B. F., Peiró, J. M., Roe, R. A., Lyon, F., Möllering, G., & Saunders, M. N. K. (2012). Trust and social capital: Challenges for studying their dynamic relationship. In F. Lyon, G. Mollering & M.N. K. Saunders (Eds.), *Handbook of research methods on trust* (pp. 61–71). Cheltenham, UK: Edward Elgar.

Blummer, B. (2008). Digital literacy practices among youth populations: A review of the literature. *Education Libraries, 31*(1), 38–45.

Boardman, J. D., Domingue, B. W., & Fletcher, J. M. (2012). How social and genetic factors predict friendship networks. *Proceedings of the National Academy of Sciences, 109*(43), 17377–17381.

Boehm, A., & Cohen, A. (2013). Commitment to community practice among social work students: Contributing factors. *Journal of Social Work Education, 49*(4), 601–618.

Bogat, G. A., & Liang, B. (2005). Gender in mentoring relationships. In D. L. DuBois & M. J. Karcher (Eds.), *Handbook of youth mentoring* (pp. 205–217). Thousand Oaks, CA: Sage.

Boje, D. M., & Jørgensen, K. M. (2014). Friendship as a way of living: Deconstruction and quantum storytelling. *Tamara Journal of Critical Organisation Inquiry, 12*(4), 33.

Bolland, J. (2003). Hopelessness and risk behavior among adolescents living in high poverty inner-city neighborhoods. *Journal of Adolescence, 26*(2), 145–158.

Bolland, J., Bryant, C., Lian, B., McCallum, D., Vazsonyi, A., & Barth, J. (2007). Development and risk behavior among African American, Caucasian, and mixed-race adolescents living in high poverty inner-city neighborhoods. *American Journal of Community Psychology, 40,* 230–249.

Bolland, J., Lian, B., & Formichella, C. (2005). The origins of hopelessness among inner- city African American adolescents. *American Journal of Community Psychology, 36,* 293–305.

Bolzan, N., & Gale, F. (2012). Using an interrupted space to explore social resilience with marginalized young people. *Qualitative Social Work, 11*(5), 502–516.

Boman, J. H., IV, Krohn, M. D., Gibson, C. L., & Stogner, J. M. (2012). Investigating friend-ship quality: An exploration of self-control and social control theories' friendship hypotheses. *Journal of Youth and Adolescence, 41*(11), 1526–1540.

Bond, M. (2014). 21st century amigos: The new age of friendship. *New Scientist, 222*(2970), 40–43.

Bonilla-Silva, E. (2004). From bi-racial to tri-racial: Towards a new system of racial stratifi-cation in the USA. *Ethnic and Racial Studies, 27*(6), 931–950.

Boocock, S. S., & Scott, K. A. (2005). *Kids in context: The sociological study of children and childhoods.* Lanham, MD: Rowman & Littlefield.

Borrero, N., Lee, D. S., & Padilla, A. M. (2013). Developing a culture of resilience for low-income immigrant youth. *Urban Review, 45*(2), 99–116.

Borrero, N. E., & Yeh, C. J. (2010). Ecological English language learning among ethnic minority youth. *Educational Researcher, 39*(8), 571–581.

Bottrell, D. (2009). Understanding "marginal" perspectives towards a social theory of resil-ience. *Qualitative Social Work, 8*(3), 321–339.

Bowers, E. P., Li, Y., Kiely, M. K., Brittian, A., Lerner, J. V., & Lerner, R. M. (2010). The five Cs model of positive youth development: A longitudinal analysis of confirmatory factor structure and measurement invariance. *Journal of Youth and Adolescence, 39*(7), 720–735.

Bowers, E. P., von Eye, A., Lerner, J. V., Arbeit, M. R., Weiner, M. B., Chase, P., & Agans, J. P. (2011). The role of ecological assets in positive and problematic developmental trajectories. *Journal of Adolescence, 34*(6), 1151–1165.

Bowker, A., & Ramsay, K. (2012). Friendship characteristics. In R. Levesque (Ed.), *Encyclopedia of adolescence* (pp. 1080–1086). New York: Springer US.

Bowlby, S. (2011). Friendship, co-presence and care: Neglected spaces. *Social & Cultural Geography, 12*(6), 605–622.

Boyer, C. B., Hightow-Weidman, L., Bethel, J., Li, S. X., Henry-Reid, L., Futterman, D., . . . Ellen, J. M. (2013). An assessment of the feasibility and acceptability of a friendship-based social network recruitment strategy to screen at-risk African American and Hispanic/Latina young women for HIV infection. *JAMA Pediatrics, 167*(3), 289–296.

Boyes-Watson, C. (2013). *Peacemaking circles and urban youth.* St. Paul, MN: Living Justice Press.

Bradford, S. (2012). *Sociology, youth and youth work practice.* New York: Palgrave Macmillan.

Bradford, S., & Cullen, F. (Eds.). (2013). *Research and research methods for youth practitioners.* New York: Routledge.

Brennan, M. A., Barnett, R. V., & Lesmeister, M. K. (2007). Enhancing local capacity and youth involvement in the community development process. *Community Development, 38*(4), 13–27.

Brenner, N. (2012). What is critical urban theory? In N. Brenner, P. Marcuse & M. Mayer (Eds.), *Cities for people, not for profit: Critical urban theory and the right to the city* (pp. 11–23). New York: Routledge.

Brenner, N., Marcuse, P., & Mayer, M. (Eds.). (2012). *Cities for people, not for profit: Critical urban theory and the right to the city.* New York: Routledge.

Brent, L. J., Chang, S. W., Gariépy, J. F., & Platt, M. L. (2014). The neuroethology of friendship. *Annals of the New York Academy of Sciences, 1316*(1), 1–17.

Brinegar, K. (2010). "I feel like I'm safe again": A discussion of middle grades organizational structures from the perspective of immigrant youth and their teachers. *RMLE Online: Research in Middle Level Education, 33*(9), 1–14.

Britton, M. L. (2014). Latino spatial and structural assimilation: Close intergroup friendships among Houston-area Latinos. *Journal of Ethnic and Migration Studies, 40*(8), 1192–1216.

Broberg, A., Kyttä, M., & Fagerholm, N. (2013). Child-friendly urban structures: Bullerby revisited. *Journal of Environmental Psychology, 35*, 110–120.

Bronk, K. C. (2011). A grounded theory of the development of noble youth purpose. *Journal of Adolescent Research, 27*(1), 78–109.

Brotherton, D. C. (2015). *Youth street gangs: A critical appraisal.* New York: Routledge.

Brown, A. (Ed.). (2006). *Contested space: Street trading, public space, and livelihoods in developing cities.* Ruby, UK: Intermediate Technology.

Brown, B. B., & Klute, C. (2003). Friendships, cliques, and crowds. In B. B. Brown, C. A. Klute, R. Gerald, & M. D. Berzonsky (Eds.), *Blackwell handbook of adolescence* (pp. 330–348). Malden, MA: Blackwell.

Brown, C. (2014). Researching children's schooling identities: Towards the development of an ethnographic methodology. *Review of Education, 2*(1), 69–109.

Brown, L. D., Redelfs, A. H., Taylor, T. J., & Messer, R. L. (2015). Comparing the functioning of youth and adult partnerships for health promotion. *American Journal of Community Psychology, 56*(1), 25–35.

Brown, M. M., & Grumet, J. G. (2009). School-based suicide prevention with African American youth in an urban setting. *Professional Psychology: Research and Practice, 40*(2), 111.

Brown, R. K. (2011). Religion, political discourse, and activism among varying racial/ethnic groups in America. *Review of Religious Research, 53*(3), 301–322.

Browning, C. R., & Soller, B. (2014). Moving beyond neighborhood: Activity spaces and ecological networks as contexts for youth development. *Cityscape* (Washington, DC), *16*(1), 165.

Bruening, J. E., Dover, K. M., & Clark, B. S. (2009). Preadolescent female development through sport and physical activity: A case study of an urban after-school program. *Research Quarterly for Exercise and Sport, 80*(1), 87–101.

Bruun, E. L., & Michael, S. (2014). *Not on speaking terms: Clinical strategies to resolve family and friendship cutoffs.* Lewisville, TX: WW Norton & Company.

Bryan, D. M. (2012). *Top 10 tips for building friendships.* New York: The Rosen Publishing Group.

Bucholtz, M. (2010a). *White kids: Language, race, and styles of youth identity.* New York: Cambridge University Press.

Bucholtz, M. (2010b). Styles and stereotypes: The linguistic negotiation of identity among Laotian American youth. *Pragmatics, 14*(2), 127–147.

Buckholz, L. L. (2014). *Peer conversations about inter-racial and inter-ethnic friendships* (Master's thesis). Portland State University.

Buckley, L., Chapman, R. L., Sheehan, M., & Cunningham, L. (2012). Keeping friends safe: A prospective study examining early adolescent's confidence and support networks. *Educational Studies, 38*(4), 373–381.

Bucknall, S. (2014). Doing qualitative research with children and young people. In A. Clark, R. Flewitt, M. Hammerseley & M. Robb (Eds.), *Understanding research with children and young people* (pp. 69–84). London: Sage.

Bugos, E., Frasso, R., FitzGerald, E., True, G., Adachi-Mejia, A. M., & Cannuscio, C. (2014). Peer reviewed: Practical guidance and ethical considerations for studies using photo-elicitation interviews. *Preventing Chronic Disease, 11*, E 189. Retrieved from http://www.ncbi.nlm.nih.gov/pmc/articles/PMC4215569/.

Buhrmester, D. (1990). Intimacy of friendship, interpersonal competence, and adjustment during preadolescence and adolescence. *Child Development, 61*(4), 1101–1111.

Bukowski, W. M., & Adams, R. (2006). Peers and culture: Details, local knowledge, and essentials. In D.C. French, B.H. Schneider & X. Chen (Eds.), *Peer relationships in cultural context* (pp. 481–488). New York: Cambridge University Press.

Bukowski, W. M., Motzoi, C., & Meyer, F. (2009). Friendship as process, function, and outcome. In K.H. Rubin, W.M. Kukowski & B. Larsen (Eds.), *Handbook of peer interactions, relationships, and groups* (pp. 217–231), New York: Guilford Press.

Bulanda, J. J., Szarzynski, K., Siler, D., & McCrea, K. T. (2013). "Keeping it real": An evaluation audit of five years of youth-led program evaluation. *Smith College Studies in Social Work, 83*(2–3), 279–302.

Bulanda, J. J., Tellis, D., & Tyson McCrea, K. (2015). Cocreating a social work apprenticeship with disadvantaged African American youth: A best-practices after-school curriculum. *Smith College Studies in Social Work, 85*(3), 285– 310.

Bundick, M. J. (2011). Extracurricular activities, positive youth development, and the role of meaningfulness of engagement. *Journal of Positive Psychology, 6*(1), 57–74.

Bunnell, T., Yea, S., Peake, L., Skelton, T., & Smith, M. (2012). Geographies of friendships. *Progress in Human Geography, 36*(4), 490–507.

Burke, K. J., Greene, S., & McKenna, M. K. (2016). A critical geographic approach to youth civic engagement reframing educational opportunity zones and the use of public spaces. *Urban Education, 51*(2), 143–169.

Buskirk-Cohen, A. A. (2015). Effectiveness of a creative arts summer camp: Benefits of a short-term, intensive program on children's social behaviors and relationships. *Journal of Creativity in Mental Health, 10*(1), 34–45.

Butler, P. (2010). *Let's get free: A hip-hop theory of justice.* New York: New Press.

Cahill, H. (2015). Approaches to understanding youth well-being. *Handbook of Children and Youth Studies,* 95–113.

Caine, B. (Ed.). (2014). *Friendship: A history.* New York: Routledge.

Caldwell, L. L., & Smith, E. A. (2013). Leisure as a context for youth development and delinquency prevention. *Pathways and Crime Prevention,* 271–297.

Callahan, R. M., & Obenchain, K. M. (2012). Finding a civic voice: Latino immigrant youths' experiences in high school social studies. *High School Journal* (Chapel Hill, NC), *96*(1), 20.

Callina, K. S., Johnson, S. K., Buckingham, M. H., & Lerner, R. M. (2014). Hope in context: Developmental profiles of trust, hopeful future expectations, and civic engagement across adolescence. *Journal of Youth and Adolescence, 43*(6), 869–883.

Calvert, M., Emery, M., & Kinsey, S. (Eds.). (2013). *Youth programs as builders of social capital: New directions for youth development*(Vol. 138). New York: John Wiley & Sons.

Camiré, M., Forneris, T., Trudel, P., & Bernard, D. (2011). Strategies for helping coaches facilitate positive youth development through sport. *Journal of Sport Psychology in Action, 2*(2), 92–99.

Cammarota, J. (2011). From hopelessness to hope: Social justice pedagogy in urban education and youth development. *Urban Education, 46*(4), 828–844.

Cammarota, J., & Fine, M. (Eds.). (2010). *Revolutionizing education: Youth participatory action research in motion.* New York: Routledge.

Campbell, G. (2014). *Mapping community with African-Canadian youth newcomers: Settlement narratives and welcoming communities* (Doctoral dissertation). University of Waterloo.

Campbell, K., Holderness, N., & Riggs, M. (2015). Friendship chemistry: An examination of underlying factors. *Social Science Journal, 52*(2), 239–247.

Carlo, G., Randall, B. A., Rotenberg, K. J., & Armenta, B. E. (2010). A friend in need is a friend indeed: Exploring the relations among trust beliefs, prosocial tendencies, and friendships. In K.J. Rosenberg (Ed.), *Interpersonal trust during childhood and adolescence* (pp. 270-294). New York: Cambridge University Press.

Carnegie, D. (2010). *How to win friends and influence people.* New York: Simon and Schuster.

Case, A. D., & Hunter, C. D. (2012). Counterspaces: A unit of analysis for understanding the role of settings in marginalized individuals' adaptive responses to oppression. *American Journal of Community Psychology, 50*(1–2), 257–270.

Case, S., & Haines, K. (2014). Reflective friend research: The relational aspects of social scientific research. In K. Lumsden & A. Winter (Eds.), *Reflexivity in criminological research: Experiences with the powerful and the powerless* (pp. 58–74). New York: Palgrave Macmillan.

Casper, D. M., & Card, N. A. (2010). "We were best friends, but . . .": Two studies of antipathetic relationships emerging from broken friendships. *Journal of Adolescent Research, 25*(4), 499–526.

Castleden, H., Mulrennan, M., & Godlewska, A. (2012). Community-based participatory research involving indigenous peoples in Canadian geography: Progress? An editorial introduction. *Canadian Geographer, 56*(2), 155–159.

Cattaneo, L. B., & Chapman, A. R. (2010). The process of empowerment: A model for use in research and practice. *American Psychologist, 65*(7), 646.

Cauce, A. M., Cruz, R., Corona, M., & Conger, R. (2011). The face of the future: Risk and resilience in minority youth. In G. Carlo, L.J. Crockett & M.A. Carranza (Eds.), *Health disparities in youth and families* (pp. 13–32). New York: Springer.

Chan, G. H. Y., & Lo, T. W. (2014). Do friendship and intimacy in virtual communications exist? An investigation of online friendship and intimacy in the context of hidden youth in Hong Kong. *Revista de Cercetare și Intervenţie Socială* (47), 117–136.

Chan, W. Y., Ou, S. R., & Reynolds, A. J. (2014). Adolescent civic engagement and adult outcomes: An examination among urban racial minorities. *Journal of Youth and Adolescence, 43*(11), 1829–1843.

Chanan, G., & Miller, C. (2013). *Rethinking community practice: Developing transformative neighbourhoods*. Bristol, UK: Policy Press.

Chang, J. (2007). *Can't stop won't stop: A history of the hip-hop generation*. New York: Macmillan.

Chang, J. (2013). Affect, trust and friendship: A case study of Chinese and Zambian relationships at the workplace. *International Journal of Business Anthropology, 4*(1), 38–61.

Chappell, P., Rule, P., Dlamini, M., & Nkala, N. (2014). Troubling power dynamics: Youth with disabilities as co-researchers in sexuality research in South Africa. *Childhood, 21*(3), 385–399.

Cheadle, J. E., & Schwadel, P. (2012). The "friendship dynamics of religion," or the "religious dynamics of friendship"? A social network analysis of adolescents who attend small schools. *Social Science Research, 41*(5), 1198–1212.

Checkoway, B. (1996). *Adults as allies*. Ann Arbor: University of Michigan School of Social Work.

Checkoway, B. (2011). What is youth participation? *Children and Youth Services Review, 33*(2), 340–345.

Checkoway, B., & Aldana, A. (2013). Four forms of youth civic engagement for diverse democracy. *Children and Youth Services Review, 35*(11), 1894–1899.

Checkoway, B., & Richards-Schuster, K. (2003). Youth participation in community evaluation research. *American Journal of Evaluation, 24*(1), 21–33.

Checkoway, B. N., & Gutierrez, L. M. (2006). Youth participation and community change: An introduction. *Journal of Community Practice, 14*(1–2), 1–9.

Chen, J., & Brooks-Gunn, J. (2015). Neighborhoods and cognitive development. Emerging trends in the social and behavioral sciences: an interdisciplinary, searchable, and linkable resource. Retrieved from http://works.bepress.com/roslynn_brain/118/

Chen, X., French, D. C., & Schneider, B. H. (Eds.). (2006). *Peer relationships in cultural context*. New York: Cambridge University Press.

Chen, X., & Graham, S. (2015). Cross-ethnic friendships and intergroup attitudes among Asian American adolescents. *Child Development, 86*(3), 749–764.

Chen, Y. W. (2013). Facing a crisis of "unlikely" relationships? Discourses of friendship and alliance across differences. *Journal of Multicultural Discourses, 8*(3), 266–271.

Chentsova-Dutton, Y. E., & Vaughn, A. (2012). Let me tell you what to do: Cultural differences in advice-giving. *Journal of Cross-Cultural Psychology, 43*(5), 687–703.

Cherng, S., Turney, K., & Kao, G. (2014). Less socially engaged? Participation in friendship and extracurricular activities among racial/ethnic minority and immigrant adolescents. *Teachers College Record.* Retrieved from http://works.bepress.com/grace_kao/47/

Ciairano, S., Rabaglietti, E., Roggero, A., Bonino, S., & Beyers, W. (2007). Patterns of adolescent friendships, psychological adjustment and antisocial behavior: The moderating role of family stress and friendship reciprocity. *International Journal of Behavioral Development, 31*(6), 539–548.

Clark-Ibanez, M. (2007). Inner-city children as sharper focus: Sociology of childhood and photo elicitation interviews. In C.C. Stanczak (Ed.), *Visual research methods: Image, society, and representation,* (pp. 167–196). Los Angeles: Sage.

Chen, X., Wang, L., & DeSouza, A. (2006). Temperament, socioemotional functioning, and peer relationships in Chinese and North American children. In X. Chen, D. French & B. Schneider (Eds.), *Peer relationships in cultural context* (p. 123–147). New York: Cambridge University Press.

Chhuon, V. (2014). "I'm Khmer and I'm not a gangster!": The problematization of Cambodian male youth in US schools. *International Journal of Qualitative Studies in Education, 27*(2), 233–250.

Childers-McKee, C. D. (2014). Forging bonds and crossing borders with youth participatory action research. *Urban Education Research and Policy Annuals, 2*(1). Retrieved from https://journals.uncc.edu/urbaned/article/view/238/267

Chow, C. M., & Buhrmester, D. (2011). Interdependent patterns of coping and support among close friends. *Journal of Social and Personal Relationships, 28*(5), 684–705.

Christens, B. D. (2012). Toward relational empowerment. *American Journal of Community Psychology, 50*(1–2), 114–128.

Christens, B. D., & Dolan, T. (2011). Interweaving youth development, community development, and social change through youth organizing. *Youth & Society, 43*(2), 528–548.

Christens, B. D., & Peterson, N. A. (2012). The role of empowerment in youth development: A study of sociopolitical control as mediator of ecological systems' influence on developmental outcomes. *Journal of Youth and Adolescence, 41*(5), 623–635.

Chu, C. M., Daffern, M., Thomas, S., Yaming, A., Long, M., & O'Brien, K. (2015). Determinants of gang affiliation in Singaporean youth offenders: Social and familial factors. *Journal of Aggression, Conflict and Peace Research, 7*(1), 19–32.

Chung, Y. S. C. (2014). *Across the colonial divide: Friendship in the British empire, 1875–1940* (Doctoral dissertation). New Zealand: University of Auckland.

Clark, A. (2014). Case studies. In A. Clark, R. Flewitt, M. Hammerseley & M. Robb (Eds.), *Understanding research with children and young people* (pp. 200–209). London: Sage.

Clark, A., Flewitt, R. Hammersley, M., & Robb, M. (2014a). Understanding research with children and young people: Introduction. In A. Clark, R. Flewitt, M. Hammerseley & M. Robb (Eds.), *Understanding research with children and young people* (pp. 1–9). London, England: Sage.

Clark, A., Flewitt, R. Hammersley, M., & Robb, M. (2014*b*). (Eds.). *Understanding research with children and young people*. London: Sage.

Clay, A. (2012). *The hip-hop generation fights back: Youth, activism, and post- civil rights politics*. New York: New York University Press.

Coad, J., Gibson, F., Horstman, M., Milnes, L., Randall, D., & Carter, B. (2015). Be my guest! Challenges and practical solutions of undertaking interviews with children in the home setting. *Journal of Child Health Care, 19*(4), 432–443.

Coakley, J. (2011). Youth sports: What counts as "positive development?" *Journal of Sport & Social Issues, 35*(3), 306–324.

Coard, S. I., & Sellers, R. M. (2005). African American families as a context for racial socialization. In V.C. McLoyd, N.E. Hill & K.A. Dodge (Eds.), *African American family life: Ecological and cultural diversity* (pp. 264–284). New York: Guilford Press.

Coburn, A. (2010). Youth work as border pedagogy. In J. Batsleer & B. Davies (Eds.), *What is youth work?* (pp. 33–46). Exeter, UK: Learning Matters.

Cocking, D. (2013). Friendship. In *The international encyclopedia of ethics*. Wiley Online Library. Retrieved from http://onlinelibrary.wiley.com/doi/10.1002/9781444367072. wbiee774/abstract?us erIsAuthenticated=false&deniedAccessCustomisedMessage=

Cohassey, J. (2014). *Hemingway and pound: A most unlikely friendship*. Jackson, NC: McFarland.

Cohen, M. L., Silber, L. H., Sangiorgio, A., & Iadeluca, V. (2012). At-risk youth: Music-making as a means to promote positive relationships. In C. Kinginger (Ed.), *The Oxford handbook of music education* (Vol. 2, pp. 185–202). New York: Oxford University Press.

Cohen, P. N. (2015). Divergent responses to family inequality. In P.R. Amato, A. Booth, S.M. McHale & J. Van Hook (Eds.), *families in an era of increasing inequality* (pp. 25–33). Heidelberg: Springer International.

Colby, S. L., & Ortman, J. M. (2015). *Projections of the size and composition of the US population: 2014 to 2060*. Retrieved from https://www.census.gov/content/dam/Census/library/publications/2015/demo/p25-1143.pdf

Coleman, J. A. (2013). Researching whole people and whole lives. In C. Kinginger (Ed.), *Social and cultural aspects of language learning in study abroad* (pp. 17–44). Amsterdam/Philadelphia: John Benjamins Publisher.

Coller, R. J., & Kuo, A. A. (2014). Youth development through mentorship: A Los Angeles school-based mentorship program among Latino children. *Journal of Community Health, 39*(2), 316–321.

Collin, P., & Burns, J. (2009). The experience of youth in the digital age. In A. Furlong (Ed.), *Handbook of youth and young adulthood: New perspectives and agendas* (pp. 283–290). New York: Routledge.

Collins, C. R., Neal, J. W., & Neal, Z. P. (2014). Transforming individual civic engagement into community collective efficacy: The role of bonding social capital. *American Journal of Community Psychology, 54*(3–4), 328–336.

Collins, R., Grimes, K., & Franklin, R. (2014). Serving our youth in 2025. *Reclaiming Children and Youth, 23*(3), 41.

Conn, S. (2014). *Americans against the city: Anti-urbanism in the twentieth century*. New York: Oxford University Press.

Cook, T., & Hess, E. (2007). What the camera sees and from whose perspective: Fun methodologies for engaging children in enlightening adults. *Childhood, 14*(1), 29–45.

Cooley-Strickland, M. R., Griffin, R. S., Darney, D., Otte, K., & Ko, J. (2011). Urban African American youth exposed to community violence: A school-based anxiety preventive intervention efficacy study. *Journal of Prevention & Intervention in the Community, 39*(2), 149–166.

Cooper, B. (2014). Building a learning community through the power of mentoring relationships. *National Civic Review, 103*(2), 21–22.

Cooper, C. (2012). Imagining "radical" youth work possibilities–challenging the "symbolic violence" within the mainstream tradition in contemporary state-led youth work practice in England. *Journal of Youth Studies, 15*(1), 53–71.

Cooper, M., & Cooper, G. (2008). *Overcoming barriers to the positive development and engagement of ethno-racial minority youth in Canada* (pp. 446–469). Alberta, Canada: Department of Canadian Heritage.

Cooper, V. (2014). Designing research for different purposes. In A. Clark, R. Flewitt, M. Hammerseley & M. Robb (Eds.), *Understanding research with children and young people* (pp. 51–68). London: Sage.

Coplan, R. J., & Bullock, A. (2012). Temperament and peer relationships. In M. Zentner & R.L. Shiner (Eds.), *Handbook of temperament* (pp. 442–461). New York: Gilford Press.

Corasani, N. Perez-Pena, R., & Alvarez, L. (2015, June 19). Races unite for nine killed by gunman at Black church. *New York Times,* A1, A16.

Cordelli, C. (2015). Distributive justice and the problem of friendship. *Political Studies, 63*(3), 679–695.

Corsaro, W. A. (2006). Qualitative research on children's peer relations. In X. Chen, D. French & B. Schneider (Eds.), *Peer relationships in cultural context* (pp. 96–121). New York: Cambridge University Press.

Costandius, E., Rosochacki, S., & le Roux, A. (2014). Critical citizenship education and community interaction: A reflection on practice. *International Journal of Art & Design Education, 33*(1), 116–129.

Costanza-Chock, S. (2012). *Youth and social movements: Key lessons for allies.* Retrieved from http://cyber.law.harvard.edu/sites/cyber.law.harvard.edu/files/KBWYoutha ndSocial-Movements2012_0.pdf

Coster, W., Law, M., Bedell, G., Khetani, M., Cousins, M., & Teplicky, R. (2012). Development of the participation and environment measure for children and youth: Conceptual basis. *Disability and Rehabilitation, 34*(3), 238–246.

Côté, J. (2014). *Youth studies: Fundamental issues and debates.* London/New York: Palgrave Macmillan.

Cotterell, J. (2007). *Social networks in youth and adolescence* (Vol. 1). New York: Routledge.

Cotterell, J. (2013). *Social networks in youth and adolescence* (2nd ed). New York: Routledge.

Coussée, F. (2009). The relevance of youth work's history. In G. Verschelden, F. Coussee, T. Van de Walle & H. Williamson (Eds.), *The history of youth work in Europe and its relevance for youth policy today.* Council of Europe Publishing. Retrieved from http://pjp-eu.coe.int/documents/1017981/3084932/History_of_youth_policy_text.pdf/ad512916-c671-43e6-8ae6-d2919326e676

Cox, K. (2008). Tools for building on youth strengths. *Reclaiming Children and Youth, 16*(4), 19–24.

Cramer, E. D., Gonzalez, L., & Pellegrini-Lafont, C. (2014). From classmates to inmates: An integrated approach to break the school-to-prison pipeline. *Equity & Excellence in Education, 47*(4), 461–475.

Creasey, G., & Jarvis, P. A. (Eds.). (2013). *Adolescent development and school achievement in urban communities: Resilience in the neighborhood.* New York: Routledge.

Crépel, A. L. (2014). Friendship: Shaping ourselves. *International Journal of Philosophical Studies, 22*(2), 184–198.

Creswell, J. W. (2013). *Qualitative inquiry and research design: Choosing among five approaches*(3rd ed.). Thousand Oaks, CA: Sage.

Crocetti, E., Erentaitė, R., & Žukauskienė, R. (2014). Identity styles, positive youth development, and civic engagement in adolescence. *Journal of Youth and Adolescence, 43*(11), 1818–1828.

Cronin, A. M. (2014). Between friends: Making emotions intersubjectively. *Emotion, Space and Society, 10*(1), 71–78.

Crosnoe, R. (2000). Friendships in childhood and adolescence: The life course and new directions. *Social Psychology Quarterly, 63*(4), 377–391.

Crosnoe, R., Cavanagh, S., & Elder, G. H. (2003). Adolescent friendships as academic resources: The intersection of friendship, race, and school disadvantage. *Sociological Perspectives, 46*(3), 331–352.

Crosnoe, R., Erickson, K. G., & Dornbusch, S. M. (2002). Protective functions of family relationships and school factors on the deviant behavior of adolescent boys and girls reducing the impact of risky friendships. *Youth & Society, 33*(4), 515–544.

Cummins, I. (2016). Reading Wacquant: Social work and advanced marginality. *European Journal of Social Work, 19*(2), 263–274.

Cunningham, D., & Warwick, A. (2013). Unnoticed apocalypse: The science fiction politics of urban crisis. *City, 17*(4), 433–448.

Curry, O. S., & Dunbar, R. I. (2013). Sharing a joke: The effects of a similar sense of humor on affiliation and altruism. *Evolution and Human Behavior, 34*(2), 125–129.

Cushing, D. L., Love, E. W., & van Vliet, W. (2012). Through the viewfinder: Using multimedia techniques to engage Latino youth in community planning. In M. Rios, L. Vasquez & L. Miranda (Eds.), *Dialogos: Placemaking in Latino communities* (pp.172–185). New York: Routledge.

Cutter-Mackenzie, A., Edwards, S., & Quinton, H. W. (2015). Child-framed video research methodologies: Issues, possibilities and challenges for researching with children. *Children's Geographies, 13*(3), 343–356.

Dagg, A. I. (2011). *Animal friendships.* New York: Cambridge University Press.

Daniel, S. (2013). *Immigrant and non-immigrant youth in Canada: Cultural orientation, ethnicity of friends, and life satisfaction among four ethnic groups.* (Masters thesis). University of Windsor.

Daniel, S., & Hakim-Larson, J. (2013). *Multicultural youth in Canada: Comparing friendships and perceived social support.* University of Windsor, Canada. Retrieved from http://scholar.uwindsor.ca/arabyouthsymp/conference_posters/conference posters/6/

Danby, S. J., Thompson, C., Theobald, M. A., & Thorpe, K. J. (2012). Children's strategies for making friends when starting school. *Australasian Journal of Early Childhood, 37*(2), 63–71.

Dang, M. T. (2014). Social connectedness and self-esteem: Predictors of resilience in mental health among maltreated homeless youth. *Issues in Mental Health Nursing, 35*(3), 212–219.

Darrah, J., & DeLuca, S. (2014). "Living here has changed my whole perspective": How escaping inner-city poverty shapes neighborhood and housing choice. *Journal of Policy Analysis and Management, 33*(2), 350–384.

Davies, B. (2015). Youth work: A manifesto for our times–revisited. *Youth & Policy, 114*(2), 96–117.

Davies, K., & Heaphy, B. (2011). Interactions that matter: Researching critical associations. *Methodological Innovations Online, 6*(3), 5–16.

Davies, K., Tropp, L. R., Aron, A., Pettigrew, T. F., & Wright, S. C. (2011). Cross-group friendships and intergroup attitudes: A meta-analytic review. *Personality and Social Psychology Review, 15*(4), 332–351.

David, P. (2014). Bidding for intimacy. In P. David (Ed.), *Pair bonding & repair: Essays on intimacy & couple therapy* (pp. 13–15). Self-published reader. Retrieved from http://pauldavidphd.com/wp-content/uploads/Pair-Bonding-Repair.pdf

Davies, K., Tropp, L. R., Aron, A., Pettigrew, T. F., & Wright, S. C. (2011). Cross-group friendships and intergroup attitudes: A meta-analytic review. *Personality and Social Psychology Review, 15*(4), 332–351.

Davis, K. (2008). *Trust in the lives of young people: A conceptual framework to explore how youth make trust judgments.* Retrieved from http://thegoodproject.org/wp-content/uploads/2012/09/52-Trust-in-the-Lives-of- Young-People.pdf

Dawes, N. P., & Larson, R. (2011). How youth get engaged: Grounded-theory research on motivational development in organized youth programs. *Developmental psychology, 47*(1), 259–269.

De Goede, I. H., Branje, S. J., & Meeus, W. H. (2009). Developmental changes and gender differences in adolescents' perceptions of friendships. *Journal of Adolescence, 32*(5), 1105–1123.

De Guzman, M. R. T. (2007). *Friendships, peer influence, and peer pressure during the teen years.* Lincoln: University of Nebraska.

De La Haye, K., Robins, G., Mohr, P., & Wilson, C. (2011). How physical activity shapes, and is shaped by, adolescent friendships. *Social science & medicine, 73*(5), 719–728.

DeLay, D., Hartl, A. C., Laursen, B., Denner, J., Werner, L., Campe, S., & Ortiz, E. (2014). Learning from friends: Measuring influence in a dyadic computer instructional setting. *International Journal of Research & Method in Education, 37*(2), 190–205.

DeLay, D., Laursen, B., Kiuru, N., Salmela-Aro, K., & Nurmi, J. E. (2013). Selecting and retaining friends on the basis of cigarette smoking similarity. *Journal of Research on Adolescence, 23*(3), 464–473.

Delgado, M. (1979). A grass-roots model for needs assessment in Hispanic communities. *Child Welfare, 57*(7), 571–576.

Delgado, M. (1998). *Social work practice in non-traditional urban settings.* New York: Oxford University Press.

Delgado, M. (1999). *Community capacity enhancement practice within an urban context.* New York: Oxford University Press.

Delgado, M. (2000). *New arenas for community social work practice with urban youth: The use of the arts, humanities, and sports.* New York: Columbia University Press.

Delgado, M. (2002). *New frontiers for youth development in the twenty-first century: Revitalizing and broadening youth development.* New York: Columbia University Press.

Delgado, M. (2006). *Designs and methods for youth-led research.* Thousand Oaks, CA: Sage.

Delgado, M. (2007). *Social work practice with Latinos using a cultural assets paradigm.* New York: Oxford University Press.

Delgado, M. (2011). *Latinos, small businesses and the American dream: Community social work and economic and social development.* New York: Columbia University Press.

Delgado, M. (2013). *Social justice and the urban obesity crisis.* New York: Columbia University Press.

Delgado, M. (2015). *Urban youth and photovoice.* New York: Oxford University Press.

Delgado, M. (2016a). *Celebrating urban community life: Fairs, festivals, parades and community practice.* Toronto: University of Toronto.

Delgado, M. (2016b). *Community practice and urban youth: Social justice service-learning and civic engagement.* New York: Routledge.

Delgado, M., & Humm-Delgado, D. (2013). *Asset assessments and community social work practice.* New York: Oxford University Press.

Delgado, M., Jones, L.K. & Rohani, M. (2005). *Social work practice with immigrant and refugee youth in the United States.* Boston: Allyn & Bacon.

Delgado, M., & Staples, L. (2008). *Youth-led community organizing: Theory and action.* New York: Oxford University Press.

Delgado, M., & Staples, L. (2013). Youth-led organizing: Community engagement and opportunity creation. In M. Weil (Eds.), *Handbook of community practice* (2nd ed.). Thousand Oaks, CA: Sage.

Delgado, M., & Zhou, H. (2008). *Youth-led health promotion in urban communities: A capacity enhancement perspective.* Lanham, MD: Rowman & Littlefield.

DelPriore, D. J., Butterfield, M. E., & Hill, S. E. (2013). Friends with benefits, but without the sex: Straight women and gay men exchange trustworthy mating advice. *Evolutionary Psychology, 11*(1), 132–147.

de Luce, J. (2009). Teaching Cicero's Laelius de Amicitia. *Classical World, 103*(1), 71–76.

de Medeiros, K., Saunders, P. A., & Sabat, S. R. (2012). Friendships and the social environments of people with dementia: Introduction to the Special Issue. *Dementia, 11*(3), 281–285.

Demir, M., & Özdemir, M. (2010). Friendship, need satisfaction and happiness. *Journal of Happiness Studies, 11*(2), 243–259.

Demir, M., Özen, A., Doğan, A., Bilyk, N. A., & Tyrell, F. A. (2011). I matter to my friend, therefore I am happy: Friendship, mattering, and happiness. *Journal of Happiness Studies, 12*(6), 983–1005.

Demir, M., Özen, A., & Procsal, A. D. (2014). *Friendship and happiness* (pp. 2359– 2364). Rotterdam: Springer Netherlands.

Demir, M., & Urberg, K. A. (2004). Friendship and adjustment among adolescents. *Journal of Experimental Child Psychology, 88*(1), 68–82.

Demır, M., & Weitekamp, L. A. (2007). I am so happy 'cause today I found my friend: Friendship and personality as predictors of happiness. *Journal of Happiness Studies, 8*(2), 181–211.

Denison, J. A., Tsui, S., Bratt, J., Torpey, K., Weaver, M. A., & Kabaso, M. (2012). Do peer educators make a difference? An evaluation of a youth-led HIV prevention model in Zambian Schools. *Health education research, 27*(2), 237–247.

Denscombe, M., Szulc, H., Patrick, C., & Wood, A. (2014). Ethnicity and friendship. In M. Hammersley & P. Woods (Eds.), *Gender and ethnicity in schools: Ethnographic accounts* (pp. 127–144).

Densley, J. A. (2014). It's gang life, but not as we know it. The evolution of gang business. *Crime & Delinquency, 60*(4), 517–546.

Deptula, D. P., & Cohen, R. (2004). Aggressive, rejected, and delinquent children and adolescents: A comparison of their friendships. *Aggression and Violent Behavior, 9*(1), 75–104.

Derlega, V. J. (Ed.). (2013). *Communication, intimacy, and close relationships.* Atlanta: Elsevier.

Derlega, V. J., & Winstead, B. A. (Eds.). (2012). *Friendship and social interaction.* New York: Springer Science & Business Media.

DeRosier, M. E., & Marcus, S. R. (2005). Building friendships and combating bullying: Effectiveness of SS GRIN at one-year follow-up. *Journal of Clinical Child and Adolescent Psychology, 34*(1), 140–150.

Desai, A., & Killick, E. (Eds.). (2013). *The ways of friendship: Anthropological perspectives.* New York: Berghahn Books.

DeScioli, P., & Kurzban, R. T. (2012). The company you keep: Friendship decisions from a functional perspective. In J. Krueger (Ed.), *Social judgment and decision making* (p. 209). New York: Psychology Press.

de Souza Briggs, X. (2007). "Some of my best friends are . . .": Interracial friendships, class, and segregation in America. *City & Community, 6*(4), 263–290.

Deutsch, N., & Hirsch, B. (2002). A place to call home: Youth organizations in the lives of inner city adolescents. In T. M. Brinthaupt & R. P. Lipka (Eds.), *Understanding early adolescent self and identity: Applications and interventions* (pp. 293–320). Albany, NY: State University of New York Press.

Deutsch, N. L., & Jones, J. N. (2008). "Show Me an Ounce of Respect" Respect and Authority in Adult-Youth Relationships in After-School Programs. *Journal of Adolescence, 23*(6), 667–688.

Deutz, M. H., Lansu, T. A., & Cillessen, A. H. (2015). Children's observed interactions with best friends: Associations with friendship jealousy and satisfaction. *Social Development, 24*(1), 39–56.

Devine, K. A., Holmbeck, G. N., Gayes, L., & Purnell, J. Q. (2012). Friendships of children and adolescents with spina bifida: Social adjustment, social performance, and social skills. *Journal of Pediatric Psychology, 37*(2), 220–231.

Dhariwal, A., & Connolly, J. (2013). Romantic experiences of homeland and diaspora South Asian youth: Westernizing processes of media and friends. *Journal of Research on Adolescence, 23*(1), 45–56.

Dickie, C. (2009). Exploring workplace friendships in business: Cultural variations of employee behaviour. *Research and Practice in Human Resource Management, 17*(1), 128–137.

Dickson, K., Vigurs, C. A., & Newman, M. (2013). *Youth work: A systematic map of the research literature.* Retrieved from http://www.lenus.ie/hse/handle/10147/306851

DiDonato, A. (2014). *New directions in social competence research: Examining developmental trajectories and language minority populations* (Doctoral dissertation). Arizona State University.

Diemer, M. A., & Li, C. H. (2011). Critical consciousness development and political partici-pation among marginalized youth. *Child Development, 82*(6), 1815–1833.

Diener, E., & Diener, M. (2009). Cross-cultural correlates of life satisfaction and self-esteem. In E. Diener (Ed.), *Culture and well-being* (pp. 71–91). Rotterdam: Springer Netherlands.

Digeser, P. E. (2013). *Friendship as a family of practices.* Retrieved from http://amityjournal.leeds.ac.uk/files/2013/11/AmityjournalfirstissuePGD28.09.13FI NAL.pdf

DiMaggio, P., & Garip, F. (2012). Network effects and social inequality. *Annual Review of Sociology, 38*, 93–118.

Dimitriadis, G. (2003). *Friendship, cliques, and gangs: Young Black men coming of age in urban America.* New York: Teachers College Press.

Di Nicola, P. (2002). *Amichevolmente parlando. La costruzione di relazioni sociali in una società di legami deboli.* Milano, Italy: FrancoAngeli.

Dinsmore, B. (2014). *"Chicks be like": Masculinity, femininity, and gendered double standards in youth peer cultures on social media.* Retrieved from http://digitalcommons.conncoll.edu/sociologyhp/3/?utm_source=digitalcommons. conncoll.edu%2Fsociologyhp%2F3&utm_medium=PDF&utm_campaign=PDFCo verPages

Diprose, K. (2014). Resilience is futile: The cultivation of resilience is not an answer to aus-terity and poverty. *Soundings: A Journal of Politics and Culture, 58*(1), 44– 56.

Doey, L., Coplan, R. J., & Kingsbury, M. (2014). Bashful boys and coy girls: A review of gender differences in childhood shyness. *Sex Roles, 70*(7–8), 255–266.

Dolcini, M. M., Harper, G. W., Watson, S. E., Catania, J. A., & Ellen, J. M. (2005). Friends in the 'hood: Should peer-based health promotion programs target nonschool friendship networks? *Journal of Adolescent Health, 36*(3), 267.e6–267.e15.

Donato, K. M., & Sisk, B. (2015). Children's migration to the United States from Mexico and Central America: Evidence from the Mexican and Latin American Migration Projects. *Journal on Migration and Human Security, 3*(1), 58–79.

Donlan, A. E., Lynch, A. D., & Lerner, R. M. (2015). Peer relationships and positive youth development. In E.P. Bowers, G.L. Geldhof, S.N. Johnson, L.J. Hilliard, R.M. Hershberg, J.V. Lerner & R.M. Lerner (Eds.), *Promoting positive youth development: Lessons from the 4-H Study* (pp. 121–136). New York: Springer.

Douglass, R. P., & Duffy, R. D. (2015). Strengths use and life satisfaction: A moderated mediation approach. *Journal of Happiness Studies,16*(3), 619–632.

DuBois, B. L., & Miley, K. K. (2013). *Social work: An empowering profession.* New York: Pearson Higher Ed.

Due, C., Riggs, D. W., & Augoustinos, M. (2014). Research with children of migrant and refugee backgrounds: A review of child-centered research methods. *Child Indicators Research, 7*(1), 209–227.

Duke, N. N., Borowsky, I. W., & Pettingell, S. L. (2012). Adult perceptions of neighbor-hood: Links to youth engagement. *Youth & Society, 44*(3), 408–430.

Dulai, J., Friessen, S., Le, D., Pagalan, L., Reynolds, K., & Sang, J. (2014). *Stories uncovered by the Investigaytors.* Community Based Research Centre. Retrieved from http://cbrc.net/sites/default/files/Investigaytorsr_GOL_X2_B.pdf

Duncombe, J., & Jessop, J. (2002). *"Doing rapport" and the ethics of "faking friendship"* (pp. 108–121). London: Sage.

Du Plessis, K., & Corney, T. (2011). Trust, respect and friendship: The key attributes of significant others in the lives of young working men. *Youth Studies Australia, 30*(1), 17–26.

Durán, R. J. (2010). Gang organization: Slangin', gang bangin' and dividin' by generation. *Latino Studies, 8*(3), 373–398.

Durlak, J. A., Weissberg, R. P., & Pachan, M. (2010). A meta-analysis of after-school programs that seek to promote personal and social skills in children and adolescents. *American Journal of Community Psychology, 45*(3–4), 294–309.

Duvdevany, I., & Arar, E. (2004). Leisure activities, friendships, and quality of life of persons with intellectual disability: Foster homes vs community residential settings. *International Journal of Rehabilitation Research, 27*(4), 289–296.

Dyck, K. T., & Holtzman, S. (2013). Understanding humor styles and well-being: The importance of social relationships and gender. *Personality and Individual Differences, 55*(1), 53–58.

Echetebu, M. C. (2014). *"We don't call it Bristol Park": Engaging African American youth in urban neighborhood redevelopment planning* (Doctoral dissertation). University of Illinois at Urbana-Champaign.

Eddles-Hirsch, K., Vialle, W., McCormick, J., & Rogers, K. (2012). Insiders or outsiders: The role of social context in the peer relations of gifted students. *Roeper Review, 34*(1), 53–62.

Edling, C., & Rydgren, J. (2012). Neighborhood and friendship composition in adolescence. *Sage Open, 2*(4). doi: 10.1177/2158244012466249

Edwin, K., & Rosenblatt, P. (2015). "I Do Me": Young Black men and the struggle to resist the street. In O. Patterson (Ed.), *The cultural matrix: Understanding Black youth* (pp. 229–251). Cambridge, MA: Harvard University Press.

Einarsdottir, J. (2014). Children's perspectives on play. In L. Brooker, M. Blaise & S. Edwards (Eds.), *SAGE handbook of play and learning in early childhood* (pp. 319–329). Thousand Oaks, CA: Sage Publication.

Elaine, S. C., Holosko, M. J., & LO, T. W. (Eds.). (2008). *Youth empowerment and volunteerism: Principles, policies and practices.* Hong Kong: City University of Hong Kong Press.

Elias Rodas, D. M. (2011). *Looking through their eyes: An emic approach to community assets and strengths for African American youth.* (Doctoral dissertation). Wichita State University.

Elmore, C. A., & Gaylord-Harden, N. K. (2013). The influence of supportive parenting and racial socialization messages on African American youth behavioral outcomes. *Journal of Child and Family Studies, 22*(1), 63–75.

Elsaesser, C. M., & Voisin, D. R. (2015). Correlates of polyvictimization among African American youth: An exploratory study. *Journal of Interpersonal Violence, 30*(17), 3022–3042.

Emmeche, C. (2014). Robot friendship: Can a robot be a friend? *International Journal of Signs and Semiotic Systems, 3*(2), 26–42.

Emond, R. (2014). Longing to belong: Children in residential care and their experiences of peer relationships at school and in the children's home. *Child & Family Social Work, 19*(2), 194–202.

Engelberg, J., Gao, P., & Parsons, C. A. (2012). Friends with money. *Journal of Financial Economics, 103*(1), 169–188.

Epstein, J. L., & Karweit, N. (Eds.). (2014). *Friends in school: Patterns of selection and influence in secondary schools.* Atlanta: Elsevier.

Erni, J. N., & Fung, A. (2010). Clever love: Dislocated intimacies among youth. *Emotion, Space and Society, 3*(1), 21–27.

Erstad, O. (2012). The learning lives of digital youth—beyond the formal and informal. *Oxford Review of Education, 38*(1), 25–43.

Erwin, P. (1998). *Friendship in childhood and adolescence.* New York: Routledge.

Evans, A. B., Banerjee, M., Meyer, R., Aldana, A., Foust, M., & Rowley, S. (2012). Racial socialization as a mechanism for positive development among African American youth. *Child Development Perspectives, 6*(3), 251–257.

Evans, R., & Holt, L. (2011). Diverse spaces of childhood and youth: Gender and other socio-cultural differences. *Children's Geographies, 9*(3–4), 277–284.

Evans, S. D., & Prilleltensky, I. (2007). Youth and democracy: Participation for personal, relational, and collective well-being. *Journal of Community Psychology, 35*(6), 681–692.

Ezaki, J. M. (2014). *Expert urban youth workers and the stories they tell: A narrative of lived experience* (Doctoral dissertation). University of Minnesota.

Fagan, A. A., Hanson, K., Hawkins, J. D., & Arthur, M. W. (2008). Bridging science to practice: Achieving prevention program implementation fidelity in the Community Youth Development Study. *American Journal of Community Psychology, 41*(3–4), 235–249.

Fainstein, S. S. (2005). Cities and diversity should we want it? Can we plan for it? *Urban Affairs Review, 41*(1), 3–19.

Fales, J. L., Forgeron, P., Gulak, R. R., & Bennett, S. M. (2014). The importance of friendships in youth with chronic pain: The next critical wave of research. *Pediatric Pain Letter.* Retrieved from http://childpain.org/ppl/issues/v16n3_2014/v16n3_fales.pdf

Faris, R., & Ennett, S. (2012). Adolescent aggression: The role of peer group status motives, peer aggression, and group characteristics. *Social Networks, 34*(4), 371–378.

Felluga, D. F. (2015). *Critical theory: The key concepts.* New York: Routledge.

Fergus, S., & Zimmerman, M. A. (2005). Adolescent resilience: A framework for understanding healthy development in the face of risk. *Annual Review of Public Health, 26,* 399–419.

Ferguson, C. J., & Olson, C. K. (2013). Friends, fun, frustration and fantasy: Child motivations for video game play. *Motivation and Emotion, 37*(1), 154–164.

Ferguson, I. (2007). *Reclaiming social work: Challenging neo-liberalism and promoting social justice.* Thousand Oaks, CA: Sage.

Ferrera, M. (2015, November). *Chicago Area Youth Health Service Corps: Preliminary findings and lessons learned from using a CBPR approach.* Presented at the 143rd APHA Annual Meeting and Exposition, Chicago, IL.

Ferrer-Chancy, M. (2012). *The importance of friendships to children.* Gainsville, FL: University of Florida, IFAS Extension.

Fields, A., Snapp, S., Russell, S. T., Licona, A. C., & Tilley, E. H. (2014). Youth voices and knowledges: Slam poetry speaks to social policies. *Sexuality Research and Social Policy, 11*(4), 310–321.

Fields, D. J. (2015). Overtown: Reclaiming a sense of place. *The Black Archives.* Retrieved from http://www.theBlackarchives.org/about-2/overtown-reclaiming-a-sense-of-place/

Fine, M. (2012). Youth participatory action research. In N. Lesko & S. Talburt (Eds.), *Keywords in youth studies: Tracing affects, movements, knowledges* (pp. 318–324). New York: Routledge.

Fine, M., & Ruglis, J. (2009). Circuits and consequences of dispossession: The racialized realignment of the public sphere for US youth. *Transforming Anthropology, 17*(1), 20–33.

Fisher, C. B., Busch-Rossnagel, N. A., Jopp, D. S., & Brown, J. L. (2012). Applied developmental science, social justice, and socio-political well-being. *Applied Developmental Science, 16*(1), 54–64.

Fisher, C. S. (1982). What do we mean by "friend?" An inductive study. *Social Network, 3,* 287–306.

Fitzgerald, A., Fitzgerald, N., & Aherne, C. (2012). Do peers matter? A review of peer and/or friends' influence on physical activity among American adolescents. *Journal of Adolescence, 35*(4), 941–958.

Flam, H., & Kleres, J. (Eds.). (2015). *Methods of exploring emotions.* New York: Routledge.

Flanagan, C. A., & Christens, B. D. (2011). Youth civic development: Historical context and emerging issues. *New Directions for Child and Adolescent Development, 2011*(134), 1–9.

Flasher, J. (1978). Adultism. *Adolescence, 13,* 517–523.

Fletcher, J. M., & Ross, S. L. (2012). *Estimating the effects of friendship networks on health behaviors of adolescents* (No. w18253). Cambridge, MA: National Bureau of Economic Research.

Flewitt, R. (2014). Interviews. In A. Clark, R. Flewitt, M. Hammerseley & M. Robb (Eds.), *Understanding research with children and young people* (pp. 136–152). London, England: Sage.

Flora, C. (2014). Just friends. *Scientific American Mind, 25*(1), 30–35.

Flora, C. B., & Flora, J. L. (2014). Developing entrepreneurial rural communities. *Sociological Practice, 8*(1), 21.

Foley, K. R., Blackmore, A. M., Girdler, S., O'Donnell, M., Glauert, R., Llewellyn, G., & Leonard, H. (2012). To feel belonged: The voices of children and youth with disabilities on the meaning of wellbeing. *Child Indicators Research, 5*(2), 375–391.

Forgeron, P. A. (2011). *My friends don't really understand me: Examining close friendships of adolescents with chronic pain.* (Doctoral dissertation). Dalhousie University.

Foster, K. T., Hicks, B. M., Iacono, W. G., & McGue, M. (2015). Gender differences in the structure of risk for alcohol use disorder in adolescence and young adulthood. *Psychological medicine, 45*(14), 3047–3058.

Forster, M., Grigsby, T. J., Bunyan, A., Unger, J. B., & Valente, T. W. (2015). The protective role of school friendship ties for substance use and aggressive behaviors among middle school students. *Journal of School Health, 85*(2), 82–89.

Foster, B. B. (2014). "Everybody gotta have a dream": Rap-centered aspirations among young Black males involved in rap music production–A qualitative study. *Issues in Race & Society, 2*(2), 25–47.

Foster, K., & Spencer, D. (2013). "It's just a social thing": Drug use, friendship and borderwork among marginalized young people. *International Journal of Drug Policy, 24*(3), 223–230.

Fotouhi, B., Momeni, N., & Rabbat, M. G. (2014). Generalized friendship paradox: An analytical approach. In A. Nadamoto (Ed.), *Social informatics* (pp. 339–352). Heidelberg: Springer International.

Fowler, J. H., Settle, J. E., & Christakis, N. A. (2011). Correlated genotypes in friendship networks. *Proceedings of the National Academy of Sciences, 108*(5), 1993–1997.

France, A., & Roberts, S. (2015). The problem of social generations: A critique of the new emerging orthodoxy in youth studies. *Journal of Youth Studies, 18*(2), 215–230.

Francis, D., & Hemson, C. (2009). Youth as research fieldworkers in a context of HIV/AIDS. *African Journal of AIDS Research, 8*(2), 223–230.

Fraser, N. (2009). Social justice in the age of identity politics. In G. Hemderson & H. Waterstone (Eds.), *Geographic thought: A praxis perspective* (pp. 72–91). New York: Routledge.

Fraser, S., Flewitt, R., & Hammersley, M. (2014). What is research with children and young people? In A. Clark, R. Flewitt, M. Hammerseley & M. Robb (Eds.), *Understanding research with children and young people* (pp. 34–50). London: Sage.

Fredricks, J. A., & Simpkins, S. D. (2012). Promoting positive youth development through organized after-school activities: Taking a closer look at participation of ethnic minority youth. *Child Development Perspectives, 6*(3), 280–287.

Fredricks, J. A., & Simpkins, S. D. (2013). Organized out-of-school activities and peer relationships: Theoretical perspectives and previous research. *New Directions for Child and Adolescent Development, 2013*(140), 1–17.

Freeman, M., & Mathison, S. (2009). *Researching children's experiences.* New York: Guilford.

French, D. C., Pidada, S., & Victor, A. (2005). Friendships of Indonesian and United States youth. *International Journal of Behavioral Development, 29*(4), 304–313.

French, R., Case, P., & Gosling, J. (2009). Betrayal and friendship. *Society and Business Review, 4*(2), 146–158.

Frey, W. H. (2015). *Diversity explosion: How new racial demographics are remaking America.* Washington, DC: Brookings Institution.

Friese, H. (2013). Notions of friendships in philosophical and anthropological thought. In A.K. Giri & J. Clammer (Eds.), *Philosophy and anthropology: Border crossing and transformations* (pp. 341–355). Anthem Press.

Friesem, E. (2014). A story of conflict and collaboration: Media literacy, video production and disadvantaged youth. *Journal of Media Literacy Education, 6*(1), 44–55.

Froh, J. J., Fan, J., Emmons, R. A., Bono, G., Huebner, E. S., & Watkins, P. (2011). Measuring gratitude in youth: Assessing the psychometric properties of adult gratitude scales in children and adolescents. *Psychological Assessment, 23*(2), 311–324.

Fry, M. D., & Gano-Overway, L. A. (2010). Exploring the contribution of the caring climate to the youth sport experience. *Journal of Applied Sport Psychology, 22*(3), 294–304.

Fry, M. D., Guivernau, M., Kim, M. S., Newton, M., Gano–Overway, L. A., & Magyar, T. M. (2012). Youth perceptions of a caring climate, emotional regulation, and psychological well-being. *Sport, Exercise, and Performance Psychology, 1*(1), 44.

Fujimoto, K., & Valente, T. W. (2012). Decomposing the components of friendship and friends' influence on adolescent drinking and smoking. *Journal of Adolescent Health, 51*(2), 136–143.

Fuligni, A. J., Yip, T., & Tseng, V. (2002). The impact of family obligation on the daily activities and psychological well-being of Chinese American adolescents. *Child Development, 73*(1), 302–314.

Fuller, B., Lizárraga, J. R., & Gray, J. H. (2015). *Digital media and Latino families.* ERIC. Retrieved from http://eric.ed.gov/?id=ED555583

Fultz, M., & Chen, S. (2012). A close look at the diversity of lacrosse. *Kentucky Association of Health, Physical Education, Recreation and Dance, 50*(1), 15–18.

Furgang, A., & Furgang, K. (2012). *Cultivating positive peer groups and friendships.* New York: Rosen Publishing Group.

Furman, G. (2012). Social justice leadership as Praxis developing capacities through preparation programs. *Educational Administration Quarterly, 48*(2), 191–229.

Furman, R., Collins, K., Garner, M. D., Montanaro, K. L., & Weber, G. (2009). Using social work theory for the facilitation of friendships. *Smith College Studies in Social Work, 79*(1), 17–33.

Furman, W., & Buhmester, D. (1985). Children's perceptions of the personal relationships in their social networks. *Developmental Psychology, 21*, 1016–1024.

Fusco, D. (Ed.). (2012). *Advancing youth work: Current trends, critical questions.* New York: Routledge.

Gaita, R. (2009). *The philosopher's dog: Friendships with animals.* New York: Random House.

Galloway, L. L. (2014). *Exploration of friendship experiences in adolescent eating disorders.* Retrieved from https://www.era.lib.ed.ac.uk/handle/1842/9723

Galupo, M. P., Krum, T. E., Hagen, D. B., Gonzalez, K. A., & Bauerband, L. A. (2014). Disclosure of transgender identity and status in the context of friendship. *Journal of LGBT Issues in Counseling, 8*(1), 25–42.

Gamble, D. N., & Weil, M. (2010). *Community practice skills: Local to global perspectives.* New York: Columbia University Press.

Gandy, M. (2006). Urban nature and the ecological imaginary. In N. Heynen & M. Kalka (Eds.), *In the nature of cities: Urban political ecology and the politics of urban metabolism* (pp. 63–74). New York: Routledge.

Gant, L. M., Shimshock, K., Allen-Meares, P., Smith, L., Miller, P., Hollingsworth, L. A., & Shanks, T. (2009). Effects of photovoice: Civic engagement among older youth in urban communities. *Journal of community practice, 17*(4), 358–376.

Garcia, M. (2014). *Spanish-English code switching in slam poetry.* Retrieved from http://triceratops.brynmawr.edu:8080/dspace/handle/10066/12514

Garrison, J. S. (2014). *Friendship and queer theory in the Renaissance: Gender and sexuality in early modern England.* New York: Routledge.

Garst, B. A., Browne, L. P., & Bialeschki, M. D. (2011). Youth development and the camp experience. In R. Allen & R.J. Barcelona (Eds.), *New Directions for Youth Development,* (Vol. 130, pp. 73–87). New York: Wiley & Sons.

Gartzke, E., & Weisiger, A. (2013). Fading friendships: Alliances, affinities and the activation of international identities. *British Journal of Political Science, 43*(01), 25–52.

Gaylord-Harden, N. K., Burrow, A. L., & Cunningham, J. A. (2012). A cultural-asset framework for investigating successful adaptation to stress in African American youth. *Child Development Perspectives, 6*(3), 264–271.

Geddes, L. (2014). Survival of the friendliest. *New Scientist, 224*(2998), 30–31.

George, R. (2007). Urban girls, "race" friendship and school choice: Changing schools, changing friendships. *Race Ethnicity and Education, 10*(2), 115–129.

Gerhardt, S., McCallum, A., McDougall, C., Keenan, S., & Rigby, P. (2015). The goal of making friends for youth with disabilities: Creating a goal menu. *Child: Care, health and development, 41*(6), 1018–1029.

Gettings, P. E., & Wilson, S. R. (2014). Examining commitment and relational maintenance in formal youth mentoring relationships. *Journal of Social and Personal Relationships, 31*(8), 1089–1115.

Ghandi, M. http://www.wisdomcommons.org/author/Mahatma%20Gandhi

Gifford-Smith, M. E., & Brownell, C. A. (2003). Childhood peer relationships: Social acceptance, friendships, and peer networks. *Journal of School Psychology, 41*(4), 235–284.

Gilbert, D. (2014). *The American class structure in an age of growing inequality.* Thousand Oaks, CA: Sage.

Gilhooly, D., & Lee, E. (2014). The role of digital literacy practices on refugee resettlement. *Journal of Adolescent & Adult Literacy, 57*(5), 387–396.

Gillard, A., & Witt, P. (2008). Recruitment and retention in youth programs. *Journal of Park and Recreation Administration, 26*(2), 177–188.

Gillespie, B. J., Lever, J., Frederick, D., & Royce, T. (2015). Close adult friendships, gender, and the life cycle. *Journal of Social and Personal Relationships, 32*(6), 709–736.

Gilliard-Matthews, S., Stevens, R., Nilsen, M., & Dunaev, J. (2015). "You see it everywhere. It's just natural.": Contextualizing the role of peers, family, and neighborhood in initial substance use. *Deviant Behavior, 36*(6), 492–509.

Ginwright, S. (2011). Hope, healing, and care: Pushing the boundaries of civic engagement for African American youth. *Liberal Education, 97*(2), 34–39.

Ginwright, S., Cammarota, J., & Noguera, P. (2005). Youth, social justice, and communities: Toward a theory of urban youth policy. *Social Justice, 32*(3), 24–40.

Ginwright, S., & James, T. (2002). From assets to agents of change: Social justice, organizing, and youth development. *New Directions for Youth Development, 2002*(96), 27–46.

Glaeser, E. L. (2010, March 5). Why the anti-urban bias? *Boston Globe.*

Glick, G. C., & Rose, A. J. (2011). Prospective associations between friendship adjustment and social strategies: Friendship as a context for building social skills. *Developmental Psychology, 47*(4), 1117–1132.

Glover, J. A., Galliher, R. V., & Crowell, K. A. (2015). Young women's passionate friendships: A qualitative analysis. *Journal of Gender Studies, 24*(1), 70–84.

Goins, M. N. (2011). Playing with dialectics: Black female friendship groups as a homeplace. *Communication Studies, 62*(5), 531–546.

Goldthorpe, J. (1997). The "Goldthorpe" class schema: Some observations on conceptual and operational issues in relation to the ESRC review on government social classifications. In D. Rose & K. O'Reilly (Eds.),*Constructing classes: Towards a new social classification for the UK* (pp. 1–20). London: Office for National Statistics.

Goldstein, T., Gray, J., Salisbury, J., & Snell, P. (2014). When qualitative research meets theater: The complexities of performed ethnography and research-informed theater project design. *Qualitative Inquiry, 20*(5), 674–685.

Good, C. A. (2014). *Founding friendships: Friendships between Men and Women in the Early American republic.* New York: Oxford University Press.

Goodnough, K. (2014. Examining the potential of youth-led community of practice: Experience and insights. *Educational Action Research, 22*(3), 363–379.

Gomez, B. E. (2013). *Community needs assessment and asset mapping in regards to homelessness in Downey, CA.* Retrieved from http://csula-dspace.calstate.edu/handle/10211.13/857

Góngora, V. C., & Castro Solano, A. (2014). Well-being and life satisfaction in Argentinean adolescents. *Journal of Youth Studies, 17*(9), 1277–1291.

Gordon, M. (2013). *Humor, laughter and human flourishing: A philosophical exploration of the laughing animal.* New York: Springer Science & Business Media.

Gordon, M. (2014). Friendship, intimacy and humor. *Educational Philosophy and Theory, 46*(2), 162–174.

Gormally, S. (2015). "I've been there, done that . . .": A study of youth gang desistance. *Youth Justice, 15*(2), 148–165.

Gormally, S., & Coburn, A. (2014). Finding nexus: Connecting youth work and research practices. *British Educational Research Journal, 40*(5), 869–885.

Gould, D., Voelker, D. K., & Griffes, K. (2013). Best coaching practices for developing team captains. *Sport Psychologist, 27*(1), 13–26.

Graber, R., Turner, R., & Madill, A. (2016). Best friends and better coping: Facilitating psychological resilience through boys' and girls' closest friendships. *British Journal of Psychology, 107*(2), 338–358.

Grace, D. (2008). *Building developmental assets in at-risk youth: A quasi- experimental study* (Doctoral dissertation). Available from ProQuest Dissertations and Theses database. (No. 3320265)

Graham, S. (2011). *Cities under siege: The new military urbanism.* New York: Verso.

Graham, S., Munniksma, A., & Juvonen, J. (2014). Psychosocial benefits of cross-ethnic friendships in urban middle schools. *Child Development, 85*(2), 469– 483.

Graham, S., Taylor, A. Z., & Ho, A. Y. (2009). Race and ethnicity in peer relations research. In K.H. Rubin, W.M. Bukowski & B. Lauren (Eds.), *Handbook of peer interactions, relationships, and groups* (pp. 394–413). New York: Guilford Press.

Graham, T., & Langa, M. (2015). Race and community practice: Reflections from the supervision of professional training. *Journal of Community Psychology, 43*(1), 36–48.

Grayling, A. C. (2013). *Friendship.* New Haven, CT: Yale University Press.

Greco, S., Holmes, M., & McKenzie, J. (2015). Friendship and happiness from a sociological perspective. In M. Demir (Ed.), *Friendship and happiness* (pp. 19–35). Rotterdam: Springer Netherlands.

Green, G. P., & Haines, A. (2011). *Asset building & community development.* Thousand Oaks, CA: Sage.

Green, K. L. (2013). "The way we hear ourselves is different from the way others hear us": Exploring the literate identities of a Black radio youth collective. *Equity & Excellence in Education, 46*(3), 315–326.

Greene, S., Burke, K., & McKenna, M. (2013). Forms of voice: Exploring the empowerment of youth at the intersection of art and action. *Urban Review, 45*(3), 311–334.

Greenberg, M. T., & Harris, A. R. (2012). Nurturing mindfulness in children and youth: Current state of research. *Child Development Perspectives, 6*(2), 161–166.

Greenman, E. (2011). Assimilation choices among immigrant families: Does school context matter? *International Migration Review, 45*(1), 29–67.

Greif, G. (2008). *Buddy system: Understanding male friendships.* New York: Oxford University Press.

Greif, G. L., & Deal, K. H. (2012). *Two plus two: Couples and their couple friendships.* New York: Routledge.

Griffin, C. (2013). *Representations of youth: The study of youth and adolescence in Britain and America.* New York: John Wiley & Sons.

Griffin, K. M., Lahman, M. K., & Opitz, M. F. (2016). Shoulder-to-shoulder research with children: Methodological and ethical considerations. *Journal of Early Childhood Research, 14*(1), 18–27.

Grills, C., Cooke, D., Douglas, J., Subica, A., Villanueva, S., & Hudson, B. (2015). Culture, racial socialization, and positive African American youth development. *Journal of Black Psychology*.

Guerra, N. G., Dierkhising, C. B., & Payne, P. R. (2013). How should we identify and intervene with youth at risk of joining gangs? A developmental approach for children ages 0–12. In T. R. Simon, N. M. Ritter, & R. R. Mahendra (Eds.), *Chànging course* (pp. 63–74). Washington, DC: US Department of Justice/US Department of Health and Human Services. Retrieved from https://www.ncjrs.gov/pdffiles1/nij/239234.pdf#page=66

Guggenheim, N., & Taubman–Ben-Ari, O. (2015). Can friendship serve as an impetus for safe driving among young drivers? *Transportation research part F: Traffic psychology and behaviour, 30*, 145–152.

Gupta, K. (2011). *A practical guide to needs assessment.* John Wiley & Sons.

Gutierrez, C. O. N., & Hopkins, P. (2015). Introduction: Young people, gender and intersectionality. *Gender, Place & Culture, 22*(1), 383–389.

Gutierrez, L. M. (1990). Working with women of color: An empowerment perspective. *Social Work, 35*(2), 149–153.

Haavind, H. (2014). "Who does he think he is?": Making new friends and leaving others behind–on the path from childhood to youth. In R. May & D.M. Sontergaard (Eds.), *School bullying: New theories in context* (pp. 129–158). New York: Cambridge University Press.

Hacker, K. (2013). *Community-based participatory research.* Los Angeles: Sage.

Hacking, E. B., & Barratt, R. (2009). Children researching their urban environment: Developing a methodology. *Education 3–13, 37*(4), 371–383.

Hadden, J. K., & Barton, J. (1973). An image that will not die: Thoughts on the history of anti-urban ideology. *Urban Affairs Annual Review, 7*(2), 79–116.

Hage, S. M., & Kenny, M. E. (2009). Promoting a social justice approach to prevention: Future directions for training, practice, and research. *Journal of Primary Prevention, 30*(1), 75–87.

Hall, J. A. (2011). Sex differences in friendship expectations: A meta-analysis. *Journal of Social and Personal Relationships, 28*(6), 723–747.

Hall, J. A. (2012). Friendship standards: The dimensions of ideal expectations. *Journal of Social and Personal Relationships, 29*(7), 884–907.

Hall, S. M. (2009). "Private life" and "work life": Difficulties and dilemmas when making and maintaining friendships with ethnographic participants. *Area, 41*(3), 263–272.

Hallett, R. (2013). Interrupting life history: Evolution of a relationship within the research process. *Qualitative Report, 18*(14), 1–16.

Halliday, T. J., & Kwak, S. (2012). What is a peer? The role of network definitions in estimation of endogenous peer effects. *Applied Economics, 44*(3), 289–302.

Hallsworth, S., & Brotherton, D. (2011). *Urban disorder and gangs: A critique and a warning.* London: Runnymede Trust.

Hamilton, S. F. (1999). *A three-part definition of youth development.* Unpublished manuscript, Cornell University College of Human Ecology, Ithaca, NY.

Hamilton, S. F., Hamilton, M. A., & Pittman, K. (2004). Principles for youth development. In S.F. Hamilton & M.A. Hamilton (Eds.), *The youth development handbook: Coming of age in American communities* (pp. 3–22). Thousand Oaks, CA: Sage Publications.

Hammerseley, M. (2014). Research design. In A. Clark, R. Flewitt, M. Hammerseley & M. Robb (Eds.), *Understanding research with children and young people* (pp. 107–121). London: Sage.

Hancock, D. R., & Algozzine, B. (2006). *Doing case study research.* New York: Teachers College Press.

Hanlon, T. E., Simon, B. D., O'Grady, K. E., Carswell, S. B., & Callaman, J. M. (2009). The effectiveness of an after-school program targeting urban African American youth. *Education and urban society, 42*(1), 96–118.

Hannes, K., & Parylo, O. (2014). Let's play it safe: Ethical considerations from participants in a photovoice research project. *International Journal of Qualitative Methods, 13*(1), 255–274.

Hardcastle, D. A., Powers, P. R., & Wenocur, S. (2011). *Community practice: Theories and skills for social workers*(3rd ed.). New York: Oxford University Press.

Hardina, D. (2012). *Interpersonal social work skills for community practice.* New York: Springer.

Hardina, D. (2013). *Analytical skills for community organization practice.* New York: Columbia University Press.

Harding, D. J. (2008). Neighborhood violence and adolescent friendships. *International Journal of Conflict and Violence, 2*(1), 28–55.

Harley, D. (2015). Perceptions of hopelessness among low-income African-American adolescents through the lens of photovoice. *Journal of Ethnic and Cultural Diversity in Social Work, 24*(1), 18–38.

Harley, D., Hunn, V., Elliott, W., & Canfield, J. (2015). Photovoice as a culturally competent research methodology for African Americans. *Journal of Pan African Studies, 7*(9), 31+.

Harper, G. W., Dolcini, M. M., Benhorin, S., Watson, S. E., & Boyer, C. B. (2014). The benefits of a friendship-based HIV/STI prevention intervention for African American youth. *Youth & Society, 46*(5), 591–622.

Harris, P. B. (2012). Maintaining friendships in early stage dementia: Factors to consider. *Dementia, 11*(3), 305–314.

Hart, R. A. (2013). *Children's participation: The theory and practice of involving young citizens in community development and environmental care.* New York: Routledge.

Harvey, D. (2010). *Social justice and the city* (Vol. 1). Athens, Georgia: University of Georgia Press.

Haynes, K., & Tanner, T. M. (2015). Empowering young people and strengthening resilience: Youth-centred participatory video as a tool for climate change adaptation and disaster risk reduction. *Children's Geographies, 13*(3), 357– 371.

Head, B. W. (2011). Why not ask them? Mapping and promoting youth participation. *Children and Youth Services Review, 33*(4), 541–547.

Headey, B. (2014). Bottom-up versus top-down theories of life satisfaction. In A.C. Michalos (Ed.), *Encyclopedia of quality of life and well-being research* (pp. 423–426). Rotterdam: Springer Netherlands.

Healey, J. F., & O'Brien, E. (2014). *Race, ethnicity, gender, and class: The sociology of group conflict and change.* Thousand Oaks, CA: Sage.

Healy, M. (2011). Should we take the friendships of children seriously? *Journal of Moral Education, 40*(4), 441–456.

Heaphy, B., & Davies, K. (2012). Critical friendships. *Families, Relationships and Societies, 1*(3), 311–326.

Hearn, H., & Thomson, P. (2014). Working with texts, images and artefacts. In A. Clark, R. Flewitt, M. Hammerseley & M. Robb (Eds.), *Understanding research with children and young people* (pp. 154–168). London: Sage.

Heath, S., Brooks, R., Cleaver, E., & Ireland, E. (2009). *Researching young people's lives.* Thousand Oaks, CA: Sage.

Heath, S., & Walker, C. (Eds.). (2012). *Innovations in youth research.* London: Palgrave Macmillan.

Hellstern, M. (2008). *Getting along famously: A celebration of friendship.* New York: Penguin.

Helm, B. (2010). Friendship. In *Stanford encyclopedia of philosophy.* Retrieved from http://seop.illc.uva.nl/entries/friendship/

Helve, H., & Bynner, J. (Eds.). (2007). *Youth and social capital.* London: Tufnell.

Henderson, S., & Gilding, M. (2004). "I've never clicked this much with anyone in my life": Trust and hyperpersonal communication in online friendships. *New Media & Society, 6*(4), 487–506.

Hendrick, S. S., & Hendrick, C. (2006). Measuring respect in close relationships. *Journal of Social and Personal Relationships, 23*(6), 881–899.

Heron, J., & Reason, P. (2006). The practice of co-operative inquiry: Research "with" rather than "on" people. In P. Reason & H. Bradbury-Huang (Eds.), *Handbook of action research* (pp. 144–154). Thousand Oaks, CA: Sage.

Hewitt, J. M., & Lee, E. A. (2012). Building relationships through reciprocal student exchanges. *Canadian Journal of Native Education, 35*(1), 98–116.

Hiatt, C., Laursen, B., Mooney, K. S., & Rubin, K. H. (2015). Forms of friendship: A person-centered assessment of the quality, stability, and outcomes of different types of adolescent friends. *Personality and Individual Differences, 77,* 149– 155.

Higa, D., Hoppe, M. J., Lindhorst, T., Mincer, S., Beadnell, B., Morrison, D. M., . . . Mountz, S. (2014). Negative and positive factors associated with the well-being of lesbian, gay, bisexual, transgender, queer, and questioning (LGBTQ) youth. *Youth & Society, 46*(5), 663–687.

Hill, E. N., & Swenson, L. P. (2014). Perceptions of friendship among youth with distressed friends. *Child Psychiatry & Human Development, 45*(1), 99–109.

Hirsch, B. J., Deutsch, N. L., & DuBois, D. L. (2011). *After-school centers and youth development: Case studies of success and failure.* New York: Cambridge University Press.

Hoagland, E. (2013). On Friendship. *American Scholar, 82*(1), 32–43.

Hodge, K., Danish, S., & Martin, J. (2013). Developing a conceptual framework for life skills interventions. *Counseling Psychologist, 41*(8), 1125–1152.

Hoffman, B. R., Weathers, N., & Sanders, B. (2014). Substance use among gang member adolescents and young adults and associations with friends and family substance use. *Journal of Child and Adolescent Psychiatric Nursing, 27*(1), 35–42.

Hofstadter, R. (1972). *The age of reform.* New York: Knopf.

Hofstede, G. (1980). *Culture's consequences: International differences in work related values.* Beverley Hills, CA: Sage.

Holder, M. D., & Coleman, B. (2015). Children's friendships and positive well-being. In M. Demir (Ed.), *Friendship and happiness* (pp. 81–97). Rotterdam: Springer Netherlands.

Holland, N. E. (2016). Partnering with a higher power: Academic engagement, religiosity, and spirituality of African American urban youth. *Education and Urban Society, 48*(4), 299–323.

Holland, S. (2010). *Child and family assessment in social work practice*. Thousand Oaks, CA: Sage.

Hollingworth, S. (2015). Performances of social class, race and gender through youth subculture: Putting structure back in to youth subcultural studies. *Journal of Youth Studies, 18*(10), 1237–1256.

Holmes, K. (2012). Perceived difficulty of friendship maintenance online: Geographic factors. *Advances in Applied Sociology, 2*(4), 309–312.

Holmes, M., & Greco, S. (2011). Introduction: Friendship and emotions. *Sociological Research Online, 16*(1), 16.

Holoien, D. S., Bergsieker, H. B., Shelton, J. N., & Alegre, J. M. (2015). Do you really understand? Achieving accuracy in interracial relationships. *Journal of Personality and Social Psychology, 108*(1), 76.

Holt, A., & Pamment, N. (2011). Overcoming the challenges of researching "young offenders": Using assisted questionnaires–a research note. *International Journal of Social Research Methodology, 14*(2), 125–133.

Holt, N. L., & Neely, K. C. (2011). Positive youth development through sport: A review. *Revista iberoamericana de psicología del ejercicio y el deporte, 6*(2), 299–316.

Holter, M., & Guilfoyle, A. (2013). *Because she's always on my side: Identity, friendships, and parental support within a whole school pastoral care program for adolescent girls*. Retrieved from http://ro.ecu.edu.au/ecuworks2013/598/

Hooper, C. A., & Gunn, R. (2014). Recognition as a framework for ethical participatory research: Developing a methodology with looked after young people. *International Journal of Social Research Methodology, 17*(5), 475–488.

Hope, E. C., & Jagers, R. J. (2014). The role of sociopolitical attitudes and civic education in the civic engagement of Black youth. *Journal of Research on Adolescence, 24*(3), 460–470.

Hopkins, P. E. (2013). *Young people, place and identity*. New York: Routledge.

Hopkins, S., & Ryan, N. (2014). Digital narratives, social connectivity and disadvantaged youth: Raising aspirations for rural and low socioeconomic young people. *International Studies in Widening Participation, 1*(1), 28–42.

Horschelmann, K., & Van Blerk, L. (2013). *Children, youth and the city*. New York: Routledge.

Howell, J. C. (2013). Why is gang-membership prevention important? In T. R. Simon, N. M. Ritter, & R. R. Mahendra (Eds.), *Changing course* (pp. 7–18). Washington, DC: US Department of Justice/US Department of Health and Human Services.

Howes, C. (2009). Friendship in early childhood. In K.H. Rubin, W.M. Bukowski & B. Laursen (Eds.), *Handbook of peer interactions, relationships, and groups* (pp. 180–194). New York: Guilford Press.

Hruschka, D. J. (2010). *Friendship: Development, ecology, and evolution of a relationship* (Vol. 5). Berkeley, CA: University of California Press.

Huebner, E. S., & Diener, C. (2008). Research on life satisfaction of children and youth. In M. Eid & R.J. Larsen (Eds.), *The science of subjective well-being* (pp. 376–392). New York: Guilford Press.

Huebner, E. S., Gilman, R., & Ma, C. (2012). Perceived quality of life of children and youth. In K.C. Land, A.C. Michalos & J. Sirgy (Eds.), *Handbook of social indicators and quality of life research* (pp. 355–372). Rotterdam: Springer Netherlands.

Huey, S., Jr., McDaniel, D. D., Smith, C. A., Pearson, C., & Griffin Jr, J. P. (2014). Gang-involved African American youth: An overview. In K.C. Vaughans & W. Spielberg (Eds.), *The psychology of Black boys and adolescents* (p. 313). Santa Barbara, CA: ABC-CLIO, LLC.

Hughes, D. (2003). Correlates of African American and Latino parents' messages to children about ethnicity and race: A comparative study of racial socialization. *American Journal of Community Psychology, 31*(1), 15–33.

Hunt, J. (2014). *Friendship.* Peabody, MA: Rose Publishing Inc.

Hunter, B. D., Neiger, B., & West, J. (2011). The importance of addressing social determinants of health at the local level: The case for social capital. *Health & social care in the community, 19*(5), 522–530.

Hur, M. H. (2006). Empowerment in terms of theoretical perspectives: Exploring a typology of the process and components across disciplines. *Journal of Community Psychology, 34*(5), 523–540.

Hynes, K., & Hirsch, B. J. (Eds.). (2012). Career programming: Linking youth to the world of work: *New Directions for Youth Development,* Number 134 (Vol. 119). New York: Wiley.

Ife, J. (2010). Capacity building and community development. In S. Kenner & M. Clarke (Eds.), *Challenging capacity building: Comparative perspectives* (pp. 67–84). London: Palgrave Macmillan.

Ife, J. (2012). *Human rights and social work: Towards rights-based practice.* New York: Cambridge University Press.

Imasiku, L. K. (2014). *Participatory perspectives: A photovoice narrative study of Zambian vulnerable youth* (Doctoral dissertation). San Francisco State University).

Ingram, P., & Zou, X. (2008). Business friendships. *Research in Organizational Behavior, 28*, 167–184.

Intrator, S. M., & Siegel, D. (2014). *The quest for mastery: Positive youth development through out-of-school programs.* Cambridge, MA: Harvard Education Press.

Irby, D. J. (2015). Urban is floating face down in the mainstream: Using hip-hop- based education research to resurrect "the urban" in urban education. *Urban Education, 50*(1), 7–30.

Irwin, C. C., Irwin, R. L., Ryan, T. D., & Drayer, J. (2009). The mythology of swimming: Are myths impacting minority youth participation? *International Journal of Aquatic Research and Education, 3*(1), 10–23.

Irwin, S. (2013). *Rights of passage: Social change and the transition from youth to adulthood* (Vol. 4). New York: Routledge.

Iwasaki, Y. (2015). The role of youth engagement in positive youth development and social justice youth development for high-risk, marginalised youth. *International Journal of Adolescence and Youth,* 1–12.

Jackson, D. (2011). *What's so funny? Making sense of humor.* New York: Penguin.

Jacquez, F., Vaughn, L. M., & Wagner, E. (2013). Youth as partners, participants or passive recipients: A review of children and adolescents in community-based participatory research (CBPR). *American Journal of Community Psychology, 51*(1–2), 176–189.

Jamieson, L. (2012). Intimacy as a concept: Explaining social change in the context of globalisation or another form of ethnocentricism? *Sociological Research Online, 1*(1), 133–147.

Jardine, C. G., & James, A. (2012). Youth researching youth: Benefits, limitations and ethical considerations within a participatory research process. *International Journal of Circumpolar,* 71. Retrieved from http://www.circumpolarhealthjournal.net/index.php/ijch/article/view/18415

Jeffries, M. P. (2011). *Thug life: Race, gender, and the meaning of hip-hop.* Chicago: University of Chicago Press.

Jeffs, T., & Smith, M. K. (Eds.). (2010). *Youth work practice.* New York: Palgrave Macmillan.

Jennings, J., & Jordan-Zachery, J. S. (2010*a*). *Urban spaces: Planning and struggles for land and community.* Lanham, MD: Rowman & Littlefield.

Jennings, J., & Jordan-Zachery, J. S. (2010*b*). Determiing the public good and evaluating local economic development: Critique of the US Supreme Court's Kelo v. New London decision. In J. Jennings & J. S. Jordan-Zachery (Eds.), *Urban spaces: Planning and struggles for land and community* (p. 1–18). Lanham, MD: Rowman & Littlefield.

Jennings, L. B., Parra-Medina, D. M., Hilfinger-Messias, D. K., & McLoughlin, K. (2006). Toward a critical social theory of youth empowerment. *Journal of Community Practice, 14*(1–2), 31–55.

Jeon, K. C., & Goodson, P. (2015). Alcohol and sex: The influence of friendship networks on co-occurring risky health behaviors of US adolescents. *PeerJ PrePrints, 3*:e1079. Retrieved from https://doi.org/10.7287/peerj.preprints.877v1.

Jesuvadian, M. K., & Wright, S. (2014). Ethnicity in research with young children: Invitation/barrier. *Early Child Development and Care, 184*(11), 1566–1582.

Jivraj, J., Sacrey, L. A., Newton, A., Nicholas, D., & Zwaigenbaum, L. (2014). Assessing the influence of researcher–partner involvement on the process and outcomes of participatory research in autism spectrum disorder and neurodevelopmental disorders: A scoping review. *Autism, 18*(7), 782–793.

Joassart-Marcelli, P. (2010). Leveling the playing field? Urban disparities in funding for local parks and recreation in the Los Angeles region. *Environment and planning A, 42*(5), 1174.

Jocson, K. M. (2006). "There's a better word": Urban youth rewriting their social worlds through poetry. *Journal of Adolescent & Adult Literacy, 49*(8), 700–707.

Johansen, S., & Le, T. N. (2014). Youth perspective on multiculturalism using photovoice methodology. *Youth & Society, 46*(4), 548–565.

Johnson, A. J., Wittenberg, E., Haigh, M., Wigley, S., Becker, J., Brown, K., & Craig, E. (2004). The process of relationship development and deterioration: Turning points in friendships that have terminated. *Communication Quarterly, 52*(1), 54–67.

Johnson, C. M. (2014). The loss of friends to homicide and the implications for the identity development of urban African American teen girls. *Clinical Social Work Journal, 42*(1), 27–49.

Johnson, K. M., Schaefer, A., Lichter, D. T., & Rogers, L. T. (2014). *The increasing diversity of America's youth.* Retrieved from http://scholars.unh.edu/carsey/212/?utm_source=scholars.unh.edu%2Fcars ey%2F212&utm_medium=PDF&utm_campaign=PDFCoverPages

Jones, G. (2009). *Youth* (Vol. 17). Cambridge, UK: Polity.

Jones, J. N., & Deutsch, N. L. (2011). Relational strategies in after-school settings: How staff–youth relationships support positive development. *Youth & Society, 43*(4), 1381–1406.

Jones, J. S., & Watt, S. (2010). *Ethnography in social science practice.* New York: Routledge.

Jones, M. I., Dunn, J. G. H., Holt, N. L., Sullivan, P. J., & Bloom, G. A. (2011). Exploring the "5Cs" of positive youth development in sport. *Journal of Sport Behavior, 34*(3), 250–267.

Jones, R. M., Vaterlaus, J. M., Jackson, M. A., & Morrill, T. B. (2014). Friendship characteristics, psychosocial development, and adolescent identity formation. *Personal Relationships, 21*(1), 51–67.

Jose, P. E., Ryan, N., & Pryor, J. (2012). Does social connectedness promote a greater sense of well-being in adolescence over time? *Journal of Research on Adolescence, 22*(2), 235–251.

Jusdanis, G. (2014). *A tremendous thing: Friendship from the "Iliad" to the internet.* Itahca, NY: Cornell University Press.

Juvonen, J., Espinoza, G., & Knifsend, C. (2012). The role of peer relationships in student academic and extracurricular engagement. In *Handbook of research on student engagement* (pp. 387–401). New York: Springer US.

Kahn, L. (2014). *Can't we just be who we are? The experiences, identity, and beliefs of adolescents with disabilities who identify as a sexual or gender minority.* (dissertation). Eugene, OR: University of Oregon.

Kang, S. K., & Bodenhausen, G. V. (2015). Multiple identities in social perception and interaction: Challenges and opportunities. *Annual Review of Psychology, 66,* 547–574.

Kao, G., & Joyner, K. (2006). Do Hispanic and Asian adolescents practice panethnicity in friendship choices? *Social Science Quarterly, 87*(5), 972–992.

Kao, G., & Vaquera, E. (2006). The salience of racial and ethnic identification in friendship choices among Hispanic adolescents. *Hispanic Journal of Behavioral Sciences, 28*(1), 23–47.

Kaplan, E. B. (2013). *"We live in the shadow" Inner-city kids tell their stories through photographs.* Philadelphia, PA: Temple University Press.

Karcher, M. J., & Hansen, K. (2013). Mentoring activities and interactions. In D.L. DuBois & M.J. Karcher (Eds.), *Handbook of youth mentoring* (pp. 63–82). Thousand Oaks, CA: Sage.

Karlsson, J. (2012). Implementing two approaches to generating visual data. In J. Arthur (Ed.), *Research Methods and Methodologies in Education* (pp. 95–101). Thousand Oaks, CA: Sage.

Karlsson, M., & Evaldsson, A. C. (2011). "It was Emma's army who bullied that girl": A narrative perspective on bullying and identity making in three girls' friendship groups. *Narrative Inquiry, 21*(1), 24–43.

Kathiravelu, L. (2013). *Friendship and the urban encounter: Towards a research agenda.* Retrieved from http://pubman.mpdl.mpg.de/pubman/item/escidoc:1850592/component/esci doc:1850591/WP_13-10_Kathiravelu_Friendship.pdf

Kaul, C. R., Johnsen, S. K., Witte, M. M., & Saxon, T. F. (2015). Critical components of a summer enrichment program for urban low-income gifted students. *Gifted Child Today, 38*(1), 32–40.

Kawai, R., Serriere, S., & Mitra, D. (2014). Contested spaces of a "failing" elementary school. *Theory & Research in Social Education, 42*(4), 486–515.

Kazovsky, M. V. (2013). *Frienemies: "Friends" under false pretence: An investigation into intrasexual competition predicting female friendships.* (hoors thesis). University of Queensland, Australia.

Kearney, M. S., & Levine, P. B. (2015). Investigating recent trends in the US teen birth rate. *Journal of Health Economics, 1*(1), 15–29.

Kegler, M. C., Oman, R. F., Vesely, S. K., McLeroy, K. R., Aspy, C. B., Rodine, S., & Marshall, L. (2005). Relationships among youth assets and neighborhood and community resources. *Health Education & Behavior, 32*(3), 380–397.

Keijsers, L., Branje, S., Hawk, S. T., Schwartz, S. J., Frijns, T., Koot, H. M., . . . Meeus, W. (2012). Forbidden friends as forbidden fruit: Parental supervision of friendships, contact with deviant peers, and adolescent delinquency. *Child development, 83*(2), 651–666.

Keller, A. C., Semmer, N. K., Samuel, R., & Bergman, M. M. (2014). The meaning and measurement of well-being as an indicator of success. In A. C. Keller & R. Samuel (Eds.),

Psychological, educational, and sociological perspectives on success and well-being in career development (pp. 171–193). Rotterdam: Springer Netherlands.

Kelly, E. J. (2013). *Youth development through a situated learning approach* (Doctoral dissertation). University of Texas, Austin.

Kempner, S. G. (2008). *Implicit theories of friendships: Examining the roles of growth and destiny beliefs in children's friendships.* (dissertation). University of Minnesota, ProQuest. Retrieved from https://books.google.com/books?hl=en&lr=&id=SwChmS2OooMC&oi=fnd&pg=PR1&dq=Kempner,+S.+G.+(2008).+Implicit+Theories+of+Friendships:+Examining+the+Roles+of++%09Growth+and+Destiny+Beliefs+in+Children%27s+Friendships&ots=8WC-jcllIW&sig=A2IYZpmpch9U8atvGhMsgcaJGGQ#v=onepage&q&f=false

Kennedy, D. (2015). Resetting race. In R. Bangs & L. Davis (Eds.), *Race and social problems* (pp. 195–205). New York: Springer.

Kenyon, D. B., & Carter, J. S. (2011). Ethnic identity, sense of community, and psychological well-being among northern plains American Indian youth. *Journal of community psychology, 39*(1), 1–9.

Keyes, C. L. (2014). Happiness, flourishing, and life satisfaction. In W. Cockerham & R. Dingwill (Eds.), *The Wiley Blackwell encyclopedia of health, illness, behavior, and society.* New York.

Kia-Keating, M., Dowdy, E., Morgan, M. L., & Noam, G. G. (2011). Protecting and promoting: An integrative conceptual model for healthy development of adolescents. *Journal of Adolescent Health, 48*(3), 220–228.

Kiang, L., Peterson, J. L., & Thompson, T. L. (2011). Ethnic peer preferences among Asian American adolescents in emerging immigrant communities. *Journal of Research on Adolescence, 21*(4), 754–761.

Kim, J. (2014). "You don't need to be mean. We're friends, Right?" Young Korean- American children's conflicts and references to friendship. *Journal of Early Childhood Research, 12*(3), 279–293.

Kimbriel, S. (2014). *Friendship as sacred knowing: Overcoming isolation.* New York: Oxford University Press.

Kingery, J. N., Erdley, C. A., & Marshall, K. C. (2011). Peer acceptance and friendship as predictors of early adolescents' adjustment across the middle school transition. *Merrill-Palmer Quarterly, 57*(3), 215–243.

Kirmanoğlu, H., & Başlevent, C. (2014). Life satisfaction of ethnic minority members: An examination of interactions with immigration, discrimination, and citizenship. *Social Indicators Research, 116*(1), 173–184.

Kirschman, K. J. B., Roberts, M. C., Shadlow, J. O., & Pelley, T. J. (2010). An evaluation of hope following a summer camp for inner-city youth. *Child & Youth Care Forum, 39*(6), 385–396.

Kirshner, B. (2015). *Youth activism in an era of education inequality.* New York: New York University Press.

Kissner, J., & Pyrooz, D. C. (2009). Self-control, differential association, and gang membership: A theoretical and empirical extension of the literature. *Journal of Criminal Justice, 37*(5), 478–487.

Klatt, J., & Enright, R. (2009). Investigating the place of forgiveness within the Positive Youth Development paradigm. *Journal of Moral Education, 38*(1), 35–52.

Knecht, A., Snijders, T. A., Baerveldt, C., Steglich, C. E., & Raub, W. (2010). Friendship and delinquency: Selection and influence processes in early adolescence. *Social Development, 19*(3), 494–514.

Knies, G., Nandi, A., & Platt, L. (2014). *Life satisfaction, ethnicity and neighbourhoods: Is there an effect of neighbourhood ethnic composition on life satisfaction?* Retrieved from http://eprints.lse.ac.uk/55669/

Knifsend, C. A., & Juvonen, J. (2014). Social identity complexity, cross-ethnic friendships, and intergroup attitudes in urban middle schools. *Child Development, 85*(2), 709–721.

Knight, G. P., & Carlo, G. (2012). Prosocial development among Mexican American youth. *Child Development Perspectives, 6*(3), 258–263.

Knox, P., & Pinch, S. (2014). *Urban social geography: An introduction.* New York: Routledge.

Kocet, M. (2014). The role of friendships in the lives of gay men, adolescents, and boys. In M.M. Kocet (Ed.), *Counseling gay men, adolescents, and boys: A strengths-based guide for helping professionals and educators* (pp. 24–33). New York: Routledge.

Konstan, D. (1997). *Friendship in the classical world.* New York: Cambridge University Press.

Koopmans, R., Lancee, B., & Schaeffer, M. (2014). Ethnic diversity in diverse societies. In R. Koopman & B. Lancee (Eds.), *Social cohesion and immigration in Europe and North America: mechanisms, conditions, and causality* (pp. 1–18). New York: Routledge.

Kotkin, J. (2014, Feb. 6). Where the US youth population is booming. *Forbes Magazine.* Retrieved from http://www.forbes.com/sites/joelkotkin/2014/02/06/americas-future-cities-where-the-youth-populations-are-booming/#6a3014432fba

Kovacic, M. B., Stigler, S., Smith, A., Kidd, A., & Vaughn, L. M. (2014). Beginning a partnership with photovoice to explore environmental health and health inequities in minority communities. *International Journal of Environmental Research and Public Health, 11*(11), 11132–11151.

Kratke, S. (2012). The new urban growth idealogy of "creative cities." In N. Brenner, P. Marcuse & M. Mayer (Eds.), *Cities for people and not profit: Critical urban theory and the right to the city* (pp. 138–149). New York: Routledge.

Kristensen, G. K., & Ravn, M. N. (2015). The voices heard and the voices silenced: Recruitment processes in qualitative interview studies. *Qualitative Research, 15*(6), 722–737.

Krostad, J. M., & Lopez, M. H. (2015). *Hispanic population reaches record 55 million, but pace has cooled.* Washington, DC Pew Hispanic Center.

Kullman, K. (2014). Children, urban care, and everyday pavements. *Environment and Planning A, 46*, 2864–2880.

Kunt, Z. (2013). *Friendship networks of people with visual impairment* (Doctoral dissertation) Central European University, Budapest, Hungary.

Kuperminc, G. P., Thomason, J., DiMeo, M., & Broomfield-Massey, K. (2011). Cool Girls, Inc.: Promoting the positive development of urban preadolescent and early adolescent girls. *Journal of Primary Prevention, 32*(3–4), 171–183.

Kuttner, P. J. (2015). Educating for cultural citizenship: Reframing the goals of arts education. *Curriculum Inquiry, 45*(1), 69–92.

Laborde, N. D., van Dommelen-Gonzalez, E., & Minnis, A. M. (2014). Trust–that's a big one: Intimate partnership values among urban Latino youth. *Culture, Health & Sexuality, 16*(9), 1009–1022.

Lachman, P., Roman, C. G., & Cahill, M. (2013). Assessing youth motivations for join-ing a peer group as risk factors for delinquent and gang behavior. *Youth Violence and Juvenile Justice, 11*(3), 212–229.

La Greca, A. M., Bearman, K. J., & Moore, H. (2002). Peer relations of youth with pediatric conditions and health risks: Promoting social support and healthy lifestyles. *Journal of Developmental & Behavioral Pediatrics, 23*(4), 271–280.

la Haye, K., Green, H. D., Kennedy, D. P., Pollard, M. S., & Tucker, J. S. (2013). Selection and influence mechanisms associated with marijuana initiation and use in adolescent friendship networks. *Journal of Research on Adolescence, 23*(3), 474–486.

Lahman, M. (2008). Always othered: Ethical research with children. *Journal of Early Childhood Research, 6*(3), 281–300.

Lakon, C. M., Wang, C., Butts, C. T., Jose, R., Timberlake, D. S., & Hipp, J. R. (2015). A dynamic model of adolescent friendship networks, parental influences, and smok-ing. *Journal of Youth and Adolescence, 44*(9), 1767–1786.

Lal, S., Jarus, T., & Suto, M. J. (2012). A scoping review of the photovoice method: Implications for occupational therapy research. *Canadian Journal of Occupational Therapy, 79*(3), 181–190.

Lam, C. B., McHale, S. M., & Crouter, A. C. (2014). Time with peers from middle childhood to late adolescence: Developmental course and adjustment correlates. *Child develop-ment, 85*(4), 1677–1693.

Lamarche, V., Brendgen, M., Boivin, M., Vitaro, F., Pérusse, D., & Dionne, G. (2006). Do friendships and sibling relationships provide protection against peer victimization in a similar way? *Social Development, 15*(3), 373–393.

Lambert, A. (2013). *Intimacy and friendship on Facebook*. New York: Palgrave Macmillan.

Lambert, J. (2013). *Digital storytelling: Capturing lives, creating community*(4th ed.). New York: Routledge.

Larson, R. W. (2011). Positive development in a disorderly world. *Journal of Research on Adolescence, 21*(2), 317–334.

Law, B. M., Siu, A. M., & Shek, D. T. (2012). Recognition for positive behavior as a critical youth development construct: Conceptual bases and implications on youth service development. *Scientific World Journal*. Retrieved from http://www.hindawi.com/jour-nals/tswj/2012/809578/abs/

Lawson, M. A., & Lawson, H. A. (2013). New conceptual frameworks for student engage-ment research, policy, and practice. *Review of Educational Research, 83*(3), 432–479.

Lawson, W. (2006). *Friendships: The Aspie way*. Philadelphia, PA: Jessica Kingsley Publishers.

Lazarsfeld, P., & Merton, R. K. (1954). Friendships as a social process: A substantive and methodological analysis. In M. Berger (Ed.), *Freedom and control in modern society* (pp. 18–66). New York: Van Nostrand.

Leadbeater, B., Riecken, T., Benoit, C., Banister, E., Brunk, C., & Class, K. (2006). Community-based research with vulnerable populations: Challenges for ethics and research guideline. In B.J.R. Leadbeater (Ed.), *Ethical issues in community-based research with children and youth* (pp. 3–21). Toronto: University of Toronto Press.

Leaman, O. (2014). *Friendship east and west: Philosophical perspectives*. New York: Routledge.

Lee, J. A. (2013). *The empowerment approach to social work practice*. New York: Columbia University Press.

Lee, N. (2015). Migrant and ethnic diversity, cities and innovation: Firm effects or city effects? *Journal of Economic Geography, 15*(4), 769–796.

Lee, R. (2011). The outlook for population growth. *Science, 333*(6042), 569–573.

Lee, T. Y., Cheung, C. K., & Kwong, W. M. (2012). Resilience as a positive youth development construct: A conceptual review. *Scientific World Journal*. Retrieved from http://www.hindawi.com/journals/tswj/2012/390450/abs/

Legerski, J. P., Biggs, B. K., Greenhoot, A. F., & Sampilo, M. L. (2015). Emotion talk and friend responses among early adolescent same-sex friend dyads. *Social Development, 24*(1), 20–38.

Leib, E. J. (2011). *Friend v. friend: The transformation of friendship—and what the law has to do with it.* New York: Oxford University Press.

Leipert, B. D. (2013). Reslience: Grounded theory and photovoice variations on a theme: An update. In C.A. Winters (Ed.), *Rural nursing: Concepts, theory, and practice* (pp. 95–118). New York: Springer Publishers.

Lekies, K. S., Yost, G., & Rode, J. (2015). Urban youth's experiences of nature: Implications for outdoor adventure recreation. *Journal of Outdoor Recreation and Tourism, 9*(1), 1–10.

Lenhart, A., Ling, R., Campbell, S., & Purcell, K. (2010). *Teens and mobile phones: Text messaging explodes as teens embrace it as the centerpiece of their communication strategies with friends.* Washington, DC: Pew Internet & American Life Project.

Lenhart, A., Rainie, L., & Lewis, O. (2001). *Teenage life online: The rise of the instant-message generation and the Internet's impact on friendships and family relationships.* Washington, DC: Pew Internet & American Life Project.

Lenzi, M., Vieno, A., Perkins, D. D., Pastore, M., Santinello, M., & Mazzardis, S. (2012). Perceived neighborhood social resources as determinants of prosocial behavior in early adolescence. *American Journal of Community Psychology, 50*(1–2), 37–49.

Lerner, J. V., Phelps, E., Forman, Y. E., & Bowers, E. P. (2009). *Positive youth development.* New York: John Wiley & Sons.

Lerner, R. M., Alberts, A. E., Jelicic, H., & Smith, L. M. (2006). Young people are resources to be developed: Promoting positive youth development through adult-youth relations and community assets. In E. Gil Clary & J.E. Rhodes (Eds.), *Mobilizing adults for positive youth development* (pp. 19–39). New York: Springer US.

Lerner, R. M., Lerner, J. V., P Bowers, E., & John Geldhof, G. (2015). Positive youth development and relational-developmental-systems. In R.M. Lerner & M.E. Lamb (Eds), *Handbook of Child Psychology and Developmental Science.* New York: John Wiley & Sons, Inc

Lewis, D. M., Al-Shawaf, L., Russell, E. M., & Buss, D. M. (2015). Friends and happiness: An evolutionary perspective on friendship. In R.M. Lerner & M.E. Lamb (Eds.), *Friendship and happiness* (pp. 37–57). Rotterdam: Springer Netherlands.

Lewis, R. K. (2011). Promoting positive youth development by understanding social contexts. *Journal of Prevention & Intervention in the Community, 39*(4), 273– 276.

Lewis-Charp, H., Yu, H. C., & Soukamneuth, S. (2006). Civic activist approaches for engaging youth in social justice. In P. Noguera, J. Cammarota & S. Ginwright (Eds.), *Beyond resistance: Youth activism and community change* (pp. 21–35). New York: Routledge.

Li, S. T., Nussbaum, K. M., & Richards, M. H. (2007). Risk and protective factors for urban African-American youth. *American Journal of Community Psychology, 39*(1–2), 21–35.

Li, W., Garland, E. L., & Howard, M. O. (2014). Family factors in Internet addiction among Chinese youth: A review of English-and Chinese-language studies. *Computers in Human Behavior, 31*, 393–411.

Liang, B., Bogat, G. A., & Duffy, N. (2014). Gender in mentoring relationships. In D. DuBois & M. Karcher (Eds.), *Handbook of Youth Mentoring,* (pp. 159–173). Thousand Oaks, CA: Sage Publications.

Libby, M., Sedonaen, M., & Bliss, S. (2006). The mystery of youth leadership development: The path to just communities. *New Directions for Youth Development, 2006*(109), 13–25.

Lichter, D. T. (2013). Integration or fragmentation? Racial diversity and the American future. *Demography, 50*(2), 359–391.

Liebenberg, L., & Theron, L. C. (2015). Innovative qualitative explorations of culture and resilience. In L. Theron, L. Liebenberg & M. Unger (Eds.), *Youth resilience and culture* (pp. 203–215). Springer Netherlands.

Light, J. M., Greenan, C. C., Rusby, J. C., Nies, K. M., & Snijders, T. A. (2013). Onset to first alcohol use in early adolescence: A network diffusion model. *Journal of Research on Adolescence, 23*(3), 487–499.

Lightfoot, A. F., Woods, B. A., Jackson, M., Riggins, L., Krieger, K., Brodie, K., . . . Howard, D. L. (2012). "In my house": Laying the foundation for youth HIV prevention in the Black church. *Progress in Community Health Partnerships: Research, Education, and Action, 6*(4), 451–456.

Linden, J. A., & Feldman, C. I. (1998). *Youth leadership: A guide to understanding leadership development in adolescents.* San Francisco: Jossey-Bass.

Liuliu, S., & Jianwen, Y. (2014). Review on the relationship between friendship quality and social self of teenagers. *Contemporary Youth Research, 6,* 007. Retrieved from http://en.cnki.com.cn/Article_en/CJFDTotal-QING201406007.htm

Lochman, D. T., López, M., & Hutson, L. (Eds.). (2011). *Discourses and representations of friendship in early modern Europe, 1500–1700.* Surrey, UK: Ashgate.

London, R. A., Pastor, M., Jr., Servon, L. J., Rosner, R., & Wallace, A. (2006). *The role of community technology centers in youth skill-building and empowerment* (Working paper). Santa Cruz: University of California, Center for Justice, Tolerance, and Community.

London, R. A., Pastor, M., Servon, L. J., Rosner, R., & Wallace, A. (2010). The role of community technology centers in promoting youth development. *Youth & Society, 42*(2), 199–228.

Lopez, A., Yoder, J. R., Brisson, D., Lechuga-Pena, S., & Jenson, J. M. (2015). Development and validation of a positive youth development measure: The bridge-positive youth development. *Research on Social Work Practice, 25*(8), 726–736.

Love, B. L. (2012). *Hip hop's li'l sistas speak: Negotiating hip hop identities and politics in the new South.* New York: Peter Lang.

Love, B. L. (2014). Urban storytelling: How storyboarding, moviemaking, and hip-hop-based education can promote students' critical voice. *English Journal, 103*(5), 53.

Love, B. L., & Bradley, R. N. (2015). Teaching Trayvon: Teaching about racism through public pedagogy, hip hop, Black trauma, and social media. In J.L. Martin (Ed.), *Racial battle fatigue: Insights from the front lines of social justice advocacy* (pp. 255–267). Santa Barbara, CA: Praeger.

Lovell, B. (2014). *Performance: It's poetry . . . but not as you know it.* Retrieved from http://search.informit.com.au/documentSummary;dn=249263073126807;res=IEL   LCC> ISSN: 1445-2839

Lovell, S., & Baker, S. (2009). Digital narratives of youth transition: Engaging university students through blended learning. *Youth Studies Australia, 28*(4), 52.

Lubin, J. (2012). The "Occupy" movement: Emerging protest forms and contested urban spaces. *Berkeley Planning Journal, 25*(1), 184–197.

Lucero, J. E. (2013). *Trust as an ethical construct in community based participatory research partnerships* (Doctoral dissertation) University of New Mexico.

Luloff, A. E., & Wilkinson, K. P. (2014). Community action and the national rural development agenda. *Sociological Practice, 8*(1), 7.

Lundby, E. (2013). "You can't buy friends, but . . .": Children's perception of consumption and friendship. *Young Consumers, 14*(4), 360–374.

Lyons, M., David-Barrett, T., & Jokela, M. (2014). Gratitude for help among adult friends and siblings. *Evolutionary Psychology, 12*(4), 673–686.

Mabee, J. (2014). *Children and their social relationships with pet dogs: Examining links with human best friendship quality and loneliness* (Doctoral dissertation). Kent State University.

MacEvoy, J. P., & Asher, S. R. (2012). When friends disappoint: Boys' and girls' responses to transgressions of friendship expectations. *Child development, 83* (1), 104–119.

MacGeorge, E. L., Guntzviller, L. M., Hanasono, L. K., & Feng, B. (2013). Testing Advice Response Theory in Interactions with Friends. *Communication Research,* 0093650213510938.

Machell, K. A., Disabato, D. J., & Kashdan, T. B. (2015). Buffering the Negative Impact of Poverty on Youth: The Power of Purpose in Life. *Social Indicators Research,* 1–17.

MacLean, S. (2015). Alcohol and the Constitution of Friendship for Young Adults. *Sociology,* 0038038514557913.

Madrigal, D., Salvatore, A., Casillas, G., Casillas, C., Vera, I., Eskenazi, B., & Minkler, M. (2014). Health in my Community: Conducting and evaluating PhotoVoice as a tool to promote environmental health and leadership among Latino/a youth. *Progress in community health partnerships: Research, education, and action, 8* (3), 317–329.

Maher, J., & Pierpoint, H. (2011). Friends, status symbols and weapons: The use of dogs by youth groups and youth gangs. *Crime, law and social change, 55* (5), 405–420.

Maira, S. (2004). Youth culture, citizenship and globalization: South Asian Muslim youth in the United States after September 11th. *Comparative Studies of South Asia, Africa and the Middle East, 24* (1), 219–231.

Mains, D. (2013). Friends and money: Balancing affection and reciprocity among young men in urban Ethiopia. *American Ethnologist, 40* (2), 335–346.

Makhoul, J., Alameddine, M., & Afifi, R. A. (2012). "I felt that I was benefiting someone": Youth as agents of change in a refugee community project. *Health education research, 27* (5), 914–926.

Malaguzzi, L. (2014). 6 Relationships with peers: Togetherness, cooperation, friendship and belonging. *Relationship Worlds of Infants and Toddlers: Multiple Perspectives from Early Years Theory and Practice,* 88.

Mallan, K. M., Singh, P., & Giardina, N. (2010). The challenges of participatory research with "tech-savvy" youth. *Journal of Youth Studies, 13* (2), 255–272.

Mallory, C., Sears, B., Hasenbush, A., & Susman, A. (2014). *LGBTQ Youth Face Unique Barriers to Accessing Youth Mentoring Programs.*

Malone, K., & Hartung, C. (2010). Challenges of participatory practice with children. *A handbook of children and young people's participation: Perspectives from theory and practice*, 24–38.

Mallory, C., Sears, B., Hasenbush, A., & Susman, A. (2014). *Ensuring Access to Mentoring Programs for LGBTQ Youth*. Los Angeles: The Williams Institute

Manen, L. V. (2015). *Friendship quality as a protective factor against maladjustment outcomes for victimized adolescents* (Masters thesis). University of Utrecht.

Mann, A. Liley, J., & Kellett, M. (2014). Engaging children and young children in research. In A. Clark, R. Flewitt, M. Hammerseley & M. Robb (Eds.). *Understanding research with children and young people*, 285. London, England: Sage.

Mansfield, K. C., Welton, A., & Halx, M. (2012). Listening to student voice: Toward a more inclusive theory for research and practice. *Advances in Educational Administration*, 14, 21–41.

Maqubela, L. (2013). *The relationship between friendship quality, masculinity ideology and happiness in men's friendship*.

Marar, Z. (2014). *Intimacy*. New York: Routledge.

Marcuse, P. (2009). From critical urban theory to the right to the city. *City*, 13(2–3), 185–197.

Marcuse, P. (2012). Whose rights to what city? In N. Brenner, P. Marcuse, & M. Mayer (Eds.), *Cities for people, not for profit: Critical urban theory and the right to the city* (pp. 24–41). New York: Routledge.

Marcuse, P., Connolly, J., Novy, J., Olivo, I., Potter, C., & Steil, J. (Eds.). (2009). *Searching for the just city: Debates in urban theory and practice*. New York: Routledge.

Markiewicz, D., Devine, I., & Kausilas, D. (2000). Friendships of women and men at work. *Journal of Managerial Psychology*, 15(2), 161–184.

Marsh, K., Chaney, C., & Jones, D. (2012). The strengths of high-achieving Black high school students in a racially diverse setting. *Journal of Negro Education*, 81(1), 39–51.

Martin, K. E., Wood, L. J., Houghton, S., Carroll, A., & Hattie, J. (2014). "I don't have the best life": A qualitative exploration of adolescent loneliness. *Journal of Child Adolescent Behavior*, 2(169), 2.

Martinez, B., & Howe, N. (2013). Canadian early adolescents' self-disclosure to siblings and best friends. *International Journal of Child, Youth and Family Studies*, 4(2), 274–300.

Martinez, J., Tost, J., Hilgert, L., & Woodard-Meyers, T. (2013). Gang membership risk factors for eighth-grade students. *Nonpartisan Education Review*, 9(1), 1–31.

Martinussen, M. H. (2014). *The drama-free performance of authentic friends: Exploring how New Zealand men make sense of their friendships*. Retrieved from http://researcharchive.vuw.ac.nz/handle/10063/3472

Mason, M. (2014). Peer networks. In Z. Sloboda & H. Petras (Eds.), *Defining prevention science* (pp. 171–193). New York: Springer US.

Matheson, C., Olsen, R. J., Weisner, T., & Dykens, E. (2009). A good friend is hard to find: Friendship among adolescents with disabilities. *American Journal on Mental Retardation*, 112(5), 319–329.

Mathie, A., & Cunningham, G. (2003). From clients to citizens: Asset-based community development as a strategy for community-driven development. *Development in Practice*, 13(5), 474–486.

Maticka-Tyndale, E., & Barnett, J. P. (2010). Peer-led interventions to reduce HIV risk of youth: A review. *Evaluation and program planning*, 33(2), 98–112.

Maton, K. I. (2008). Empowering community settings: Agents of individual development, community betterment, and positive social change. *American Journal of Community Psychology, 41*(1–2), 4–21.

Matthews, S. H. (1983). Definitions of friendship and their consequences in old age. *Ageing and Society, 3*(2), 141–155.

Maturo, C. C., & Cunningham, S. A. (2013). Influence of friends on children's physical activity: A review. *American Journal of Public Health, 103*(7), e23–e38.

Maunder, R., & Monks, C. (2014). *When friends are not so friendly: Investigating friendship quality, participant roles in bullying situations and links to well-being in primary school children.* Retrieved from http://nectar.northampton.ac.uk/6932/

Mavin, S., Williams, J., Bryans, P., Patterson, N., & Mavin, S. (Undated). *Women's friendships at work: Power, possibilities and potential.* Retrieved from http://www.ufhrd.co.uk/wordpress/wp-content/uploads/2013/09/Mavin-et-al-full-paper.pdf

Mayer, M. (2012). The "right to the city" in urban social movements. In N. Brenner, P. Marcuse & M. Mayer (Eds.), *Cities for people and not profit: Critical urban theory and the right to the city* (pp. 63–85). New York: Routledge.

Mayer, M., & Boudreau, I. A. (2012). Urban politics: Trends in research and practice. In M. Mossberger, S.E. Clarke & P. John (Eds.), *Oxford handbook of urban politics* (pp. 273–293). New York.

Mayo, C. (2007). Intersectionality and queer youth. *Journal of Curriculum and Pedagogy, 4*(2), 67–71.

McCarthy, M. (2010). Researching children's musical culture: Historical and contemporary perspectives. *Music Education Research, 12*(1), 1–12.

McCormack, M., Adams, A., & Anderson, E. (2013). Taking to the streets: The benefits of spontaneous methodological innovation in participant recruitment. *Qualitative research, 13*(2), 228–241.

McDaniel, D. D. (2012). Risk and protective factors associated with gang affiliation among high-risk youth: A public health approach. *Injury Prevention, 18*(4), 253–258.

McDonald, J. A., Mojarro, O., Sutton, P. D., & Ventura, S. J. (2015). Adolescent births in the border region: A descriptive analysis based on US Hispanic and Mexican birth certificates. *Maternal and Child Health Journal, 19*(1), 128–135.

McDonald, K. L., Malti, T., Killen, M., & Rubin, K. H. (2014). Best friends' discussions of social dilemmas. *Journal of Youth and Adolescence, 43*(2), 233–244.

McGovern, F., & Devine, D. (2016). The care worlds of migrant children: Exploring intergenerational dynamics of love, care and solidarity across home and school. *Childhood, 23*(1), 37–52.

McGrath, B., Brennan, M. A., Dolan, P., & Barnett, R. (2014). Adolescents and their networks of social support: Real connections in real lives? *Child & Family Social Work, 19*(2), 237–248.

McIntyre, A. (2000). Constructing meaning about violence, school, and community: Participatory action research with urban youth. *Urban Review, 32*(2), 123–154.

McKay, M. M., & Paikoff, R. L. (Eds.). (2012). *Community collaborative partnerships: The foundation for HIV prevention research efforts.* New York: Routledge.

McLanahan, S., & Jacobsen, W. (2015). Diverging destinies revisited. In *Families in an era of increasing inequality* (pp. 3–23). Heidelberg: Springer International.

McLeod, S. (2007). Maslow's hierarchy of needs. Retrieved from http://www.simplypsychology.org/maslow.html.

McMillan, V. A. (2013). *Sistas on the move: An ethnographic case study of health and friendship in urban space among Black women in New Orleans* (Master's thesis). University of New Orleans.

Mendelson, T., Greenberg, M. T., Dariotis, J. K., Gould, L. F., Rhoades, B. L., & Leaf, P. J. (2010). Feasibility and preliminary outcomes of a school-based mindfulness intervention for urban youth. *Journal of Abnormal Child Psychology, 38*(7), 985–994.

Mendoza-Denton, N. (2014). *Homegirls: Language and cultural practice among Latina youth gangs.* New York: John Wiley & Sons.

Mercken, L., Sleddens, E. F. C., de Vries, H., & Steglich, C. E. G. (2013). Choosing adolescent smokers as friends: The role of parenting and parental smoking. *Journal of Adolescence, 36*(2), 383–392.

Merry, S. K. (2014). *The friend justifies the means: How modern friendship is effected, and affected* (Doctoral dissertation). Department of Information Studies, Aberystwyth University, Wales, UK.

Meyer, R. M. L. (2011). *The role of friendship for adolescent development in African American youth* (Doctoral dissertation). University of Michigan.

Miche, M., Huxhold, O., & Stevens, N. L. (2013). A latent class analysis of friendship network types and their predictors in the second half of life. *Journals of Gerontology Series B: Psychological Sciences and Social Sciences, 68*(4), 644–652.

Miller, L., Clark, A., Flewitt, R., Hammersley, M., & Robb, M. (Eds.). (2014). *Understanding research with children and young people.* Thousand Oaks, CA: Sage.

Miller, S. R. (2012). I don't want to get involved: Shyness, psychological control, and youth activities. *Journal of Social and Personal Relationships, 29*(7), 308–329.

Minkler, M. (Ed.). (2012). *Community organizing and community building for health and welfare.* New Brunswick, NJ: Rutgers University Press.

Mitchell, C. (2011). *Doing visual research.* Los Angeles: Sage.

Mitchell, F. M. (2015, November). *Promoting community-based participatory research methods in an American Indian community: Building trust, sustaining relationships, and moving forward.* Presented at the 143rd APHA annual meeting and exposition (October 31–November 4, 2015). Chicago, IL

Mitra, D., Serriere, S., & Kirshner, B. (2014). Youth participation in US contexts: Student voice without a national mandate. *Children & Society, 28*(4), 292–304.

Mitra, D. L., & Serriere, S. C. (2012). Student voice in elementary school reform examining youth development in fifth graders. *American Educational Research Journal, 49*(4), 743–774.

Mizen, P., & Ofosu-Kusi, Y. (2010). Asking, giving, receiving: Friendship as survival strategy among Accra's street children. *Childhood, 17*(4), 441–454.

Mohamad, M., Mohammad, M., & Ali, N. A. M. (2014). Positive youth development and life satisfaction among youths. *Journal of Applied Sciences, 14*(21), 2782–2792.

Mohan, L. (2014). Race and its impact on youth sport participation choice. *Journal of Sport Studies, 4*(11), 1309–1316

Montgomery, H. (2014). Particpant observation. In A. Clark, R. Flewitt, M. Hammerseley & M. Robb (Eds.), *Understanding research with children and young people* (pp. 122–135). London: Sage.

Morch, S., & Andersen, H. (2012). Becoming a gang member: Youth life and gang youth. *Psychology Research, 2*(9), 506–514.

Morgan, A., & Ziglio, E. (2010). Revitalising the public health evidence base: An asset model. In *Health assets in a global context* (pp. 3–16). New York: Springer.

Morgan, M. L., Vera, E. M., Gonzales, R. R., Conner, W., Vacek, K. B., & Coyle, L. D. (2011). Subjective well-being in urban adolescents: Interpersonal, individual, and community influences. *Youth & Society, 43*(2), 609–634.

Morgan, S. T. (2013). Social pedagogy within key worker practice: Community situated support for marginalised youth. *International Journal of Social Pedagogy, 2*(1), 17–32.

Morimoto, S. A., & Friedland, L. A. (2013). Cultivating success: Youth achievement, capital and civic engagement in the contemporary United States. *Sociological Perspectives, 56*(4), 523–546.

Moroz, H. (2010, May 9). Washington's anti-urban bias. *San Francisco Gate.* Retrieved from http://www.sfgate.com/opinion/article/Washington-s-anti-urban-bias-3264750.php

Morris, E. J. (2012). Respect, protection, faith, and love: Major care constructs identified within the subculture of selected urban African American adolescent gang members. *Journal of Transcultural Nursing, 23*(3), 262–269.

Morrison, R. L., & Nolan, T. (2009). I get by with a little help from my friends . . . at work. *Kōtuitui: New Zealand Journal of Social Sciences Online, 4*(1), 41–54.

Morton, M. H., & Montgomery, P. (2013). Youth empowerment programs for improving adolescents' self-efficacy and self-esteem: A systematic review. *Research on Social Work Practice, 23*(1), 22–33.

Mosher, J., Anucha, U., Appiah, H., & Levesque, S. (2014). From research to action: Four theories and their implications for knowledge mobilization. *Scholarly and Research Communication, 5*(3). Retrieved from http://src-online.ca/index.php/src/article/view/161

Moule, R. K., Jr., Decker, S. H., & Pyrooz, D. C. (2013). Social capital, the life-course, and gangs. In M. Maguire, R. Morgan & R. Reiner (Eds.), *Handbook of life-course criminology* (pp. 143–158). New York: Springer.

Mueller, M. K., Phelps, E., Bowers, E. P., Agans, J. P., Urban, J. B., & Lerner, R. M. (2011). Youth development program participation and intentional self-regulation skills: Contextual and individual bases of pathways to positive youth development. *Journal of Adolescence, 34*(6), 1115–1125.

Mühl, J. K. (2014). Research methodology. In *Organizational trust* (pp. 75–100). Heidelberg: Springer International.

Müller, L., & Ruch, W. (2011). Humor and strengths of character. *Journal of Positive Psychology, 6*(5), 368–376.

Mullis, E. C. (2010). Confucius and Aristotle on the goods of friendship. *Dao, 9*(4), 391–405.

Munro, L., Travers, R., St. John, A., Klein, K., Hunter, H., Brennan, D., & Brett, C. (2013). A bed of roses? Exploring the experiences of LGBT newcomer youth who migrate to Toronto. *Ethnicity and Inequalities in Health and Social Care, 6*(4), 137–150.

Murnaghan, D., Laurence, C., Bell, B., & Munro-Bernard, M. (2014). Engaging Canadian youth in conversations: Using knowledge exchange in school-based health promotion. *Gateways: International Journal of Community Research and Engagement, 7*(1), 85–100.

Muttarak, R. (2014). Generation, ethnic and religious diversity in friendship choice: Exploring interethnic close ties in Britain. *Ethnic and Racial Studies, 37*(1), 71– 98.

Nairn, A., & Clarke, B. (2012). Researching children: Are we getting it right? *International Journal of Market Research, 54*(2), 177–198.

Narendorf, S. C., Fedoravicius, N., McMillen, J. C., McNelly, D., & Robinson, D. R. (2012). Stepping down and stepping in: Youth's perspectives on making the transition from residential treatment to treatment foster care. *Children and Youth Services Review, 34*(1), 43–49.

Neal, J. W., Neal, Z. P., & Cappella, E. (2014). I know who my friends are, but do you? Predictors of self-reported and peer-inferred relationships. *Child Development, 85*(4), 1366–1372.

Nebbitt, V. E., Lombe, M., Cryer-Coupet, Q. R., & Stephens, J. K. (2015). Peers' influence and African-American youth in public housing. *Journal of Children and Poverty, 21*(1), 1–15.

Neblett, E. W., Rivas-Drake, D., & Umaña-Taylor, A. J. (2012). The promise of racial and ethnic protective factors in promoting ethnic minority youth development. *Child Development Perspectives, 6*(3), 295–303.

Neblett, E. W., Smith, C. P., Ford, K. R., Nguyen, H. X., & Sellers, R. M. (2009). Racial socialization and psychological adjustment: Can parental communication about race reduce the impact of discrimination? *Journal of Research on Adolescence, 18*(2), 477–515.

Nelson, K., & Adams, P. (Eds.). (2011). *Reinventing human services: Community- and family-centered practice.* New Brunswick, NJ: Transaction.

Newman, B. M., Lohman, B. J., Newman, P. R., Myers, M. C., & Smith, V. L. (2000). Experiences of urban youth navigating the transition to ninth grade. *Youth & Society, 31*(4), 387–416.

Nicholson, D. J. (2009). *Knowing" knowledge": Explorations with youth and other thinking friends.* (Doctoral dissertation). University of British Columbia.

Nicolas, G., Helms, J. E., Jernigan, M. M., Sass, T., Skrzypek, A., & DeSilva, A. M. (2008). A conceptual framework for understanding the strengths of Black youths. *Journal of Black Psychology, 34*(3), 261–280.

Noble, T., & McGrath, H. (2012). Wellbeing and resilience in young people and the role of positive relationships. In S. Roffey (Ed.), *Positive relationships* (pp. 17–33). Springer Netherlands.

Noddings, N. (1995). Teaching themes of care. *Phi Delta Kappan, 76*(9), 675–679.

Norris, J., & Greenlaw, J. (2012). Responding to our muses: A duoethnography on becoming writers. In J. Norris, R.D. Sawyer & D. Lund (Eds.), *Duoethnography: Dialogic Methods for Social, Health, and Educational Research* (Vol. 7, pp. 89–114). Walnut Creek, CA: Left Coast Press.

Norton, C. L., & Watt, T. T. (2014). Exploring the impact of a wilderness-based positive youth development program for urban youth. *Journal of Experiential Education, 37*(4), 335–350.

Nybell, L. M., Shook, J. J., & Finn, J. L. (Eds.). (2013). *Childhood, youth, and social work in transformation: Implications for policy and practice.* New York: Columbia University Press.

Nygreen, K., Ah Kwon, S., & Sánchez, P. (2006). Urban youth building community: Social change and participatory research in schools, homes, and community- based organizations. *Journal of Community Practice, 14*(1–2), 107–123.

Oberle, E., Schonert-Reichl, K. A., & Zumbo, B. D. (2011). Life satisfaction in early adolescence: Personal, neighborhood, school, family, and peer influences. *Journal of Youth and Adolescence, 40*(7), 889–901.

O'Brien, K., Daffern, M., Chu, C. M., & Thomas, S. D. (2013). Youth gang affiliation, violence, and criminal activities: A review of motivational, risk, and protective factors. *Aggression and Violent Behavior, 18*(4), 417–425.

O'Donnell, M. B., Bentele, C. N., Grossman, H. B., Le, Y., Jang, H., & Steger, M. F. (2014). You, me, and meaning: An integrative review of connections between relationships and meaning in life. *Journal of Psychology in Africa, 24*(1), 44–50.

Ogbu, J. I. (2013). A cultural ecology of competence among inner-city Blacks. In M.B. Spencer, W.R. Allen & G.K. Brookins (Eds.), *Beginnings: The social and affective development of Black children* (pp. 45–66). Hillsdale, NJ: Lawrence, Erlbaum Associates Publishers.

Oh, S. A. (2012). Photofriend: Creating visual ethnography with refugee children. *Area, 44*(3), 382–288.

Ohtsubo, Y., Matsumura, A., Noda, C., Sawa, E., Yagi, A., & Yamaguchi, M. (2014). It's the attention that counts: Interpersonal attention fosters intimacy and social exchange. *Evolution and Human Behavior, 35*(3), 237–244.

Ojanen, T., Sijtsema, J. J., & Rambaran, A. J. (2013). Social goals and adolescent friendships: Social selection, deselection, and influence. *Journal of Research on Adolescence, 23*(3), 550–562.

Ojanen, T., Stratman, A., Card, N. A., & Little, T. D. (2013). Motivation and perceived control in early adolescent friendships: Relations with self-, friend-, and peer- reported adjustment. *Journal of Early Adolescence, 33*(4), 552–577.

Oliveira, E., & Vearey, J. (2015). Images of place: Visuals from migrant women sex workers in South Africa. *Medical Anthropology, 34*(4), 305–318.

Oliver, M. (2001). Forward. In T. M. Shapiro & E. N. Wolff (Eds.), *Asset for the poor: The benefits of spreading asset ownership* (pp. xi–xiii). New York: Sage.

Olson, P., & Gillman, L. (2013). Combating racialized and gendered ignorance: Theorizing a transactional pedagogy of friendship. *Feminist Formations, 25*(1), 59–83.

Omerzel, D. G., & Širca, N. T. (2009). *The motivation of educational institutions for validation of non-formal and informal learning.* Retrieved from http://www.fm.upr.si/zalozba/ISBN/978-961-6573-65-8/105-116.pdf.

Onion, R. (2014, July 13). A brief history of hating cities. *Boston Globe.* Online.

Oransky, M., Hahn, H., & Stover, C. S. (2013). Caregiver and youth agreement regarding youths' trauma histories: Implications for youths' functioning after exposure to trauma. *Journal of Youth and Adolescence, 42*(10), 1528–1542.

Osgood, D. W., Ragan, D. T., Wallace, L., Gest, S. D., Feinberg, M. E., & Moody, J. (2013). Peers and the emergence of alcohol use: Influence and selection processes in adolescent friendship networks. *Journal of Research on Adolescence, 23*(3), 500–512.

Oswald, D. L., & Clark, E. M. (2003). Best friends forever? High school best friendships and the transition to college. *Personal Relationships, 10*(2), 187–196.

Owen, M., & Greeff, A. P. (2015). Factors attracting and discouraging adolescent boys in high-prevalence communities from becoming involved in gangs. *Journal of Forensic Psychology Practice, 15*(1), 1–32.

Overstreet, S., & Mathews, T. (2011). Challenges associated with exposure to chronic trauma: Using a public health framework to foster resilient outcomes among youth. *Psychology in the Schools, 48*(7), 738–754.

Ozanne, J. L., & Anderson, L. (2010). Community action research. *Journal of Public Policy & Marketing, 29*(1), 123–137.

Ozer, E. J., & Douglas, L. (2013). The impact of participatory research on urban teens: An experimental evaluation. *American Journal of Community Psychology, 51*(1–2), 66–75.

Ozer, E. J., Newlan, S., Douglas, L., & Hubbard, E. (2013). "Bounded" empowerment: Analyzing tensions in the practice of youth-led participatory research in urban public schools. *American Journal of Community Psychology, 52*(1–2), 13–26.

Pabst, J. (2014). *Empowered youth: The co-creation of youth as technological citizens and consumers within community-based technology programs* (Doctoral dissertation). Boston College.

Padilla-Walker, L. M., Fraser, A. M., Black, B. B., & Bean, R. A. (2015). Associations between friendship, sympathy, and prosocial behavior toward friends. *Journal of Research on Adolescence, 25*(1), 28–35.

Pagano, M. E., & Hirsch, B. J. (2007). Friendships and romantic relationships of Black and White adolescents. *Journal of child and family studies, 16*(3), 347–357.

Pahl, R., & Spencer, L. (2004). Personal communities: Not simply families of "fate" or "choice." *Current Sociology, 52*(2): 199–221.

Panzar, J. (2015, July 8). It's official: Latinos now outnumber Whites in California. *Los Angeles Times.* Online.

Papachristos, A. V., Braga, Piza, E., & Grossman, L. S. (2015). The company you keep? The spillover effects of gang membership on individual gunshot victimization in a co-offending network. *Criminology, 53*(4), 624–649.

Papapolydorou, M. (2014). "When you see a normal person . . .": Social class and friendship networks among teenage students. *British Journal of Sociology of Education, 35*(4), 559–577.

Paranagamage, P., Austin, S., Price, A., & Khandokar, F. (2010). Social capital in action in urban environments: An intersection of theory, research and practice literature. *Journal of Urbanism, 3*(3), 231–252.

Paris, D. (2010). "The second language of the United States": Youth perspectives on Spanish in a changing multiethnic community. *Journal of Language, Identity, and Education, 9*(2), 139–155.

Parker, P. D., Lüdtke, O., Trautwein, U., & Roberts, B. W. (2012). Personality and relationship quality during the transition from high school to early adulthood. *Journal of Personality, 80*(4), 1061–1089.

Pascal, C., & Bertram, T. (2014). In A. Clark, R. Flewitt, M. Hammerseley, & M. Robb (Eds.), *Understanding research with children and young people* (pp. 269–284). London: Sage.

Passarelli, A., Hall, E., & Anderson, M. (2010). A strengths-based approach to outdoor and adventure education: Possibilities for personal growth. *Journal of Experiential Education, 33*(2), 120–135.

Passel, J. S. (2011). Demography of immigrant youth: Past, present, and future. *Future of Children, 21*(1), 19–41.

Pattaro, C. (2015). New media & youth identity. Issues and research pathways. *Sociology of Education, 7*(1), 297–327.

Patterson, O., & Fosse, E. (Eds.). (2015). *The cultural matrix: Understanding Black youth.* Cambridge, MA: Harvard University Press.

Pattillo, M. (2013). *Black picket fences: Privilege and peril among the Black middle class.* Chicago: University of Chicago Press.

Pattman, R. (2015). Ways of thinking about young people in participatory interview research. In J. Wyn & H. Cahill (Eds.), *Handbook of children and youth studies* (pp. 79–92). Singapore: Springer Publisher.

Pavot, W., & Diener, E. (2008). The satisfaction with life scale and the emerging construct of life satisfaction. *Journal of Positive Psychology, 3*(2), 137–152.

Payne, M. (2013). What is professional social work? In V.E. Cree (Ed.), *Social work: A reader* (pp. 11–15). London, UK: Routledge.

Pellegrino, A. M., Zenkov, K., & Aponte-Martinez, G. (2014). Middle school students, slam poetry and the notion of citizenship. *Journal of Educational Controversy, 8*(1), 8. Retrieved from http://cedar.wwu.edu/jec/vol8/iss1/8/?utm_source=cedar.wwu.edu%2Fjec%2Fvol8%2Fiss1%2F8&utm_medium=PDF&utm_campaign=PDFCoverPages

Percy, A., Wilson, J., McCartan, C., & McCrystal, P. (2011). *Teenage drinking cultures.* York, England: Joseph Rowntree Foundation.

Percy-Smith, B., & Thomas, N. (Eds.). (2009). *A handbook of children and young people's participation: Perspectives from theory and practice.* New York: Routledge.

Pérez-Wilson, P., Hernán, M., Morgan, A. R., & Mena, A. (2015). Health assets for adolescents: Opinions from a neighbourhood in Spain. *Health Promotion International, 30*(3), 552–562.

Perkins, D. F., Borden, L. M., Villarruel, F. A., Carlton-Hug, A., Stone, M. R., & Keith, J. G. (2007). Participation in structured youth programs: Why ethnic minority urban youth choose to participate—or not to participate. *Youth & Society, 38*(4), 420–442.

Petermann, S., & Schönwälder, K. (2014). Immigration and social interaction: Do diverse environments matter? *European Societies, 16*(4), 500–521.

Peterson, C., & Park, N. (2009). Positive psychology. *Reclaiming Children and Youth, 18*(2), 3.

Peterson, N. A., Peterson, C. H., Agre, L., Christens, B. D., & Morton, C. M. (2011). Measuring youth empowerment: Validation of a sociopolitical control scale for youth in an urban community context. *Journal of Community Psychology, 39*(5), 592–605.

Peterson, T. H., Dolan, T., & Hanft, S. (2010). Partnering with youth organizers to prevent violence: An analysis of relationships, power, and change. *Progress in Community Health Partnerships: Research, Education, and Action, 4*(3), 235–242.

Petrucka, P., Brooks, S., Smadu, G., McBeth, B., Bassendowski, S., Mackay, A., . . . Fudger, S. (2014). At street level: Learnings, voices, experiences, and lifestyles of street involved youth. *Nursing and Health, 2*(2), 48–56.

Pew Research Center. (2015, June 11). *Multiracial Americans.* Washington, DC: Author.

Pezalla, A. E., Pettigrew, J., & Miller-Day, M. (2012). Researching the researcher-as- instrument: An exercise in interviewer self-reflexivity. *Qualitative Research, 12*(2), 165–185.

Pica-Smith, C., & Poynton, T. A. (2014). Supporting interethnic and interracial friendships among youth to reduce prejudice and racism in schools: The role of the school counselor. *Professional School Counseling, 18*(1), 82–89.

Pink, S. (2007). *Doing visual ethnography.* Los Angeles: Sage.

Pinter, A., & Zandian, S. (2015). "I thought it would be tiny little one phrase that we said, in a huge big pile of papers": Children's reflections on their involvement in participatory research. *Qualitative Research, 15*(2), 235–250.

Piquette, J. C. (2013). *Exploring the effects of friendship on risky sexual behavior: A look at female gang members* (Master's thesis). University of Massachusetts.

Pitts, J. (2009). The X-It gang desistance programme: An interview with Julia Wolton. *Safer Communities, 8*(2), 42–46.

Plante, C., Moreau, N., Jaimes, A., & Turbide, C. (2014). Motivational factors for youth recruitment in voluntary interventions: The case of a community sport program. *Sport, Education and Society,* 1–20.

Policarpo, V. (2015). What is a friend? An exploratory typology of the meanings of friendship. *Social Sciences, 4* (1), 171–191.

Ponting, J. R., & Voyageur, C. J. (2001). Challenging the deficit paradigm: Grounds for optimism among First Nations in Canada. *Canadian Journal of Native Studies, 21*(2), 275–307.

Popple, K., & Stepney, P. (2008). *Social work and the community: A critical context for practice.* London: Palgrave Macmillan.

Post, M., Hanten, G., Li, X., Schmidt, A. T., Avci, G., Wilde, E. A., & McCauley, S. R. (2014). Dimensions of trauma and specific symptoms of complex posttraumatic stress disorder in inner-city youth: A preliminary study. *Violence and Victims, 29*(2), 262–279.

Poteat, V. P., Yoshikawa, H., Calzo, J. P., Gray, M. L., DiGiovanni, C. D., Lipkin, A., . . . Shaw, M. P. (2015). Contextualizing gay-straight alliances: Student, advisor, and structural factors related to positive youth development among members. *Child Development, 86*(1), 176–193.

Poteet, M., & Simmons, A. (2014). Schooling goals and social belonging among Central American-origin male youth in Toronto. *Canadian Ethnic Studies, 46*(3), 55–75.

Poteet, M., & Simmons, A. (2015). Not boxed in: Acculturation and ethno-social identities of Central American male youth in Toronto. *Journal of International Migration and Integration,* 1–19.

Poulin, F., & Denault, A. S. (2013). Friendships with co-participants in organized activities: Prevalence, quality, friends' characteristics, and associations with adolescents' adjustment. *New Directions for Child and Adolescent Development, 2013*(140), 19–35.

Poulin, F., Kiesner, J., Pedersen, S., & Dishion, T. J. (2011). A short-term longitudinal analysis of friendship selection on early adolescent substance use. *Journal of Adolescence, 34*(2), 249–256.

Powers, J. L., & Tiffany, J. S. (2006). Engaging youth in participatory research and evaluation. *Journal of Public Health Management and Practice, 12*(1), S79–S87.

Powers, L. E., Garner, T., Valnes, B., Squire, P., Turner, A., Couture, T., & Dertinger, R. (2007). Building a successful adult life: Findings from youth-directed research. *Exceptionality, 15*(1), 45–56.

Prado, G., Lightfoot, M., & Brown, C. H. (2013). Macro-level approaches to HIV prevention among ethnic minority youth: State of the science, opportunities, and challenges. *American Psychologist, 68*(4), 286.

Preciado, P., Snijders, T. A., Burk, W. J., Stattin, H., & Kerr, M. (2012). Does proximity matter? Distance dependence of adolescent friendships. *Social Networks, 34*(1), 18–31.

Price, A. W. (1989). *Love and friendship in Plato and Aristotle.* New York: Oxford University Press.

Price, J. M. (2015). *Prison and social death.* New Brunswick, NJ: Rutgers University Press.

Prinsen, F., de Haan, M., & Leander, K. M. (2015). Networked identity: How immigrant youth employ online identity resources. *Young, 23*(1), 19–38.

Prior, R. W. (2013). Knowing what is known: The subjective objective partnership. In S. McNiff (Ed.), *Art as research: Opportunities and challenges* (pp.161–169). Bristol, UK: Intellect.

Proctor, C. L., Linley, P. A., & Maltby, J. (2009). Youth life satisfaction: A review of the literature. *Journal of Happiness Studies, 10*(5), 583–630.

Pryce, J. M., & Keller, T. E. (2013). Interpersonal tone within school-based youth mentoring relationships. *Youth & Society, 45*(1), 98–116.

Pryor, B. N. K., & Outley, C. W. (2014). Just spaces: Urban recreation centers as sites for social justice youth development. *Journal of Leisure Research, 46*(3), 272.

Ptacek, J. (2014). *I get by with a little help from my friends: A qualitative study of nurse close work friendship and social support.* (Master's thesis). Western Michigan University.

Pyrooz, D. C., Decker, S. H., & Webb, V. J. (2010). The ties that bind: Desistance from gangs. *Crime & Delinquency, 60*(1), 491–516.

Pyrooz, D. C., Sweeten, G., & Piquero, A. R. (2013). Continuity and change in gang membership and gang embeddedness. *Journal of Research in Crime and Delinquency, 50*(2), 239–271.

Pyne, K. B., Scott, M. A., O'Brien, M., Stevenson, A., & Musah, M. (2014). The critical pedagogy of mentoring: Undergraduate researchers as mentors in youth participatory action research. *Collaborative Anthropologies, 7*(1), 50–83.

Qin, D. B., Way, N., & Mukherjee, P. (2008). The other side of the model minority story: The familial and peer challenges faced by Chinese American adolescents. *Youth & Society, 39*(4), 480–506.

Quane, J. M., & Rankin, B. H. (2006). Does it pay to participate? Neighborhood-based organizations and the social development of urban adolescents. *Children and Youth Services Review, 28*(10), 1229–1250.

Quijada Cerecer, D. A., Cahill, C., & Bradley, M. (2013). Toward a critical youth policy praxis: Critical youth studies and participatory action research. *Theory into Practice, 52*(3), 216–223.

Quillian, L., & Campbell, M. E. (2003). Beyond Black and White: The present and future of multiracial friendship segregation. *American Sociological Review, 68*(4), 540–566.

Quinn, J. (2014). *The mentor: A memoir of friendship and gay identity.* New York: Routledge.

Radmacher, K., & Azmitia, M. (2006). Are there gendered pathways to intimacy in early adolescents' and emerging adults' friendships? *Journal of Adolescent Research, 21*(4), 415–448.

Raffety, E. L. (2015). Minimizing social distance: Participatory research with children. *Childhood, 22*(6), 409–422.

Ramirez, R., Hinman, A., Sterling, S., Weisner, C., & Campbell, C. (2012). Peer influences on adolescent alcohol and other drug use outcomes. *Journal of Nursing Scholarship, 44*(1), 36–44.

Rampton, B. (2014). *Crossings: Language and ethnicity among adolescents.* New York: Routledge.

Randle, M., Miller, L., Ciarrochi, J., & Dolnicar, S. (2014). A psychological profile of potential youth mentor volunteers. *Journal of Community Psychology, 42*(3), 338–351.

Rath, T., & Harter, J. (2010).Your friends and your social wellbeing. *Gallup Management Journal Online, 1.*

Rauner, D. M. (2013). *They still pick me up when I fall: The role of caring in youth development and community life.* New York: Columbia University Press.

Rawlins, W. K. (1992). *Friendship matters: Communication, dialectics, and the life course.* New York: Aldine de Gruyter.

Reamer, F. G. (2013). *Social work values and ethics.* New York: Columbia University Press.

Reed, S. J., Miller, R. L., & Adolescent Medicine Trials Network for HIV/AIDS Interventions. (2014). The benefits of youth engagement in HIV-preventive structural change interventions. *Youth & Society, 46*(4), 529–547.

Rees, C., Freng, A., & Winfree Jr, L. T. (2014). The Native American adolescent: Social network structure and perceptions of alcohol induced social problems. *Journal of Youth and Adolescence, 43*(3), 405–425.

Reimer, E. C. (2014). Using friendship to build professional family work relationships where child neglect is an issue: Worker perceptions. *Australian Social Work, 67*(3), 315–331.

Reisch, M., Ife, J., & Weil, M. (2012). Social justice, human rights, values, and community practice. In M. Weil, M.S. Reisch & M.L. Ohmer (Eds.), *Handbook of community practice* (pp. 73–103). Thosand Oaks, CA: Sage.

Reitz-Krueger, C. L., Nagel, A. G., Guarnera, L. A., & Reppucci, N. D. (2015). Community influence on adolescent development. In T.P. Gullotta & G.R. Adams (Eds.), *Handbook of adolescent behavioral problems* (pp. 71–84). Springer US.

Hirsh, B.J., & Renders, R. J. (2014). The challenge of adolescent friendship: A study of Lisa and her friends. In S.E. Hobfall (Ed.), *Stress, social support, and women* (pp. 17–28). London: Routledge.

Rendón, M. G. (2014). "Caught up": How urban violence and peer ties contribute to high school noncompletion. *Social Problems, 61*(1), 61–82.

Rendón, M. G. (2015). Dynamics of urban neighborhood reciprocity. In B. Conchas, M. Gottfried & B.M. Hinga (Eds.), *Inequality, power and school success: Case studies on racial disparity and opportunity in education* (pp. 83–109). New York: Routledge.

Reynolds, A. D., & Crea, T. M. (2015). Peer influence processes for youth delinquency and depression. *Journal of Adolescence, 43,* 83–95.

Rice, E., & Barman-Adhikari, A. (2014). Internet and social media use as a resource among homeless youth. *Journal of Computer-Mediated Communication, 19*(2), 232–247.

Rice, K., Primak, S., & Girvin, H. (2013). Through their eyes: Using photography with youth who experienced trauma. *Qualitative Report, 18*(26), 1–14.

Richards-Schuster, K. (2013, November). *Engaging youth as peer leaders for promoting instant recess in schools and communities-using a CBPR approach.* Presented at the 141st APHA annual meeting. Boston, MA.

Richards-Schuster, K. (2015, January). *Youth participatory methods for evaluating youth civic engagement: Findings from a multi-year evaluation program.* Presented at the Society for Social Work and Research 19th annual conference: The social and behavioral importance of increased longevity. New Orleans, LA,

Richardson, B. (2011). *Diversity Revealed: Photovoice methodology as a means for understanding how teens construct diversity* (Doctoral dissertation). University of North Texas.

Richardson, J. B., Jr. (2012). Beyond the playing field: Coaches as social capital for inner-city adolescent African-American males. *Journal of African American Studies, 16*(2), 171–194.

Riffe, H. A., Turner, S., & Rojas-Guyler, L. (2008). The diverse faces of Latinos in the Midwest: Planning for service delivery and building community. *Health & Social Work, 33*(2), 101–110.

Riley, A., & Anderson-Butcher, D. (2012). Participation in a summer sport-based youth development program for disadvantaged youth: Getting the parent perspective. *Children and Youth Services Review, 34*(7), 1367–1377.

Rios, M., Vasquez, L., & Miranda, L. (2012). Introduction: Place as space, action, and identity. In M. Rios, L. Vasquez, & L. Miranda (Eds.), *Dialogos: Placemaking in Latino communities* (pp.1–19). New York: Routledge.

Rivas-Drake, D., Hughes, D., & Way, N. (2008). A closer look at peer discrimination, ethnic identity, and psychological well-being among urban Chinese American sixth graders. *Journal of Youth and Adolescence, 37*(1), 12–21.

Rivernbark, W. H., III. (1971). Self-disclosure patterns among adolescents. *Psychological Reports, 28*(1), 35–42.

Roach, T. (2012). *Friendship as a way of life: Foucault, AIDS, and the politics of shared estrangement.* Albany, NY: SUNY Press, State University of New York.

Robards, B. (2013). Friending participants: Managing the researcher–participant relationship on social network sites. *Young, 21*(3), 217–235.

Roberts, D. (2009). Friendship fosters learning: The importance of friendships in clinical practice. *Nurse Education in Practice, 9*(6), 367–371.

Roberts, E. B., & Jette, S. L. (2016). Implementing participatory research with an urban American Indian community: Lessons learned. *Health Education Journal, 75*(2), 158–169.

Roberts, S. G. B., Arrow, H., Gowlett, J. A. J., Lehmann, J., & Dunbar, R. I. M. (2014). Close social relationships: An evolutionary perspective. In R. Dunbar, C. Gamble & J. Gowlett (Eds.), *Lucy to language: The benchmark papers* (pp. 151–180). New York: Oxford University Press.

Roberts, S. L. (2011). *An exploration of Key Stage 3 girls' peer group friendships outside the class-room and their influence within the class-room* (Doctoral dissertation). Open University, London, UK.

Roche, K. M., Ghazarian, S. R., & Fernandez-Esquer, M. E. (2012). Unpacking acculturation: Cultural orientations and educational attainment among Mexican- origin youth. *Journal of Youth and Adolescence, 41*(7), 920–931.

Rodríguez, L. F., & Conchas, G. Q. (2009). Preventing truancy and dropout among urban middle school youth: Understanding community-based action from the student's perspective. *Education and Urban Society, 41*(2), 216–247.

Rodriguez, M. C., & Morrobel, D. (2004). A review of Latino youth development research and a call for an asset orientation. *Hispanic Journal of Behavioral Sciences, 26*(2), 107–127.

Rodríguez, M. M. D., Baumann, A. A., & Schwartz, A. L. (2011). Cultural adaptation of an evidence based intervention: From theory to practice in a Latino/a community context. *American Journal of Community Psychology, 47*(1–2), 170–186.

Rodríguez, S. A., Perez-Brena, N. J., Updegraff, K. A., & Umaña-Taylor, A. J. (2014). Emotional closeness in Mexican-origin adolescents' relationships with mothers, fathers, and same-sex friends. *Journal of Youth and Adolescence, 43*(12), 1953–1968.

Rogers, L. O., Scott, M. A., & Way, N. (2015). Racial and gender identity among Black adolescent males: An intersectionality perspective. *Child Development, 86*(2), 407–424.

Roholt, R. V., Baizerman, M., & Hildreth, R. W. (2014). *Becoming citizens: Deepening the craft of youth civic engagement.* New York: Routledge.

Roholt, R. V., & Mueller, M. (2013). Youth advisory structures: Listening to young people to support quality youth services. *New Directions for Youth Development, 2013*(139), 79–100.

Rohrer, I. (2013). *Cohesion and dissolution: Friendship in the globalized punk and hardcore scene of Buenos Aires.* New York: Springer Science & Business Media.

Rohrer, I. (2014). Theorizing friendship. In I. Rohrer (Ed.), *Cohesion and dissolution* (pp. 47–76). Freiberg, Germany: Springer Fachmedien Wiesbaden.

Roman, C. G. (2012). *Social networks, delinquency, and gang membership: Using a neighborhood framework to examine the influence of network composition and structure in a Latino community.* Washington, DC: The Urban Institute.

Rose, A. J., Carlson, W., Luebbe, A. M., Schwartz-Mette, R. A., Smith, R. R., & Swenson, L. P. (2011). Predicting difficulties in youth's friendships: Are anxiety symptoms as damaging as depressive symptoms? *Merrill-Palmer Quarterly, 57*(3), 244–262.

Rose, A. J., Schwartz-Mette, R. A., Smith, R. L., Asher, S. R., Swenson, L. P., Carlson, W., & Waller, E. M. (2012). How girls and boys expect disclosure about problems will make them feel: Implications for friendships. *Child Development, 83*(3), 844–863.

Rose, A. J., Swenson, L. P., & Carlson, W. (2004). Friendships of aggressive youth: Considering the influences of being disliked and of being perceived as popular. *Journal of Experimental Child Psychology, 88*(1), 25–45.

Rose, G. (2012). *Visual methodologies: An introduction to researching with visual materials*(3rd ed.). Los Angeles: Sage.

Rose, T. (2013). *The hip hop wars: What we talk about when we talk about hip hop- -and why it matters.* New York: Basic Books.

Rosenbaum, M. S. (2009). Exploring commercial friendships from employees' perspectives. *Journal of Services Marketing, 23*(1), 57–66.

Rossetti, Z. (2015). Descriptors of friendship between secondary students with and without autism or intellectual and developmental disability. *Remedial and Special Education, 36*(3), 181–192.

Rossetti, Z. S. (2012). Helping or hindering: The role of secondary educators in facilitating friendship opportunities among students with and without autism or developmental disability. *International Journal of Inclusive Education, 16*(12), 1259–1272.

Rossiter, G. (2011). Some perspectives on contemporary youth spirituality. *Religious Education Journal of Australia, 27*(1). Online.

Rowe, S. L., French, R. S., Henderson, C., Ougrin, D., Slade, M., & Moran, P. (2014). Help-seeking behaviour and adolescent self-harm: A systematic review. *Australian and New Zealand Journal of Psychiatry, 48*(12), 1083–1095.

Rude, J., & Herda, D. (2010). Best friends forever? Race and the stability of adolescent friendships. *Social Forces, 89*(2), 585–607.

Rueda, H. A., Williams, L. R., & Nagoshi, J. L. (2015). Help-seeking and help-offering for teen dating violence among acculturating Mexican American adolescents. *Children and Youth Services Review, 53*, 219–228.

Ruiz-Aranda, D., & Zaccagnini, J. L. (2013). *Why women have a greater intimacy in their friendship* Retrieved from http://dspace.uma.es/xmlui/handle/10630/5906

Rumens, N. (2010). Firm friends: Exploring the supportive components in gay men's workplace friendships. *Sociological Review, 58*(1), 135–155.

Runk, J. V. (2014). Enriching indigenous knowledge scholarship via collaborative methodologies: Beyond the high tide's few hours. *Ecology and Society, 19*(4), 37.

Rusk, N., Larson, R. W., Raffaelli, M., Walker, K., Washington, L., Gutierrez, V., . . . Perry, S. C. (2013). Positive youth development in organized programs: How teens learn to manage emotions. In B. Proctor & P.A. Linley (Eds.), *Research, Applications, and Interventions for Children and Adolescents* (pp. 247–261). Rotterdam: Springer Netherlands.

Rybak, A., & McAndrew, F. T. (2006). How do we decide who our friends are? Defining levels of friendship in Poland and the United States. *Journal of Social Psychology, 146*(2), 147–163.

Saha, R., Huebner, E. S., Hills, K. J., Malone, P. S., & Valois, R. F. (2014). Social coping and life satisfaction in adolescents. *Social Indicators Research, 115*(1), 241–252.

Saimon, R., Choo, W. Y., & Bulgiba, A. (2015). "Feeling unsafe": A photovoice analysis of factors influencing physical activity behavior among Malaysian adolescents. *Asia-Pacific Journal of Public Health, 27*(2), NP2079–NP2092.

Sakyi, K. S., Surkan, P. J., Fombonne, E., Chollet, A., & Melchior, M. (2014). Childhood friendships and psychological difficulties in young adulthood: An 18-year follow-up study. *European Child & Adolescent Psychiatry, 24*(7), 815–826.

Salehi, R. (2010). Intersection of health, immigration, and youth: A systematic literature review. *Journal of Immigrant and Minority Health, 12*(5), 788–797.

Salisch, M., Zeman, J., Luepschen, N., & Kanevski, R. (2014). Prospective relations between adolescents' social-emotional competencies and their friendships. *Social Development, 23*(4), 684–701.

Salmon, N. (2013). "We just stick together": How disabled teens negotiate stigma to create lasting friendship. *Journal of Intellectual Disability Research, 57*(4), 347–358.

Sampson, R. J. (2012). Neighborhood inequality, violence, and the social infrastructure of the American city. In W.F. Tate IV (Ed.), *Research on schools, neighborhoods, and communities: Toward civic responsibility* (pp. 11–28). Lanham, MD: Roman & Littlefield.

Samuelson, B. L., Smith, R., Stevenson, E., & Ryan, C. (2013). A case study of youth participatory evaluation in co-curricular service learning. *Journal of the Scholarship of Teaching and Learning, 13*(3), 63–81.

Sanchez, Y. M., Lambert, S. F., & Cooley-Strickland, M. (2013). Adverse life events, coping and internalizing and externalizing behaviors in urban African American youth. *Journal of Child and Family Studies, 22*(1), 38–47.

Sanfey, H., Hollands, C., & Gantt, N. L. (2013). Strategies for building an effective mentoring relationship. *American Journal of Surgery, 206*(5), 714–718.

Sangalang, C. C., Ngouy, S., & Lau, A. S. (2015). Using community-based participatory research to identify health issues for Cambodian American youth. *Family & Community Health, 38*(1), 55–65.

Sanon, M. A., Evans-Agnew, R. A., & Boutain, D. M. (2014). An exploration of social justice intent in photovoice research studies from 2008 to 2013. *Nursing Inquiry, 21*(3), 212–226.

Santo, C. A., Ferguson, N., & Trippel, A. (2010). Engaging urban youth through technology: The youth neighborhood mapping initiative. *Journal of Planning Education and Research, 30*(1), 52–65.

Sassi, K., & Thomas, E. E. (2012). "If you weren't researching me and a friend . . ." The mobius of friendship and mentorship as methodological approaches to qualitative research. *Qualitative Inquiry, 18*(10), 830–842.

Scales, P. C., & Leffert, N. (2004). *Developmental assets: A synthesis of the scientific research* (2nd ed.). Minneapolis, MN: Search Institute.

Schaefer, D. R., Haas, S. A., & Bishop, N. J. (2012). A dynamic model of US adolescents' smoking and friendship networks. *American Journal of Public Health, 102*(6), e12–e18.

Schaefer, D. R., Rodriguez, N., & Decker, S. H. (2014). The role of neighborhood context in youth co-offending. *Criminology, 52*(1), 117–139.

Schäefer, N. (2012a). Finding ways to do research on, with and for children and young people. *Geography, 97*(3), 147–154.

Schäefer, N. (2012b). Using video in participatory, multi-method project on young people's everyday lives in rural East Germany: A critical reflection. In S. Heath & C. Walker (Eds.), *Innovations in youth research* (pp. 143–160). New York: Palgrave Macmillan.

Schall, J., Wallace, T. L., & Chhuon, V. (2014). "Fitting in" in high school: How adolescent belonging is influenced by locus of control beliefs. *International Journal of Adolescence and Youth*. Advance online publication. doi: 10.1080/02673843.2013.866148Scharf, M. (2014). Children's social competence within close friendship: The role of self- perception and attachment orientations. *School Psychology International, 35*(2), 206–220.

Schelbe, L., Chanmugam, A., Moses, T., Saltzburg, S., Williams, L. R., & Letendre, J. (2015). Youth participation in qualitative research: Challenges and possibilities. *Qualitative Social Work, 14*(4) 504–521.

Schmid, C. (2013). Henri Lefebvre, the right of the city, and the new metropolitan mainstream. In N. Brenner, P. Marcuse, & M. Mayer (Eds.), *Cities for people and not profit: Critical urban theory and the right to the city* (pp. 42–62). New York: Routledge.

Schmidt, M. E., & Bagwell, C. L. (2007). The protective role of friendships in overtly and relationally victimized boys and girls. *Merrill-Palmer Quarterly, 53*(3), 439–460.

Schonert-Reichl, K. A., Smith, V., Zaidman-Zait, A., & Hertzman, C. (2012). Promoting children's prosocial behaviors in school: Impact of the "Roots of Empathy" program on the social and emotional competence of school-aged children. *School Mental Health, 4*(1), 1–21.

Schoon, I. (2015). Diverse pathways: Rethinking the transition to adulthood. In P. Amato, A. Booth, S.M. McHale & J.V. Hook (Eds.), *Families in an era of increasing inequality* (pp. 115–136). Heidelberg: Springer International.

Schuh, M. C., Sundar, V., & Hagner, D. C. (2014). Friendship is the ocean: Importance of friendship, acceptance, and leadership in the transition to adulthood. *Career Development and Transition for Exceptional Individuals, 38*(3), 152– 161.

Schlueter, E. (2012). The inter-ethnic friendships of immigrants with host-society members: Revisiting the role of ethnic residential segregation. *Journal of Ethnic and Migration Studies, 38*(1), 77–91.

Schneider, B. H., Lee, M. D., & Alvarez-Valdivia, I. (2011). Adolescent friendship bonds in cultures of connectedness. In Laursen, B., & Collins, W. A. (Eds.), *Relationship pathways: From adolescence to young adulthood* (pp. 113–134). Thousand Oaks, CA: Sage.

Schunk, D. H., & Mullen, C. A. (2012). Self-efficacy as an engaged learner. In *Handbook of research on student engagement* (pp. 219–235). New York: Springer US.

Schusler, T. M., & Krasny, M. E. (2010). Environmental action as context for youth development. *Journal of Environmental Education, 41*(4), 208–223.

Scott, A. J., & Storper, M. (2015). The nature of cities: The scope and limits of urban theory. *International Journal of Urban and Regional Research, 39*(1), 1–15.

Seffrin, P. (2012). Alcohol use among Black and White adolescents exploring the influence of interracial friendship, the racial composition of peer groups, and communities. *Sociological Quarterly, 53*(4), 610–635.

Sekara, V., & Lehmann, S. (2014). The strength of friendship ties in proximity sensor data. *PloS one, 9*(7), e100915.

Seligman, M. E. (2012). *Flourish: A visionary new understanding of happiness and well-being.* New York: Simon and Schuster.

Senior, C., & Howard, C. (2014). Learning in friendship groups: Developing students' conceptual understanding through social interaction. In C. Senior (Ed), *Frontiers in Psychology* (Vol.5, pp. 25–32). Lausanne, Switzerland .

Serido, J., Borden, L. M., & Perkins, D. F. (2011). Moving beyond youth voice. *Youth & Society, 43*(1), 44–63.

Serido, J., Borden, L. M., & Wiggs, C. B. (2014). Breaking down potential barriers to continued program participation. *Youth & Society, 46*(1), 51–69.

Sesma, A., Jr., Mannes, M., & Scales, P. C. (2013). Positive adaptation, resilience and the developmental assets framework. In *Handbook of resilience in children* (pp. 427–442). New York: Springer US.

Seyfarth, R. M., & Cheney, D. L. (2012). The evolutionary origins of friendship. *Annual Review of Psychology, 63*(2), 153–177.

Shadur, J. M., & Hussong, A. M. (2014). Friendship intimacy, close friend drug use, and self-medication in adolescence. *Journal of Social and Personal Relationships, 31*(8), 997–1018.

Shank, D. B., & Cotten, S. R. (2014). Does technology empower urban youth? The relationship of technology use to self-efficacy. *Computers & Education, 70*, 184–193.

Sharabany, R. (2006). The cultural context of children and adolescents: Peer relationships and intimate friendships among Arab and Jewish children. In D.C. French, B.H. Schneider & X. Chen (Eds.), *Peer relationships in cultural context* (pp. 452–480). New York: Cambridge University Press.

Shaw, A., Brady, B., McGrath, B., Brennan, M. A., & Dolan, P. (2014). Understanding youth civic engagement: Debates, discourses, and lessons from practice. *Community Development, 45*(4), 300–316.

Shek, D. T. (2013). Recognition for positive behavior as a critical youth development construct: Conceptual bases and implications on youth service development. *Journal of Alternative Medicine Research, 5*(1), 29–35.

Shelden, R., Tracy, S., & Brown, W. (2012). *Youth gangs in American society.* Boston, MA: Cengage Learning.

Shelton, N. R., & McDermott, M. (2015). Duoethnography on friendship: Continue to breathe normally. *International Review of Qualitative Research, 8*(1), 68–89.

Shik, A. W. (2015). Transnational families: Chinese-Canadian youth between worlds. *Journal of Ethnic and Cultural Diversity in Social Work, 24*(1), 71–86.

Shiller, J. T. (2013). Preparing for democracy: How community-based organizations build civic engagement among urban youth. *Urban Education, 48*(1), 69–91.

Shin, R., Daly, B., & Vera, E. (2007). The relationships of peer norms, ethnic identity, and peer support to school engagement in urban youth. *Professional School Counseling, 10*(4), 379–388.

Shin, R. Q., Morgan, M. L., Buhin, L., Truitt, T. J., & Vera, E. M. (2010). Expanding the discourse on urban youth of color. *Cultural Diversity and Ethnic Minority Psychology, 16*(3), 421–426.

Shinn, M., & Yoshikawa, H. (Eds.). (2008). *Toward positive youth development: Transforming schools and community programs*. New York: Oxford University Press.

Short, J. R., & Mussman, M. (2014). Population change in US cities: Estimating and explaining the extent of decline and level of resurgence. *Professional Geographer, 66*(1), 112–123.

Shpigelman, C. N., & Gill, C. J. (2013). The characteristics of unsuccessful e-mentoring relationships for youth with disabilities. *Qualitative Health Research, 23*(4), 463– 475.

Shulman, S., Laursen, B., Kalman, Z., & Karpovsky, S. (1997). Adolescent intimacy revisited. *Journal of Youth and Adolescence, 26*(5), 597–617.

Siennick, S. E., & Osgood, D. W. (2012). Hanging out with which friends? Friendship-level predictors of unstructured and unsupervised socializing in adolescence. *Journal of Research on Adolescence, 22*(4), 646–661.

Silbereisen, R. K., & Lerner, R. M. (Eds.). (2007). *Approaches to positive youth development*. Thousand Oaks, CA: Sage.

Singh, A. A. (2013). Transgender youth of color and resilience: Negotiating oppression and finding support. *Sex Roles, 68*(11–12), 690–702.

Sirgy, M. J. (2012). *The psychology of quality of life: Hedonic well-being, life satisfaction, and eudaimonia* (Vol. 50). New York: Springer Science & Business Media.

Skelton, T., & Gough, K. V. (2013). Introduction: Young people's im/mobile urban geographies. *Urban Studies, 50*(3), 455–466.

Skoog, T., Sorbring, E., & Bohlin, M. (2015). Facebook as a means to make new peers among early maturing girls. *Computers in Human Behavior, 48*, 500–505.

Skott-Myhre, H. (2006). Radical youth work: Becoming visible. *Child and Youth Care Forum, 35*(3), 219–229.

Skovdal, M., & Ogutu, V. O. (2012). Coping with hardship through friendship: The importance of peer social capital among children affected by HIV in Kenya. *African Journal of AIDS Research, 11*(3), 241–250.

Slater, J. (2013). Research with dis/abled youth: Taking a critical disability "critically young" positionality. In T. Curran & K. Runswick-Cole (Eds.), *Disabled Children's Childhood Studies: Critical Approaches in a Global Context* (pp. 180–195). London, UK: Palgrave Macmillan.

Slavin, S., Mizrahi, T. P., & Morrison, J. D. (2013). *Community organization and social administration: Advances, trends, and emerging principles*. New York: Routledge.

Sletten, M. A. (2011). Long-term benefits of social ties to peers–even among adolescents with "risky" friendships? *Journal of Youth Studies, 14*(5), 561–585.

Smart, C., Davies, K., Heaphy, B., & Mason, J. (2012). Difficult friendships and ontological insecurity. *Sociological Review, 60*(1), 91–109.

Smith, A. L. (2003). Peer relationships in physical activity contexts: A road less traveled in youth sport and exercise psychology research. *Psychology of Sport and Exercise, 4*(1), 25–39.

Smith, G. M. (2014). Friendship, state, and nation. In S. Koschul & A. Oelsner (Eds.), *Friendship and International Relations* (pp. 35–50). London, UK: Palgrave Macmillan.

Snelgrove, S. (2005). Bad, mad and sad: Developing a methodology of inclusion and a pedagogy for researching students with intellectual disabilities. *International Journal of Inclusive Education, 9*(3), 313–329.

Soap, E. (2014).*Participatory politics: Next-generation tactics to remake public spheres.* Cambridge, MA: MIT Press.

Solomon, B. (1976). *Black empowerment.* New York. Columbia University Press.

Soriano, F. I. (2012). *Conducting needs assessments: A multidisciplinary approach* (Vol. 68). Thousand Oaks, CA: Sage.

Soshensky, R. (2016). Linking Research and Clinical Practice. *Music Therapy Perspectives*, miw006.

Speck, J. (2013). *Walkable city: How downtown can save America, one step at a time.* New York: Macmillan.

Spence, J. (2008). What do you youth workers do? Communicating youth work. *Youth Studies Ireland, 2*(2), 3–18.

Spencer, M. B., & Spencer, T. R. (2014). Invited commentary: Exploring the promises, intricacies, and challenges to positive youth development. *Journal of Youth and Adolescence, 43*(6), 1027–1035.

Spencer, M. B., & Swanson, D. P. (2013). Opportunities and challenges to the development of healthy children and youth living in diverse communities. *Development and Psychopathology, 25*(4 Pt 2), 1551–1566.

Spencer, S. (2011). *Visual research methods in the social sciences: Awakening visuals.* New York: Routledge.

Springett, J. (2010). *Participatory practice: Community-based action for transformative change.* University of Bristol, England: Policy Press.

Stanczak, G. C. (2007). *Visual research methods: Image, society, and representation.* Los Angeles: Sage.

Stanton-Salazar, R. D., & Spina, S. U. (2005). Adolescent peer networks as a context for social and emotional support. *Youth & Society, 36*(4), 379–417.

Staples, L. (2012). Community organizing for social justice: Grassroots groups for power. *Social Work with Groups, 35*(3), 287–296.

Stark, A., & Newton, M. (2014). A dancer's well-being: The influence of the social psychological climate during adolescence. *Psychology of Sport and Exercise, 15*(4), 356–363.

Stebner, E. J. (1997). *The women of Hull House: A study in spirituality, vocation, and friendship.* Albany, NY: SUNY Press.

Stegenga, K., & Burks, L. M. (2013). Using photovoice to explore the unique life perspectives of youth with sickle cell disease: A pilot study. *Journal of Pediatric Oncology Nursing, 30*(5), 269–274.

Stephanou, G., & Balkamou, K. (2011). Children's attributions and emotions for their friendships with their best friend. *Psychology Research, 1*(6), 17–34.

Stern-Gillet, S. (1995). *Aristotle's philosophy of friendship.* Albany, NY: SUNY Press.

Stern-Gillet, S., & Gurtler, G. M. (Eds.). (2014). *Ancient and medieval concepts of friendship.* Albany, NY: SUNY Press.

Stevenson, H. C., & Arrington, E. G. (2009). Racial/ethnic socialization mediates perceived racism and the racial identity of African American adolescents. *Cultural Diversity and Ethnic Minority Psychology, 15*(2), 125–136.

Stewart, S., & Liddicoat, K. (2014, January). Measuring youth development outcomes of camp and a camp-themed after-school program. Presented at the *Coalition for Education in the Outdoors twelfth biennial research symposium*, Martinsville, IN.

Stoddard, S. A., McMorris, B. J., & Sieving, R. E. (2011). Do social connections and hope matter in predicting early adolescent violence? *American Journal of Community Psychology, 48*(3–4), 247–256.

Stodolska, M., Sharaievska, I., Tainsky, S., & Ryan, A. (2014). Minority youth participation in an organized sport program: Needs, motivations, and facilitators. *Journal of Leisure Research, 46*(5), 612–634.

Stoecker, R. (2013). *Research methods for community change: A project-based approach.* Los Angeles: Sage.

Stolle, D., & Harell, A. (2013). Social capital and ethno-racial diversity: Learning to trust in an immigrant society. *Political Studies, 61*(1), 42–66.

Stone, L. L., Giletta, M., Brendgen, M., Otten, R., Engels, R. C., & Janssens, J. M. (2013). Friendship similarities in internalizing problems in early childhood. *Early Childhood Research Quarterly, 28*(2), 210–217.

Strachan, L., Côté, J., & Deakin, J. (2011). A new view: Exploring positive youth development in elite sport contexts. *Qualitative Research in Sport, Exercise and Health, 3*(1), 9–32.

Strachan, L., & Davies, K. (2015). Click! Using photo elicitation to explore youth experiences and positive youth development in sport. *Qualitative Research in Sport, Exercise and Health, 7*(2), 170–191.

Strobel, K., Kirshner, B., O'Donoghue, J., & Wallin McLaughlin, M. (2008). Qualities that attract urban youth to after-school settings and promote continued participation. *Teachers College Record, 110*(8), 1677–1705.

Strohmeier, D. (2012). *Friendship homophily among children and youth in multicultural classes.* M. Messner, R. Schroeder & R. Wodak (Eds.) (pp. 99–109). Vienna, Austria: Springer.

Strohmeier, D., & Spiel, C. (2012). *Peer relations among immigrant adolescents: Methodological challenges and key findings.* M. Messner, R. Schroeder & R. Wodak (Eds.) (pp. 57–65). Vienna, Austria: Springer.

Suárez-Orozco, M. M., Suárez-Orozco, C., & Qin-Hillard, D. (Eds.). (2014). *The new immigrant in American society: Interdisciplinary perspectives on the new immigration.* New York: Routledge.

Sudak, D. M., & Arbuckle, M. R. (2013). "Louis, I think this is the beginning of a beautiful friendship": A mentoring journey. *Academic Psychiatry, 37*(6), 441–441.

Suddock, J. (2012, October 8). Latino youth seek to play key roles in elections. *Orange County Register.* Retrieved from http://www.ocregister.com/articles/latino-373946-vote-election.html

Sugrue, T. J. (2014). *The origins of the urban crisis: Race and inequality in postwar Detroit.* Princeton, NJ: Princeton University Press.

Sukarieh, M., & Tannock, S. (2011). The positivity imperative: A critical look at the "new" youth development movement. *Journal of Youth Studies, 14*(6), 675–691.

Suldo, S. M., & Huebner, E. S. (2004). Does life satisfaction moderate the effects of stressful life events on psychopathological behavior during adolescence? *School Psychology Quarterly, 19*(2), 93–105.

Suleiman, A. B., Soleimanpour, S., & London, J. (2006). Youth action for health through youth-led research. *Journal of Community Practice, 14*(1–2), 125–145.

Sullivan, T., Mwangi, W., Miller, B., Muhammad, D., & Harris, C. (2012). *The emerging majority.* United for a Fair Economy. Retrieved from http://urbanhabitat.org/files/2012_State_of_the_Dream.pdf

Sullivan, T. N., Helms, S. W., Kliewer, W., & Goodman, K. L. (2010). Associations between sadness and anger regulation coping, emotional expression, and physical and relational aggression among urban adolescents. *Social Development, 19*(1), 30–51.

Sutton-Brown, C. A. (2014). Photovoice: A methodological guide. *Photography and Culture, 7*(2), 169–185.

Sutton-Spence, R., & de Quadros, R. M. (2014). "I am the book"—Deaf poets' views on signed poetry. *Journal of Deaf Studies and Deaf Education, 19*(4), 546–558.

Suyemoto, K. L., Day, S. C., & Schwartz, S. (2014). *Exploring effects of social justice youth programming on racial and ethnic identities and activism for Asian American youth.* Retrieved from http://psycnet.apa.org/psycinfo/2014-39103-001/

Sweeten, G., Pyrooz, D. C., & Piquero, A. R. (2013). Disengaging from gangs and desistance from crime. *Justice Quarterly, 30*(3), 469–500.

Syed, M., & Juan, M. J. D. (2012). Birds of an ethnic feather? Ethnic identity homophily among college-age friends. *Journal of adolescence, 35*(6), 1505–1514.

Taft, J. (2007). Racing age: Reflections on anti-racist research with teenage girls. In A. Best (Ed.), *Representing youth: Methodological issues in critical youth studies* (pp. 203–225). New York: New York University Press.

Taiapa, K., Barnes, H. M., & McCreanor, T. (2013). *"I don't want this to stop; I want it to keep going" Waimarino Youth Photovoice Report.* Retrieved from http://www.communityresearch.org.nz/wp-content/uploads/formidable/Waimarinoreportfinal-09dec2013.pdf

Tani, F., Smorti, A., & Peterson, C. (2015). Is friendship quality reflected in memory narratives? *Journal of Social and Personal Relationships, 32*(3), 281–303.

Tassara, M. H. (2014). *The role of friendships among Latino male adolescent immigrants who are unauthorized* (Doctoral dissertation). Milwaukee, WI: Marquette University.

Tavernise, S. (2015, May 19). Rise in suicide by Black children surprises researchers. *New York Times,* p. A14.

Taylor, C. S., & Smith, P. R. (2013). The attraction of gangs: How can we reduce it? In T. R. Simon, M. N. Ritter, & R. R. Mahendra (Eds.), *Changing course* (pp. 19–30). Washington, DC: US Department of Justice/US Department of Health and Human Services.

Taylor, J. (2011). The intimate insider: Negotiating the ethics of friendship when doing insider research. *Qualitative Research, 11*(1), 3–22.

Taylor, J., & Dwyer, A. (2014). Queer youth research/ers: A reflexive account of risk and intimacy in an ethical (mine) field. In P. Kelley (Ed.), *A critical youth studies for the 21st century* (pp. 251–266). Leiden, Netherlands: Brill Publisher.

Teixeira, S. (2015). "It seems like no one cares": Participatory photo mapping to understand youth perspectives on property vacancy. *Journal of Adolescent Research, 30*(3), 390–414.

Teja, Z., & Schonert-Reichl, K. A. (2013). Peer relations of Chinese adolescent newcomers: Relations of peer group integration and friendship quality to psychological and school adjustment. *Journal of International Migration and Integration, 14*(3), 535–556.

Te Riele, K., & Brooks, R. (2013). *Negotiating ethical challenges in youth research.* New York: Routledge.

Terrell, J. E. (2014). *A talent for friendship: Rediscovery of a remarkable trait.* New York: Oxford University Press.

Theobald, M., Danby, S., Thompson, C., & Thorpe, K. (2014). Friendships in the early years. In S. Gravis & D. Pendergast (Eds.), *Health and wellbeing in the early years* (pp. 115–132). New York: Cambridge University Press.

Thomas, T. L. (2013). *"Hey, those are teenagers and they are doing stuff": Youth participation in community development* (Doctoral dissertation). University of Pittsburgh.

Thomason, M. E., Marusak, H. A., Tocco, M. A., Vila, A. M., McGarragle, O., & Rosenberg, D. R. (2015). Altered amygdala connectivity in urban youth exposed to trauma. *Social Cognitive and Affective Neuroscience, 10*(1), 1460–1468.

Thompson, A., & Shockley, C. (2013). Developing youth workers: Career ladders for sector stability. *Children and Youth Services Review, 35*(3), 447–452.

Thompson, M. G. (2012). *Best friends, worst enemies.* Retrieved from http://www.chatham-nj.org/cms/lib/NJ01000518/Centricity/Domain/471/Best_Friends_Worst_Enemies_Handout.pdf

Thomson, N. R., & Zand, D. H. (2010). Mentees' perceptions of their interpersonal relationships the role of the mentor-youth bond. *Youth & Society, 41*(3), 434–445.

Thomson, P. (Ed.). (2009). *Doing visual research with children and young people.* New York: Routledge.

Thor, P. (2014). *The effects of ropes courses as an intervention for at risk youth: A meta-analysis* (Doctoral dissertation). California State University, Stanislaus.

Thurber, C. A., Scanlin, M. M., Scheuler, L., & Henderson, K. A. (2007). Youth development outcomes of the camp experience: Evidence for multidimensional growth. *Journal of Youth and Adolescence, 36*(3), 241–254.

Tietjen, A. M. (2006). Cultural influences on peer relations: An ecological perspective. In X. Chen, D.C. French & B.H. Schneider (Eds.), *Peer relationships in cultural context* (pp. 52–74). New York: Cambridge University Press.

Tilley, E. H., & Barnett, M. A. (2015). Bridging the gap: Fertility timing in the United States, effective public policy, and prevention design. *Sexuality Research and Social Policy, 12*(2), 92–100.

Tillmann-Healy, L. M. (2003). Friendship as method. *Qualitative Inquiry, 9*(5), 729–749.

Tilton-Weaver, L. C., Marshall, S. K., & Darling, N. (2014). What's in a name? Distinguishing between routine disclosure and self-disclosure. *Journal of Research on Adolescence, 24*(4), 551–563.

Titzmann, P. F., Brenick, A., & Silbereisen, R. K. (2015). Friendships fighting prejudice: A longitudinal perspective on adolescents' cross-group friendships with immigrants. *Journal of Youth and Adolescence, 44*(6), 1318–1331.

Todd, J. M. (2012). Female friendships in Jane Austen's novels. *Journal of the Rutgers University Libraries, 39*(1). Retrieved from http://dx.doi.org/10.14713/jrul.v39i1.1561

Tolan, P. (2014). Forward thinking: Preparing our youth for the coming world. *Journal of Research on Adolescence, 24*(3), 411–416.

Tonnies, F. (1887). *Gemeinschaft und gesellschaft.* Mineola, NY: Dover Publications Inc.

Toy, J. (2011). Urban gang violence: The implications for practice. *Safer Communities, 10*(2), 11–17.

Travis, R., & Leech, T. G. (2014). Empowerment-based positive youth development: A new understanding of healthy development for African American youth. *Journal of Research on Adolescence, 24*(1), 93–116.

Treger, S., Sprecher, S., & Erber, R. (2013). Laughing and liking: Exploring the interpersonal effects of humor use in initial social interactions. *European Journal of Social Psychology, 43*(6), 532–543.

Trevatt, D. (2014). Understanding peer relations in adolescence–group or gang? In L. French & R. Klein (Eds.), *Therapeutic practice in schools: Vol. 2. The contemporary adolescent: A clinical workbook for counsellors, psychotherapists and arts therapists* (pp. 146–152). New York: Routledge.

Triandis, H. C. (1990). *Cross-cultural studies of individualism and collectivism.* Lincoln: University of Nebraska Press.

Tropp, L. R., O'Brien, T. C., & Migacheva, K. (2014). How peer norms of inclusion and exclusion predict children's interest in cross-ethnic friendships. *Journal of Social Issues, 70*(1), 151–166.

Troutman, D. R., & Fletcher, A. C. (2010). Context and companionship in children's short-term versus long-term friendships. *Journal of Social and Personal Relationships, 27*(8), 1060–1074.

Trumbull, H. C. (1908). *Friendship the master-passion: Or, the nature and history of friendship, and its place as a force in the world.* New York: Chales Scribner's Son.

Tuck, E., & Yang, K. W. (Eds.). (2013). *Youth resistance research and theories of change.* New York: Routledge.

Turnbull, A. P., Blue-Banning, M., & Pereira, L. (2000). Successful friendships of Hispanic children and youth with disabilities: An exploratory study. *Mental Retardation, 38*(2), 138–153.

Tutenges, S., & Sandberg, S. (2013). Intoxicating stories: The characteristics, contexts and implications of drinking stories among Danish youth. *International Journal of Drug Policy, 24*(6), 538–544.

Twelvetrees, A. (2008). *Community work.* New York: Palgrave Macmillan.

Tyler, K. A., & Melander, L. A. (2011). A qualitative study of the formation and composition of social networks among homeless youth. *Journal of Research on Adolescence, 21*(4), 802–817.

Ule, M. (2013). "I trust my mom the most": Trust patterns of contemporary youth. In M. Ule (Ed.), *Participation, citizenship and trust in children's lives* (pp. 174–193). New York: Spinger.

Ungar, M. (2013). Social ecologies and their contribution to resilience. In D.S. Becvar (Ed.), *Handbook of family resilience* (pp. 13–31). New York: Springer.

Ungar, M. (2013). Family resilience and at-risk youth. In D.S. Becvar (Ed.), *Handbook of family resilience* (pp. 137–152). New York: Springer.

United States Census Bureau. (2011). *Overview of race and Hispanic origin: 2010.* Washington, DC: Author.

United States Census Bureau. (2012a). *Most children younger than age 1 are minorities.* Washington, DC: Author.

United States Census Bureau. (2012*b*). *Growth in urban population outpaces rest of nation, Census Bureau reports*. Washington, DC: Author.

Updegraff, K. A., Kim, J. Y., Killoren, S. E., & Thayer, S. M. (2010). Mexican American parents' involvement in adolescents' peer relationships: Exploring the role of culture and adolescents' peer experiences. *Journal of Research on Adolescence, 20*(1), 65–87.

Urban, J. B., Lewin-Bizan, S., & Lerner, R. M. (2009). The role of neighborhood ecological assets and activity involvement in youth developmental outcomes: Differential impacts of asset poor and asset rich neighborhoods. *Journal of Applied Developmental Psychology, 30*(5), 601–614.

Urciuoli, B. (2013). *Exposing prejudice: Puerto Rican experiences of language, race, and class*. Long Grove, IL: Waveland.

Urgent Inc. (2015). Retrieved from http://urgentinc.org/drupal/?q=content/about-us

Văetiși, Ş. (2013). Anti-urban ideologies and practices in the evolution of the American city. *Transylvanian Review, 22*(Suppl 3), 82–95.

Valdez, C. R., Lambert, S. F., & Ialongo, N. S. (2011). Identifying patterns of early risk for mental health and academic problems in adolescence: A longitudinal study of urban youth. *Child Psychiatry & Human Development, 42*(5), 521–538.

Valdivia, C. S. (2013). *Virtual youth spaces in public libraries: Developing an evaluative framework* (Doctoral dissertation). College Park, MD: University of Maryland.

Valencia, R. R. (2012). Deficit thinking paradigm. *Encyclopedia of Diversity in Education, 2*, 611–613.

Vallor, S. (2012). Flourishing on Facebook: Virtue friendship & new social media. *Ethics and Information Technology, 14*(3), 185–199.

Valois, R. F. (2014). Life satisfaction and youth developmental assets. *Encyclopedia of Quality of Life and Well-Being Research*, 3581–3589.

Valois, R. F., Zullig, K. J., Huebner, E. S., & Drane, J. W. (2009). Youth developmental assets and perceived life satisfaction: Is there a relationship? *Applied Research in Quality of Life, 4*(4), 315–331.

Van Baren, E., Meelen, M., & Meijs, L. (2014). Promoting youth development around the world: The Duke of Edinburgh's International Award. *Jeugdbeleid, 8*(3–4), 95–102.

Van Dommelen-Gonzalez, E., Deardorff, J., Herd, D., & Minnis, A. M. (2015). Homies with aspirations and positive peer network ties: Associations with reduced frequent substance use among gang-affiliated Latino youth. *Journal of Urban Health, 92*(2), 322–337.

Van Hoogdalem, A. G., Singer, E., Eek, A., & Heesbeen, D. (2013). Friendship in young children: Construction of a behavioural sociometric method. *Journal of Early Childhood Research, 11*(3), 236–247.

Vanhoutte, B., & Hooghe, M. (2012). Do diverse geographical contexts lead to diverse friendship networks? A multilevel analysis of Belgian survey data. *International Journal of Intercultural Relations, 36*(3), 343–352.

Van Liempt, I., van Aalst, I., & Schwanen, T. (2015). Introduction: Geographies of the urban night. *Urban Studies, 52*(3), 407–421.

Van Willigen, J. (2005). Community assets and the community-building process: Historical perspectives. In S.E. Hyland (Ed.), *Community building in the 21st century* (pp. 25–44). Santa Fe, New Mexico: School for American Research Press.

Van Zantvliet, P. I., & Kalmijn, M. (2013). Friendship networks and interethnic union formation an analysis of immigrant children. *Journal of Social and Personal Relationships, 30*(7), 953–973.

Vaquera, E., & Kao, G. (2008). Do you like me as much as I like you? Friendship reciprocity and its effects on school outcomes among adolescents. *Social Science Research, 37*(1), 55–72.

Vasechko, L. (2015). Mentor–A trustee for disadvantaged youth. In *Proceedings of the International Scientific Conference: Vol. 3. Society, Integration, Education* (pp. 424–431). Retrieved from http://journals.ru.lv/index.php/SIE/article/view/369

Veits, G. (2014). *Exposure to community violence and conflict during adolescence: Does conflict within a friendship contribute to higher levels of aggression?* (Doctoral dissertation). Bowling Green State University, Bowling Green, OH.

Verjee, B. (2010). Service-learning: Charity-based or transformative. *Transformative Dialogues: Teaching & Learning Journal, 4*(2), 1–13.

Verkuyten, M., & Martinovic, B. (2006). Understanding multicultural attitudes: The role of group status, identification, friendships, and justifying ideologies. *International Journal of Intercultural Relations, 30*(1), 1–18.

Vernon, M. (2005). *The philosophy of friendship.* Retrieved from http://philpapers.org/rec/VERTPO-10

Vierimaa, M., Erickson, K., Côté, J., & Gilbert, W. (2012). Positive youth development: A measurement framework for sport. *International Journal of Sports Science and Coaching, 7*(3), 601–614.

Vigil, J. D. (2008). Female gang members from East Los Angeles. *International Journal of Social Inquiry, 1*(1), 47–74.

Vigil, J. D. (2010). *Gang redux: A balanced anti-gang strategy.* Long Grove, IL: Waveland.

Visscher, A. (2015). Integrating outdoor and nature-based play in community programs. Liberty University. Retrieved from http://digitalcommons.liberty.edu/honors/529/

Vitaro, F., Boivin, M., & Bukowski, W. M. (2009). The role of friendship in child and adolescent psychosocial development. In K.H. Rubin, W.M. Bukowski & B. Lauren (Eds.), *Handbook of peer interactions, relationships, and groups* (pp. 568–585). New York: Guilford Press.

Voisin, D. R., Bird, J. D., Shiu, C. S., & Krieger, C. (2013). "It's crazy being a Black, gay youth." Getting information about HIV prevention: A pilot study. *Journal of Adolescence, 36*(1), 111–119.

Volti, R. (2014). Car country: An environmental history. *Environmental History, 19*(1), 141–142.

Von Salisch, M., Lüpschen, N., & Kanevski, R. (2012). [Having and losing friends: Necessary social-emotional competencies in adolescents]. *Praxis der Kinderpsychologie und Kinderpsychiatrie, 62*(3), 179–196.

Voorend, C. G., Norris, S. A., Griffiths, P. L., Sedibe, M. H., Westerman, M. J., & Doak, C. M. (2013). "We eat together; today she buys, tomorrow I will buy the food": Adolescent best friends' food choices and dietary practices in Soweto, South Africa. *Public Health Nutrition, 16*(03), 559–567.

Waasdorp, T. E., Bagdi, A., & Bradshaw, C. P. (2009). Peer victimization among urban, predominantly African American youth: Coping with relational aggression between friends. *Journal of School Violence, 9*(1), 98–116.

Wade, R., Shea, J. A., Rubin, D., & Wood, J. (2014). Adverse childhood experiences of low-income urban youth. *Pediatrics, 134*(1), e13–e20.

Wagaman, M. A. (2011). Social empathy as a framework for adolescent empowerment. *Journal of Social Service Research, 37*(3), 278–293.

Waite, S. (2015). Put me in, coach: The political promise of competitive coaching. *Literacy in Composition Studies, 3*(1), 108–121.

Walker, K. C. (2011). The multiple roles that youth development program leaders adopt with youth. *Youth & Society, 43*(2), 635–655.

Walker, M. D. (2015). *How Black LGBQ youths' perceptions of parental acceptance and rejection are associated with their self-esteem and mental health* (Doctoral dissertation). Drexel University, Philadelphia, PA.

Walklate, S., Hope, T., & Sparks, R. (2012). Trust and the problem of community in the inner city. In T. Hope & R. Sparks (Eds.), *Crime risk and insecurity: Law and order in everyday life and political discourse* (pp. 50–64). New York: Routledge.

Wallace, P. (2014). Internet addiction disorder and youth. *EMBO Reports, 15*(1), 12–16.

Walsh, C. A., Casselman, P. J., Hickey, J., Lee, N., & Pliszka, H. (2015). Engaged in Research/Achieving Balance: A Case Example of Teaching Research to Masters of Social Work Students. *Contemporary Issues in Education Research (CIER), 8* (2), 93–102.

Wang, H., Chin, A., & Wang, H. (2011, March). Interplay between social selection and social influence on physical proximity in friendship formation. In *SRS 2011 workshop*. Hangzhou, China.

Ward, R., Howorth, M., Wilkinson, H., Campbell, S., & Keady, J. (2012). Supporting the friendships of people with dementia. *Dementia, 11*(3), 287–303.

Warschauer, M., & Matuchniak, T. (2010). New technology and digital worlds: Analyzing evidence of equity in access, use, and outcomes. *Review of Research in Education, 34*(1), 179–225.

Watkins, D., & Gioia, D. (2015). *Mixed methods research*. New York: Oxford University Press.

Watkins, N. D., Larson, R. W., & Sullivan, P. J. (2007). Bridging intergroup difference in a community youth program. *American Behavioral Scientist, 51*(3), 380–402.

Watson, D., & West, J. (2006). *Social work process and practice: Approaches, knowledge and skills*. New York: Palgrave Macmillan.

Watts, R. J., & Flanagan, C. (2007). Pushing the envelope on youth civic engagement: A developmental and liberation psychology perspective. *Journal of Community Psychology, 35*(6), 779–792.

Way, N. (1996). Between experiences of betrayal and desire: Close friendships among urban adolescents. In B.J. Ross Leadbeater & N. Way (Eds.), *Urban girls: Resisting stereotypes, creating identities* (pp. 173–192). New York: new York university Press.

Way, N. (2006). The cultural practice of close friendships among urban adolescents in the United States. In X. Chen, D.C. French & B.H. Scbeider (Eds.), *Peer relationships in cultural context* (pp. 403–425). New York: Cambridge University Press.

Way, N., Santos, C., & Cordero, A. (2012). "Sometimes you need to spill your heart out to somebody." The cultural practice of close friendships among urban adolescents in the United States. In P. Noguera, A. Hurtado & E. Fergus (Eds.), *Understanding the disenfranchisement of Latino men and boys: Invisible no more* (pp. 255–275). New York: Routledge.

Way, N. (2013). Boys' friendships during adolescence: Intimacy, desire, and loss. *Journal of Research on Adolescence, 23*(2), 201–213.

Way, N., & Chen, L. (2000). Close and general friendships among African American, Latino, and Asian American adolescents from low-income families. *Journal of Adolescent Research, 15*(2), 274–301.

Way, N., Gingold, R., Rotenberg, M., & Kuriakose, G. (2005). Close friendships among urban, ethnic-minority adolescents. *New Directions for Child and Adolescent Development, 2005*(107), 41–59.

Way, N., & Greene, M. L. (2006). Trajectories of perceived friendship quality during adolescence: The patterns and contextual predictors. *Journal of Research on Adolescence, 16*(2), 293–320.

Way, N., & Rogers, O. (2014). 17 "They say Black men won't make it, but I know I'm gonna make it": Ethnic and racial identity development in the context of cultural stereotypes. In K.C. McLean & M. Syed (Eds.), *The Oxford handbook of identity development* (pp. 269–284). New York: Oxford University Press.

Wearing, M. (2011). Strengthening youth citizenship and social inclusion practice—The Australian case: Towards rights based and inclusive practice in services for marginalized young people. *Children and Youth Services Review, 33*(4), 534–540.

Webb, H. J., & Zimmer-Gembeck, M. J. (2015). Body image and body change strategies within friendship dyads and groups: Implications for adolescent appearance-based rejection sensitivity. *Social Development, 24*(1), 1–19.

Webb, N. B. (2011). *Social work practice with children.* New York: Guilford.

Weerman, F. M., Lovegrove, P. J., & Thornberry, T. (2015). Gang membership transitions and its consequences: Exploring changes related to joining and leaving gangs in two countries. *European Journal of Criminology, 12*(1), 70–91.

Wehrens, R. (2014). Beyond two communities: From research utilization and knowledge translation to co-production? *Public Health, 128*(6), 545–551.

Wei, H. S., & Jonson-Reid, M. (2011). Friends can hurt you: Examining the coexistence of friendship and bullying among early adolescents. *School Psychology International, 32*(3), 244–262.

Weichselgartner, J., & Truffer, B. (2015). From knowledge co-production to transdisciplinary research: Lessons from the quest to produce socially robust knowledge. In *Global sustainability* (pp. 89–106). Heidelberg: Springer International.

Weil, M., Reisch, M. S., & Ohmer, M. L. (Eds.). (2012). *The handbook of community practice.* Thousand Oaks, CA: Sage.

Weiner, L. (2006). Challenging deficit thinking. *Educational Leadership, 64*(1), 42–45.

Weinstein, T. A., & Capitanio, J. P. (2012). Longitudinal stability of friendships in rhesus monkeys (Macaca mulatta): Individual-and relationship-level effects. *Journal of Comparative Psychology, 126*(1), 97–108.

Weisman, J. (2015, June 19). Scene of carnage has long history of pain, pride and dignity. *New York Times,* pp. A1, A18.

Weiss, M. R., Bolter, N. D., & Kipp, L. E. (2014). Assessing impact of physical activity-based youth development programs: Validation of the Life Skills Transfer Survey (LSTS). *Research Quarterly for Exercise and Sport, 85*(3), 263–278.

Weiss, M. R., & Smith, A. L. (1999). Quality of youth sport friendships: Measurement development and validation. *Journal of Sport & Exercise Psychology, 21*(2), 145–166.

Weiss, M. R., & Smith, A. L. (2002). Friendship quality in youth sport: Relationship to age, gender, and motivation variables. *Journal of Sport and Exercise Psychology, 24*(4), 420–437.

Weller, S. (2003). "Teach us something useful": Contested spaces of teenagers' citizenship. *Space and Polity, 7*(2), 153–171.

Wells, C., Vraga, E., Thorson, K., Edgerly, S., & Bode, L. (2015). Youth civic engagement. In S. Coleman & D. Freelon (Eds.), *Handbook of digital politics* (pp. 199–220). Edward Edgar: Northampton, MA.

Wells, K. J. (2015). A housing crisis, a failed law, and a property conflict: The US urban speculation tax. *Antipode*. Retrieved from http://onlinelibrary.wiley.com/doi/10.1111/anti.12146/full

Weng, S. S., & Lee, J. S. (2016). Why do immigrants and refugees give back to their communities and what can we learn from their civic engagement? *Voluntas, 27*(2), 509–524.

Wernick, L. (2015, January). *LGBTQQ youth's innovative use of PAR in direct action and evaluation of organizing model.* Presented at the Society for Social Work and Research 19th annual conference: The social and behavioral importance of increased longevity, New Orleans.

Wernick, L. J., Woodford, M. R., & Kulick, A. (2014). LGBTQQ youth using participatory action research and theater to effect change: Moving adult decision-makers to create youth-centered change. *Journal of Community Practice, 22*(1–2), 47–66.

Wesley, D. L. (2015). *Reimagining two-spirit community: Critically centering narratives of urban two-spirit youth.* Retrieved from http://qspace.library.queensu.ca/jspui/handle/1974/13024

West, E., & Petrik, P. (Eds.). (1992). *Small worlds: Children & adolescents in America, 1850–1950.* Manhattan: University Press of Kansas.

Wexler, L., & Eglinton, K. A. (2015). Reconsidering youth well-being as fluid and relational: A dynamic process at the intersection of their physical and social geographies. In J. Wyn & H. Cahill (Eds.), *Handbook of children and youth studies* (pp. 127–137). Singapore: Spinger.

Wexler, L., Gubrium, A., Griffin, M., & DiFulvio, G. (2013). Promoting positive youth development and highlighting reasons for living in Northwest Alaska through digital storytelling. *Health promotion practice, 14*(4), 617–623.

Whalon, K. J. (2014). *Friendship 101: Helping students build social competence.* J.E. Hart Barnett & K.J. Whalon (Eds.) (Vol. 8). Arlington, VA: Council for Exceptional Children.

Whitaker, R. (2011). The politics of friendship in feminist anthropology. *Anthropology in Action, 18*(1), 56–66.

White, D. J., Shoffner, A., Johnson, K., Knowles, N., & Mills, M. (2012). Advancing positive youth development: Perspectives of youth as researchers and evaluators. *Journal of Extension, 50*(4). Retrieved from http://www.joe.org/joe/2012august/pdf/JOE_v50_4a4.pdf

White, R., & Wyn, J. (2008). *Youth & society: Exploring the social dynamics of youth experiences.* New York: Oxford University Press.

Whiting, L. S., Kendall, S., & Wills, W. (2013). Rethinking children's public health: The development of an assets model. *Critical Public Health, 23*(2), 146–159.

Whitmore, C. B., & Dunsmore, J. C. (2014). Trust development: Testing a new model in undergraduate roommate relationships. *Journal of Genetic Psychology, 175*(3), 233–251.

Whittington, A., & Mack, E. N. (2010). Inspiring courage in girls: An evaluation of practices and outcomes. *Journal of Experiential Education, 33*, 166–180.

Wickenden, M., & Kembhavi-Tam, G. (2014). Ask us too! Doing participatory research with disabled children in the global south. *Childhood, 21*(3), 400–417.

Willeto, A. P. A. A. (2015). Friendship and happiness in Navajos (Bik'éí Diné Baa'Hózhó). In M. Demir (Ed.), *Friendship and happiness* (pp. 209–223). Rotterdam: Springer Netherlands.

Williams, C. A. (2012). *Reading Roman friendship*. New York: Cambridge University Press.

Williams, J. L., Aiyer, S. M., Durkee, M. I., & Tolan, P. H. (2014). The protective role of ethnic identity for urban adolescent males facing multiple stressors. *Journal of Youth and Adolescence, 43*(10), 1728–1741.

Williams, L. R., & Adams, H. L. (2013). Friends with benefits or "friends" with deficits? The meaning and contexts of uncommitted sexual relationships among Mexican American and European American adolescents. *Children and Youth Services Review, 35*(7), 1110–1117.

Wilson, N., Dasho, S., Martin, A. C., Wallerstein, N., Wang, C. C., & Minkler, M. (2007). Engaging young adolescents in social action through photovoice the youth empowerment strategies (YES!) project. *Journal of Early Adolescence, 27*(2), 241–261.

Wilson, R. E., Harris, K., & Vazire, S. (2015). Personality and friendship satisfaction in daily life: Do everyday social interactions account for individual differences in friendship satisfaction? *European Journal of Personality, 29*(2), 173–186.

Wimsatt, M. A. (2014). *Humor and friendship quality in middle childhood* (Doctoral dissertation). University of Maryland, College Park, MD.

Windzio, M., & Wingens, M. (2014). Religion, friendship networks and home visits of immigrant and native children. *Acta Sociologica, 57*(1), 59–75.

Winterrowd, E., Canetto, S. S., & Chavez, E. L. (2011). Friendship factors and suicidality: Common and unique patterns in Mexican American and European American youth. *Suicide and Life-Threatening Behavior, 41*(1), 50–65.

Witt, P. A., & Caldwell, L. L. (2010). *The rationale for recreation services for youth: An evidenced based approach*. Asburn, VA: National Recreation and Park Association.

Witten, K., Kearns, R., & Carroll, P. (2015). Urban inclusion as wellbeing: Exploring children's accounts of confronting diversity on inner city streets. *Social Science & Medicine, 133*(May), 349–357.

Wolf, A., & Gutierrez, L. (2012). *It's about time: Prevention and intervention services for gang-affiliated girls*. Oakland, CA: National Council on Crime and Delinquency.

Wong, N. T., Zimmerman, M. A., & Parker, E. A. (2010). A typology of youth participation and empowerment for child and adolescent health promotion. *American Journal of Community Psychology, 46*(1–2), 100–114.

Wood, J. L. (2014). Understanding gang membership: The significance of group processes. *Group Processes & Intergroup Relations, 17*(6), 710–729.

Wood, J. L., & Giles, H. (2014). Group and intergroup parameters of gang activities: An introduction and research agenda. *Group Processes & Intergroup Relations, 17*(6), 704–709.

Wood, L., Martin, K., Christian, H., Nathan, A., Lauritsen, C., Houghton, S., . . . McCune, S. (2015). *The pet factor: Companion animals as a conduit for getting to know people, friendship formation and social support*. Retrieved from http://journals.plos.org/plosone/article?id=10.1371/journal.pone.0122085

Woodbury-Fariña, M. A., & Antongiorgi, J. L. (2014). Humor. *Psychiatric Clinics of North America, 37*(4), 561–578.

Woodland, M. H. (2014). After-school programs: A resource for young black males and other urban youth. *Urban Education*.

Woodman, D. (2013). Researching "ordinary" young people in a changing world: The sociology of generations and the "missing middle" in youth research. *Sociological Research Online, 18*(1), 7.

Woodman, D., & Wyn, J. (2013). Youth policy and generations: Why youth policy needs to "rethink youth." *Social policy and Society, 12*(02), 265–275.

Wray-Lake, L., Rote, W. M., Gupta, T., Godfrey, E., & Sirin, S. (2015). Examining correlates of civic engagement among immigrant adolescents in the United States. *Research in Human Development, 12*(1–2), 10–27.

Wright, B. L. (2011). I know who I am, do you? Identity and academic achievement of successful African American male adolescents in an urban pilot high school in the United States. *Urban Education, 46*(4), 611–638.

Wright, M. O. D., Masten, A. S., & Narayan, A. J. (2013). Resilience processes in development: Four waves of research on positive adaptation in the context of adversity. In S.Goldstein & R.B. Brooks (Eds.), *Handbook of resilience in children* (pp. 15–37). New York: Springer US.

Wright, P. M., & Li, W. (2009). Exploring the relevance of positive youth development in urban physical education. *Physical Education and Sport Pedagogy, 14*(3), 241–251.

Wright, R., Alaggia, R., & Krygsman, A. (2014). Five-year follow-up study of the qualitative experiences of youth in an afterschool arts program in low-income communities. *Journal of Social Service Research, 40*(2), 137–146. Yan, A. F., Voorhees, C. C., Beck, K. H., & Wang, M. Q. (2014). A social ecological assessment of physical activity among urban adolescents. *American Journal of Health Behavior, 38*(3), 379–391.

Yanez, C. (2015). Hispanic children: Pioneers for cultural change. *2014 NCUR.* Retrieved from http://www.ncurproceedings.org/ojs/index.php/NCUR2014/article/view/1097

Yang, C. (2014). A retrospect on the attitudes to the city of the early Americans. In *Proceedings of the 2014 International Conference on Education, Management and Computing Technology (ICEMCT-14).* Tiajin, China: Atlantis Press. Retrieved from http://www.atlantis-press.com/php/pub.php?publication=icemct-14

Yang, H. C. (2014). Young people's friendship and love relationships and technology: New practices of intimacy and rethinking feminism. *Asian Journal of Women's Studies, 20*(1), 93–124.

Yang, H. H., & Wu, C. I. (2013). Evolution of friendship network and daily activities of high school students. In *Advances in Social Networks Analysis and Mining (ASONAM), 2013 IEEE/ACM International Conference* (pp. 1221–1228). ACM: New York. Retrieved from http://dl.acm.org/citation.cfm?id=2500300

Yefimova, K., Neils, M., Newell, B. C., & Gomez, R. (2015, January). Fotohistorias: Participatory photography as a methodology to elicit the life experiences of migrants. In *System Sciences (HICSS), 2015 48th Hawaii International conference* (pp. 3672–3681). Retrieved from http://ieeexplore.ieee.org/xpl/login.jsp?tp=&arnumber=7070258&url=http%3A%2F%2Fieeexplore.ieee.org%2Fxpls%2Fabs_all.jsp%3Farnumber%3D7070258

Yeh, C. J., Borrero, N. E., & Shea, M. (2011). Spirituality as a cultural asset for culturally diverse youth in urban schools. *Counseling and Values, 55*(2), 185–198.

Yonas, M. A., Burke, J. G., Rak, K., Bennett, A., Kelly, V., & Gielen, A. C. (2009). A picture's worth a thousand words: Engaging youth in CBPR using the creative arts. *Progress in Community Health Partnerships: Research, Education, and Action, 3*(4), 349–358.

Yoshida, S. C., Craypo, L., & Samuels, S. E. (2011). Engaging youth in improving their food and physical activity environments. *Journal of Adolescent Health, 48*(6), 641–643.

Zaff, J. F., Donlan, A. E., Jones, E. P., & Lin, E. S. (2015). Supportive developmental systems for children and youth: A theoretical framework for comprehensive community initiatives. *Journal of Applied Developmental Psychology, 40*(1), 1–7.

Zaleski, N., Martin, P., & Messinger, J. (2015). Given and chosen: Youth-led research on family-supported conversations about sexuality. *Family & Community Health, 38*(1), 131–140.

Zalk, V., Walter, M. H., Kerr, M., Branje, S. J., Stattin, H., & Meeus, W. H. (2010). It takes three: Selection, influence, and de-selection processes of depression in adolescent friendship networks. *Developmental Psychology, 46*(4), 927–938.

Zanoni, J. P. (2013). Cultivating experiential knowledge: Peer educators working disciplinary borders. *Postcolonial Directions in Education, 2*(2), 186–225.

Zeldin, S., Christens, B. D., & Powers, J. L. (2013). The psychology and practice of youth-adult partnership: Bridging generations for youth development and community change. *American Journal of Community Psychology, 51*(3–4), 385–397.

Zenkov, K., & Harmon, J. (2009). Picturing a writing process: Photovoice and teaching writing to urban youth. *Journal of Adolescent & Adult Literacy, 7*, 575–584.

Zenkov, K., & Harmon, J. (2014). Through students' eyes: Using "photovoice" to help youth make sense of school. In K. Adams (Ed.), *Expressive writing: Classroom and community* (p. 53). Lanham, MD: Rowman & Littlefield, 53–80.

Zhao, X., & Gao, M. (2014). "No time for friendship": Shanghai mothers' views of adult and adolescent friendships. *Journal of Adolescent Research, 29*(5), 587–615.

Zolkoski, S. M., & Bullock, L. M. (2012). Resilience in children and youth: A review. *Children and Youth Services Review, 34*(12), 2295–2303.

AUTHOR INDEX

SUBJECT INDEX